JOHN A. BURNS

JOHN A. BURNS

The Man and His Times

Dan Boylan and T. Michael Holmes

To Dr. Felicetti —
A little introduction
to Hawaiʻi's politics. Happy
reading!
 Aloha,
 Dan Boylan

A Latitude 20 Book
University of Hawaiʻi Press
Honolulu

Published with support from the Gannett Foundation
and *The Honolulu Advertiser*

© 2000 University of Hawai'i Press
All rights reserved
Printed in the United States of America
00 01 02 03 04 05   5 4 3 2 1

Library of Congress Cataloging-in-Publication Data

Boylan, Dan.
John A. Burns : the man and his times / Dan Boylan and T. Michael Holmes.
p. cm.
Includes bibliographical references and index.
ISBN 0-8248-2277-3 (cloth : alk. paper) — ISBN 0-8248-2282-x (pbk. : alk. paper)
1. Burns, John Anthony, 1909– 2. Hawaii—Politics and government—1959–
I. Holmes, T. Michael, 1934– II. Title.
DU627.82.B87 B69 2000
996.9'04'092—dc21
[B]   99–046543

The photographs in this book are from the following sources: Moana
Guerrero, Haunani Burns, Sheenaugh Burns, Judge James S. Burns, the
John A. Burns Foundation, Betty Tokunaga, *Honolulu Advertiser*, and
Honolulu Star-Bulletin. Printed with permission.

University of Hawai'i Press books are printed on acid-free paper and meet the
guidelines for permanence and durability of the Council on Library Resources.

Designed by Nighthawk Design
Printed by the Maple-Vail Manufacturing Group

To Glo, Erin, and Peter, for their patience
—Dan Boylan

To my parents, Eve and Jack Holmes
—T. Michael Holmes

CONTENTS

PART IV: The Making of a Consensus (1962–1975)

PREFACE

THE ORIGINS OF THIS biography predate the death of John A. Burns in April 1975. As it became clear that Governor Burns' illness was terminal, James S. Burns, the governor's younger son and now chief judge of the state intermediate court of appeals, and Stuart Ho, son and heir to entrepreneur Chinn Ho, decided to approach the University of Hawaii about capturing the record of the governor in an ambitious oral history project.

During the final weeks of his life, Burns spent many hours with University of Hawaii Professor Stuart Gerry Brown and two assistants, Dan Boylan and Paul Hooper. The result was a 230-page transcript. Burns' language was not elegant; indeed he would frequently lapse into pidgin, the language he had learned as a child on the streets of Kalihi. But his insights into Hawaii's mid-century society and politics were profound.

The interviews with Governor Burns were never completed; death took him too soon for that. But there followed a procession of other contributors to the John A. Burns Oral History Project—almost one hundred of them. Most loved and respected Burns. Most recognized him as the most significant figure in Hawaii's political life for the thirty years following the end of World War II. They would have agreed that these were "The Burns Years."

Brown, Boylan, and Hooper shared in the early interviews, sometimes working together. As time went on, Boylan became the principal interviewer for the project. In the late 1970s his interest in Burns had grown sufficiently that, with Bea Burns' permission, he began work on a biography of her husband. By the mid-1980s, however, Boylan's manuscript on the life of John A. Burns was gathering dust in an office drawer. Teaching responsibilities, parenthood, and freelance writing had undermined his resolve.

It was at this point that I met Dan Boylan. My doctoral dissertation at the University of Hawaii, completed under the supervision of Professor Walter Johnson, was entitled "The Specter of Communism in Hawaii." It dealt with the McCarthy era in Hawaii; the anticommunist crusade of businessmen and their representatives against growing union power; and the Smith Act trial of leaders of the International Longshoremen and Warehousemen's Union and their supporters.

My feelings about Burns, as I studied Hawaii's history from 1947 to 1953, were that he had shown great courage in not being intimidated by those who sought to portray the Democratic Party as being under the influence of the "Communists" who ran the ILWU. But I also saw him as a peripheral figure in the events chronicled in *The Specter*. While Burns was willing to go to bat for ILWU Regional Director Jack Hall as a loyal American, he did not want to open the door for the union to control the Democratic Party.

I left Hawaii in 1976 for a career that would take me out of academe and into the financial services industry. In 1991, determined to return to the academic world, I decided the best way back was through the University of Hawaii Press and the publication of *The Specter of Communism in Hawaii*. With the encouragement of Iris Wiley, an outstanding editor who has since retired from the U.H. Press, I quit my job in California and returned to Hawaii to update *The Specter*. Dan Boylan helped guide me through the John A. Burns Oral History Project in search of material relevant to the postwar red scare.

The Specter of Communism in Hawaii was completed in 1992 and published by the University of Hawaii Press in 1994. I then asked Boylan if he would like a collaborator on his dormant Burns biography. He immediately assented, and with financial help from the John A. Burns Foundation I devoted the next year to work on the manuscript.

We hoped to complete the book by 1995, the twentieth anniversary of the former governor's death. But Boylan became bogged down in the manuscript once again, and I had taken a teaching job at Iolani School, a one-year replacement position that turned into a four-year tenure. So much for our 1995 deadline.

What it finally took to get the Burns biography finished was marriage and my moving away from Hawaii. In 1997 I met a wonderful lady from San Diego. As we began to talk about marriage, it became clear that my work as a writer and teacher was more portable than her consulting business with nonprofit organizations in San Diego. And so I resigned my teaching post at Iolani and returned to my native State of California in the summer of 1998.

Suddenly, I found myself with two very precious things—time and a wife, Anita, who is, among her many talents, a great proofreader. And that is how, after five months of polishing the manuscript, the Burns biography was finally completed in the spring of 1999. The delay allowed us to include material from the recent memoirs of George Ariyoshi and Matsuo ("Matsy") Takabuki and a biography of William Quinn, all three of which were released after the 1993 Burns manuscript had been completed.

At the end of a 1982 luncheon interview in Austin, Texas, *Hawaii* author James Michener was asked whether he thought John A. Burns was worth a biography. Michener hesitated, then replied: "I don't know if he deserves a full-scale biography, but there's a need for something entitled 'John A. Burns and His Times.'"

This is our attempt to fill that need.

T. Michael Holmes, Ph.D.

ACKNOWLEDGMENTS

MANY PEOPLE TALKED to me over the years about Jack Burns, some as part of the John A. Burns Oral History Project, some more informally. I appreciate their graciousness and generosity. They include: Kazuhisa Abe, Robert Alderman, Dan Aoki, Yasuki Arakaki, George Ariyoshi, Bobby Baker, Byron Baker, Ed Beechert, Tadao Beppu, Doug Boswell, Kenneth Brown, Beatrice Burns, Edward Burns, James S. Burns, John A. Burns, Jr., Sheenaugh Burns;

J. Russell Cades, George Chaplin, Tom Coffman, Elmer Cravalho, John Craven, Margaret Mary Curtis, Robert Cushing, Lowell Dillingham, Nelson Doi, Buck Donham, O. Vincent Esposito, Elizabeth Farrington, Dante Fascell, Tom Gill, H. Tucker Gratz, John Griffin, Thomas Hamilton, James B. Hatcher, Seichi Hirai, Don Horio, Robert Hughes, John Hulten;

Andrew Ing, Daniel K. Inouye, Mary Isa, Henry "Scoop" Jackson, Lowell Jackson, Lady Bird Johnson, Jack Kawano, Ernest Lehman, Kanemi Kanazawa, Gerry Keir, Monsignor Charles A. Kekumano, Jack Kellner, Robert Kennedy, Mitsuyuki Kido, Shunichi Kimura, Bert Kobayashi, Richard Kosaki, Lefty and Clarissa Kuniyoshi, Herman Lemke;

Malcolm McNaughton, Fujio Matsuda, Chuck Mau, Eugene McCarthy, Dave McClung, Robert McElrath, Norman Meller, Benjamin Menor, Ralph Miwa, Ernest Murai, William Norwood, "Major" Okada, Tadao Okimoto, Robert Oshiro, Kenneth Otagaki, Martin Pence;

William Quinn, William Richardson, Juanita Roberts, Paul Rogers, Ed Rohrbough, Toshio Serizawa, Ed and Sally Sheehan, Leon Strauss, A.E. "Bud" Smyser, Matsuo Takabuki, Sakae Takahashi, Hiroshi "Scrub" Tanaka, Rene Tillich, Turk Tokita, Mike Tokunaga, Bob and Jean Trumbull, Dan Tuttle, Henry Walker, Bambi Weil, Jim Wright, Tom Yagi, Pundi Yokouchi, Nadao Yoshinaga.

I have received friendship, moral support, and constant needling from Dave Heenan, Ned Shultz, Mark Helbling, Dave "Stretch" Pellegrin, and Gaylord Wilcox; all of those things plus a fine editorial hand from Vic Lipman; and the repeated assurances that it would not be in vain from Gerry Keir, Sandy Zalburg, and Tom Coffman (Tom and I still haven't finished our conversation about JAB). George Chaplin, bless him, opened wide the Hawaii Newspaper Agency's clipping files to me.

My extraordinarily fine students at the University of Hawaii–West Oahu, people like Kenny Miller, Jana Centeio, Bob Castro, Lani Nedbalek, and scores of others, have sustained me.

My particular thanks to the University of Hawaii–West Oahu for two sabbatical leaves to work on the Burns book, and to both the University of Hawaii Foundation and the John A. Burns Foundation for travel grants. Stuart Ho and the Chinn Ho Foundation helped finance both the Burns Oral History Project and the publication of this book.

Bea Burns, the most courageous woman I've ever known, and her son Jim never lost faith. Neither did Bob Oshiro. The Burns family, Sheenaugh, Jack, Jr., Brother Ed, Sister Margaret Mary, all, always, lent their gracious support.

Many thanks as well to Mona Nakayama, who was there at the beginning to transcribe the Burns Oral History Project and at the end to provide research help. Megumi Kuwada, Megan Turner, and Stacey Sawa guided me through the horrors of preparing the manuscript on a new computer, checking footnotes, and formatting text. Pam Kelly at the University of Hawai'i Press kept me on schedule, or at least close to it.

Finally, my greatest debt is to Mike Holmes, a fine writer and scholar, who dragged me, kickin' and screamin', over the finish line. He finished the book, and it is truly his achievement.

To all, *mahalo nui loa,*
Dan Boylan

P·R·O·L·O·G·U·E

Death of a Leader

AT 4:05 P.M. ON Saturday afternoon, 5 April 1975, John Anthony Burns died peacefully at his home on a modest side street in the Coconut Grove district of Kailua, on the windward side of the Island of Oahu. The end came just five days after his 66th birthday, scarcely three months after he had left office as the State of Hawaii's second governor. Death came as no surprise to Burns' family and close friends. It followed an eighteen-month battle with colon cancer, a battle that had left him largely incapacitated during the final fifteen months of his third administration.

Death came too late in the day for the afternoon *Honolulu Star-Bulletin* to get the story in their Saturday edition. Fittingly, it was the jointly produced *Sunday Star-Bulletin & Advertiser* that informed the majority of the people of Hawaii of Burns' death. They were clearly prepared. Since 11 April 1974, when Governor Burns delivered his aloha address to a joint session of the state legislature, a major effort to evaluate the impact of John A. Burns upon the history of the Territory and State of Hawaii had been under way. This effort ranged from the creation of the John A. Burns Oral History Project at the University of Hawaii, a project that is at the core of this work, to the individual efforts of reporters who knew that they would soon be writing their tributes to a man who looms as the most significant political figure in Hawaii during the last half of the twentieth century. The outpouring of praise and adulation over the next four days was unlike anything Hawaii had seen since the deaths of Kalakaua and Kuhio.

Who was this man who left so indelible an imprint upon the State he loved so much? All who knew him would agree that he was an unlikely candidate to have filled such a role. Burns was born into a military

1

family at Fort Assiniboine, Montana, in 1909. The family followed Sergeant Major Harry Burns to Hawaii in 1913, only to be deserted by him shortly after he was discharged from the U.S. Army for stealing company funds. From 1918, Burns and his three siblings were raised by a remarkable woman by the name of Anne Florida Burns—Flo, to all who knew her well. It was Flo Burns who, against heavy odds, gave her firstborn the religious foundation of his remarkable life.

But the strength he was to show later was not evident in young Jack Burns. An indifferent student who frequently found himself at odds with authority at St. Louis High School, Burns was sent to Kansas to live with his uncle for two years. After dropping out of school and serving in the U.S. Army for a year, Burns returned to Hawaii, where he graduated from St. Louis at the advanced age of 21. Burns drifted into the University of Hawaii, but within a year he was married to an Army nurse and had dropped out of school. The Great Depression had begun and Burns bounced from job to job—and from Hawaii to California and back. He and his wife Bea began to build their family on a very tenuous foundation.

It wasn't until 1934, when Burns was 25 years old, that he got his first job with career potential—as an officer in the Honolulu Police Department. Then, just as things seemed to be going well for the young Burns family, tragedy struck. On 7 October 1935, Bea Burns, seven months pregnant, was struck down by polio. Bea lost her third child and lay in her bed of pain, a helpless invalid. Both Bea and Jack Burns' lives stood at the abyss. Out of this experience, Bea would emerge as the second powerful woman in the life of John A. Burns.

The precariousness of John Burns' existence was made evident when, on 14 December 1935, the day after Bea Burns came home from the hospital, the young, off-duty police officer was involved in an automobile accident in which it was reported that he had been drinking. At this crucial point in his life, when John Burns could have gone either way, his mother stepped forward. Flo Burns gave her son a large dose of what today would be called "tough love." It changed his life.

The rest, as they say, is history. Burns began to fashion a successful career with the Honolulu Police Department; but the coming of World War II gave Lieutenant Burns an assignment that would change his life every bit as much as had the tragic events of 1935. In early 1941, when war with Japan loomed on the horizon, Burns was made the head of the

Honolulu Police Department's Espionage Bureau. His job was to investigate the loyalty of the Japanese community in Hawaii, a community that represented 37 percent of the population of the Territory, to be sure that any security risks would be quickly identified and detained in the event of war. Through this assignment Burns came to know the Japanese community intimately. When the war broke out, he was prepared to vouch for the loyalty of Hawaii's Japanese, making it possible for Hawaii to avoid the tragic excesses that were heaped upon the Japanese-American population on the West Coast. Few Hawaii Japanese were relocated to military concentration camps.

By the end of World War II, Captain John A. Burns of the Honolulu Police Department was ready to take on his final vocation. He abandoned the job security of the police department to become a politician. He became a politician to work a revolution. As the *Sunday Star-Bulletin & Advertiser* put it on the day after his death, "He was a mid-Pacific Jacksonian, surrounded by social, economic and racial elitists." He vowed to put an end to privilege and to give every citizen an equal opportunity to realize his "impossible dream." Success did not come quickly or easily. It would be nine years before "The Revolution of 1954" would take place in Hawaii and eleven years before John Burns would win his first elective office. When it finally came, Hawaii's revolution, to borrow a phrase from the American Revolution, turned Hawaii's political world "upside down."

Burns built his political success on four pillars. The first three—the Democratic Party, the Japanese-American war veterans, and organized labor—are all a part of the public record. The fourth pillar was his religious faith, personal character, and determination, which had been hammered out on an anvil of hardship and tragedy that would have broken a lesser man. He was not without his faults and he was not without his enemies, but ultimately he transcended his faults and won the grudging respect of most of his enemies.

Twice elected Hawaii's delegate to Congress, John A. Burns was the man who brought statehood to Hawaii. Three times governor, Burns helped to shape a Hawaii that is still visible as we enter the new millennium. When he left it a quarter of a century ago, the Islands wept. In an emotional eulogy, Governor George Ariyoshi, the nation's first Asian governor and Burns' lieutenant governor, tearfully told the mourners who had gathered at the National Memorial Cemetery of the Pacific at

Punchbowl that he had "lost another father." Ariyoshi focused upon his mentor's unselfish approach to the challenges he had faced:

> In all his work, he sought no personal recognition. He wanted all of Hawaii's people to take part in the process by which his successes were achieved and he gave to them the full measure of credit for shaping their own destiny. . . .
>
> A giant has walked among us, and many have been privileged to walk with him. Governor Burns fought the good fight throughout his life, and he kept the faith. He dedicated his entire life, his total energies, his whole being to Hawaii's people. He leaves us an enormous legacy.

Ariyoshi concluded his eulogy with the immortal lines from Hamlet, "Now cracks a noble heart. Goodnight sweet prince. And flights of angels sing thee to thy rest."

John Anthony Burns was laid to rest in a private ceremony in a secluded corner of the Punchbowl Cemetery. He was given a soldier's burial next to an Army infantry private from the State of Michigan who had died in World War II in the Pacific. His grave was also close to a number of Japanese-American veterans who had died in Europe. The spot had been chosen for the convenience of Mrs. Burns so that she could visit her husband's final resting place in her wheelchair with a maximum of privacy.

Gregg Kakesako and Pierre Bowman of the *Star-Bulletin* movingly described the end of the burial ceremony:

> At the cemetery following taps, four Air National Guard F-102 jets flew overhead in a tribute to their former commander-in-chief. National Guardsmen carefully folded the flag from Burns' coffin and presented it to Mrs. Ariyoshi, who handed it to Mrs. Burns. Mrs. Burns, who had been holding more than a dozen strands of golden ilima, gave them to her son, James, who placed them on the casket. Ariyoshi, one of the last to offer his condolences, knelt by Mrs. Burns; she expressed her thanks for all Ariyoshi had done for her husband.
>
> As the limousine bearing the former governor's family drove away, one of the children was heard saying: "Good-bye, Grandpa."

PART I

The Making of the Man
(1909–1945)

O·N·E

Youth

THERE WAS LITTLE about the origins of John Anthony Burns to suggest that he would become the most significant political figure in the Territory and State of Hawaii during the thirty years following World War II. The physical environment into which he was born on 30 March 1909 stood in sharp contrast to that of the islands he would call home for most of his life. Fort Assiniboine, a military outpost on the plains of Montana, was known to have winter temperatures approaching fifty degrees below zero.

Nor was there anything in the experience of his parents to suggest that Burns would, in any way, be exceptional. Harry Jacob Burns, a career Army man with six years of service under his belt, married Anne Florida Scally, daughter of a military family, in 1905. Within months of their marriage, Harry was off to the Far East for service in the Philippines.

Sergeant Burns returned to stateside duty in 1908. When Harry and Flo, as she was known to family and friends throughout her life, reported to their new assignment in Montana, Mrs. Burns was already pregnant with their first son. At his birth, the couple christened him Harry John Burns. (He would become "John Anthony" at his teenage confirmation.) The young family led an uneventful life until 1911, when Sergeant Burns was transferred to Fort Shafter on the Island of Oahu, in the Territory of Hawaii. When he departed for Hawaii, Burns left a pregnant wife and a 2-year-old son behind, in the care of Flo's brother, Elmer Scally.

Scally, who was also an enlisted man in the Army, was stationed at Fort Des Moines, Iowa. The understanding was that after the Burns' second child was old enough to travel, the family would be united in

Hawaii. But the family received neither word nor support from Harry Burns. When Scally was transferred to Pittsburgh, he took Flo and her two sons with him. Finally, having had enough, Scally wrote Harry Burns' commanding officer in Hawaii, explaining that he could not raise two families on the salary of an enlisted man and pointing out that Burns should be required to meet his obligations as a husband and a father.

Scally's letter got results. On 30 May 1913, two months after his 4th birthday, Harry John Burns first set foot in Hawaii. He was accompanied by his mother and his brother, Elmer ("Elmer," until, like his brother, he changed his name at his confirmation ceremony—to "Edward"), who was just shy of his 2nd birthday. Reunited with now Sergeant Major Harry Burns, the family took up residence in Kalihi, awaiting the completion of military housing at Fort Shafter. Ten months later, the Burns family grew to five members with the birth of a daughter, Helen.

Sergeant Major Burns cut a romantic figure, especially in the eyes of his children. His rank entitled him to a mount, and years later Edward would recall that his father "rode a white horse home to lunch every day. I was very impressed by it." One of the Burns children's happiest memories was of being lifted onto the saddle of their father's horse for a ride with their dad.

Harry Burns was a man's man. He played a good game of baseball in the military leagues and qualified as a sharpshooter in Army rifle competition. He was also subject to two of the more notorious afflictions in military life, drinking and gambling. He did neither well. Harry's drinking led to an occasional brawl, but his gambling led to the end of his military career. Responsible for certain company funds, Harry dipped into them from time to time to cover some of his gambling losses. When an audit discovered his transgressions, Harry admitted what he had done and was cashiered from the Army in 1916. Ironically, his dismissal from the Army may have saved Burns' life. The United States was less than a year away from entering World War I and a time when seasoned noncommissioned officers were badly needed on the front lines.

The family, of course, lost the military housing they had finally acquired and moved back to Kalihi. Harry Burns' first civilian job was with the Hawaiian Electric Company, putting up telephone poles. Harry Burns thought such labor beneath his dignity. He quit to take a sales position with a company that manufactured guava jelly and jam. Harry made a fair living selling guava products and other goods at the wholesale level. Flo Burns brought in additional income from her employment as a cook and housekeeper for the owner of the guava factory. But Flo could do only so much work because she was soon pregnant with their fourth child, Margaret Mary, who was born in September 1917. The Burns family was now complete.

It wasn't a happy family. Harry Burns continued drinking and, according to his eldest son, "went out with other women all the time." On occasion, he physically abused his children. Jack took the brunt of his father's abuse. But Harry Burns beat his children at his own peril. Flo Burns would not allow it and, according to Edward, she "put the fear of God in Harry Burns." By 1918, Flo Burns was running the family, which had moved four times in the two years after Harry's dismissal from the Army.

Things got worse in 1918 when the guava factory went broke and Harry Burns went to the mainland to look for work, promising Flo that he would send money for the family. For a while, Flo received letters from Harry, but no money. Soon, even the letters stopped. Flo maintained contact with her mother-in-law, receiving occasional reports about her husband's whereabouts. The last that was heard was that Harry Burns had died in an automobile accident in 1929 or 1930. He left his children a legacy of parental irresponsibility and indifference. For his eldest son, Jack, the pain was carefully masked and rarely expressed.

Flo Burns' legacy, on the other hand, was that of a deeply religious, caring, sometimes indulgent single mother who would make any sacrifice necessary to raise her four children properly. For a time after Harry's departure, Flo took in laundry from Tripler Hospital. But laundry did not pay the bills, so in 1919 Flo Burns applied for an opening as postmistress at Fort Shafter.

Educated in one-room schoolhouses on frontier Army posts, Flo Burns did not know how far she had progressed in school. She thought she had completed the eighth grade. But Flo was smart and finished second on the civil service examination required for a position with the Postal Service. She got the job at Fort Shafter and, thanks to her brother's intercession, housing on the base. A salary of $75 per month in 1919 would provide for few luxuries, but it was adequate to meet the needs of her young family.

As hard as Flo worked, supervising her children proved difficult. Jack's headstrong, often sullen behavior didn't make it any easier. At age

12, Jack Burns was an unpredictable child. Edward recalled an occasion when a local club, to which he and Jack belonged, found Jack's behavior unacceptable. They decided to arrest Jack and bring him to their club-house for a trial. When the young vigilantes arrived at the Burns home and demanded that Jack present himself, they were in for a big surprise. Not amused with their idea of a mock trial, Jack appeared on the front porch bearing his departed father's twelve-gauge shotgun. "Don't come near," he warned, "or I'll blast this thing." Not taking him seriously, they proceeded up the path to make their arrest. Jack fired the shotgun over their astonished heads. "God! You should have seen the troops scatter," Ed Burns remembered, "including me. I was just flabbergasted.... There was a big investigation and poor Mom almost had to move us out of there because of that."

Flo Burns decided that the Catholic Church, not the U.S. Army, was more likely to provide the role models her children needed. When she received a transfer to the main post office in Honolulu, Flo moved her family to Kaimuki to be close to St. Louis School, which both of her sons attended. The girls were boarding students at Sacred Hearts Academy. Flo Burns insisted that her children have a solid Catholic foundation. Her Catholicism defined her, as it would one day define her eldest son, Jack. Flo's granddaughter Sheenaugh, a trained psychologist, has written that "the Church became her substitute for a supportive husband, and she used its assistance to raise her children to be decent, God-fearing adults. Although it was a severe financial hardship, she insisted that her children attend Catholic schools to receive proper discipline and religious training. Her parish priest, Father Alphonsus Boumeister, SS.CC., became a close family friend and a model of nurturance for young Jack Burns."

Stories about Flo Burns' religiosity abound, including one that Jack's wife, Bea, had heard and loved to tell. According to her daughter-in-law, "every evening, after the children had gone to bed, Flo Burns went about the house in her nightgown, her hair in a single braid down her back, sprinkling holy water on everyone and everything."

There was, of course, a more practical side to Flo's Catholicism. Because she was a member of the Third Order of Saint Francis, Flo Burns and her children were caught up in a regular cycle of church activities. When she wasn't dragging her children off to attend another church fair, she was helping to run one. "Mother was always in charge of the hot dog booth," Margaret Mary recalled. "She was the only one who could make money off of it." Flo would go to Loves Bakery and the Metropolitan Meat Market to negotiate the best price she could get, "but she never asked them to provide them for free." Both at work and in her community service, Flo Burns had developed a solid reputation as a person you could count on.

In some respects, Jack was a son in whom Flo Burns could take pride. In his early teens, Jack along with brother Edward served as an altar boy at Sacred Hearts Church. Jack was also a good athlete. To help his mother make ends meet, he held down a paper route at Fort Shafter and worked as a soda jerk and delivery boy for the Kaimuki Drug Store. The girls considered him handsome and did not hesitate to use his sisters as a conduit for messages.

But there was another, more troubling side to Jack Burns. In his later years, Burns would acknowledge that he had been tough to handle as a teenager. "I was spoiled," he reflected, "being the eldest and sort of the apple of Mama's eye. Why, I caused her more gray hair than half a dozen kids cause their parents." This was particularly true in school where, in his eighth-grade year, Jack played hooky fifty-eight times before being marched up to the school's principal, Brother Adolph, by his mother. Brother Adolph made a lasting impression upon the teenager. "I think he weighed 210 [pounds], or something like that. He said if I didn't show up to school he was going to mop the floor up with me."

For the rest of his eighth-grade year and the beginning of his freshman year of high school, Jack Burns followed the straight and narrow. Then a problem reminiscent of his father arose. After a swimming meet at Punahou School, Jack and some of his schoolmates dropped by a bootleg liquor establishment. The boys returned to the school dormitories drunk. Things got worse after school let out. "We were living in Waikiki," Ed Burns later recalled, "and Jack was getting a little rambunctious. After all, my mother worked all day and she was concerned about his lack of discipline and his running around with some older boys that she didn't want him to be with."

In the summer of 1925, Flo Burns decided that her 16-year-old son needed a man's influence. She sent him to live with her brother, Jack Scally, who, like Elmer, had made a career in the U.S. Army. Uncle Jack was stationed at Fort Leavenworth, Kansas. That fall, young Jack Burns enrolled as a sophomore in Immaculata High School in Fort Leavenworth. Jack's experience in Hawaii's barefoot football leagues served him well and he soon found himself the starting quarterback for the school's team, beating out a returning letterman for the spot. A painful shoulder injury cut short his season, however.

In spite of that injury, which took three months to heal, Jack was already thinking about the next football season. But he didn't want to return to Immaculata; he wanted to attend St. Benedict's High School in nearby Atchison, Kansas. Jack had seen St. Benedict's defeat Immaculata by a score of 12 to 0, and he wanted to be a part of St. Benedict's superior program. St. Benedict's coach encouraged him to make the switch. Jack persuaded his mother to allow him to enroll as a boarding student. Burns later reflected on the move, saying, "I don't know how I could be so selfish. That's the thoughtlessness of a 16-year-old, because she had three kids at home and was working as a postal clerk. If she was making $110 a month she was lucky."

But Jack tried to help financially. In the summer of 1926, he worked in the Kansas wheat fields, toiling by the side of working men much older than himself. During that same summer, Jack spent the month of August at a Citizens Military Training Camp. This, plus the influence of his Uncle Jack, caused Burns to set his sights on an appointment to West Point and a career in the U.S. Army. By the end of his junior year in high school, Jack had earned high marks at both Immaculata and St. Benedict's, especially in history. Thinking that his best chance of making it into West Point lay within the ranks, Burns asked his mother's permission to drop out of school and enter the Army. Daughter of the Army that she was, Flo Burns agreed.

Jack Burns would not realize his ambition of attending West Point. At eighteen, he was unwilling to knuckle under to Army discipline. "I still drank like hell," Burns admitted near the end of his life, "and I didn't study too damn much. I did attend my courses, but I didn't study enough to impress my captain, and he didn't like my drinking. Somebody open the bottle and I was ready."

Burns' proclivity for drink placed him in a curious position with regard to racial matters. Having grown up in multiracial, multiethnic Hawaii, he was comfortable with people of all races. He often drank with blacks at Fort Leavenworth or nearby communities. He recalled that this became "a little bit of a problem because a lot of the officers were southern officers and their families would be southern, and me, I just couldn't understand the stuff. I'd go down there drinking in a Negro place, fine with me." Burns made no gestures in the direction of righting the wrongs of racial intolerance in the mid-1920s, but he did demonstrate a color-blindness that remained with him throughout his life.

At the end of a year, Burns received an honorable discharge from the U.S. Army and returned to Hawaii. By any standard, he returned home a failure. He was a 19-year-old high school dropout. He had failed to obtain an appointment to West Point. To top it off, he arrived in Hawaii too late to enroll at St. Louis for his senior year of high school.

Jack spent the 1928–1929 school year out of school and unemployed. His sister, Margaret Mary, held a dim view of her oldest brother that year: "He'd come home drunk sometimes, sneaking by Mother. He slept until 11:00 each morning and then he'd expect Helen or me to fix him breakfast." About all he was doing "was dating Army nurses at Fort Shafter and playing basketball."

Margaret Mary also became upset by Jack's attempts to get money from their hardworking mother. She described an episode in which Flo Burns had refused to give her son any money, citing specifics of family finances. Jack told Flo Burns that if she would hand over her paycheck, "I'll show you how to manage your money." Flo responded, "When you make it, you can manage it." Jack came back with a smart remark, and his mother slapped him. He was clearly a difficult young man to handle.

During the spring semester of 1929, Edward Burns came down with rheumatic fever, creating an open spot in the senior class at St. Louis for the next fall. In September, Jack was back in school, a 20-year-old high school senior. In 1975 he observed that he "just barely" made it to graduation. By his own admission, he was a lazy student. "I could always get by and never mind opening the book. But what I heard in class I could remember and what I happened to read once, . . . enough of it would stick that I could get by." Things may have come too easily to Jack. At the time of his high school graduation, Jack seemed a bundle of unrealized potential, drifting through an unfocused life.

In the spring of 1930, the editors of the St. Louis annual, *Ka Lamaku*, provided a cryptic characterization of the future governor of Hawaii: "Jackie is one of those crazy army boys. A born debater, Jack always maintains the courage of his convictions. That he also uses his talents in other ways than argument is seen from the interest he displays in his studies."

The following fall, Jack Burns enrolled at the University of Hawaii. His academic interests remained uncertain, but he talked about majoring in journalism. He was approached by the football coach, Otto Klum, about coming out for football. Klum had heard about Jack's exploits in the barefoot leagues, and he needed a quarterback. He promised Jack a campus job, paying twenty-five cents an hour, if he would join the squad. Jack thought about it, but turned Klum down. Instead, he took a thirty-five-cents-an-hour job as the night switchboard operator for the *Honolulu Star-Bulletin*. He was also given the opportunity to write about university events on a space-rates basis.

The *Star-Bulletin* gave Jack Burns his first insight into Hawaii's power structure. One evening he picked up a call from Frank C. Atherton, chairman of Castle & Cooke and one of the Territory's most powerful men. Atherton instructed Burns to tell Wallace Rider Farrington that he wanted to see him right away. Burns relayed the message and, moments later, Farrington came trotting down the stairs and went across the street to Atherton's office in the Castle & Cooke building. "It just amazed me," Burns recalled. "This man [Farrington] being governor of the territory, publisher of the paper. The boss was the other guy." Burns would later learn that the Athertons "damn nearly owned the paper. Whatever stock in there that the Farringtons had had been sold to them by the grace of the Athertons."

Burns enjoyed the activity surrounding the newspaper and became acquainted with some of the young reporters. He loved to drink with them and to listen to their stories. One afternoon, while drinking with a couple of newspaper pals at a bootleg bar on Miller Street, they were joined by two young businessmen, Harry Spellman and George Pickering. They urged Jack to join them for a picnic with some Army nurses from Schofield Barracks. Jack went along and met a fragile 24-year-old beauty named Beatrice Van Vleet. She was his date. She would soon become his wife.

Bea was three years older than Jack Burns. Her mother came originally from Nebraska. Her father, an itinerant schoolteacher, hailed from Iowa. They moved west, living in California, Oregon, and Nevada during most of their adult lives. While Bea and her brother, William, were in school, the Van Vleets moved twenty-eight times.

In 1928, Bea Van Vleet completed nurses training at San Jose Hospital. She felt no particular attraction to nursing as a vocation, but went into it because "nothing else was available." She found she liked it, how-ever, and after graduation joined the Army Nurse Corps, hoping to see something of the world. For eighteen months she saw nothing but the inside of Merriam Hospital in San Francisco. When she requested a transfer, the Army told her to list her top three choices. She put the Hawaiian Islands at the top of her list. When she was notified that she would be going to Hawaii, Bea recalled that she "almost turned hand-springs in the head nurse's office."

Shortly after her arrival, Bea Van Vleet agreed to join two other nurses for a picnic with their dates and a third young man they had found for her. She was charmed. When they arrived at Hanauma Bay, Jack im-pressed Bea when he removed his coat so she could sit on the sand. In their conversations that day and during their courtship, Bea discovered more than mere gallantry. Bea found Jack to be a gentleman and a ro-mantic. And he possessed a quality discernible even on their first meet-ing. "I think his integrity came out," she recalled thirty-six years later. "I think that's what impressed me more than anything else."

After that first evening together, Jack Burns became a regular visi-tor to Schofield Barracks. And when she was in town, Bea would stop by the *Star-Bulletin* to see Jack. In time, Jack took Bea to meet his fam-ily. Looking back, Bea could not remember a proposal of marriage, but somehow they both knew they would be married.

There were many reasons why Bea Van Vleet and Jack Burns should have postponed marriage in Depression year 1931. To begin with, Bea would have to leave her job in the Army Nurse Corps; and Jack would not be able to continue in college. Bea's father also questioned the ad-visability of the match. But in the end, love won out. In February 1931, Jack Burns dropped out of the University of Hawaii and accepted a job George Pickering had gotten for him as a straw boss in the warehouse of the Hawaiian Pineapple Company. The pay was $75 a week during the canning season; $27.50 a week in the off season. On 8 June 1931, Bea and Jack were married.

When a Catholic Army chaplain, Father Edward R. Martin, blessed the marriage, Flo Burns expressed her concern, for she knew that Bea was not a Catholic. "It's all right," the priest reassured her, "she's going to become one." And she did. The wedding and reception, both of which took place at Schofield Barracks, were attended by the officers and ladies of the medical regiment and assorted family friends.

The young couple began their married life in a $50-a-month apartment in Waikiki. Bea continued to work at Schofield Barracks as a private nurse while Jack threw himself into the peak of the canning season. But as the Great Depression deepened, the demand for pineapple dropped. By fall, it became clear that Jack's days in the pineapple industry were numbered. His loss of a job could not have come at a less opportune time; Bea was pregnant with their first child.

After considerable thought, Jack accepted an offer from Bea's father to live and work on the family's fifty-five-acre farm in California's Redwood Valley. "Tell your father I'll come up there and do the job, and in the meantime your folks can see what kind of damn fool you married." The idea seemed to make sense, with Mr. Van Vleet living and teaching three hundred miles away in Merced. But Jack, of course, had absolutely no experience as a farmer.

The Burns' Redwood Valley accommodations proved disappointing. The house had neither electricity nor running water. Roofed with tar paper, it was little more than a shack. The Burns family's only entertainment came from a crank-operated phonograph. Jack chafed at the idea of taking the torrents of advice his father-in-law sent from Merced. Instead, he read everything he could lay his hands on and he talked with other farmers in the vicinity.

At first, Bea thought she might have married "a lazy hunk." But Jack proved her wrong. "All that time I thought he was just lying around being lazy he was learning. . . . And once he got going, once he got things laid out in his mind, then he worked like a dog from early morning until late at night. That's the sort of person he was, and he was infuriatingly right. Always right."

When Bea's father arrived to inspect Jack's work, the farm had the best stand of oats in the county. As Mr. Van Vleet happily explained his success to the neighbors, not suspecting that Jack had done it his own way, his son-in-law said nothing.

Life on the farm was not destined to last. In the spring of 1932, Bea gave birth to John Anthony Burns, Jr. Now three mouths had to find subsistence from the $10 per month Jack was being paid by his father-in-law, a cow, some chickens, and the food they could grow on the small farm. The final blow came at the end of the 1931–1932 school year. Bea's father lost his job teaching in Merced when the school board passed a measure against the employment of teachers whose primary residence was not in the district. Mr. and Mrs. Van Vleet joined the Burns family on the farm. What had been crowded now became impossible. Even if they could have agreed on how to work the land, which they couldn't, the small farm would not sustain five people. The following spring, with money borrowed from his mother, Jack and his family returned to Hawaii.

The Burns family found a small house in Kalihi for $18 a month rent and Jack went to work stacking cans at Libby Pineapple. It was the peak of the canning season. The pay was low and the job did not last long. Jack's next job was as a milkman for Dairyman's, one of Hawaii's three dairies. The pay wasn't bad, $145 a month, but the hours were terrible. Burns rose at 10:00 P.M. every evening and went to work. In those days, milkmen worked seven days a week. He loaded his truck and made his deliveries, finishing at 7:00 A.M. After breakfast, he returned to work, collecting from his customers and trying to sell them additional dairy products.

In his spare time, Jacked played for the Dairyman's basketball team in the Honolulu Businessmen's League. A friend of Jack's at the time, Elmer Leehman, remembers him as "a pretty good guard, but not outstanding." The schedule was hard on Jack, but even harder on Bea. "He was never at home," she recalled, "and I was caught between feeding him and taking care of the baby. That part was hard. And I was alone. He was not at home. This was true most of our married life."

In spite of his best efforts, commissions from selling more dairy products were slow in coming during the depths of the Depression. Early in 1934, when Bea became pregnant with their second child, Jack Burns decided he must find a better job. When he heard of possible openings at the Honolulu Police Department, Jack signed up to take the examination. It was a decision that changed his life. As he approached his 25th birthday, the future governor of Hawaii took his first step in the direction of a real career. The last vestiges of youth were ending.

T·W·O

Policeman

THE POLICE DEPARTMENT to which John A. Burns applied in 1934 was a department under siege. At the heart of the problem lay the smoldering question of race. Most Americans saw the annexation of the Hawaiian Islands in 1898 as a part of the nation's strategic plan for the Pacific. The Organic Act of 1900 provided a carefully circumscribed area within which local government was allowed to function.

One of the areas of civilian government that was granted to each county in the Territory of Hawaii was its own police department. But when local police came in conflict with those who represented the strategic interests of the United States, the military, the whole arrangement was called into question. This was particularly true in 1931–1932, when the Massie case focused the nation's attention on Hawaii.

On 12 September 1931, Thalia Massie, the wife of a young lieutenant in the U.S. Navy, claimed to have been raped and beaten by five young local men. The case against the five was doubtful, at best, and their first trial ended with a hung jury. While awaiting a second trial, one of the defendants, a Hawaiian named Joseph Kahahawai, was abducted by Thalia Massie's husband, her mother, Grace Fortescue, and two accomplices recruited by Lieutenant Massie from the Navy's local boxing team. In a rented home in Manoa, Lieutenant Massie, his mother-in-law (described in the local press as a "southern gentlewoman"), and their accomplices killed Kahahawai. The four perpetrators were arrested while attempting to dispose of the body near Hanauma Bay.

For their crimes, the four were found guilty of second-degree murder. On 4 May 1932, the four were sentenced to ten years at hard labor in Oahu Prison. Then, in a deal struck between Clarence Darrow, the defense attorney, and the federally appointed governor of the Territory of Hawaii, Lawrence M. Judd, the prisoners' sentences were commuted to one hour, to be served in the custody of the high sheriff.

Throughout the Massie case, mainland newspapers and U.S. Navy officers in the Islands questioned whether a white person could receive justice in Hawaii. Critics called for a permanent military government for Hawaii. Governor Judd called a special session of the territorial legislature. The governor's message was clear: if we cannot maintain law and order in Hawaii, the military will do it for us.

The legislature responded by creating a five-member police commission charged with the reorganization of the Honolulu Police Department and the selection of a new police chief. The commissioners chose William A. Gabrielson, a veteran of police work in Berkeley, California.

Gabrielson was a disciplined, tough, somewhat autocratic cop. He stressed professionalism in the Honolulu Police Department. This meant, among other things, competitive testing for new officers, regular instruction and training, and frequent evaluation of the force. These reforms opened the doors of the Honolulu Police Department to Jack Burns.

When Chief Gabrielson looked at the results of the police examinations taken in March 1934, the name John A. Burns stood at the top of the list. Burns also came highly recommended by Riley Allen, editor of the *Honolulu Star-Bulletin;* D. L. Conkling, treasurer of the City and County of Honolulu; and Father Alphonsus, friend and spiritual adviser to the Burns family. The fingerprints of Flo Burns were all over the recommendations, but the test score was Jack's alone.

On 1 April 1934—April Fool's Day, as Burns delighted in pointing out—Burns joined three others as probationary officers of the Honolulu Police Department. The entire Burns family celebrated. Bea Burns made clear her principal reason for joy on that day: "We were delighted because of the larger income."

Like most probationary officers, Burns began his police career walking a beat. He covered the area around Queen's Hospital, lower Makiki, Kakaako, and Punchbowl. Jack's friend, Leon Strauss, remembered Burns as "a quiet but effective street cop." All of the fitness reports during his probationary period indicated that Jack Burns would have a promising future with the Honolulu Police Department. On 26 October 1934, he was promoted to motor patrolman and granted a coveted automobile allowance.

The Burns family had much to celebrate between Thanksgiving and Christmas 1934. Jack was doing well in his new job. His promotion meant more money for the family. But most important, on 7 December 1934, Bea had given birth to their second child, a healthy girl they named Mary Elizabeth.

On 1 April 1935, Jack's probationary period ended. He was now a permanent member of the HPD. In June, Burns was transferred to the vice division, a position tendered only to officers who were considered to be particularly trustworthy. One month later he was moved to the detective division. His career appeared to be on a steep, upward trajectory. His growing family was healthy and happy.

Then, on 7 October 1935, Jack Burns' world was shattered. Early that morning, while everyone else in the house slept, Bea Burns, seven months pregnant, got up to go to the bathroom. On the way, a sudden paralysis gripped her and she fell to the floor. Unable to move her legs, she pulled herself back to bed. She didn't want to wake her sleeping husband. He had been working so hard, she thought, let him sleep. The paralysis would be gone by the time they had to get up. But it wasn't.

When the ambulance arrived and the attendants attempted to move her, Bea was in excruciating pain. She was fighting simply to breathe. Her life seemed to hang in the balance. The doctors had some difficulty in diagnosing her problem, infantile paralysis being unusual among adults. Three days after entering the hospital, Bea went into labor. The following morning, she delivered her third child, a red-haired boy, two months early. They baptized him William; he lived only four hours.

For the next twenty-four hours, nobody had the heart to tell Bea that her baby had died. When she was finally told by one of the nurses, Bea Burns lay very still. "And I thought," she recalled years later, "if I cry I'll die because I can't breathe, so I won't cry." And she didn't. It wasn't because she didn't feel the loss of her child, and it wasn't because she was being brave; to her it was simply a matter of life or death. To cry might make her choke and die, and she wasn't ready to die.

Over the years, people often praised Bea Burns for her courage. "Oh, you're so brave, you accepted your disability," they would say. "Well, I didn't have a choice. Nobody said, 'Will you have polio or won't you?' I got it. And what do you do? There's no other course. You go along." Throughout her private and public life, Bea Burns showed not the slightest hint of self-pity.

While Bea struggled to regain her health, Jack and his family rallied to her support. They decided that when Bea got out of the hospital, the family would move to Kailua, where they would share a house with Jack's mother. Flo Burns still worked at the post office, so she would be unable to assume the central role of raising Jack's children. Somehow they would get by.

The family's problems were compounded when, in the early morning hours of 14 December 1935, the day after Bea had come home from the hospital, Jack Burns had an automobile accident on the Nuuanu Pali Road. Burns, accompanied by another officer and a woman, somehow swerved across the center line, striking an oncoming motorist. Burns admitted having been drinking, off and on, during much of the preceding day. He had not been on duty. The police report stated, "Officer J. A. Burns, at the time he was questioned . . . smells [of] liquor, but was not drunk at the time of my arrival." Burns and his fellow officer were immediately suspended by Chief Gabrielson, pending an investigation.

Fortunately, no one was seriously injured in the accident, but a police officer involved in a traffic accident while under the influence of alcohol was a serious matter. Flo Burns understood this and on the same day as her son's suspension she wrote a letter to Chief Gabrielson explaining the pressures Jack Burns had been living and working under and begging him to give her son another chance. Then she had a three-hour, heart-to-heart discussion with her son. They talked about his father and the role drinking had played in his development as an abusive husband and father; she would not allow her son to follow the same path. At the end of their meeting, Jack Burns made a pledge to his mother that he would never drink again, a pledge he kept for the rest of his life.

A careful reading of the response from Chief Gabrielson to Flo Burns seems to indicate that Gabrielson was well aware of Jack's circumstances and that they had been taken into consideration when he was suspended, rather than dismissed. Even so, the manner in which Gabrielson responded to Flo Burns on 18 December 1935, shows that they were thinking along the same lines:

Dear Mrs. Burns,

I am very sorry for the actions of your son, which necessitated me to take disciplinary action; and regret that I had to be severe, but liquor and police work cannot go together. Liquor is the ruination of any police officer.

Taking into consideration the condition of his wife and the fact that it is difficult for a young man to secure a job on this island, I gave him another chance; otherwise, I would have been compelled to dismiss him. I sincerely hope that this incident will make a better man of him.

It did. This combination of events, coupled with the foundation his mother had laid for him, helped forge Burns' character. The result was a man of both strength and compassion. Those close to him felt both, although not necessarily at the same time.

When he returned to the HPD after his brief suspension, Burns had been demoted from detective to motor patrolman. For the next year, those officers who evaluated his work questioned whether he would be able to overcome the extreme personal pressures under which he labored. No one doubted his ability; they only wondered about his endurance.

At home, the question was how he would relate to Bea as an invalid. Jack answered it, at least in part, when Bea became pregnant less than a year after she had been stricken with polio. The pregnancy demonstrated Jack's ability to continue to think of Bea as his wife, rather than an object of pity. "He expected as much of me as he would have if I hadn't had polio," Bea Burns said simply in 1976. Yet both Jack and Bea recognized that carrying another child to term in her condition could be very dangerous.

The conventional medical wisdom of the time dictated that, to save her own life, Bea should have an abortion. Neither she nor Jack would agree to that. Instead, Jack Burns took his wife to see Professor Henry Seishiro Okazaki, owner of the Nikko sanatorium on South Hotel Street in downtown Honolulu. The young couple and Professor Okazaki were warned against what they were proposing to do, but they were determined.

So Bea took a small room near the sanatorium and began daily treatments. These included hot baths in seaweed water *(wakame)* and vigorous massage. Bea remembered that Okazaki "did all sorts of horrible things, almost killed me, but it worked. He bent my knees, whether they'd bend or not, and finally one day it didn't hurt." Okazaki's rigorous ministrations proved successful. On 19 April 1937, Bea gave birth to a healthy eight-pound boy. In honor of the proprietor of the Nikko Sanatorium, the child was named James Seishiro Burns. The birth of this child seemed like a gift from God to the young couple.

In the meantime, Jack Burns' career, which had been in question for the year following the onset of his wife's polio, began to soar. His superiors singled him out for special training, including classes in public speaking. Chief Gabrielson felt that the department needed leaders who could communicate with the public. Although he was never a great public speaker, the training he had as a police officer surely helped to prepare Jack Burns for a political career that no one dreamed of in 1937.

Leon Strauss, who would later become an assistant chief in the Honolulu Police Department, remembered Burns' work habits with a mixture of admiration and frustration: "Jack had a very, very keen and probing mind, but he didn't work fast enough for me. When I got a lead on a case, I wanted to bust in; ask questions later. But Jack evaluated a lead first. He looked at it from all aspects." Burns would later look back with pride on his methodology. Speaking of the need for meticulous preparation in obtaining convictions, Burns recalled, "In the whole time that I went into circuit court, I lost only one little minor part of a case."

During his eleven years as a police officer, Jack Burns saw a good deal of the seamy side of life. He dealt with everything from wife-beaters, gamblers, prostitutes, and bootleggers to muggers and murderers. He saw the underside of a harbor town and a massive military complex. He also saw the rising aspirations of those who made Hawaii's economy work: dock workers, plantation workers, and those who had left the plantation to find a better life in the city. In the process, he acquired an understanding of human nature—and Hawaii—that went beyond that of most men. His lessons were those of the street rather than the academy, but they were every bit as instructive.

Beneath the carefully controlled exterior of Jack Burns in the late 1930s, there lay a smoldering volcano. It is not difficult to imagine how trapped he must have felt by the untimely reduction of his wife to the status of an invalid. The disorder this tragedy had brought into his life led to a yearning for order in other aspects of his life, particularly with his children. Taking care of a family was not easy for a man who worked a policeman's hours. When he was home, Burns proved a strict, exacting, and occasionally physically abusive parent. "There were never any broken bones," Mary Beth recalled, "but it was very bad. After an explosion of anger, he would stand very still, then go for a walk among the ironwood trees to cool down."

It was a confusing situation for the Burns children, who were getting mixed signals from a submissive invalid mother, a dominating but very busy grandmother, a long succession of hired girls from the Koolau

Home, and the occasional application of stern paternal discipline. Mary Beth provided a daughter's perspective:

> He was very strict with himself, and he was equally strict with his children. We were extensions of him. He didn't know what to do with kids. He had no father image of his own. My father was like a god you feared and admired. You could trust him totally. He never let you down. But he was always telling you your faults, and you knew what he said was right.

He may have been right, but being held up to their father's rigid standards was no pleasant experience for the young Burns children. Bea Burns knew it:

> He was too strict. I think later on he may have felt so, too, but there was a lot he didn't know. Jack, Jr., particularly, had a rough time. . . . I think that Jack, with the bad examples he saw in the police department, he felt that he had to be overly strict. He did it with the best intentions. He felt . . . that I was too soft, probably due to my physical condition, so he was very strict. But they knew that he loved them; they knew that he was interested in them.

The three Burns children had distinctly different personalities. Jack, Jr., the eldest, was the most sensitive and creative of the three. He was "a poet" in the eyes of his sister, Mary Beth. He was also afraid of his father. In childhood, he developed a stutter which Mary Beth attributed to their father's constant criticism. "Jack, Jr. hardly got a sentence out and Dad was on him," she recalled years later.

Mary Beth considered herself a gawky, unattractive child. It was not until she went away to college that she began to understand and appreciate her father. One reason for the resentment of the older children may well have been the dramatic appearance of James Seishiro Burns, the "miracle baby," in 1937, just as they were becoming accustomed to their mother as an invalid. Mary Beth would later recall that the whole world seemed to revolve around the third Burns child: "Jim was in charge of everything. The world was his oyster."

Jack Burns had a softer side. Mary Beth recalled seeing it when she had her tonsils removed. As her father drove her home from the hospital, she threw up in the back seat of the car, a car in which Jack Burns took a policeman's pride. His daughter was terrified, but terror turned to astonishment as her father turned to her and said, "You think I'm mad about that, don't you? Well, I'm not. You couldn't help it."

Mary Beth could also recall moments of playful fatherly affection. One that came to mind involved Jack Burns' extensive collection of phonograph records. Mary Beth recalled times when her father was listening to his favorite records and he would hold out his arms and say, "Come dance with me, bug."

At work, there were those who still doubted Jack Burns' competence. In his 1937 year-end report, one of Jack's superior officers, Don J. Hays, marked Burns "unsatisfactory" in the areas of "initiative" and "force." Hays wrote, "At times he acts as if he were in a trance; probably domestic difficulties. Some outside influence [is] retarding his progress. [He] appears to force himself at times to go on. In my opinion, he will never develop."

Hays' 1937 criticisms constituted the last negative report police officer Burns ever received; but that, and other earlier reports, hung like an albatross around his neck. Burns later complained of the frustration and embarrassment he felt about his failure to rise within the department. "I was at the top of the [promotion] list three times running," Burns recalled, "and I know sixteen promotions were made from below during this period of time." When friends would ask him why he wasn't getting promoted, Jack would respond, "Don't ask me, ask the boss [Gabrielson], he's running the ship. I don't make promotions." Burns recalled that there were several of his friends who did go to Gabrielson and ask why he wasn't being promoted. "This got under his skin a bit."

The logjam finally broke in June 1940, when Jack Burns became a temporary captain, in charge of the vice squad. It was a one-year appointment. Gabrielson felt that a year was about as long as a man could be expected to resist the temptations faced by a member of the vice squad. In 1940, the military population of Hawaii was growing rapidly in anticipation of an eventual military struggle with Japan. Every day saw the arrival of another ship, filled with men and equipment. Other ships arrived with women to fill the rooms of Hawaii's bordellos. Although prostitution was technically illegal, the HPD did not enforce the laws against it. Instead, they were charged with the regulation of the world's oldest profession.

Women who came to Hawaii to engage in prostitution came as contract workers, much as the plantation workers of the late nineteenth and early twentieth centuries had come. The contract was written for the protection of the military and civilian populations of Hawaii. Those who came under this contract found that their civil rights were very narrowly defined. Upon arrival from the mainland, prostitutes were required to go directly to their place of employment; they were not allowed to visit Waikiki; they were not allowed to patronize "better class" restaurants; they could not own automobiles or real estate; they were not allowed to have boyfriends or to be seen in public with men; they could not marry service personnel; they could not wire money to the mainland or telephone the mainland without permission from the madam in charge of the house in which they worked; and they were required to be in their houses after 6:00 P.M. except for five days each month.

The basic idea behind the contract was to have the operators of these licensed houses of prostitution regulate themselves. The threat was: if you don't regulate your girls, you lose your license. And a license to operate a house of prostitution in Hawaii just before and during World War II was a license to print money. Jack Burns' job was to keep tabs on the operators. If one of the girls complained to him about their loss of civil rights, his reply was, "If you want civil rights, go back to the mainland. Come back as a civilian—stay out there, don't go prostituting, fine. Otherwise we put you in jail."

Burns gained a reputation as a fair, honest captain of the vice squad. His integrity was such that Chief Gabrielson assigned him to two tours of duty in that position. The first was in 1940; the second in 1942. During his second stint, Burns came as close as he ever would to getting "busted" for being on the take. In the final analysis, he did nothing wrong, but the situation gave the impression to some that he had.

It all began in the summer of 1942 when a dispute broke out between the military police and the madams of the downtown houses. The MPs closed them all down. One madam appealed to Burns. He replied to her that the HPD no longer had jurisdiction over the licensing of houses of prostitution. He could not help her, but he would not try to stop her should she reopen. That was between her and the MPs. She did reopen, enjoying great profits in the process. Then, shortly before Christmas in 1942, a Philco combination radio and phonograph mysteriously appeared at the Burns house. The girl who signed for it, Rosalind Kubo, assumed that it had been purchased by Mr. Burns.

When Burns got home, he immediately tracked down the store

where the "music box," as he called it, had been purchased. When he discovered who had ordered it, he descended on the madam who had sent it to him. "I was only nice to you because I had to be, my official business," Burns told her. "But if you think I did you a favor, that you owe me an obligation, this is not the way to do it. I can't go that route. . . . This is you and me, me and my conscience, so I can't keep it, *pau* [that's the end of it]!" Burns reported the whole incident to Chief Gabrielson.

The episode with the Philco "music box" came close to hurting Burns in the spring of 1943. Summoned to police headquarters, Burns was confronted by George W. Sumner, chairman of the police commission; Charles E. Weber, a former chief of police who was now on the police commission; Chief Gabrielson; and the receipt for the Philco, which had been signed by Rosalind Kubo. During the course of the conference, Gabrielson admitted that he had been informed about the gift and its return the preceding December. Why Gabrielson did not inform the commissioners of this before Burns was called in is not clear. Burns was disillusioned by his superior's failure to do so.

In September 1943, Burns was promoted to the permanent rank of captain of the uniformed patrol division. Soon after assuming his new command, Jack Burns told his brother, Edward, that he had discovered one of his officers asking questions about his past, "looking for dirt." The officer told those who asked that he was acting upon the instructions of George W. Sumner. The officer also told people that Sumner believed that Burns got his promotion because "[Burns] had so much on the chief [Gabrielson], the Chief had to give him his captaincy."

During his political career, John A. Burns ran for public office nine times. In some of those campaigns there were rumors about possible indiscretions during his tenure with the Honolulu Police Department, but never a shred of hard evidence. Many of his political opponents would have paid dearly for something solid against Burns, but nothing ever turned up. In the extensive investigations of vice squad wrongdoing after the end of World War II, investigations that resulted in the resignation of Chief Gabrielson, Burns came out clean. Jack Burns always resented any effort to portray him as anything but the honest cop he was. Of course, his work on the vice squad was only a small, and relatively unimportant, part of what John A. Burns did as a police officer between 1941 and 1945. The more important part would provide his springboard to greatness.

T·H·R·E·E

Loyalty

FROM AN HISTORICAL perspective, the work of John A. Burns as head of the Honolulu Police Department's vice squad during the 1940–1943 period was of little consequence. It was his work as head of the HPD's Espionage Bureau that lay the foundation for Burns' later political success in Hawaii. The manner in which he mitigated the burdens borne by Hawaii's Japanese-American community, which represented 37 percent of the Territory's population in 1940, provided Burns with a constituency that allowed him to lead a political revolution in 1954.

When Chief Gabrielson tapped Burns to head the Espionage Bureau in December 1940, few doubted that Imperial Japan represented an imminent threat to the security of American interests in Asia and the Pacific. Plans to move the Pacific Fleet to Hawaii, which took place in May 1941, were well under way by the end of 1940. The proposal to establish the Espionage Bureau was made jointly by Chief Gabrielson and the FBI and was approved by the mayor and the board of supervisors on the Island of Oahu, where virtually all of the United States' military assets in Hawaii were based.

The loyalty of people of Japanese ancestry, living and working in the Islands, had long been a concern in Hawaii. The original expectation of the sugar planters who imported Asian labor to Hawaii had been that the contract workers would finish their terms of service—generally a period of five years—and go home. Indeed, most contract laborers who came to Hawaii shared this expectation. As matters developed, however, substantial numbers of the contract laborers simply moved into the towns and cities of Hawaii after their contracts had expired. Their children who were born in Hawaii automatically became citizens of the United States by right of birth. This troubled many Americans.

Speaking before a congressional immigration hearing in 1920, Walter F. Dillingham, whose family construction business had been responsible for the creation of Pearl Harbor as a U.S. naval base, stated the issue in terms that struck a resonant chord for many:

> Supposing, for the sake of example, that the Japanese on one of her mandated islands in the Pacific should develop the island by bringing in a great number of American citizens, and finally they had a situation where 110,000 red-blooded Americans were on the island where there were 18,000 pure-blooded Japanese. How would I feel having a college roommate visit me, to usher him from the boat to the house, kick off sandals and toss on a kimono and say, "This is my home. My wife and I came here fifteen years ago, and we have made our home here and have entered into the spirit of the life. I want you to meet my boy." In comes a fine upstanding boy, fifteen years of age. I say, "He is going to the University of Japan. He reads, writes and speaks Japanese better than he does English, and if we ever have a rumpus with Uncle Sam that boy is true blue; he is going to fight for the Empire." Now just imagine pointing with pride to your son and saying that and you realize what you're asking of the Japanese in Hawaii.

Erroneous demographic and sociological assumptions notwithstanding, Dillingham had, indeed, framed the question of Japanese loyalty for many among Hawaii's economic and military elite.

During a strike of Japanese plantation workers in 1920, the *Honolulu Star-Bulletin* came at the Japanese question from another direction:

> Never lose sight of the real issue: Is Hawaii to remain American or become Japanese? A compromise of any nature or any degree with alien agitators would be a victory for them and an indirect but nonetheless deadly invasion of American sovereignty in Hawaii. The American citizen who advocates anything less than resistance, to the bitter end, against the arrogant ambition of the Japanese agitators is a traitor to his own people.

The strike was harshly put down by the economic oligarchy in Hawaii. Hawaii's plantation workers would wait another quarter century, with the rise of the International Longshoremen's and Warehousemen's Union

(ILWU) after World War II, before becoming effectively organized to assert their economic interests.

In 1938, approximately 150,000 people of Japanese ancestry lived in the Territory of Hawaii. Of that number, roughly 113,000 were recognized as U.S. citizens, virtually all by right of birth. The intricacies of exclusionary immigration and naturalization legislation passed in the 1920s make it exceedingly difficult to track the citizenship aspirations of the remaining 37,000 Japanese living in Hawaii during this period. But the reaction of the Japanese population in Hawaii to Imperial Japan's military success at the time of the Russo-Japanese War of 1905 and, more important, to the Sino-Japanese War which began in 1931, led many to look upon the Japanese with suspicion. Hawaii's older Japanese, in particular, had cheered these victories.

During the early stages of the Sino-Japanese War, many issei (first-generation Japanese immigrants) women prepared comfort bags, which were sent to Japanese soldiers in China. Thousands of dollars were raised among members of the Japanese community to support the war effort in China. When Japanese ships docked in Hawaii, hundreds of local Japanese would greet the ships and attend open houses on board. Prosperous Japanese businessmen in Hawaii entertained Japanese naval personnel in their homes. Few issei homes were without a picture of Emperor Hirohito and a Japanese flag. In Honolulu, four Japanese banks kept the deposits of most of Hawaii's alien Japanese community. Japanese-language schools sought to maintain Japanese language, culture, and patriotism. Some parents went so far as to send their children to Japan to be educated. All children of Japanese immigrants knew a degree of cultural schizophrenia, especially those who were born in Hawaii and educated in Japan, the *kibei*.

By 1941, the Japanese and Japanese-American population in Hawaii had risen to 158,000. None served in the territorial legislature. None presided over any of the territorial courts. None held significant appointive office in county or territorial governments. Japanese intelligence calculations assumed that as many as 75 percent of those of Japanese ancestry in Hawaii would be loyal to the emperor in the event of war with the United States. U.S. military intelligence estimates were much lower, with the maximum figure being about 10 percent.

In January 1941, Jack Burns stepped down from the temporary rank of captain to the rank of lieutenant to assume command of the newly formed Espionage Bureau. He assembled a staff of four, three of whom spoke Japanese fluently. Having grown up in Hawaii, Burns rejected the stereotype that all people of Japanese ancestry were inherently disloyal to the United States. He insisted upon a presumption of innocence until the weight of the evidence proved otherwise. This made a great difference in the way in which the bureau operated and the way in which it was perceived by the Japanese community.

Much of what the Espionage Bureau did, Burns would later recall, was in response to questions raised by the FBI. The questions, according to Burns, generally followed this form:

> We received information that Hachiro Yamamoto has a relative who is a member of the general staff of the Japanese navy and that he has further links with the Imperial government. Will you investigate his background, general reputation and activities to ascertain whether, in the event of hostilities between this country and Japan, his interests would be inimical to those of the United States?

Kanemi Kanazawa, a member of Burns' staff at the Espionage Bureau, recalled that their work was different than that of a normal police unit. "The investigations," Kanazawa pointed out, "were done discreetly and indirectly. You couldn't just walk up to a man and ask whether his interests were inimical to those of the United States. Our investigations were based upon second or third-hand hearsay evidence. It would never have stood up in a court of law."

The Japanese of Hawaii were fortunate in the FBI's choice for an agent in charge of the Honolulu office. Robert Shivers was a man of demonstrated sensitivity when it came to matters of race and ethnicity. He had acted wisely when he decided to work with Chief Gabrielson and the Espionage Bureau. Something akin to what happened on the West Coast of the United States could have happened in Hawaii had it not been for the ameliorating influence of the local authorities regarding Japanese loyalty.

"The high-powered mainland FBI could not understand the local situation," Kanazawa would later assert. "Naval intelligence had the most bizarre, textbook approach to understanding the Japanese. They saw only barbaric Japanese, rather than the products of a 2,500-year-old culture." Kanazawa remembered having long talks with Jack Burns about Japanese feelings. He found that his superior officer lent an interested and sympathetic ear.

On occasion, Burns found himself with serious questions about some of the tactics used by military intelligence. One such occasion took place when Burns received a report that the Japanese owner of a laundry in Kailua, a man whose last name was Abe, was going around town trying to borrow $2,000 for some unknown reason. After a preliminary visit by two of his staffers, Burns sat down with Mr. Abe and his family in a three-hour session. What emerged was a story of entrapment and extortion by a young Japanese-American who was working for Navy intelligence.

Abe was approached by this young man in early 1941. He told Abe that he was a *kibei,* just returned from Japan. He said that he would soon be returning to Japan to report to the Japanese government on certain people from various prefectures. He questioned Abe about his past, his business, and his clan chief in Japan. Then he produced a card for Abe to sign. The card said, "I pledge myself to support the government of Japan." Abe said he signed the card to protect members of his family who were still living in Japan.

But the card did not go to Japan. It was taken to naval intelligence, where it was photocopied. The young man who had passed himself off as a *kibei* kept the original. He then returned to see Abe, telling the hapless laundryman that a U.S. government intelligence agency had gotten a copy of his pledge. He painted a picture of the dire consequences Abe might face in light of the approaching war with Japan. Having thus baited the hook, he then showed Abe a way out. He knew a person who worked at the intelligence agency who could destroy the evidence for $2,000. That was the real reason Mr. Abe was trying to borrow $2,000.

Jack Burns was outraged and had the extortionist, named Mitoshi, arrested. The arresting officers found a slip of paper in Mitoshi's pocket with the telephone number of Navy intelligence. Burns called the captain in charge of the unit and informed him of Mitoshi's arrest. "For what?" the captain asked. "For obtaining money under false pretenses, lying, deceit, fleecing," Burns responded. "You can't lock him up," the captain said, "he is doing a great service for the Navy." Eventually, Burns unearthed nine or ten such cases involving Mitoshi. Although he was indicted, Mitoshi was never tried. The U.S. Attorney in Hawaii told Burns that the case would never go to trial. The reason was simple: "Because the major defendant is Navy intelligence."

As relations between the United States and Japan deteriorated in 1941, members of the Japanese-American community became more concerned. Six months before the attack on Pearl Harbor, Japanese community leaders called a public meeting at McKinley High School, a place where so many of them had learned their lessons about what it meant to be an American. The leaders at the meeting proposed the organization of Japanese-Americans to police the Japanese community in the event of war between the United States and Japan. The FBI and Chief Gabrielson agreed that such an organization was not acceptable. But they did have an alternative.

The alternative was a group to be called the Police Contact Group, a network of loyal Japanese-Americans who would report regularly to the Honolulu Police Department, through Jack Burns. Gabrielson asked Burns to coordinate the effort and to submit names to the FBI for clearance. While this was going on, Congressman John Rankin of Mississippi made a proposal that civilian government be replaced by military government in the Territory of Hawaii. Rankin's attack on civilian government in Hawaii led Jack Burns to make a public expression of his support of the Japanese community in Hawaii.

On 18 November 1941, less than three weeks before the Japanese attack on Pearl Harbor, a guest editorial appeared in the *Honolulu Star-Bulletin.* The piece was entitled, "Why Attack the People of Hawaii?" Riley Allen, editor of the *Star-Bulletin,* introduced the author, identified only by the initials J. B., as someone who is "known to the editor, is a long time resident of the islands and has had an unusual opportunity, in his schooling and in his profession, to know Americans of Oriental ancestry. He is an American of Caucasian ancestry." Burns wrote:

> The introduction of the "martial law" bill in congress, opening the way for the substitution of military instead of civil government in Hawaii calls for comment.
>
> What would the attitude of the people of the state of Pennsylvania, Minnesota, West Virginia, or any other state, be should such a bill be introduced regarding that state? There are in those states, and in others, large blocks of aliens, some of whom have preserved intact their old country traditions, methods of speech, etc., to such an extent that if you were to suddenly find yourself in the district you would not know that you were in America.
>
> Are those states different from Hawaii? Is not Hawaii entitled to the same treatment that each state receives? And can it reasonably be asserted, with any element of proof that our citizens and aliens are un-American? . . .
>
> Regarding the loyalty of our citizens and aliens, there is a lot of

loose talk. It is said that the Japanese maintain their own schools, teach their own language, maintain their traditions and respect for those traditions. . . . They are not alone in this. Figures have been published and vouched for which show that many of the published papers, etc., in the United States are in a foreign language.

Again, it can be shown that they are good, law abiding citizens. The records of our police departments will show this. Where can the explanation for this be found, if not in their maintenance of their traditions and way of life.

As to our Japanese aliens, there is no [evidence] showing that they are disloyal to the United States! That they have some love for Japan or things Japanese may be admitted, but without that love how can we expect them to be good American aides or loyal to anything American? There are probably two loves present and those units which have been investigating [them] have not found facts which would indicate or prove disloyalty but rather the reverse.

"Let's be Americans." Basically that means equal justice. Let us demand that justice be done us. Our pride in ourselves and our ability to fulfill our obligations as Americans dictates that we also be jealous of our rights—that we should not allow ourselves to be condemned or our people condemned without proper reason. And this bill does that. It condemns our aliens on improper information.

Burns' prose may not have been memorable, but the message was. It would not be forgotten by those on whose behalf it was written.

Opposition to martial law was not the only public issue Burns would address in 1941. Late that year, Roy Vitousek, Speaker of the Territorial House of Representatives and chairman of the Republican Party in Hawaii, announced his plans for an official trip to Washington, D.C. Vitousek represented the moderate wing of the Republican Party and had a reputation for being sympathetic to all racial and ethnic groups in Hawaii. Burns approached Vitousek about lobbying for changes in the nation's naturalization laws, particularly the National Origins Act of 1924, which prevented Japanese aliens from applying for U.S. citizenship.

More than 37,000 issei lived in Hawaii in 1941. Most had lived in Hawaii for their entire adult lives. They had proven themselves to be exemplary members of the community: law-abiding, industrious, and family-oriented. Their children were U.S. citizens by right of birth and yet they could not even apply for American citizenship. Vitousek agreed to present the case if Burns would write it up for him. Burns handed him a ten-page paper on the subject before Vitousek departed for the nation's capital.

When Vitousek returned, he reported to Burns that the message had been well received, but that the timing was not propitious for a change in the law. Burns continued to fight for changes in the National Origins Act. In 1942, he managed to get the Kailua Lions' Club to pass a resolution "asking for a change in the nationality act so that anybody legally admitted to this country . . . could become a citizen."

Roy Vitousek came back to Burns in 1942, asking for a return of his favor the year before. Caught in a tough race for reelection to the Territorial House of Representatives, Vitousek sought Burns' help with Japanese-American voters. Vitousek represented the fourth district, which included Moiliili, a largely Japanese residential area. Burns demurred: "I don't want to get involved in politics and particularly I don't want this organization that I have—the Police Contact Group, which exists for a different purpose—involved in politics."

When Vitousek persisted, he and Burns struck a deal. Burns would help Vitousek with personal introductions within the Japanese community, outside the context of the Police Contact Group, if Vitousek would pledge to prevent any action by the territorial legislature that would discriminate against the Japanese community in Hawaii. Vitousek agreed and won reelection by the razor-thin margin of twelve votes.

When the territorial legislature met in 1943, a Republican senator introduced a measure that would have prevented any individual of Japanese ancestry from being on the legislative payroll. Burns called Vitousek, who protested that this measure was before the Senate, not the House of Representatives. "I don't care," Burns barked back. "Our agreement was that you do it wherever it happens. . . . I don't care how many they employ, I don't care if they don't employ any, but I don't want any resolution adopted." Vitousek called back shortly to inform Burns that the resolution had been rescinded. By the end of 1943, there were two Japanese-Americans on the legislative payroll.

Returning to 1941, the organizational meeting of the Police Contact Group had been scheduled for Monday, 8 December. That meeting had to be canceled after the 7 December bombing of Pearl Harbor, but the group would soon prove its worth. In the meantime, Burns had work to do.

One week before the Japanese attack, Burns was summoned to the

FBI office by Robert Shivers. When he arrived, Shivers called Burns into his office and said, "Close the door. I'm not telling my men this, but I'm telling you. We're going to be attacked before the week is out." Burns recalled that Shivers had tears in his eyes when he spoke. The head of the FBI office in Honolulu asked Burns to send his staff from the Espionage Bureau out to "take the pulse" of the Japanese community.

After leaving the FBI office, Burns assembled his staff and gave them the following instructions: "You go around and see your friends every day, . . . at least ten or fifteen. See if it looks like a catastrophe is coming, . . . are they expecting anything? . . . I want reports back and give me names." In spite of a week of intensive investigation, Burns and his staff could turn up no evidence that anyone in the Japanese community knew of an imminent invasion. They received no reports of anyone acting suspiciously and no evidence of espionage taking place.

On Sunday, 7 December 1941, Jack Burns was attending Mass at St. Anthony's in Kailua. It was daughter Mary Beth's 7th birthday. When Burns saw Japanese dive bombers descending upon the Kaneohe Naval Air Station, he called Bob Shivers of the FBI. Shivers instructed Burns to do a damage assessment of Kaneohe and then report to FBI headquarters in Honolulu. Burns took a quick look at the fires raging along the lines of naval aircraft at Kaneohe, then drove twelve-and-one-half miles across the Old Pali Road to Honolulu.

Along the way, Burns noted U.S. Army guards, some of Japanese ancestry, patrolling the steep, winding, narrow highway. It occurred to him that the road would have been a prime target for local saboteurs, had any existed. It would have been a simple task to have created an obstruction that would have cut one side of the island off from the other. Yet the road was intact.

Burns arrived at FBI headquarters at 10:20 A.M. By noon, he was closeted with Robert Shivers of the FBI and Colonel George W. Bicknell, head of counterintelligence for the U.S. Army in Hawaii. Together, they went over lists of possible security risks. By the evening of 8 December, 482 individuals had been rounded up. Of that number, 370 were Japanese; 98 were German; and 14 were Italian. Japan's having joined the Axis Powers in 1938, of course, meant that the attack against the United States on 7 December 1941 was done in the name of Germany and Italy as well.

Burns recalled the manner in which the security risks were identified. As they went through the lists of potential internees, each of the three men present had a vote. "If two of us voted yes," Burns said, "he was a risk." Burns was willing to sacrifice the civil rights of some to protect the many. But he was unwilling to agree to wholesale internment of individuals because of their race or national origin.

Those at the top of the suspect list included reserve officers of the Japanese army, mostly *kibei*, consular agents, and Japanese-language school principals. Those identified as security risks were picked up by the Honolulu Police Department, working with military security officers, and taken to the U.S. Immigration and Naturalization Service facility or to Sand Island. They were later taken to the Honouliuli internment camp. The total number of Japanese internees from Hawaii during World War II was 1,444. Of that number, 534 were American citizens. By the end of the war, only 277 were still being held.

This was a far cry from the situation that existed on the West Coast of the United States, where 120,000 people of Japanese ancestry were relocated to internment camps during World War II. Hawaii's Japanese population of 158,000 was spared in large measure because it represented 37 percent of the Territory's prewar population. Japanese constituted the backbone of Hawaii's civilian labor force. The logistical problem of placing Hawaii's Japanese population in internment camps would have been horrendous; but in the minds of some, it was not unthinkable. Navy Secretary Frank Knox was one who recommended internment. Lieutenant General Delos C. Emmons, the military governor of Hawaii under the martial law that was declared on 7 December, suggested that one thousand Japanese per month be interned. Still others suggested that the Island of Molokai be converted into an internment camp. Jack Burns did everything in his power to avoid such a move.

Within a week of the attack on Pearl Harbor, federal authorities stopped consulting Burns and his Espionage Bureau about who should be interned; but they continued to use his unit to track down a variety of rumors. There were stories of flares set out to guide the Japanese pilots to their targets, directional signals cut into the cane fields, pointing toward Pearl Harbor. Some reports told of snipers shooting at U.S. troops, of sightings of Japanese paratroopers, of unauthorized shortwave radio sets in the possession of Japanese in Hawaii. All leads were checked out. None led to any evidence of espionage.

The attack on Pearl Harbor created turmoil in the Japanese community. In the first hours following the bombing, military authorities searched all Japanese homes within two miles of Pearl Harbor, seizing radios and any weapons they found. Japanese-language newspapers were shut down. Burns himself encouraged the closure of Shinto shrines, believing that Shintoism was more a tool of the Japanese Imperial government than a religion. He also advised the Japanese community to give up many of their public customs, at least for a while. These customs included the wearing of kimonos or geta (Japanese slippers) in the streets, the deep bow as an act of greeting and respect, and the use of the Japanese language in public. "I knew a lot of this stuff was silly on its face," Burns later said, "but we wanted to avoid incidents from a lot of haoles (Caucasians) who were too ignorant of our people to know the meaning of what they saw." The haoles to whom Burns referred were not the locals, but the hundreds of thousands of servicemen and war workers who doubled the size of Hawaii's population during the war and had no experience with the Territory's multiracial population.

There were many spontaneous efforts to avoid race-related problems among the local population of Hawaii. A Morale Committee, composed of citizens of various racial and ethnic groups, was organized under the leadership of Charles Loomis, Shigeo Yoshida, and Hung Wai Ching. Their primary goal was to quell any potential for racial hysteria. Japanese and Americans of Japanese ancestry created the Emergency Service Committee, chapters of which popped up in every Oahu neighborhood where the Japanese population was concentrated. They engaged in an unending stream of patriotic activities, from blood drives to war bond drives. Burns initially coordinated the efforts of these groups with both the Espionage Bureau and the Police Contact Group.

By April 1942, security matters had been so completely taken over by the military that Chief Gabrielson reassigned the major portion of Jack Burns' time to the vice squad. Burns continued to work with the Espionage Bureau, the Morale Committee, and the Emergency Service Committee, but it was no longer his full-time responsibility. The off-duty military and defense workers of Hawaii's inflated wartime population increasingly commanded his attention.

Burns continued, however, to address the question of how the Japanese community might serve their country during wartime. When the war began, the Territorial Guard had been called out. The first to assemble were the cadet officers of the Reserve Officers Training Corps (ROTC) at the University of Hawaii. For six weeks, the ROTC members served as an integral part of the Guard, standing watch wherever they were needed. Then, on 21 January 1942, General Emmons ordered all 317 Japanese-American members of the Territorial Guard to be relieved of their duties and dismissed.

Still wanting to assist in the war effort, in spite of this slap in the face, 150 of the dismissed guardsmen, almost all of them students at the University of Hawaii, immediately volunteered to go to work for the U.S. Army Corps of Engineers in a unit called the Varsity Victory Volunteers (VVV). For $90 a month, they dug trenches, built roads, and strung barbed wire.

Emmons had another, larger problem of a similar nature. The National Guard, as distinguished from the Territorial Guard, in Hawaii had 1,400 nisei (second-generation Japanese) in its ranks. The Army was simply too short of men to dismiss them, so they were sent to the mainland for training under the name of the Hawaiian Provisional Infantry Battalion. They sailed from Honolulu in June 1942, having been relieved of their arms in advance.

Their destination was Camp McCoy, Wisconsin, where they were given a new name, "the 100th Infantry Battalion (Separate)." They didn't have to be told that they were separate. That was evident. After six months in the friendly environs of Wisconsin, the 100th was transferred to Camp Shelby, Mississippi. The contrast was dramatic. As Gavan Daws pointed out in *a Shoal of Time*, "In Wisconsin the weather was frigid, but the people . . . were surprisingly warm. A weekend leave in Hattiesburg, Mississippi was something else."

In January 1943, General Emmons, who had one year earlier ordered all Japanese-Americans to be discharged from the Territorial Guard, had a change of heart. "Open to distrust because of their racial origin, and discriminated against in certain fields of the defense effort, they nevertheless have borne their burdens without complaint and have added materially to the strength of the Hawaiian area." Emmons called for 1,500 volunteers from Hawaii for an all-Japanese (except for officers) fighting unit that would eventually be called the 442nd Regimental Combat Team.

Within one month, more than nine thousand Japanese-Americans volunteered from Hawaii. Jack Burns took an active role in the recruitment effort. "We went all over the place," he recalled in 1975. "Every one of my Contact Group members." Burns recalled putting the matter to the young Japanese like this:

Okay, Uncle Sam has kicked you in the ass, you're entirely right to be mad about it. In fact, if you weren't, why you wouldn't make a good American anyway. But that doesn't answer the question. The question is, are you an American? Are you willing to give your life for your country? Do you believe in your country? If you don't, [if] you're not willing to die for your country, don't volunteer, please.

Fewer than three thousand volunteers were eventually chosen to form the 442nd. In April 1943 they arrived at Camp Shelby, Mississippi, where the 100th was still in training. These two units (eventually merged into the 442nd) represented sixty percent of Hawaii's fighting forces during World War II, and suffered eighty percent of the Territory's casualties. As it was so eloquently expressed in November 1945 by Katsumi Kometani, one of the original members of the 100th Battalion:

> The highest aspiration of our boys in uniform is to return to a Hawaii where a citizen, irrespective of ancestry, will share and share equally in the rights as well as the responsibilities of citizenship. We have helped win the war on the battlefront, but we have not yet won the war on the homefront. We shall have won [that war] only when we attain those things [to] which our country is dedicated, namely, equality of opportunity and the dignity of man.

For the last three years of World War II, Jack Burns was as busy thinking about the issues raised by Kometani in 1945 as he was in working for ways to ease the wartime burden of the people in the Japanese community. Understanding the importance of the symbols of democracy, Burns went to his old friend at the *Honolulu Star-Bulletin*, Riley Allen, and asked him to guide the paper into using the more positive term, Americans of Japanese ancestry, or AJA for short, instead of the more negative Japanese-Americans.

More than anything else, Jack Burns began to talk with those who would help shape a new future for Hawaii. John A. Burns, the man, was fully formed. His values reflected those lessons he had finally learned so well, if belatedly, from his Church, his family, and his community. What was taking place during the final years of World War II was the transformation of Burns from a policeman to a politician. The preceding five years of his life had provided Jack Burns with an education that no university could have duplicated.

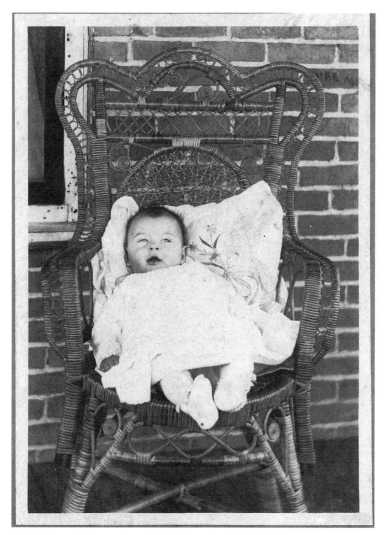

Harry John Burns, later christened John Anthony Burns, 1909. The picture was taken at Fort Assiniboine, Montana.

One-year-old "Jack" Burns on a swing between family friend Beatrice Ely and his mother, Anne Florida Burns.

Harry Jacob Burns, two friends, and Flo and her firstborn watching a baseball game at Fort Assiniboine, Montana.

Jack is standing with his arm around his mother. Sitting in her lap is Jack's new brother Edward, 1912.

Flo *(top center)* and her boys joined Sergeant Major Harry Burns in Hawaii in 1913. In 1916, the Burns family was visited by Flo's brother Elmer (the heavy-set gentleman next to Flo). Immediately in front of Flo stands daughter Helen, seated in front of her is Edward, and on Flo's left, in a sailor suit, is Jack.

Flo and her brood at a house they rented in Kaimuki. *From the left:* Helen, Edward, Margaret Mary, and Jack.

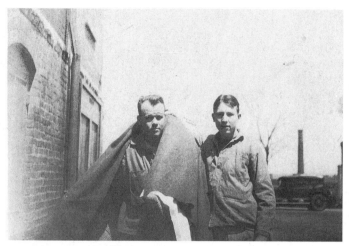

Burns dropped out of high school in Kansas to join the U.S. Army. In this 1927 picture, Jack *(right)* and another soldier pose at Fort Leavenworth.

St. Louis College, Class of 1928, at College Walk

The St. Louis High School class of 1928. In the second row, fourth from left, wearing dark jacket, dark shirt, patterned tie, and slicked-back hair: Hawaii's future governor, John A. Burns.

Flo and her grown-up children. *From left to right:* Margaret Mary, Edward, Flo, Jack, and Helen.

A lei-bedecked and lovely Flo Burns. All but a few of her gray hairs were given her by her firstborn, John Anthony.

Bea with the Burns' first child, John A. Burns, Jr. Bea and Jack were attempting to ride out the Depression on a farm in northern California owned by Bea's father.

Bea with her daughter, Mary Beth, during the summer of 1935, three months before Bea was stricken with polio.

Here Bea stands propped up against a car with an arm around her husband. Jack, Jr., and Mary Beth look dourly at the camera.

The Honolulu Police Department was a choice job for a young man in Depression Hawaii. Here Sergeant John A. Burns tries to look the tough cop.

Detective Burns in 1941.

Despite her paralysis from polio, Bea Burns delivered a healthy son, James Seishiro Burns. He was named for Seishiro Okazaki, the Japanese massage therapist who prepared Bea for the delivery.

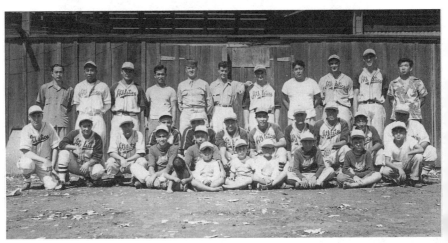

With the outbreak of World War II, Hawaii's Japanese baseball league had to "Americanize." Burns (kneeling, in uniform *on the far left*) took over the management of the Asahis, renamed the Athletics for the duration of the war. Note batboys Jack, Jr., (*second from right, front row*, dark shirt) and Jim (*fifth from right, front row*).

Bea Burns, circa 1940.

Bea in 1942, just after her return from a year-and-a-half in California where she received therapy to mitigate her paralysis.

Jack Burns in 1946, the first year he ran for public office.

Burns was a dedicated Lion. Here he is (*back row, second from right*) with his beloved Koolaupoko Lions Club.

Burns and Oren Long, whom the resurgent Democrats supported for territorial governor in 1950 in hopes of getting some patronage.

Elected delegate to Congress in 1956, Burns made statehood for Hawaii his crusade. Here he and New York Congressman Leo O'Brien, a co-author of the Hawaii Statehood Bill, present a statehood petition to Sam Rayburn, the powerful Speaker of the House of Representatives.

Burns developed good relationships with the Irish Catholic members of the House. Here he and Massachusetts Congressman John McCormick examine a new 50-star flag.

Territorial Governor William Quinn visits Delegate Burns in the company of
Father Charles A. Kekumano, a member of the Hawaii Statehood Commission.

On his 50th birthday (30 March 1959), Bea baked a cake for Delegate Burns.
Mary Isa stands in the middle of the picture. Administrative Assistant Dan
Aoki looks over Isa's shoulder.

Burns' Washington staffers show their support during his 1958 delegate reelection bid *(from left)*: Seichi "Shadow" Hirai, Nobleen Kauhane, Mary Isa, and Bea.

In 1959, Dan Inouye announced his intentions to seek U.S. Senate seat. *From left:* Aoki, Mrs. Inouye, Dan Inouye, and Inouye loyalist Henry Giugni.

Burns lost his race for governor in 1959, but he returned to Washington to see his political protégé sworn in as the first Japanese-American member of the U.S. Congress.

When Burns won elections, he did a lot of this: one-on-one at coffee hours and *pau hana* parties.

Vice President Lyndon Baines Johnson made a flying visit to Hawaii on 20 October 1962, less than two weeks before the general election. Although courtesy demanded that Governor Quinn and Republican Senator Hiram Fong get in the picture, there's little question Johnson favors Democrats Inouye and Burns.

Burns on election night 1962, checking the numbers with "cell gang" member and loyalist Mike Tokunaga.

Burns with the crowd at his campaign headquarters.

Burns was no speaker, to which the expressions of the people on this dias attest.

PART II

The Making of a Politician (1951–1962)

F·O·U·R

Peace

To UNDERSTAND JACK BURNS' postwar political base, it is necessary to examine the relationships he developed during the war. World War II required that the Japanese community in Hawaii maintain a delicate balance. Dr. Ernest Murai, a mainland-trained dentist who served on both the Police Contact Group and the Emergency Service Committee, constantly reassured his fellow ethnic Japanese, "This is a democracy. Our government will take care of us provided we don't do anything subversive."

Murai, who would become one of Burns' closest allies in the shaping of Hawaii's Democratic Party after the war, urged his fellow Japanese to be sensitive to the haole elite—both civilian and military—who controlled the Islands during the war. He also warned them against creating bad feelings within Hawaii's non-Japanese Asian community. The atrocities of the Japanese Imperial forces against the Chinese, Koreans, and Filipinos had explosive potential in the Territory of Hawaii.

Most plantation managers were pleased to cooperate with the Emergency Service Committee, but not all. Hans L'Orange, manager of Oahu Sugar's big plantation at Waipahu, refused to allow Burns to organize any meetings on the premises, feeling that it would be disruptive for his workers. When Burns pressed him about the need to educate the Japanese community about their rights and responsibilities during the war, L'Orange remained intransigent. Both Burns and military intelligence felt that Waipahu, a virtual Japanese ghetto, strategically located next to Pearl Harbor, had to participate in the program. Colonel Bicknell was so angry that he wanted to have L'Orange arrested. Burns asked Bicknell to be patient while he pursued another approach. Burns went to the Hawaii Sugar Planters' Association (HSPA) and urged them to

63

get the Waipahu plantation manager to cooperate. The HSPA got back to Burns within days, telling him that L'Orange was now more than happy to participate in the program.

The Emergency Service Committee meetings on the plantations were well attended, with an average turnout of roughly one hundred. Dr. Murai recalled that martial law dictated the timing of the meetings: "They had to be off the street at eight o'clock, so we had to rush out there, maybe at 4:30 or 5:00—some of them would just get through work and come to the meeting in their work clothes before they go home." At the meetings, Burns kept a low profile, letting people like Dr. Murai, Mitsuyuki "Mits" Kido, Baron Goto, and Masatoshi Katagiri do the talking. They gave their listeners hard-headed, practical advice. But not all of their listeners appreciated what they heard.

The most difficult were the issei. Many were troubled by any suggestion that they should turn their backs on the two-thousand-year-old culture that had shaped their lives. There was also a small number of ultranationalists who called themselves the *katta gumi* (the winning group). They quietly applauded each Japanese victory at the beginning of the war and looked forward to the day when Japanese forces would come to claim the Hawaiian Islands for the Japanese Empire. Some found it hard to admit, even after V-J Day, that the Japanese Empire had been defeated. These nationalists thought of Murai, Kido, Goto, Katagiri, and the haole cop they traveled with as *inu*—dogs. But most members of the Japanese community listened carefully and did their best to demonstrate their American patriotism.

Burns grew increasingly more familiar with the leaders of the Japanese community. He would drive the members of the Emergency Service Committee to the meetings. They all had police permits to drive during the blackout, but they were still Japanese. The young mainland military police who enforced the blackout laws could not be trusted to know the difference between a Japanese national and an American of Japanese ancestry. With Burns driving, there were no problems. Driving to and from these meetings not only gave Burns a chance to get to know his passengers, it also gave the leaders of the Japanese community a chance to get to know him. In time they came to sense his genuine concern for their community and to develop a feeling of trust in him.

Jack Burns was not an easy man to know. Dr. Murai recalled, "My first impression of him was that he was a man of few words. He just listens, and I thought that probably this was a position a police officer should take." Mits Kido was less generous in his first impression. "The first time I met him," Kido recalled, "I thought he was very cold and a hard person to work with. Never smiled much. Very businesslike. Abrupt, almost curt in his response when you talked to him. . . . He didn't strike me as a person you could get close to, . . . so I kept my distance."

Another Japanese-American who worked with Burns during the war was Jack Kawano, a longshoreman and one of the leaders of the International Longshoremen's and Warehousemen's Union (ILWU). "I didn't like him," Kawano said, recalling his first impression of Burns. "To me, he didn't know how to smile. To me, he was just a policeman. Nothing friendly about him." In time, Kawano's feelings would change.

For Kawano, and many others, understanding came over a cup of coffee. Whether it was in the coffee shop beneath his office in the Dillingham Transportation Building, the Emergency Service Committee's office at the Nuuanu YMCA, or in their homes, coffee was for Jack Burns the lubricant for conversation. "I remember many times he used to come to my house," Kawano recalled. "He'd come around midnight and he'd stay until around three o'clock . . . in the morning. All I had was coffee for him."

Ultimately, it was Burns' sincerity that won over the Japanese-American leaders. "He was not primarily concerned for the Japanese, per se," Murai reasoned, "but I think I sensed that he was concerned about the whole people of the Territory of Hawaii. If he can help, he was trying to prevent any racial incident to happen on the plantation between the Japanese and either the Caucasians, or the Filipinos, or the Chinese, or the Puerto Ricans." Kawano, too, came to see the compassion and egalitarianism that lay hidden beneath Burns' tough exterior. "After we got a little acquainted, I see that this man is a very sentimental guy. . . . He's the kind of guy, if you cry, he'll comfort you. . . . He was a good man to have around. . . . He grew up in Kalihi—he has no feeling of 'big shot.'"

His work with the Police Contact Group and the Emergency Service Committee, in addition to his full-time duty with the vice squad, left Jack Burns with little time for his family. Nevertheless, with a wife who was an invalid, he had to pitch in with family chores. One of those chores was to drive the two oldest children—Jack, Jr., who attended St. Louis, and Mary Beth, who attended Sacred Heart—to and from school every day. Living in Kailua, this was no small task. One evening, when a meeting at Waipahu ran late, Burns turned to Dr. Murai in horror, "My God, I forgot my children!" As a driver for the Red Cross, Murai's wife had a pass to drive during the blackout. After a call from her husband, she picked up the Burns children, took them home, and fed them dinner while they waited for their father to return from his meeting.

Having been supportive of the 100th Battalion and active in encouraging young AJAs to enlist in the 442nd Regimental Combat Team, Burns took great interest in the welfare of these young soldiers and their families. When stories came back to Hawaii about the hospitality shown to members of the 100th by the citizens of Wisconsin, Burns decided to reciprocate. "We told the military," Burns recalled, "you give us five hundred guys from Wisconsin." The Emergency Service Committee put on a luau for the Wisconsin soldiers which was attended by three thousand. Throughout the war, Burns maintained personal correspondence with Earl Kubo of the 442nd and William T. Hiraoka of the little-publicized, but very important Military Intelligence Service. He encouraged members of the Police Contact Group and the Emergency Service Committee to write to AJAs in the service to let them know that they were being remembered and that their families in Hawaii were doing well.

Years later, Mits Kido commented on the importance of those letters:

> What triggered me into politics was the fact that youngsters we enrolled in the 442nd [Regimental] Combat Team . . . wrote letters from their hospital beds in Italy and said, "We're willing to sacrifice our lives and everything—are we coming back to a second class society? What are we going to do when we get back?" We read some of those letters and decided something had to be done. We felt that one way of bringing about full recognition of the people who made this supreme sacrifice was to get into politics to change [the] political life of the community to be more democratic—to bring about . . . equality of opportunity.

Beginning in 1944, Jack Burns joined four other men to discuss, informally, the political future of the Territory of Hawaii: Dr. Ernest Murai, the dentist; Mits Kido, a University of Hawaii-trained social studies teacher; Jack Kawano, a Big Island-born labor leader; and Chuck Mau, a Chinese-American lawyer and a member of the Honolulu board of supervisors (now known as the Honolulu City Council). Out of their meetings, the new Democratic Party of the Territory of Hawaii would emerge. They had no mandate to do this, only a passion born out of an understanding of prewar social conditions and the wartime experience of those who wanted to return to a more just society than they had left.

Kawano, who knew that the future of the ILWU depended upon an altered political landscape in Hawaii, was the prime mover in the formation of this group in its earliest days. "It was through his auspices," Mau recalled, "that the five of us got together. . . . And he was powerful . . . because he had an organization behind him. None of [the rest of] us had an organization behind us." Mau may have been excessively modest about what he and the others contributed, but the postwar Democratic Party relied heavily on the ILWU to provide manpower to register voters and organize the precincts. Jack Kawano—not Jack Hall, the man generally credited with the rise of the ILWU after the war—led that charge.

The five men met weekly, usually at the home of Chuck Mau, the only one of the group with any direct political experience. They drank coffee, ate cookies and talked long into the night. As they discussed the future, Jack Kawano and the ILWU showed it to them. In June 1944, Jack Hall became regional director of the ILWU, a position that Kawano had wanted very much, thought he deserved, and might have had if he had not been a Japanese-American. After all, the reasoning went, the United States was still at war with Japan. Would it be wise for the ILWU to present as its most visible leader someone of Japanese ancestry?

Hall and Kawano both knew that the fortunes of their union would be limited without a change in the laws, which would allow them to organize all plantation workers, including agricultural workers. Hall had been working in this direction since 1938, when he organized the Kauai Progressive League. The war had interrupted his efforts. But in 1944, utilizing a political technique created by the Congress of Industrial Organizations (CIO)—the political action committee (PAC)—the ILWU quietly moved into Hawaii's politics, catching the economic and political oligarchy completely off guard. In the November 1944 legislative elections, fifteen of the nineteen House candidates endorsed by the PAC were elected; six of eight PAC-endorsed Senate candidates won as well. Central to the success of the ILWU/PAC campaign was a voter registration drive headed by Jack Kawano.

The ILWU/PAC endorsements were not made strictly along Party lines, but in accordance with the willingness of the nominee to recognize labor's right to organize. The territorial legislature elected in 1944 was still controlled by the Republican Party. The GOP majority in the House of Representatives was 21 to 9; in the Senate it was 7 to 6. It may have been a Republican majority, but it was a majority that was mindful of the potential political power of the ILWU and willing to support the union's principal objective, the right to organize all of Hawaii's plantation workers.

On 21 May 1945, the new legislature passed the Hawaii Employee Relations Act, often referred to as the Little Wagner Act. The measure had been written by Jack Hall of the ILWU, who had worked in the Territorial Department of Labor and Industrial Relations during the war, and it was the key to the union's postwar success. With only nine hundred members at the beginning of 1944, the ILWU would grow to a membership of over thirty thousand by 1947. The lesson of the 1944 elections was not lost on those who met weekly with Jack Kawano; if the ILWU had that kind of power, they wanted the union on the side of the Democratic Party.

The rise of the Democratic Party in Hawaii after World War II received its impetus from two sources: the ILWU and the Japanese-American veterans of the 100th and the 442nd. But not all veterans were immediately available for political activity. Many were busy taking advantage of the G.I. Bill of Rights, getting the education that would qualify them to be the leaders of the future. In the first years after the war, it was the ILWU, not the AJA veterans, that led the way in the creation of the new Democratic Party. But it was not until the veterans were added to the equation that the Democrats were able to fashion their revolution in 1954.

In spite of Jack Burns' brief political liaison with Republican Chairman Roy Vituosek in 1942, there was no question about which party the five would select as the object of their political intentions. It had to be the Democratic Party. Since 1902, when the leadership of the Republican Party secured Prince Jonah Kalanianaole Kuhio as their political ally, the Republican Party had been the political instrument of upper-class haole. The Big Five companies, Alexander & Baldwin, American Factors, C. Brewer, Castle and Cooke, and Theo. H. Davies, controlled both the economy and the politics of the Islands. Kuhio became, and remained until his death in 1920, Hawaii's nonvoting delegate to Congress for his part in the deal. The Republican Party got something far more important: the political allegiance of the Hawaiian and part-Hawaiian population, then the largest single voting bloc in the Islands. This assured the Republicans control of the territorial legislature. It also gave the Hawaiians a considerable amount of patronage. In Hawaii, as elsewhere, jobs and votes were never very far apart.

The Democratic Party, by contrast, was a shambles. A Democrat would occasionally win countywide office on the Island of Oahu, as Chuck Mau had, or a few seats in the territorial legislature, but Party factionalism destroyed any significant effort to share power. Mits Kido best expressed the thinking of his colleagues as they looked to the Democratic Party organization in 1944:

The Democratic Party ... was made up of various cliques—the Holts and the Heens and the Trasks and a few others—disgruntled people. And the *malihini* (newcomer) haoles, like the Stainbacks and the Huberts and a few southern Democrats that were here. So there was not an organization, and we felt that if we got into the Democratic Party we would be able to control it, set up a machinery, and offer the people of Hawaii an alternative.

Making the Democratic Party into an instrument of social change would require more than conversation in Chuck Mau's living room. Someone would have to take on the onerous, slightly disreputable task of full-time organizing. Lacking volunteers, Jack Burns decided that he would be the one. On 8 August 1945, two days after the dropping of an atomic bomb on Hiroshima had sealed the fate of the Japanese empire, Jack Burns submitted a letter of resignation from the Honolulu Police Department to Chief Gabrielson.

In his letter, Burns explained that he was leaving the police force because he had acquired a combination liquor and grocery store. In fact, the decision to leave the HPD had been coming for some time. As early as 1943, he was looking elsewhere. In that year, Hawaii County changed from an elected sheriff to an elected police commission and a civil service chief of police. There is some debate about whether Burns was actually offered the job, but there is no doubt that there were those on the Big Island who were very interested in having him assume the post. There is also no doubt that extensive discussions had taken place with Burns about the job. Whether he declined the job, or merely took himself out of the running, Burns decided that the newly constituted Hawaii County Police Commission would not give him sufficient freedom to do the job as he saw fit. Burns had experienced interference by the police commission in Honolulu, and he wanted none of it on the Big Island.

In the waning days of World War II, both Jack Burns and his brother Ed—who had followed his older sibling into the HPD—were growing restive under the increasingly arbitrary leadership of Chief

Gabrielson. The beginning of the end came in 1944 when Chief Gabrielson overrode the decision of a three-man promotion board on which both Burns brothers and Assistant Police Chief Hoopai had served. The three had submitted a list, ranked from 1 to 5, of candidates for promotion to sergeant. Instead of accepting their recommendation, Gabrielson reached down and promoted a man who ranked seventeenth on the promotion list. When this led to a confrontation between Gabrielson and Police Commission Chairman George W. Sumner, the chief turned on the Burns brothers and Assistant Chief Hoopai with a vengeance, giving them a tongue-lashing they would never forget—or forgive. Then Gabrielson went after Sumner, actively and successfully lobbying all fifteen members of the territorial senate in the process. "When I found out they had dumped Sumner," Ed Burns said, "I was ready to quit the same day." Ed Burns resigned in January 1945; Jack waited until August.

Dissatisfaction with Chief Gabrielson may have been the primary reason Ed Burns left the HPD, but the final trigger for Jack was political. Following the ILWU surprise in 1944, the Republican leadership in the territorial legislature demanded closer adherence to the Party line. This was evident when the legislature next convened. "After the '45 session," Burns stated, "I made up my mind—period—that I was gonna help build the Democratic Party, so long as I could make a living some way."

Jack Burns had no intention of making his mark as the proprietor of a liquor store, but it was a way to earn an income while he was doing his political work. He acquired the Kalama Liquor Store from his brother-in-law, Jimmy Trask, in exchange for the forgiveness of a $6,500 loan. It wasn't much, but in August 1945 it was Jack Burns' largest single asset. The application for transfer of the liquor license required an inventory of the prospective owner's assets. Those declared by Jack Burns were:

Cash on hand	$ 500
Territorial retirement plan	1,000
War bonds	1,500
Oahu Railroad and McBryde stock	2,000
Equity in Kailua home ($1,800 loan balance)	5,700
1940 Chevrolet sedan	800
Unsecured note from Jimmy Trask	6,500
Total assets	$18,000

Burns also obtained a real estate license, hoping for an occasional commission along the way.

When Ed Burns left the HPD, it was to pursue a career in business. It seemed natural for him to become a member of the Republican Party. He encouraged his brother to do the same. When Ed told Roy Vitousek of Jack's plans to leave the police force to build the Democratic Party, the Republican Party chairman tried to get him to change his mind. Vitousek told Jack Burns that he could get him elected to any office he wanted—as a Republican, of course. Burns told his old friend that he didn't want to run for any office, he just wanted to build a Party of opportunity for the people of Hawaii. "I knew labor belonged in the ranks of the Democratic Party because they always had been," Burns reasoned, "[and] I knew that the young veterans should be Democrats."

Burns looked to the Democratic Party establishment in Hawaii for help. FDR appointee Ingram M. Stainback had been the territorial governor since 1942. Burns urged him to use his federal patronage to help Democrats, something Stainback had rarely done. As Lawrence Fuchs pointed out in *Hawaii Pono*, "He filled ten of the top thirteen positions with members of the GOP, and throughout his eight years in office, two-thirds of his major appointments were Republicans." The supplications of a socially, and at that point politically, unimportant Kailua liquor store owner did not make Governor Stainback change his thinking. "Stainback took the flat position," Burns remembered bitterly, "that he was not named [by FDR] as a Democrat, that he was named as Stainback."

Burns himself had the occasion to seek an appointive position from Governor Stainback. When the position of postmaster of Kailua opened up, Burns asked friends to urge Stainback to appoint him. Burns thought it was a natural since the post office was right next door to his liquor store. Burns had neglected to consider an important point, however. Had he taken the position, the Hatch Act would have prevented him from active participation in Party politics. When he discovered this prohibition, Burns rejected the offer. There is no evidence that Stainback made the offer with the strictures of the Hatch Act in mind, but it is clear that he saw Jack Burns as a threat to business as usual for the Democratic Party of Hawaii.

During the first two years after his resignation from the police force, Burns did alright financially. The liquor store put food on the Burns' family table. But increasingly Burns' community and political activities took him away from the business. "He let the store go," Bea remembered.

Jack hired others to run the store, but their salaries ate up the business' income. "I said (to him), 'Well, this is great. (While) you're taking care of the community, who's going to take care of us?' . . . I grumbled." Burns took over the operation of the store himself. "But by then the only reason we didn't go bankrupt was we didn't file," Bea recalled.

Then one summer day, Jack announced that he had to go into Honolulu to pick up supplies. He asked Bea to mind the store. When she protested, he pointed out that their teenage son Jim would be there to help, but it was against the law for him to handle the liquor. Bea worked that summer, certain that when school started in the fall and Jim returned to classes she would not be able to continue. But she did, all day, every day, as her husband's political activity expanded.

"I didn't know a blasted thing about liquor," Bea remembered. "The liquor salesmen were so great. They were beautiful. They were so good to me. . . . I remember the day we got up to a hundred dollars gross. Jack was in Washington, D.C., and I was so thrilled. Then from then on it was a daily thing." Jack would usually drop her off at the store in the morning. Jim would often "push me home, from Oneawa Street . . . with the money box in my lap." Bea's most difficult obstacle was the store's lack of a restroom: "I had no john. I just didn't drink."

While Bea watched the store, Jack was getting a few friends to sign Democratic Party cards and persuading them to attend a precinct meeting that would elect him to the Party's county and territorial central committees. With the Democratic Party all but moribund, especially on the windward side of the island, there was little competition for these positions.

Burns recalled that there were sixteen members present at his first meeting as a member of Oahu's County Democratic Central Committee. "The chair announced that he had the proxies of thirty-odd more votes," Burns recalled, "and since there were seventy-two precincts at that time, that constituted a quorum. . . . That was the state of the Party." Those proxies not only constituted a quorum, they created a majority in the hands of a single person. Burns wondered at the time whether the procedure was entirely legal. Legal or not, Burns managed to get himself elected as second vice chairman. It wasn't much, but it was a start in his effort to take over the reins of the Democratic Party of Hawaii.

In the meantime, on the leeward side of the island, Dr. Murai was having a similar experience. Murai later recalled:

The Democratic precincts they used to have [were] controlled by a few
. . . haoles. They'd have a meeting at their home and maybe only their
family would meet and elect so-and-so president, vice-president, secretary. That's the only kind of meeting they had. But we insisted in
meeting at a public school. This is where I became president of the St.
Louis Heights precinct.

In 1946, to broaden this penetration into the inner workings of the Democratic Party, Burns, Murai, Kido, Kawano, and Mau decided that they
would attempt to bring the former members of Burns' Police Contact
Group into the fold. Each member was asked to organize meetings in
his own election precinct. Their efforts were just under way when the
1946 elections took place.

As the elections approached, the ILWU was going through its
defining moment, the successful 1946 sugar strike. Jack Hall, the pragmatic leader of the ILWU, decided that the political action committees
should avoid the appearance of partisanship in the elections. After all,
they had been successful in 1944 by endorsing across Party lines. Hall
also saw the benefit of having the union endorse Delegate Joseph R. Farrington, the Republican publisher of the *Honolulu Star-Bulletin*. If he
could neutralize one of the major daily papers during the strike, public
opinion might be more favorable to the ILWU. It was a strategy that
may have worked for the union, but it certainly slowed the progress of
the Democratic Party. It was also a strategy that was opposed by Jack
Kawano within the ILWU and may, at least in part, account for his increasing isolation from the union's leaders. Burns and his friends came
to realize that, for the time being, the ILWU's preference for the Democratic Party was clear, but it was not automatic.

The major challenge of the Democratic Party in 1946 was to find
viable candidates who were willing to face well-financed, incumbent Republicans. For example, when the Oahu County Democratic Committee looked at the races for the board of supervisors, they wanted a full
slate of six candidates to challenge the Republicans. The way in which
elections were run in the Territory of Hawaii in those days required that
all candidates run at-large, meaning that each member represented all
of the voters of Oahu, rather than those of a smaller electoral district.
Six candidates from each Party would advance from the primary to the
general election. In the general election, the top six vote-getters would

be elected to the board of supervisors. When it appeared that the Democrats could not field a full slate of candidates, Burns volunteered to run. As it turned out, he need not have run; on primary day he was one of seven Democratic candidates on the ballot.

When Burns announced his candidacy, the *Honolulu Star-Bulletin* carried the following story:

> John A. Burns, a member of the Oahu County Democratic Committee, Tuesday announced his candidacy for the board of supervisors. He is basing his candidacy on the development of a parks and playground system and on direct representation of rural districts on the board. He is: vice-president of the Koolaupoko Lions Club, president of St. Anthony's Holy Name Society, and a member of the Mid-Pacific Country Club.

Although the announcement was short on anything that reflected Burns' true political motivation, it did identify three passions of his life: his service club, his church, and his golf game.

But election to the Oahu County board of supervisors in 1946 required substantial name recognition, islandwide, as all members were elected on an at-large basis. Burns was short of name recognition and, in addition to that, he lived on the wrong side of the island. In the primary election, Burns finished dead last among the seven Democratic candidates. He was the only one who did not make it onto the ballot for the general election.

There were friends who sought to help Jack Burns in his 1946 supervisor's race, even Republican friends. One of those was T. G. S. Walker, whom Jack had met during the war when Walker was serving as territorial director of Civil Defense. Walker, who had been the prewar manager of Kahuku Sugar Company, wrote the following letter to Harry Shigemitsu, a resident of rural Kahuku:

> You may think it strange that a staunch Republican like myself should be backing a Democratic candidate, but I am so convinced that Jack would make such an excellent "Supervisor" that I believe his election would be very beneficial to the efficient running of our local government.
>
> As you probably know, Jack Burns was a police captain and acted as a liaison between the Police Department, F.B.I. and military intelligence during the war and in that capacity was a great help in warding off discriminatory action against portions of our civilian population.

It would have been clear to a man named Shigemitsu exactly what "portions" of the population Walker was referring to in his letter. Thus it was a haole Republican who was the first to articulate, in a semipublic way, the basis of John A. Burns' eventual leadership of the Democratic Party in Hawaii. Walker sent a note to Burns with a copy of his letter. In the note, Walker joked that he had "told the same lies" to six others, four of whom were identified as Republicans, two as independents.

For Burns, the election proved educational. He learned, for example, what happened on the plantations when Democrats campaigned there. At Kahuku, Burns heard David K. Trask deliver a stem-winding, full-dress oration to a gathering of eight. When he asked Trask why he had given so much for so few, the veteran Democrat replied that this was the first election in which a Democrat had been allowed anywhere near the plantations and he was going to make the most of it. From other political veterans, Burns heard how, in the past, Democrats had been forced to use loudspeakers on public roads in the hope that their message might carry to a few plantation workers who were interested enough to listen from behind roadside bushes. Aside from the education, the campaign was a dismal failure.

Mits Kido succeeded in 1946 while Burns and Chuck Mau were going down to defeat. Kido ran for the territorial house of representatives in Oahu's fifth district. In the urban part of his district, which included everything west of Nuuanu Avenue, Kido had been well known as a social studies teacher at Kalakaua Intermediate School and Farrington High School for sixteen years. In the rural areas, Jack Kawano opened doors for Kido. In the general election, Kido's 10,619 votes placed him first in a field of twelve. His vote count even exceeded that of the fabled Republican vote-getter Hiram Fong, who received 9,721 votes.

On several occasions during the 1946 primary campaign, Kido shared the stump with Burns and Mau. Kido saw Burns' oratorical style as a significant drawback to his candidacy. "He was stiff," Kido recalled, "not one of those effusive guys that would generate enthusiasm." Chuck Mau agreed: "Jack was never a good speaker. He never had that personality that could exude out and permeate the people. . . . He always had a dour expression. Not only that, his voice didn't carry. . . . He really had a hard time."

While his lack of oratorical skills may have been a problem for him, Burns did have two qualities which left their mark on those voters who took the trouble to listen to this earnest ex-cop who was trying to make it in politics. The first, remembered well by Mits Kido, was that Burns "always spoke about the principles of the Party, spoke for the team. Never once did I hear him say, 'Vote for Jack Burns,' or even intimate that. His talk was always about [the] Democratic Party, what the Party can do for the people of Hawaii." The second quality, recalled by Chuck Mau, was his tenacity and his ability to overcome adversity. Burns lost badly in his first two attempts at public office—for supervisor in 1946 and for delegate to Congress in 1948. "It took a lot of courage to be knocked on the head each time," Mau said. "He had no funds—we had no funds. Nobody had any money to support him and what little organization there was, was only Jack Kawano's group, plus a few friends that the rest of us had." Kawano agreed, adding: "He had determination. . . . He was very persistent. . . . He'd never give up."

A. A. "Bud" Smyser, who would later become editor of the *Honolulu Star-Bulletin*, was a cub reporter in 1946. He covered politics and he remembered Jack Burns well: "I can recall him appearing up at the [board of supervisors] chamber to watch activities there, and . . . innumerable conversations with him on street corners." Smyser saw little potential for Burns as a politician, nor did he accept Burns' dream for the future of the Democratic Party of Hawaii. "Even then," Smyser recalled, "he was espousing what he held to over all the years, the importance of bringing labor and the AJAs together in politics, the importance of challenging the established hierarchy. . . . [He was] a Don Quixote . . . with whom I could sympathize, but I wasn't sure he was ever going to pull it off."

Smyser concluded his assessment of Jack Burns with these words:

> He certainly was not the most intelligent man I ever met, he wasn't the sweetest man I ever met, he wasn't the most ingenious man, nor the shrewdest man or anything else I ever met. I've asked myself what was uncommon about this essentially common man. I believe the uncommon thing about him was a great inner sense of direction, a very strong personal sense of what was right and wrong. I think that Jack was able, in the course of defeats that would have discouraged other people, to still feel that his own sense of direction was right and to hold to it, and in the end to rally people around him and win respect. . . . [That is what] separated him from people more intelligent, more able, more everything else than he might be.

Two important races in the 1946 elections might have been seen as hopeful for the Democratic Party of Hawaii. In the contest for delegate to Congress, William Borthwick, a Stainback Democrat, gave Joseph R. Farrington a surprisingly tough race. Farrington, who had received the endorsement of the ILWU, received 45,765 votes to a respectable 37,209 for Borthwick, the territorial tax commissioner. Farrington had run virtually unopposed in 1944. In the other high visibility race, Democrat "Johnny" H. Wilson edged out Herbert "Monty" Richards for mayor of Honolulu by a mere sixteen votes—26,752 to 26,736. This was a remarkable comeback for the part-Hawaiian Wilson, who had previously served as Honolulu's mayor 1920–1926 and 1929–1930, but neither Borthwick's relatively strong showing nor Wilson's victory can be viewed as a harbinger of things to come for the Democratic Party in 1946.

In 1946, the war was over, the troops were back from the front and off to college, the ILWU was on the march, and the Democratic Party was gaining strength. Power would not come immediately, but come it would. And although it was far too early for most to recognize it, the Party's leader—Jack Burns—was already in place. Burns, who had failed so badly in his own election efforts in 1946, soon fashioned the coalition which would dominate Hawaii's politics for the last half of the twentieth century.

F·I·V·E

Emerging Leadership

BUILDING A POLITICAL COALITION in Hawaii was a highly personal process, one for which Jack Burns was admirably suited. His unique combination of selflessness, determination, and patience enabled him to overcome a lack of charisma, particularly in the Japanese-American community. This was certainly one of the keys to his special relationship with the young veterans of the 100th and 442nd who were just entering politics. Burns, who seemed to value their personal success more than his own, would become their leader and mentor. But the process would not take place overnight.

That Jack Burns was not a great public speaker did not mean that he was a poor communicator. Many locals treated people who were too articulate with suspicion. Jack Burns spoke the language of the common people of Hawaii. And while he might have appeared remote and colorless in a public forum, Burns was a different man in private. As Bud Smyser observed, "In a one-for-one relationship [Jack] was charming and likable. He was a different man in front of a group."

Burns was also very good with small groups, as we have seen from his association with the Police Contact Group and his political strategy sessions with Dr. Murai, Mits Kido, Jack Kawano, and Chuck Mau. Another small group that met with Jack Burns right after the end of the war was his Friday lunch club. This consisted of Bill Norwood, Tom Walker, his brother Ed, and two or three others who would rotate in and out. They first met at the Kewalo Inn, then at the Beaver Grill on Merchant Street. Jack Burns was not a loner. He made his decisions only after having looked at an issue through the eyes of trusted friends, an absolute requirement for a consensus builder.

In 1946, Jack Burns began to take his message to the neighbor islands. In his first foray, he went to Kauai while the sugar strike was still in progress. One morning in Lihue, Burns walked into the farm supply store of Toshio Serizawa, a young independent businessman. As Serizawa recalled the meeting, Burns arrived, unannounced, and said: "I'm Jack Burns. I want to talk politics." Not wanting to be seen talking with a Democratic Party organizer, Serizawa invited Burns to go into the back room. "Being a Democrat," Serizawa explained, "was [for a man in his business] like having leprosy."

Serizawa recalled that Burns stayed in his store the entire morning, talking about the veterans who were coming back to their homes in Hawaii, about the kind of employment they would find, about the opportunities their children would enjoy. He also talked about the working men who had built Hawaii's plantations.

"Why do you think all these guys are on strike on the sugar plantation?" Burns asked Serizawa.

"What I read, Mr. Burns, in the newspapers," Serizawa replied, "is that Communists are behind this sugar strike."

"It's not communism," Burns shot back, "it's economics. . . . Don't tell me these thousands of people in the plantations—your own brother-in-law, . . . your sister-in-law—are Communists." Seeking to defuse the issue of communism, Burns went on to say, "There's always a rotten apple someplace in the barrel, but don't condemn all of them." The overwhelming majority of the strikers, Burns told Serizawa, "are going to be Democrats." Burns then went to the heart of the reason for his visit: "But we've got to get the independent people—nonplantation employees—involved. This is why I've come to talk to you."

Burns left Serizawa's store that afternoon with a new recruit. Two years later, Serizawa went to Honolulu as a delegate to the 1948 territorial Democratic Convention. That same year, he ran for the Kauai board of supervisors, as a Democrat, and won. In this highly personal way, Burns and his friends began the geometric progression that would result in the creation of a new Democratic Party. "We knew," Chuck Mau recalled, "that we wanted the young people to come in and take part because they were going to be the eventual leaders. We never thought that any one of the five [of us] would really become a strong enough leader in the community to lead the Party."

One of the major risks of a Democratic Party that was built on a base of plantation workers and veterans of the 100th and 442nd was that it would become racially isolated. Burns, Mau, and the others understood this. "The wider the racial group," Mau said, "the better it is for us. . . . So we were constantly looking . . . for Caucasians." But it wasn't easy, for, as Mau said, "if they belonged to the Democratic Party they were ostracized, just like we were. Not only economically, but socially as well. We had a hard time."

Not all haoles were afraid to join the Democratic Party in Hawaii. Beginning in 1940, a flood of new workers came into the Territory's rapidly expanding job market. Many were laborers, mechanics, and defense workers who had been supporters of the New Deal on the mainland during the 1930s. They brought their politics with them.

O. Vincent Esposito, then a young lawyer who was destined to become one of the top leaders of the postwar Democratic Party, remembered this group. "A lot of them stayed here and they began to swell the ranks of the Democrats and started to give sustenance and stability and meaning to Democratic politics."

Esposito notwithstanding, "a lot" was a relative term. In fact, they were few in actual numbers and they were handicapped by that most pernicious of all Island labels, they were *malihini*. But given their political weakness, Burns and his friends could not afford to discriminate against newcomers, whatever their background. And so it was that David Benz, a young Jewish printing executive with the Tongg Printing Company, was welcomed into their midst. Politicians need printing like ducks need water and Benz became an intimate of the five, frequently attending their meetings.

As the 1948 political season approached, Burns and his friends hoped to recruit enough attractive candidates to challenge the Republicans in every electoral contest. One of the places they looked was on the campus of the University of Hawaii at Manoa. All across the United States World War II veterans, supported by the G.I. Bill, were changing the face of American higher education. They would soon change the face of the nation. Nowhere was this phenomenon more dramatic than in Hawaii. In the years immediately following the war, Manoa teemed with bright young men, returned from the war, eager to get on with their education and their lives. Their battlefield experiences had given them maturity far beyond their years. They demonstrated a seriousness of purpose never before seen on the campus. They listened attentively to devoted teachers like Gregg Sinclair, Allan Saunders, and Thomas Murphy.

One such veteran, a member of the 442nd Regimental Combat Team, had lost his right arm to a German rifle grenade during the war.

Daniel K. Inouye was a pre-law student at the University of Hawaii and was already looking beyond Manoa. Inouye and his friends from the 442nd knew Jack Burns and about the friendship and support he had given to the Japanese community during the war. When they organized the 442nd Veterans Club, they made Burns an honorary member.

In the summer of 1947, Inouye became a member of the Democratic Party, in spite of the suggestion of some of his friends that he might find a more promising political future as a Republican. After all, Inouye recalled being told, "What's the difference between them, except that the Republicans are in and the Democrats never will be." Inouye's response was quick: "The difference between them is that the Republicans' chief concern is property, things, what we own; the Democrats worry about people, what we are."

As the 1948 filing deadline drew near and the Democrats found themselves without a credible candidate to challenge Joe Farrington, the incumbent Republican delegate to Congress, Jack Burns stepped up as he had in 1946. He would challenge the unbeatable Farrington because he could not allow the Democratic Party to let the position go to the Republicans by default. When he read Burns' announcement in the newspaper, Dan Inouye called him. Inouye told Burns that he would like to ask him a few questions. Burns told him to fire away. Inouye remembered that his first question—"Do you think you can win the race for delegate?"—led to the following exchange:

BURNS: No, but that's not going to keep me from trying my hardest.

INOUYE: But if you did win, you'd give it everything you had, right? You'd be a good delegate?

BURNS: I think I'd be a good delegate. Yes. I have strong feelings about Hawaii and its people. I think I can express to Congress our great desire for statehood.

INOUYE: Jack, do you need some help?

BURNS: No one ever needed it more. Can I count on you?

INOUYE: For anything at all.

Inouye expected to be stuffing envelopes or performing some other menial task. Instead, the 24-year-old war hero joined the executive board of Burns' campaign committee.

The 442nd Veterans Club did not rush to Burns' support. They liked Joe Farrington and did not want to waste their time or vote on someone who had no chance of winning. They were also more interested in their education, jobs, and families than politics. Inouye recalled that, even as a member of the board of directors of the 442nd Veterans Club, he had to beg to get Burns on an upcoming program to which Farrington had been invited. Even then, it was with the understanding that each candidate had only three minutes to speak and that they would not be allowed to talk about politics. It was only after some of their members began to run for public office that the 442nd Veterans Club became decidedly more political.

In 1948, Inouye failed to persuade many of his friends to support the man he would later call his "political godfather." But he helped to open the door, ever so slightly, which would later be torn from its hinges. The military structure which had helped the men of the 442nd survive in time of war remained in place in time of peace. To many, Dan Inouye would always be Captain Inouye, their battlefield leader to whom they would continue to look for leadership in civilian life. Unlike similar organizations on the mainland, the veterans of the 442nd did not scatter themselves throughout the United States. They were concentrated on six small islands in the middle of the Pacific Ocean and they possessed enormous organizational power.

Had the organization of the Democratic Party been as simple as uniting the political clout of the ILWU and the AJA veterans, it might have been achieved sooner than it was. But there was a serious hurdle the Democratic Party had to overcome before it would achieve power. That hurdle was the issue of communism. The specter of communism had been raised in Hawaii, from time to time, since the 1920s. It was a club the Big Five used to beat down early efforts to unionize Hawaii's agricultural workforce. As with the mainland, it did not take on the dimensions of a life-and-death struggle until the Cold War emerged at the end of World War II.

Ironically, the first political campaign to be hit with charges of communist influence was that of the Republican delegate to Congress, Joe Farrington. Farrington's refusal to repudiate the endorsement of the ILWU's political action committee in 1946 resulted in strong expressions of concern. Roy Vitousek, chairman of the territorial Republican Central Committee, commented: "We want a government run by and for the people of the Territory, instead of for the PAC, other organized minorities, communist front organizations, and pressure groups." Some were less restrained than Vitousek. Jack Hall's biographer, Sanford Zalburg, recounted one such reaction from realtor Lindsley Austin, who "was so incensed that upon meeting Farrington at a polling place on election day, he tried to hit him. 'You communist,' Austin shouted." But talk of communism in 1946 was a small ripple when compared to the tidal wave that hit the Islands in 1947.

On 11 November 1947, in an Armistice Day speech, Governor Ingram M. Stainback announced that a communist conspiracy was on the loose in Hawaii. He read a portion of what he called the "plan for the communists under which they have operated in the Territory for many years." Governor Stainback had warned of the communist menace in 1947 speeches given on Navy Day, during Army week, on the Fourth of July, on Labor Day, and again as recently as 24 October, before a gathering of the American Federation of Labor (AFL). Stainback's Armistice Day speech, however, was different in that it spoke of "a communist plan" for Hawaii. It made reference to the "mastermind" of that plan and made clear his intention to expose that evil force.

Less than a week after Stainback's Armistice Day speech, a pamphlet was released under the ominous title, *The Truth About Communism in Hawaii*. The thirty-two-page pamphlet, purportedly written by a former ILWU officer from Kauai, Ichiro Izuka, named forty-seven individuals as members of the Communist Party in Hawaii. It hit at the very heart of the ILWU. With the ILWU recognized as one of the key elements in the emerging Democratic Party of Hawaii, the taint of communism came with it.

On 25 November 1947, the "mastermind" of the Communist Party of Hawaii was revealed to be Dr. John E. Reinecke, a teacher at Farrington High School. Reinecke was suspended from his teaching position, without pay, pending a hearing that would determine whether he possessed the "ideals of democracy" which were requisite for such a position of public trust. For good measure, Reinecke's wife Aiko, a teacher at Waialae Elementary School, was also suspended.

For the better part of a year, the Reinecke case remained in front of the Hawaiian public. On 29 October 1948, the territorial Department of Education fired John and Aiko Reinecke. These two teachers, with a combined total of almost forty years of teaching the children of Hawaii, would never teach again. John Reinecke had, indeed, been a member of the Communist Party, although he would neither affirm nor deny the charge during his ordeal. The "communist plan" Reinecke was accused of writing turned out to be a paper he had written for his own benefit, while a graduate student at the University of Hawaii, to clarify his thinking, in 1934 or 1935. He made the mistake of sharing it with a couple of friends from the university. During World War II, the paper found its way into the hands of military intelligence who, in turn, shared it with Governor Stainback.

Interestingly enough, the paper was written two or three years before there was a Communist Party in Hawaii. Reinecke actually joined the Communist Party in New Haven, Connecticut, during the 1935–1936 academic year, while studying for his doctorate at Yale University. He became a member of the Communist Party in Hawaii in 1938.

Whether Reinecke's unpopular political views indicated a failure to possess the "ideals of democracy" was clearly in the eyes of the beholder. The Territory presented no evidence that Reinecke ever sought to promote his views in class. The entire outcome hinged on whether he was a member of the Communist Party. The territorial commissioners of public instruction were satisfied that he was and that this membership, on the face of it, precluded the possibility that John Reinecke could possibly possess the "ideals of democracy." The fact that the Communist Party was a legal organization in the United States was, to them, irrelevant.

Hawaii was caught up in the early stages of what later came to be known as the "McCarthy Era," named for that reckless anticommunist senator from Wisconsin, Joe McCarthy. As on the mainland, Hawaii's Republicans were all too willing to use the communist issue as a blunt instrument against their Democratic opponents. Hawaii would also imitate the mainland in the way in which the issue of communism created schisms within the Democratic Party. Right wing, or simply frightened, Democrats fell all over themselves trying to show that they were more anticommunist than the Republicans.

In retrospect, it was a sad chapter in America's and Hawaii's history. From 1947 through 1954, communism was an issue through which careers in public service were made and broken. On the mainland, the anticommunist tide began in earnest in 1947–1948, when Richard Nixon overwhelmed his hapless victim, Alger Hiss. It had largely spent itself by 1954, as counsel for the U.S. Army pounded a bewildered Senator

McCarthy into submission. In Hawaii, it began in 1947–1948 with the Reinecke case and rapidly declined at the conclusion of the 1953 Smith Act trial, in which seven of Hawaii's alleged top Communists were tried and convicted of conspiring to teach and advocate the overthrow of the American government by force and violence. None of the so-called Hawaii Seven served a single day of their sentences and the Smith Act was ultimately declared to be unconstitutional by the U.S. Supreme Court.

The Izuka pamphlet, which was first distributed in November 1947, breathed new life into the charges which had been made against Delegate Joe Farrington in the 1946 elections. Sensing the spirit of the times, the ILWU announced in December 1947 that its political action committee would, henceforth, address only "educational concerns" and get out of the business of endorsing candidates. This did not mean that the ILWU was out of politics. As Jack Hall had written to Louis Goldblatt, the ILWU's international secretary-treasurer, on 4 September 1947: "We are moving politically to take over the local Democratic Party and its convention in April [1948], including the Territorial Committee, the national committeeman and woman, and delegates to the national convention."

Jack Burns well understood the ILWU's strategy. They would take over the local precinct organizations by encouraging their members to become active in neighborhood politics. Hall's chief agents in this effort were Jack Kawano, who was identified as a member of the Communist Party in the Izuka pamphlet, and Wilfred Oka, who would later be charged with contempt of Congress for his unwillingness to testify before the House Un-American Activities Committee. The ILWU did a good deal of organizing for the Democratic Party, but the union fell far short of its goal of Party domination. Looking back in 1962, Jack Hall said in a Labor Day speech:

> Our union has always followed a program of independent political action except for a sorry period when some of us incorrectly thought we could pick up the dead carcass of a jackass [the Democratic Party] and rejuvenate it into an intelligent, vigorous, loyal, and honest animal that might lead the rest of us to progress, decency, and a better way of life.

Jack Burns, of course, knew what the ILWU was doing to get their members to register to vote and to become involved with precinct politics. When he was asked in March 1948 about the possibility of an ILWU takeover of the Democratic Party, he expressed no concern. "We don't question the motives of those who join the Democratic Party," Burns told an *Advertiser* reporter. "It's not up to us to judge whether they are Communists, ILWU, or anything else. If, after joining it, they fail to abide by the Party rules and Party policies, then the Party itself has the power to act." Burns knew better than Jack Hall that the ILWU could not swallow up the Democratic Party; it was simply too big a bite. But he welcomed their help, whatever their motivation.

At the territorial Democratic Convention, which began on 2 May 1948, there were many contests over the seating of delegates and the precinct organizations that had sent them to the convention. Most were decided in favor of the ILWU precinct organizers. In protest, Ed Berman, a labor lawyer who once had aspirations of leading the ILWU in Hawaii, announced the formation of a group called the Independent Democrats of Hawaii. Berman, a friend and adviser to Ichiro Izuka, had been a strong supporter of William Borthwick in his 1946 race for delegate to Congress. He was a Stainback Democrat and he hated Jack Hall, the man he felt had denied him his rightful place in Hawaii's labor history. The efforts of the Stainback–Berman wing of the Democratic Party went nowhere in 1948, but they would be a harbinger of 1950, when the Democratic Party would come apart.

Less than two weeks after the Democratic Convention, the Democratic Women's Organization of Hawaii met and declared themselves unalterably opposed to communism in the Territory of Hawaii. They also pledged their support for President Truman and Governor Stainback in their efforts to combat the communist menace. On 25 May, one of their leading lights, Victoria K. Holt, declared herself as a candidate for the Democratic nomination for delegate to Congress. The majority of the Democratic Party leaders, including Jack Burns, were caught off guard. They thought they had put the issue of communism to rest at the convention, and here was a candidate for the only territorywide elective office announcing that she would run a campaign in which the *only* issue would be communism.

The Democratic Party leaders, even those who were strongly anticommunist, were appalled by the lack of substance in Victoria Holt's campaign. In late August, as the primary election drew close, many urged William Borthwick, who had given Joe Farrington a good run for his money in 1946, to declare again. In his public response, Borthwick made two things clear: First, that Mrs. Holt had nothing on him when it came to being against communism; he declared, "If I am defeated by Delegate Farrington, it will show conclusively that subversive elements are in control of Hawaii." Second, he would run only if Mrs. Holt would withdraw from the race. When she did not, Borthwick withdrew. The day after Borthwick's withdrawal, Jack Burns, ever the team player, announced that he would run against Mrs. Holt.

During the campaign that followed, Mrs. Holt and others in the Stainback wing of the Democratic Party regularly accused Burns of being a communist sympathizer. Burns ducked the charges as best he could, trying to focus on what he saw as the more substantive issues of the campaign. Allegations of communism notwithstanding, Jack Burns defeated Victoria Holt in the Democratic primary by a vote of 7,947 to 5,021. Holt carried urban Honolulu by 400 votes. Burns won the election on the neighbor islands, where the ILWU's strength lay.

In the meantime, Joe Farrington was facing an anticommunist challenger of his own, Walter H. Dillingham, who declared, "My decision to run is based entirely upon patriotic reasons. I feel I can be of service to Hawaii and our country as delegate and I can be counted upon to make an all-out fight against communism." Over and over, Dillingham called upon Farrington to repudiate his 1946 endorsement by the ILWU's political action committee. Farrington refused to be stampeded and won the Republican primary easily by a vote of 49,128 to 23,703.

A cursory glance at the number of votes in each primary—73,000 in the Republican compared to 13,000 in the Democratic—made it clear that Farrington would be the overwhelming favorite in the general election. In his first speech of the general election campaign, Burns told two hundred of the Democratic faithful who were gathered at the Beretania Playground, "I haven't a chance of a snowball in Hades of being elected." When the *Advertiser* treated the comment as a concession, Burns backtracked. "I don't *appear* to have a chance," he corrected himself the next day. He then put on a brave face in the form of an appeal for the AJA vote: "I was once made an honorary member of the 442nd, and I've adopted the slogan that carried it over the top. I'm going to 'go for broke.'" In 1948, that appeal would be too little, too late.

During the campaign between Burns and Farrington, communism was never mentioned. Burns, as he had in 1946, focused his campaign on the Democratic Party rather than himself. He painted the choice for the voters as one between the common people and the privileged. He pointed out that his campaign operated at a considerable disadvantage to his opponent's since he did not own a newspaper as his opponent did.

Burns called for a national minimum wage and a change to immigration laws to allow Japanese, Samoans, Maoris, and other Pacific peoples to have the right to become citizens of the United States. Above all, he tried to portray himself as a friend of labor and as a friend of the Japanese community. It was a gallant effort, but when the votes were counted, Farrington had trounced him by a vote of 75,725 to 24,920. Farrington carried 163 of the Territory's 168 precincts. In a graceful concession, Jack Burns told Joe Farrington, "I know of no one to whom I would rather lose."

In the 1948 elections, the Republican Party had won fifty-five of ninety-one elective offices. They had a nine to four majority in the territorial senate and a twenty to ten margin in the house. Only on the local level did the Democrats have anything to cheer about. Johnny Wilson was reelected as mayor of Honolulu, a highly personal victory. Wilson also got a seven to five majority on the Oahu County board of supervisors. This was the first time the Democrats had controlled both city hall and the board of supervisors since 1920, during Wilson's first term as mayor.

After studying the 1948 election returns on the mainland, which included Harry S Truman's victory over Thomas E. Dewey for president and the Democratic Party's return to majority status in both houses of Congress, Burns wrote a commentary piece for the newspapers. He expressed his regret that "the people of Hawaii did not 'keep in step' with the people of this nation." He attributed their failure to do so to Hawaii's history of one-party Republican rule and to the Republican Party's overwhelming control of the media in the Territory. He continued with an interesting insight into his political philosophy:

> The era of selfishness and unfettered greed is and must remain dead. It has been recognized by some observers that . . . there must be some retreat from the economic individualism of our fathers. However, those who have recognized this have not been the ones who could do anything about it. Those not recognizing the situation are in the field of management and they have taken unto themselves functions and powers not rightfully theirs.

Next, Burns turned to the thorny question of communism. "We do not want government control or ownership which develops into a collectivist state. Yet, if we fail to solve the problems on the social, economic, and political fields, we will have such collectivism." Burns was not threatening, merely warning. It was a warning he would repeat endlessly, in both public and private discussions. Communism was no danger so long as capitalism could maintain a human face. "We must definitely recognize," Burns continued, "the equality of man and practice it publicly and privately; we must assure all men . . . a salary that will enable them to save and be property holders as their right; a salary that will enable them to make suitable provision for protection from periods of illness, unemployment, and old age."

Burns lectured management on its duties in this process: "The brains of our community, particularly as represented by management, must approach this as their responsibility along with giving capital a return on its investment." Returning to the theme of the Republican defeat on the national political scene, Burns had a warning for the Republicans:

> We must assure all men equal political status. The Democrats have offered the only efforts in this regard by their social measures over the past fourteen years, from 1932 to 1946, and the failure of the Republicans and those whom they represent has been readily answered by their removal from office. . . . Locally, the Republicans are going to have to act like Democrats or be out of step.

These were the words of a man who had just been defeated by a 3 to 1 margin. But John A. Burns did not feel like a man defeated in 1948. He was a Democrat and the Democratic Party had won a stunning victory; it was just a bit slow arriving in Hawaii. But it would come. Of that, Burns had no doubt. It would be six long years before the political revolution Burns envisioned for Hawaii would be completed; eight years before he would get his personal political reward. But in 1948, John A. Burns was still only 39 years old. He could wait.

S·I·X

Roadblocks

IN 1949, HAWAII'S longshoremen staged a 177-day strike, the longest and most traumatic work stoppage in Island history. The ILWU was seeking to catch up with West Coast wages for dock workers, having fallen forty-two cents behind for comparable work. In their first offer, the union asked for thirty-two cents. The employers offered eight cents. Before the strike actually began, Jack Hall and Lou Goldblatt of the ILWU reported that the employers had raised their offer to fifteen cents to match the increase recently granted to the West Coast longshoremen. Hall and Goldblatt told Alexander G. "Pinky" Budge of Castle & Cooke that they would take a sixteen-cents offer to the membership. Even if it were by only one penny, they had to present an offer that at least began to close the gap with the West Coast. This sequence of events was subsequently disputed by the employers, but the evidence weighs heavily in favor of its veracity. If true, it means that for a single penny an hour the Territory of Hawaii was subjected to a strike that eventually cost an estimated $100 million.

On 1 May 1949, two thousand dock workers walked off their jobs. By midsummer, thirty-four thousand residents of Hawaii were out of work. To generate public opinion against the ILWU, the employers orchestrated a campaign that included the creation of two organizations: "We, the Women," and its dockside auxiliary called "The Broom Brigade"; and the Hawaii Residents' Association, better known as IMUA, (a Hawaiian word meaning "forward, charge.") from their publication *IMUA Spotlight*. Both groups argued that the strike was communist-inspired. As Jack Burns pointed out in a 1964 interview, "The Big Five called it a political strike. They called it communist. What else could they do? Their position was completely untenable."

The Hawaii longshoremen's strike attracted national attention. In June 1949, Republican Hugh Butler of Nebraska, a member of the Senate Committee on Interior and Insular Affairs, published a report entitled *Statehood for Hawaii: Communist Penetration of the Hawaiian Islands.* Butler's research for the project turned out to be a composite of Governor Stainback's revelations of November 1947, the Izuka pamphlet, and the Reinecke hearing. John Reinecke's 1934 ruminations were once again trotted out as the centerpiece of an alleged communist plot for Hawaii.

By the end of July 1949, Jack Hall asked Burns to go to Washington D.C., to explain to public officials that this was an economic strike, not a communist plot, and to head off the possibility of a public hearing in Hawaii by the House Un-American Activities Committee (HUAC) while the strike was in progress. Burns, traveling at ILWU expense, convinced Labor Secretary Maurice Tobin that it was, indeed, an economic strike. He revealed to Tobin, whom he happily referred to as "another fish-eater [i.e., Roman Catholic]," the maze in interlocking directorates among various companies controlled by the Big Five.

Burns' presentation so impressed Tobin that he put the ILWU's designated representative in touch with Cyrus Ching, the noted negotiator with the National Mediation and Conciliation Service. Burns convinced Ching that it might be productive to get both sides to come to New York for serious negotiations. Burns also appears to have convinced Alex Campbell, chief of the Department of Justice's Criminal Division, to delay the government's pending prosecution of ILWU leaders Harry Bridges, Bob Robertson, and Henry Schmidt for having perjured themselves at Bridges' 1945 naturalization hearing. Finally, he convinced Frank Tavenner, chief counsel of HUAC, to delay hearings in Hawaii until after the conclusion of the dock strike. All in all, Burns' efforts in behalf of the ILWU in the nation's capital were most effective, even if they did not result in an immediate end to the strike. They would long be remembered by the union's leadership.

By August, Island shippers had pressured the territorial legislature into passing the Dock Seizure Act, thinking that control of the docks in Hawaii would break the logjam and free the Territory's economy. Neither the shippers nor the legislators had understood the solidarity that West Coast dock workers would show for their brothers in Hawaii. ILWU longshoremen up and down the West Coast staunchly refused to unload any ships from Hawaii that had been loaded by scab labor.

When the strike was finally resolved on 23 October 1949, both sides claimed victory. The shippers bragged that they had held the pay increase to fourteen cents. The union boasted of a twenty-one-cents settlement—fourteen cents immediately and an additional seven cents on 1 May 1950. However victory is measured, and it seems clear that the ILWU was the victor, the people of Hawaii were the major losers. The legacy of the 1949 dock strike was bitterness, recrimination, and the revitalization of the communist issue in Hawaii's politics. Whatever hopes Burns had of putting the communist issue to rest in 1948 were destroyed in 1949 by the fallout from this six-month ordeal.

Jack Burns returned to Washington, D.C., in January 1950. This time he traveled at Democratic Party expense. His mission was to discuss patronage and to make the case against the reappointment of Ingram M. Stainback as territorial governor. Stainback, the titular head of the Democratic Party in Hawaii, had parceled out embarrassingly few jobs to hardworking Party loyalists. Since 1946, Stainback had maintained a drumbeat of criticism against organized labor in Hawaii, threatening to alienate one of the natural constituencies of the Democratic Party. Stainback had to go.

On his side, Governor Stainback had a powerful advocate in Senator Kenneth MacKeller of Tennessee. Stainback had come to Hawaii from Tennessee in 1912 and still had many prominent family members in his home state who had the ear of Tennessee's senior senator. "I couldn't talk to MacKeller worth five cents," Burns later lamented. "I said, 'Is the fact that this man is from Tennessee the only reason you are supporting him?' And that was just about the answer."

Having determined that the Tennessee connection was the problem, Burns proposed an alternative: another Tennessean for the job. Burns' man was Robert L. Shivers, former head of the FBI office in Hawaii. In 1950, Shivers was serving as the Territory's collector of customs. Shivers had several advantages. First, he was from Ashland, Tennessee; second, Burns had worked effectively with Shivers during World War II on matters of the internal security of the Territory; third, in light of the red-baiting going on in Hawaii, Shivers possessed an impeccable set of anticommunist credentials.

Burns returned to Hawaii on 15 March 1950, after almost two months in the nation's capital. He returned thinking he had assurances that Stainback would be replaced when his term expired in August. The usually tight-lipped Burns let slip to a reporter that his mission to Washington, D.C., had been "to counteract the false statements and innuendoes Governor Stainback and others were giving out about certain Party members here." He also went on record saying that Stainback would not be reappointed in August. Stainback, however, had no intention of leaving in August. If he did, he wouldn't go quietly.

In the month that followed Burns' return from Washington, two events took place that helped Governor Stainback to maintain his position and to widen the breach that existed within the Democratic Party of Hawaii. At the same time that there was a territorial Constitutional Convention for the purpose of drafting a Constitution in anticipation of statehood, the House Un-American Activities Committee opened hearings in the Iolani Palace on the subject of communism in the Territory of Hawaii.

Prospects for Hawaiian statehood in the spring of 1950 looked deceptively good. In March, the U.S. House of Representatives had passed HR49, a measure granting statehood for Hawaii, by a two-to-one margin. In June, the Senate Interior and Insular Affairs Committee sent the measure to the Senate floor by a 9 to 1 vote. But there it languished as southern Democrats like Richard Russell of Georgia and Allen Ellender of Louisiana made it abundantly clear that they would filibuster the measure should an attempt be made to bring it to a vote. The southerners disguised a deeply felt racism with charges that communist infiltration made the Territory of Hawaii unfit for statehood.

When the HUAC hearings began, the first witness called by the committee was Richard Kageyama, a member of Oahu County's board of supervisors. Only six days earlier, Kageyama had taken an oath at the Constitutional Convention that he had not, for the past five years, been a member of the Communist Party. Now, before an overflow crowd in the territorial senate chamber, Kageyama told how, in February 1947, he had been duped into becoming a member of the Communist Party of Hawaii by his former teacher at Farrington High School, John E. Reinecke.

Kageyama then described how he had left the Communist Party in 1949. He then proceeded to name his former associates in the Party. He also explained that he had been instructed by the Party to consult with ILWU counsel, Harriet Bouslog, about his testimony before HUAC. For his efforts, Kageyama received the thanks of HUAC chairman, Francis Walter, a Democrat from Pennsylvania. Kageyama's final gesture, clearly orchestrated by HUAC counsel, was his resignation as a delegate to the Constitutional Convention. "Further attendance at the Constitutional Convention as a delegate," Kageyama wrote in his letter of resignation, "would embarrass my fellow delegates and prejudice the cause of statehood for Hawaii."

Lau Ah Chew, chairman of the Democratic Central Committee for the Territory of Hawaii, was livid. "Kageyama has struck a foul blow not only at the Democratic Party," he declared, "but primarily at our hopes for statehood." In a bit of tortured logic, Lau then argued that Kageyama was not a member of the Democratic Party, having automatically given up his membership when he became a member of the Communist Party in 1947. Lau was so incensed about the role of HUAC in the Kageyama episode that he wired President Truman, complaining bitterly that Chairman Walter was intruding into Hawaii's internal politics. As he was leaving Hawaii, after the conclusion of the HUAC hearings, Walter took a parting shot at the territorial Democratic chairman: "Lau Ah Chew," he said, "is not my kind of Democrat."

HUAC's next witness was Ichiro Izuka. The former longshoreman told the same story he had set out in his 1947 pamphlet and had repeated around town for the past two and one-half years. Izuka's testimony was followed by a parade of thirty-nine witnesses, most of whom he had identified as Communists. All pled their Fifth Amendment right against self-incrimination as they were urged to do by ILWU counsel, Harriet Bouslog. For having done so, they were cited for contempt of Congress and branded as the "Reluctant Thirty-Nine." Twenty-six of the thirty-nine were either officers or employees of the ILWU.

A new name in Izuka's testimony was that of Frank G. Silva, ILWU business agent from Kauai and a delegate to the Constitutional Convention. Although Izuka's testimony was confused and contradictory, Silva's decision to plead the Fifth Amendment was reason enough for his fellow delegates to send him back to Kauai by a 53 to 7 vote. Silva later explained that he was not, and never had been, a member of the Communist Party. But in light of what happened to Alger Hiss because of his testimony before HUAC in 1948, he had opted not to subject himself and his family to the possibility of a charge of perjury. Izuka was never able to explain why Silva's name had not come up before in his many recitations about the threat of communism in Hawaii, giving Silva's testimony a ring of authenticity. Izuka enjoyed immunity from cross-examination during the HUAC hearings, a luxury he would not have during the Smith Act trial of 1952–1953.

One ILWU official deviated from the recommended testimony. Jack Kawano, a member of Jack Burns' inner circle during his early efforts in behalf of the Democratic Party, answered one question asked by HUAC counsel. Kawano stated that he was not a member of the Communist Party. He declined, however, to answer any questions about whether he had ever been a member or to name any others who might have been members of the Communist Party of Hawaii. For his refusal to do so, Kawano was included with the other thirty-eight witnesses who were cited for contempt of Congress. But Jack Kawano, who had a falling out with the ILWU leadership during the 1949 dock strike, would go to Washington, D.C., in July 1951 to tell his whole story before a closed session of HUAC.

The Democratic Party suffered another blow when Wilfred Oka, secretary of Oahu's County Democratic Central Committee and an employee of the ILWU, was identified as a member of the Communist Party of Hawaii. Oka and Kawano had been the key figures in the organization of precinct clubs during the 1948 political season.

Throughout the Constitutional Convention and the HUAC hearings, Jack Burns maintained a stoic silence. Mercifully, the precinct elections had taken place during the first week of April, before the fireworks had begun. The results had assured that the Burns wing of the Democratic Party would control the territorial Democratic Convention, which would begin on 30 April. The Democratic Party's two national committee members, Charles Kauhane and Victoria Holt, attempted to obtain permission from the Democratic National Committee to reorganize Hawaii's Democratic Party before the convention, but to no avail. On 24 April, Governor Stainback called together a group of his Party loyalists, including Kauhane and Holt, to discuss the possibility of postponing the Party convention, but once again with no success.

When the 1950 Democratic Party Convention convened on the last day of April, fourteen delegates and two alternates were found to be members of the so-called "Reluctant Thirty-Nine." A walkout was precipitated when Maurice Sapienza, a right-wing delegate, introduced a motion to deny accreditation to fifteen of the sixteen delegates and alternates who had been cited by HUAC for contempt of Congress. The exception was Jack Kawano. When Sapienza's motion failed, Ernest

Heen and Harold Rice led ninety-one delegates, controlling 118 of the 510 convention votes, including proxies, out of the auditorium at Kalakaua Intermediate School and into the American Legion Hall, where they reconvened.

Thus, the Democratic Party divided into what came to be known as the "Standpat" (or left-wing) and "Walkout" (or right-wing) factions. After the departure of the right-wing Democrats, Jack Burns was unanimously elected chairman of the convention and Vince Esposito declared to one and all: "This is the new Democratic Party." Esposito was clearly on target that day, for the "Standpat Democrats" represented the nucleus of the Democratic Party which would assume political control of Hawaii in the so-called Revolution of 1954, with John A. Burns as their leader. By maintaining solidarity with the ILWU delegates at the 1950 Democratic Convention, Burns had demonstrated once again his conviction that the Democratic Party in Hawaii would be nothing without the support of the labor movement. Still, Burns knew that ILWU support came at a steep price to the Party's immediate success.

Jack Burns was unwilling to have the Democratic Party smeared with the communist label. After the walkout, he insisted on the creation of an affidavit, to be signed by all members of the territorial Democratic Convention, stating that they were not members of the Communist Party. In its original form, the document contained some equivocal language, including a statement that it was being signed "reluctantly." Five delegates were unwilling to sign even this statement and were expelled from the convention. A sixth, Adele Kensinger, resigned from the Party because such an affidavit was being required of the delegates. Nine signed.

In mid-July, when the public outcry over the equivocal nature of the affidavit wouldn't go away, a new one was drafted. It was the essence of simplicity and clarity, stating,

> To Whom It May Concern:
> I am NOT a Communist. I am a member of the Democratic Party of Hawaii. I endorse the principles of the Democratic Party and pledge my support of its rules and platforms.

This time it was signed by all thirty Democrats among the "Reluctant Thirty-Nine," not just the fifteen delegates to the territorial Democratic Convention.

After his election as chairman of Oahu's County Democratic Central Committee on 12 May, Burns made another move to remove the taint of communism from the Democratic Party. The other key post on that committee was secretary, a position held by Wilfred Oka, now one of the "Reluctant Thirty-Nine." Burns approached his protégé, Dan Inouye, a new member of the committee, and asked him to run for secretary against Oka. With some reluctance, Inouye jumped into the contest, winning by a margin of 33 to 30. Burns was sure that the pragmatic leadership of the ILWU would understand. Besides, where else would they go?

The "Standpat Democrats," considering themselves to be the keepers of the Democratic Party flame in Hawaii, appointed two new members from Hawaii to the Democratic National Committee (DNC): Mayor Johnny Wilson and Harriet Magoon. When the DNC met in Chicago in mid-May, Wilson, Magoon, Charles Kauhane, and Victoria Holt all presented themselves to fill Hawaii's two seats on the committee. Not wanting to become involved in a local matter, the DNC sidestepped the issue by saying that only death or resignation could have disqualified Kauhane and Holt from retaining their seats at that time. The two "Walkout Democrats" took their seats. When they departed, it was with instructions from the DNC to go back to Hawaii and help build a unified Party.

The "Walkout Democrats" chose to interpret the DNC's instructions as a mandate to reorganize the Democratic Party of Hawaii, a convenient flight of fancy. When presented with the Kauhane–Holt interpretation of the DNC's admonition, Johnny Wilson bristled. "They are going to have one hell of a time reorganizing the Party when they get back. . . . Our precinct clubs are already organized and they are not going to reorganize."

That certainly didn't mean that they wouldn't try. That effort was made when Leon K. Sterling, Sr., chairman of the "Walkout" version of the territorial Democratic Central Committee and Honolulu's city clerk, tried to use these positions to change the face of the Democratic Party. On 5 June, Sterling issued a "proclamation" stating, "No one is authorized to solicit or accept funds, or to incur any indebtedness in the name of the Democratic Party unless authorized by me." Sterling went on to declare that all "true Democrats" should reregister between 10 June and 10 July. Jack Burns scornfully denounced Sterling's announcements, calling them "an attempt to rule by minority." Sterling's efforts were to no avail; only 1,181 voters chose to reregister during the month-long campaign. The "Walkout Democrats" had been aiming for at least ten thousand.

The actual elections of 1950 produced no great surprises. The deep divisions within the Democratic Party gave the Republicans a golden opportunity to extend their traditional political hegemony in the Territory. The only race of real interest was for mayor of Honolulu. Ernest Heen, one of the leaders of the "Walkout Democrats," challenged Johnny Wilson, who had remained with the "Standpat Democrats." Wilson won the Democratic primary by a margin of 15,608 to 10,058. Wilson's personal popularity probably played a larger role in his victory than the contestants' differences on Democratic Party politics.

Meanwhile, time was running short on the question of Stainback's reappointment as governor of the Territory of Hawaii. On 25 June 1950, Honolulu businessman Tucker Gratz was dining in Washington, D.C., with President Truman, Vice President Alben Barkley, House Speaker Sam Rayburn, Interior Secretary Oscar Chapman, and two or three other Truman intimates. Truman spent most of the evening discussing his decision that day to commit U.S. troops in Korea, but eventually the conversation turned to Hawaii. Much to his surprise, Gratz found himself being offered either the governorship, the office of territorial secretary (the equivalent of lieutenant governor), or the position of collector of customs. Not wanting a position of high visibility, Gratz opted for the customs job. He told Truman and Chapman that he would return to Hawaii and report back with recommendations for the other two positions. Gratz returned to Washington, D.C., within a month, prepared to lobby for the appointment of Robert Shivers, Burns' choice, as governor. While Gratz was on his way to the nation's capital, Shivers died of a heart attack. The governorship would not be resolved until the spring of 1951.

Burns and his advisers cast their net once again for an acceptable candidate. One of the names being bandied about was that of Ernest Kai. Kai had two important points in his favor. First, he had served as territorial secretary, so he knew his way around the territorial government; second, he was part-Hawaiian and thus would be a popular choice with one of the Territory's largest ethnic voting blocs. Kai, however, had a fatal drawback in Burns' eyes—he had long been affiliated with Territorial Senator Ernest Heen, one of the leaders of the "Walkout Democrats." In addition, it was unclear what Kai's attitude would be with regard to federal patronage, a key to building Hawaii's Democratic future.

Burns and his friends decided to take Kai's candidacy to the next level. "We were practical," Mits Kido recalled. "We wanted to know what he'd do for the so-called Burns group, what kind of directions would he take? What kind of cabinet would he have if he were confirmed? And so, a delegation of boys—including Jack Burns, Dan Aoki, and Mike Tokunaga—went to see Ernie Kai." Kai was very interested in the job and exuded confidence that he could be confirmed by the U.S. Senate, but he would make no promises about patronage. That decision cost him the governorship.

The next name the Burns group put forward was that of the current territorial secretary, Oren E. Long. Kido's wife had worked as a house-maid for the Long family while he was the territorial superintendent of public instruction and had been well treated. As a schoolteacher, Kido had been favorably impressed with Long's stewardship of Hawaii's pub-lic schools. That Long's wife was a member of a prominent Tennessee family would sit well with Senators MacKeller and Estes Kefauver.

More important, as territorial secretary under Stainback, Long had not fallen into the red-baiting ways of the governor. Long's words to the "Walkout Democrats" had been a message of conciliation:

> A development of this kind sometimes is essential and such develop-ments have the possibility of building a much stronger Democratic Party.... But let us be careful of labels and name calling. Let us be cer-tain that we keep in our ideal of democracy that which will make Americans of great diversity of opinion feel at home.

Another point in Long's favor was that, although personally conserva-tive, he appreciated the contribution that organized labor had made to the lives of Hawaii's workers.

Burns harbored serious doubts about Long's forcefulness as gover-nor or as a Party leader, but the alternative seemed to be Ernest Kai, and Kai simply would not do. On New Year's Day in 1951, Long met with Burns, Kido, Murai, and David Benz at Benz's home. Long seemed ea-ger to accommodate the group's patronage demands—a cabinet position for Burns, territorial secretary for Kido, attorney general for Mau—all of which sounded fine to Long. They parted having pledged their sup-port of Long's candidacy. Little did they know how long confirmation would take.

In the spring of 1951, Jack Burns found himself the beneficiary of a different kind of patronage than that which he had discussed with Oren Long. On 8 March, Mayor Johnny Wilson had Burns appointed as Oahu's disaster relief administrator. The position had distinct advantages for Burns. It gave him a much needed salary of $500 per month and a downtown Honolulu office where he could have free rein to play politics—and get paid for it. The appointment, clearly a political plumb, aroused what the *Star-Bulletin* called "stiff opposition" among disaster relief officials and the Honolulu Chamber of Commerce.

Wilson responded to the *Star-Bulletin's* criticism with a letter to the editor on 12 March in which he cited Burns' "long residence on the island of Oahu, his experience in police and FBI work in World War II and his almost unlimited acquaintance not only with the island's people, but with their ancestral habits and customs, as well as his exact knowledge of the geography of the islands." Burns' experience with the Honolulu Police Department was undoubtedly the strongest counter to such opposition.

The disaster relief appointment came at a crucial time for the Burns family. His first son, John A. Burns, Jr., would be entering Notre Dame University in the fall and Jack Burns needed something to help pay the mounting expenses his family demanded. The proceeds from the Kalama store were being sorely stretched.

On 10 March 1951, two days after Burns had been appointed disaster relief administrator, he was off to Philadelphia for a four-day civil defense exercise, representing the City of Honolulu. After the meeting, Burns went down to Washington, D.C., to see what could be done to expedite the appointment of Oren Long as territorial governor. Upon arrival, he found that papers had been prepared for the nomination of Ernest Kai as governor of the Territory of Hawaii. They only needed President Truman's signature. An announcement had been planned for the following day. Burns asked for twenty-four hours to get things straightened out. Using the good offices of Interior Secretary Oscar Chapman, Burns managed to have the name on the appointment changed from Ernest Kai to Oren E. Long.

Burns and his friends were ecstatic. For the first time, they had flexed their muscles with the national Democratic Party and gotten results. Now all they had to do was to cash in their chips with Governor Long— or so they thought. But when Long returned from Washington, D.C., he brought bad news. First, he informed the group that Interior Secretary Chapman had vetoed the appointment of Mits Kido as territorial secretary. The reason was that Kido had been one of the original 1948 investors in the radical labor newspaper, the *Honolulu Record*. Both Koji

Ariyoshi, editor and publisher of the *Record*, and Jack Kimoto, Ariyoshi's number two man at the paper, had been identified before HUAC as members of the Communist Party and now stood indicted for contempt of Congress. Chapman wanted no part of anyone who had, however innocently, associated himself with Ariyoshi and Kimoto.

Second, Long revealed that the best he could do for Burns was the position of high sheriff of the Territory of Hawaii, "a mere figurehead who served papers for a fee." Finally, confirming that bad news comes in threes, Long told those who had supported his candidacy that Democratic Senator Pat McCarran of Nevada, chairman of the Senate subcommittee on internal security, had nixed Chuck Mau's nomination as territorial attorney general. McCarran's rejection was said to have been based upon certain "indiscretions" in Mau's personal life. The source of this information was not revealed. In the final analysis, the only member of the Burns group—although not a member of the inner circle—to benefit from a Long appointment was Sakae Takahashi, who was named territorial secretary. At least Stainback was out of the way, having been appointed to the territorial supreme court as a consolation prize.

Throughout the fall of 1950 there had been rumors that HUAC would be returning to Hawaii. The return trip did not materialize and anticommunist zeal waned in Hawaii when the "Reluctant Thirty-Nine" were acquitted of contempt of Congress. Writing the unanimous decision of the Supreme Court, which served as the basis for acquittal, *Blau v. United States* (340 U.S. 159), Justice Hugo Black asserted that in light of the conviction of eleven top officials of the Communist Party for violating the Smith Act, Mrs. Blau's fear of prosecution was more than "a mere imaginary possibility; she could reasonably fear that criminal charges might be brought against her if she admitted employment by the Communist Party or intimate knowledge of its workings." In January 1951, all of the "Reluctant Thirty-Nine" were found not guilty of contempt of Congress.

While this may have been the end of HUAC's business in Hawaii, the committee would hear more testimony about Hawaii from the no longer reluctant Jack Kawano. On 6 July 1951, accompanied by Chuck Mau, the former ILWU leader appeared before HUAC in closed session in Washington, D.C., and told all that he knew about communism in Hawaii, including his interpretations of how Communist Party decisions had been transformed into decisions of the Democratic Party.

In extensive interviews which were conducted in 1975 as a part of the John A. Burns Oral History Project, each member of the original Burns group—Burns, Mau, Murai, and Kido—and Dan Inouye as well, all claim to have been surprised when they were told by Jack Kawano in 1950 that he had, indeed, been a member of the Communist Party for twelve years, from 1937 until 1949. They expressed incredulity that he could have been a member of the Communist Party while he sat with them on a weekly basis to discuss the formation of the new Democratic Party in Hawaii.

While this may seem hard to believe, especially since Ichiro Izuka had identified Kawano as a member of the Communist Party in 1947, it can convincingly be explained. Burns harbored no illusions about Communist Party assistance to the ILWU in their early organizing efforts. Burns knew that the union had to get their members to think of themselves as members of the working class—the proletariat, in Marxist terminology—rather than members of different ethnic groups. Burns knew that the Big Five had used one ethnic group against another to defeat virtually every effort of organized labor to build a union movement in Hawaii before World War II. Burns also knew that the union had used the California Labor School in San Francisco to train many of its leaders and that the California Labor School was reputed to be an instrument of the Communist Party of California. "They used the Communist Party cell formation to organize and develop a labor union. . . . Who else [was] going to help them?"

Jack Burns knew very well that there were members of the Communist Party in Hawaii. His exposure to military intelligence during World War II made it impossible for him not to know that. His mother had even alerted him to the flow of communist literature into the Territory of Hawaii when she worked in general delivery at the downtown Honolulu post office. But Jack Burns never accepted the idea that membership in the Communist Party in Hawaii automatically made someone "a conscious agent of an international communist conspiracy." He believed that the ILWU used some of the ideas and techniques of communism to achieve a particular goal—the unionization of Hawaii. When that goal was achieved, they discarded communism as no longer useful to them. This is, in fact, what happened in Hawaii.

In their contact with Jack Kawano, beginning in 1944, the Burns group was dealing with a man who had been rejected by the ILWU leadership in San Francisco as the union's regional director. It is logical to assume that Kawano was looking for another path to achieve his goals and that he had hitched his star to the emerging Democratic Party for that purpose. Perhaps he thought he could use the Democratic Party, as the ILWU had used the Communist Party, to reclaim the position in the labor movement he felt was rightfully his. Whatever his intentions, Kawano's role in union circles diminished as his role in Democratic Party circles increased. By the time HUAC came to Hawaii in 1950, Kawano was irrelevant within the ranks of the ILWU and damaged goods within the ranks of the Democratic Party.

Whatever the case, Jack Kawano's Democratic Party friends were prepared to sacrifice their colleague for the sake of cleansing the Democratic Party of the taint of communism. According to Chuck Mau, he took the initiative to get Kawano back to Washington, D.C., in the summer of 1951. "Jack," he said, "I think it's time to have you go to Washington and testify, and since these people in the ILWU are treating you like dirt, anyway, you might as well come out and tell the whole truth about the communist apparatus in Hawaii." Kawano agreed to go on the condition that Mau accompany him. Burns, in the meantime, had moved beyond his original inner circle, having built a younger one that was dominated by the AJA veterans from the 100th and the 442nd. Mau's trip to Washington, D.C., with Kawano merely accelerated that process.

The fifty-three pages of Kawano's testimony before HUAC in July 1951 reveal a bitter man who was attempting to shade every interpretation of events in such a way that it would place the ILWU leadership in the worst possible light. It contained no new or dramatic revelations, but Kawano's stature in the community and his importance in the union gave his testimony far more credibility than that of Ichiro Izuka. The most important thing about his testimony was that the Justice Department had found, in Kawano, their star witness for the Smith Act trial they were contemplating for Hawaii.

In the early morning hours of 28 August 1951, less than two months after Kawano's testimony in Washington, D.C., twenty-one FBI agents moved simultaneously to arrest seven alleged leaders of the Communist Party of Hawaii. The seven, who came to be known as the "Hawaii Seven," were: Koji Ariyoshi, editor and publisher of the *Honolulu Record*; Jack Kimoto, an employee of the *Honolulu Record*; Charles Fujimoto, self-proclaimed chairman of the Communist Party of Hawaii; Eileen

Fujimoto, wife of Charles and secretary to Jack Hall at the ILWU; John E. Reinecke, former teacher; Jim Freeman, mechanic; and Jack Hall, regional director of the ILWU. Hall, of course, was the centerpiece of the Justice Department's case. The seven were charged with having violated Section Two of the Smith Act by conspiring "to advocate and teach the duty and necessity of overthrowing the Government of the United States by force and violence," and having organized the Communist Party of Hawaii for that purpose.

Jack Kawano's testimony before HUAC in Washington, D.C., destroyed what was left of his personal and public life. His admission that he had belonged to the Communist Party while helping to build both the ILWU and the Democratic Party of Hawaii had turned him into a virtual untouchable. Three members of the original Burns group made an effort to help their former colleague. Chuck Mau helped Kawano secure loans to start up a small liquor and grocery store on Kukui Street. Mits Kido contributed $2,700 and Dr. Murai another $1,700. But Kawano was no businessman and the store failed within a year and a half. There was a string of menial jobs, but at the end of the Smith Act trial in 1953, Jack Kawano went into virtual exile from his native Hawaii. The U.S. Attorney's office helped Kawano get a job with Lockheed Aircraft in Burbank, California, where he spent the rest of his life.

Jack Burns kept a low profile during the Smith Act trial. He was willing to become involved, but as the situation developed it became clear that the prosecution saw no value in calling Burns as a witness and the defense saw no benefit in sacrificing his reputation for the meager return it might bring the defendants. In 1975, Burns recalled the exploratory efforts of the prosecution to enlist his support:

> I told the counsel for the FBI, . . . "Okay, just expect me to answer the questions honestly. I've never lied on the witness stand yet, and I'm not gonna start now." What does that mean? I said, "It means that when Shivers and Bicknell, Fielder . . . all testify to me that Jack Hall is one hell of an American, I got to have some belief that he's some hell of an American." They were not very interested in having me as a witness. So I offered to Jack [Hall] and Koji [Ariyoshi], I'd be happy to testify as a witness for the defense. But they decided they didn't want to throw me to the wolves. It was Jack's decision.

On 19 June 1953, almost two years after their original arrest, the Hawaii Seven were found guilty of having violated the Smith Act. Jack

Hall was immediately released on bail, pending an appeal, and never served a single day of his five-year sentence. The others languished in jail for a week while bail was being raised. That was the full extent of their time in jail. On 17 June 1957, almost four years after the original verdict, the U.S. Supreme Court, in *Yates v. United States* (354 U.S. 298), rendered the decision which would lead to a reversal of the conviction of the Hawaii Seven. But by the end of the Smith Act trial the issue of communism in Hawaii politics had largely burned itself out, removing the last major roadblock to the Democratic Revolution of 1954.

PART III

The Making of a Governor
(1951–1962)

S·E·V·E·N

Revolution

IF 1950 WAS THE YEAR the Democratic Party of Hawaii came apart, 1951 was the year in which it started to come together for the final push to power. The original Burns group of Chuck Mau, Jack Kawano, Ernest Murai, and Mits Kido was no longer the core of the new Democratic Party. Kawano had become anathema to the ILWU wing of the Democratic Party for his February 1951 attempt to get rank-and-file union members to repudiate the leadership of Jack Hall and for his July 1951 testimony before the House Un-American Activities Committee in Washington, D.C. Mau was similarly discredited because of his open support for Kawano and for his efforts to get the Justice Department to bring Smith Act charges against Jack Hall and six other alleged communist leaders in Hawaii. Murai and Kido remained elder statesmen of the new Democratic Party, but their proximity to Burns had been eclipsed by the so-called cell gang.

The cell referred to Jack Burns' basement office in Honolulu Hale, the city hall, where he had his office as civil defense administrator. Here, Burns met with a group made up mostly of young AJA war veterans. The stated purpose of their meetings was to learn parliamentary procedure and Party organization. The meetings invariably turned to the vision these young activists shared for the future of Hawaii. While there might be from fifteen to twenty present at these meetings, the stalwarts included AJAs Dan Inouye, Dan Aoki, Mike Tokunaga, Sakae Takahashi, Matsuo "Matsy" Takabuki, Seichi "Shadow" Hirai, Elton "Curly" Sakamoto, Taro Sukinaga, and Shigeto Kanemoto. Not all of those who attended were AJAs. Herman Lum was Chinese-American. And, very important, in Burns' mind, Bill Richardson and Herman Lemke were

109

part-Hawaiian. Burns knew well that the haoles, the AJAs, and the part-Hawaiians constituted the three largest voting blocs in the Islands. Any winning combination would have to include significant numbers from each group.

While Dan Inouye had been the first of the AJA veterans to join Burns, perhaps no individual was more representative of the group than Dan Aoki, a man who claimed politics as his profession but never held a public office. Aoki stood at the side of Jack Burns as his chief of staff for the better part of a quarter-century, guarding the "old man's" flank and keeping "the boys" from the 442nd in line.

Dan Aoki was the son of a Congregational minister who had originally come to Hawaii as a contract laborer. He was born in Kealakekua, on the Island of Hawaii, in 1918. In 1926, when Aoki was 7 years old, his father moved the family to Puunene, Maui, to answer the call of another Congregational parish. Aoki spent most of his youth on Maui. There he became conscious of the exclusion of his people from many of the better things of life. Looking back in 1975, Aoki recalled the Maui of his youth: "They had sections . . . where only the haole used to stay. And they also had a community hall, tennis courts, swimming pools, recreational areas which were only for the haole people. . . . They wouldn't even let us watch them play tennis."

Dan Aoki graduated from high school in the spring of 1937. In the fall, he enrolled in the University of Hawaii with an eye to becoming a dentist. Aoki's dormitory mates included Tadao Beppu, a future speaker of the state house of representatives; Sakai Takahashi, a future state senator; and Spark Matsunaga, a future U.S. Senator. During his junior year, Aoki postponed his dental ambitions, dropping out of school to earn some money. After a brief stint as a longshoreman, he and Beppu found jobs clerking for Castle & Cooke terminals on the Honolulu waterfront. At the time of the Japanese attack on Pearl Harbor, Aoki and Beppu were talking with Jack Kawano about organizing a clerks' union. Martial law froze union activity, but it did not freeze firings. Castle & Cooke let Aoki and Beppu go, claiming a shortage of work. Both believed that they had been dismissed for their union activities.

Aoki found a job with the Honolulu Fire Department and was stationed at the Pearl City fire station. When the call came for volunteers for the 442nd Regimental Combat Team in early 1943, Aoki signed up. He had plenty of company from among his old university classmates: Matsunaga and Takahashi were already serving in the 100th Battalion and Beppu volunteered with Aoki for the 442nd. Aoki downplayed his accomplishments as a soldier, but by the time he left Camp Shelby for Europe he was a sergeant. Overseas he made first sergeant, earned a Purple Heart, and gained the respect of his fellow soldiers. He had become a leader.

Discharged in 1946, Dan Aoki returned to the University of Hawaii on the G.I. Bill, still harboring thoughts of dentistry. Once again his education was interrupted, this time by marriage and by the arrival of his first of three children in 1947. After a brief stint working for the territorial Department of Education, Aoki moved to the Apprenticeship Council of the territorial Department of Labor. In his off hours, he became heavily involved in efforts to unite Club 100 and the 442nd Veterans' Club. Club 100 members resisted these efforts. Some still resented their unit's incorporation into the 442nd during the war. Most feared that the money they had begun to collect while still overseas to purchase a small clubhouse might benefit the more numerous but less provident members of the 442nd.

One of the projects designed to bring the two groups together was the cosponsorship of a touring Japanese circus in 1951. Aoki was president of the 442nd Club that year; Sakae Takahashi was president of Club 100. During the planning of the event, Aoki came to know Mike Tokunaga, chairman of Club 100's activities committee. The two clubs never did combine, but Aoki, Takahashi, and Tokunaga discovered the common goals which would lead them into the Burns camp. Within the Burns group, distinctions between the 100th and the 442nd quickly vanished. Dan Inouye had opened the door; his fellow AJA veterans followed closely behind.

Another charter member of the new Burns group, and the only woman to attend regular meetings of the cell gang, was Mary Isa. Born and raised on the Big Island, Isa was the only child of a plantation family. She attended Hilo High School and Hilo Commercial College. Upon graduation, Isa took the civil service examination and scored among the top five in the Territory of Hawaii. Burns saw her name on a civil service list and asked Teruo "Terry" Ihara, a 442nd veteran and Big Island teacher, to interview her. Thus, Mary Isa became Burns' administrative secretary at the Oahu Civil Defense Agency. She would remain with him for most of the next quarter-century, including all of the years he held public office. Mary Isa played the role of gatekeeper and frequently frustrated keeper of the schedule that Burns found so difficult to keep. Shunning marriage, Isa devoted the major part of her life to her boss. She even converted to Roman Catholicism, as she witnessed the spiritual foundation the Church provided for a man she so deeply admired.

Jack Burns came to have a profound impact upon his largely AJA following. He encouraged them to enter politics in order to provide themselves and their families a better life. He was the source of political lessons in organization, in the necessity of multiethnic appeal, in the uses of patronage, and in the realities of power. Burns was their *genro*, their elder statesman. They would call him, in jest, "Old Stone Face." They referred to him with affection as "The Old Man," or "Papa," or even "The Great White Father." But he was also their *sensei*, their teacher, perhaps the most revered object of respect in the system of Confucian relationships. He taught them well, he never let them down, and he always retained their highest regard.

James Michener took up residence in Hawaii during the late 1940s. He spent much of the next decade researching and writing his enormously successful novel *Hawaii*. He also dabbled in Democratic Party politics. The emerging leaders of Hawaii's Democrats met three or four times each year in his apartment. He watched the relationship between Burns and the AJAs develop with a sense of awe: "The young Japanese adored Burns," Michener remembered, "and rightly so. He taught them strategy, he gave them strength, ability, character, and hope. Far more than any of the rest of us, Burns understood the Japanese-Americans."

In 1975, Dan Inouye reflected upon two reasons for Burns' role as the elder statesman—age and ethnicity. "My contemporaries were all brought up to respect our elders," Inouye commented. "It took me a long time to get to the point where I [could] call [him] Jack. . . . I would call him Mr. Burns and he would call me Dan." The matter of ethnicity was more telling:

> You should remember that for the most part my . . . Japanese contemporaries came from the lowest rung of the social ladder. Our immediate ancestors were for the most part failures, otherwise they wouldn't have come here. My grandparents and all the others had been brought up to look up to superior men, and in the case of Hawaii the superior man was a haole.

Thus, the paradox facing the young AJA veterans: In spite of having been tested by war and having returned to their homes with a superior education—thanks to the G.I. Bill—they retained a sense of inferiority. They needed the leadership a Jack Burns could provide.

For men confronting a sense of inferiority, Burns provided a certain level of comfort. In casual conversation he lapsed quickly into pidgin, the lingua franca of the plantation and the lower-class urban communities of Hawaii. Inouye observed that Burns "was not a very talkative fellow, . . . [but] when he opened up, boom, there'd be quiet and we'd listen to him. And when he quieted down, the rest of us talked." Burns made it a point to see that they did most of the talking, to test their ideas and communication skills. He guided the future leaders of Hawaii into an understanding of the meaning of democracy as it had been enunciated by his two favorite American political figures, Thomas Jefferson and Andrew Jackson.

Other haoles would seek to lead the AJAs, particularly Tom Gill, Frank Fasi, and Vince Esposito. They were better educated, more articulate, and at least as committed to the cause of social equality as Burns; but the very strengths these men possessed caused them to be seen by many AJAs as a threat. Burns had two advantages over his haole rivals: he made the AJAs feel comfortable and he was seen as having paid his dues. Above all, it was widely felt by Burns' followers that he cared more about their success than his own.

The members of Burns' cell gang were much in evidence at the 1952 territorial Democratic Convention. As in 1950, Burns was elected convention chairman. Bill Richardson, one of Burns' young protégés, was chosen to serve as the convention's secretary. Others from the Burns group—Aoki, Tokunaga, Sakamoto, Takahashi, and Kido—served as delegates. Dan Inouye, meanwhile, was at George Washington University in Washington, D.C., working on a degree in law and developing an appetite for the nation's capital that he would never lose.

Much of the bitterness that had divided the 1950 territorial Democratic Convention had subsided by 1952. Ingram Stainback's removal from the political scene had defused much of the red-baiting that had characterized the preceding years. The trial of the Hawaii Seven was slowly working its way through the federal court system, desensitizing the public along the way. The former "Walkout Democrats" had divided into factions and, lacking leadership, were no longer a force.

The more important division in the Democratic Party was to be found within the former "Standpat" wing of the Party. Burns led the largest of the factions, occupying the philosophical center of the Party. The Burns wing, the political home for AJA veterans since Dan Inouye signed on to help in Burns' 1948 delegate's race, was being energized by the return of many of these veterans from America's colleges and universities, where they had been the beneficiaries of the G.I. Bill. They were young and energetic and possessed a strong sense of organization and discipline. They maintained their ranks in the 1952 territorial Democratic Convention in much the same way the ILWU faction had done in past Democratic conventions.

Another faction of the former "Standpat" Democrats was, in 1952, dubbed by Hawaii's conservative press as the "Left Wing" Democrats. Its titular leader was Mayor Johnny Wilson, but its leaders in fact were Vince Esposito and Wilson's proxy, Takaichi Miyamoto. Another senior member of the "Left Wing" Democrats was the liberal judge, Delbert Metzger. Because of Jack Hall's paramount position among the defendants in the Smith Act trial, the ILWU took a low profile at the 1952 territorial Democratic Convention, but their interests were being tended to by their friends in the left wing of the Party.

With the disintegration of the "Walkout" Democrats, the right wing of the Party devolved into small splinter groups led by old-timers like Charles Kauhane and a relative newcomer to Island politics by the name of Frank Fasi. A native of Hartford, Connecticut, Fasi first came to Hawaii as a young marine during World War II. He stayed on, went into the salvage business, married a local girl, and decided to enter politics. A fiery red-baiter in his own right, Fasi ran an unsuccessful but attention-getting campaign for the territorial house of representatives in 1950. He was among those who walked out of the 1950 territorial Democratic Convention and aimed much of his anticommunist campaign rhetoric at the ILWU and Jack Burns. Basically a populist, Fasi often spoke of his own immigrant roots, working-class origins, and union background.

Working from the center of the Party, but wanting to maintain as large a tent as possible for the Democratic Party of Hawaii, John Burns had some difficult problems to deal with at the 1952 territorial Democratic Convention. One was how to select a new member of the Democratic National Committee (DNC). It was particularly awkward for Burns because Johnny Wilson, a man to whom he owed much, badly wanted the position. Burns knew that Wilson, infirm and 80 years old, would not be able to handle the frequent trips to the mainland the position entailed. In a move which was seen by many as supporting Frank Fasi for membership on the DNC, Burns opposed his old friend Johnny Wilson. In 1975, Dan Aoki explained the meaning of this move as the "tail end of the struggle [between] the ILWU and the Democratic Party." Aoki continued:

> It was a question of whether we were a part of the ILWU or the ILWU was a part of the Democratic Party, . . . and we just could not see Mayor Wilson—deserving as he may have been—we couldn't quite see him as the national committeeman because we knew . . . that if he got elected . . . Vincent Esposito would be the man that would be going to all the meetings and he would be representing the opposite faction from our side. Frank Fasi was not our candidate for national committeeman, but he won by default.

By the time it became apparent that Wilson was not going to respond favorably to Burns' request that he withdraw from the contest for national committeeman, it was too late for the Burns group to offer a candidate of their own. As Aoki explained it: "We would have had no qualms about putting any man against Fasi," who had vigorously advanced his own candidacy, "but we didn't want to put anybody against Wilson."

Mits Kido's recollection of the 1952 contest for national committeeman is in total agreement with Aoki regarding the ILWU connection, but he went further with regard to the Burns group's involvement with Frank Fasi at that time. Kido described a quid pro quo which was offered by the Burns group to Fasi in exchange for their support of his candidacy. As Kido pointed out, Fasi "had been calling us Communists or pro-Communists and reds and radicals and so on. He promised at that meeting that if we joined forces with him, that he'd stop all this name-calling and any public statements he'd make, he'd clear with Jack Burns."

Fasi's pledges of fealty to Jack Burns were short-lived. But when Fasi attacked Burns in the future, the response he got was a stony silence. As Burns is reputed to have said, "Why get into a pissing contest with a goddam skunk?" This was the same Frank Fasi about whom Tom Gill, a maverick in his own right, made the following assessment:

> Frank has always been Frank; that's his bag. Everybody else is either to be used or to be ignored or yelled at or something. But he's never really had any close friends or support in the Party. . . . Frank is only

for Frank. He's a complete egotist. . . . He's wherever he thinks the cause is most immediately newsworthy. . . . He had no particular ideology except to try to get elected, and God knows he tried long enough.

That Burns was willing, in 1952, to reach out to Frank Fasi was consistent with his big tent view of the Democratic Party of Hawaii. It was also consistent with his effort to keep the ILWU under that tent, but just inside the flap.

Burns was also trying to get Tom Gill into the tent before the territorial Democratic Convention of 1952. The instrument of this effort was Matsy Takabuki, who had known Gill as a fellow student at the University of Hawaii before World War II. After the war, both Takabuki and Gill had gone to the mainland to study—Takabuki to the University of Chicago, Gill to the University of California at Berkeley. Both became attorneys and by 1952, both had returned to Hawaii. Takabuki, a 442nd Club friend of Inouye and Aoki, arranged for a luncheon meeting with Gill at the old South Seas restaurant in Waikiki.

When Aoki and Takabuki met with Gill, they had a proposal for the young attorney. As Aoki recalled it, Takabuki opened the subject, saying, "Eh, you know we're forming this Democratic Party and . . . we think you'd make, you know, a good Democrat . . . and we sure would like to have you join us." Gill's response according to Aoki was, "Join you guys? How about you guys joining me?" That ended what Aoki remembered as "a very short lunch."

For the next twelve years, Burns would continue to try to find positive roles for the talented Gill within the mainstream of the Democratic Party of Hawaii, ultimately at great risk to his own career. Gill saw every effort of Burns to bring him into the fold as an attempt to co-opt him. But in 1974, when asked which one he would vote for if faced with the choice of Tom Gill or Frank Fasi, Burns is reported to have said without hesitation that he would vote for Gill, "because he's at least an honest man."

Johnny Wilson was not the only old-timer who left the 1952 territorial Democratic Convention disappointed. Chuck Mau, chairman of the territorial Democratic Central Committee and a Burns intimate from 1944 through 1950, sought selection as a delegate to the Democratic National Convention in 1952. As a delegate to the 1948 Democratic National Convention, Mau had made a name for himself with a forceful and well-orchestrated effort in behalf of Hawaiian statehood. These efforts had been rewarded by a statehood plank in the 1948 Democratic Party Platform and by a nomination to the federal bench in 1950. Neither of these efforts came to fruition: the statehood bill passed by the House of Representatives in 1950 never made it out of committee in the Senate, and Mau's nomination to the federal bench was blocked in 1951 by Pat McCarran of the Senate Judiciary Committee.

There would be more disappointment for Mau in 1952, for he was now tainted by his close association with Jack Kawano. Looking back in 1975, Mau said somewhat ruefully, "I was left out in the cold. Naturally, having won the plank [in 1948], I thought that probably I should have been asked to go again and see what else we could do in getting some of the senators and congressmen to fight for statehood in Congress." But Chuck Mau's day in Hawaii's Democratic Party leadership had passed. The day after the 1952 territorial Democratic Convention adjourned, Mau resigned his chairmanship of the Party's Central Committee. The Party's delegates to the Democratic National Convention in 1952 were Jack Burns, Mits Kido, and Governor Oren E. Long.

The greatest achievement of the 1952 territorial Democratic Convention was its Platform, which outlined the basic program the Democratic Party would pursue throughout the 1950s and into John A. Burns' first term as governor. The Platform consisted of six planks:

1. We believe that the people of Hawaii want and are entitled to the full privileges of citizenship which only immediate statehood for Hawaii can bestow.
2. To make a thorough-going revision of the present tax structure of the Territory and to enact tax laws based upon ability to pay and reject any tax that is not based on ability to pay.
3. To aid the cause of small business in Hawaii as a counter-balance to the economic power of Hawaii's economic oligarchy.
4. To enact laws which will make land available for purchase in fee simple for home construction and for small farming and ranching and to amend existing laws and to enact new laws to require that leases be granted for sufficient periods of time to enable lessees to plant long-range crops and to justify expenditures for sound conservation practices. To support the overall economic

development of these islands through intelligent and comprehensive economic research and planning.

5. To create a high-quality public school system from kindergarten through a first-class university, placing emphasis upon facilities, small classes and a substantial reduction of university tuition. To enact legislation providing for home rule for each county.

6. To support war veterans and their families and to support the rights and needs of labor.

Three weeks after the end of the convention, the territorial Democratic Central Committee turned to the selection of a new chairman. Burns had made his interest in the position well known, telling the press that he would like to make the chairmanship "a more active position in the leadership of the Democratic Party." One small problem existed, however. Burns was not a member of the Central Committee and some questioned whether or not it would be legal to make him chairman of a committee to which he did not belong. In what amounted to a comedy of motions, the Central Committee finally said, in essence, "To hell with legalisms, Burns is our man."

Party Chairman John A. Burns intended to create greater discipline within the Democratic Party of Hawaii. He recognized that control of patronage was the indispensable tool for the effective exercise of his new position. In a 23 June 1952 letter to the county committees, Burns wrote: "Nothing has caused the Party more trouble and more harm than patronage. The dissension and ill-feeling aroused as a result of endorsement or nonendorsement of particular individuals for particular appointments have contributed to a major breach in the ranks of a party whose essential need is unity." Continuing with this theme, Burns recognized that as long as Hawaii remained a territory there would be severe limits to their ability to control patronage completely. "We have had ample examples," Burns pointed out, "of the fact that the appointive authority [i.e., the president of the United States] pays no attention to the Party endorsements. . . . This is and has been the fact."

In this same letter, we see Burns calling his forces to battle, citing the formidable foe they faced and the reason for their inevitable victory: "The Democratic Party has for its opposition a Republican Party which has at its command every possible resource—money, social position, and individual prestige. Democratic strength is in the correctness of its program and the numbers of citizens who want that program for themselves and their children." In retrospect, this moment after the 1952 territorial Democratic Convention marks the beginning of the final drive to power by the Democratic Party of Hawaii. All of the key players were in place and the theme of their victory had been sounded by their leader, John A. Burns. But the inevitability of their victory was anything but clear in 1952.

The irony of Burns' move into territorial leadership is that his old power base, the Oahu County Committee, fell into the hands of non-Burns people. The new chairman of the Oahu County was John Akau, an old Stainback loyalist who had given the former governor the so-called communist plan for Hawaii that was the cornerstone of the case against John and Aiko Reinecke in 1947. Tom Gill, who had shunned Burns' efforts to make him a part of his leadership group, was elected vice president and secretary of the Oahu County Committee.

As a matter of fact, Tom Gill came very close to becoming a Republican when he returned to Hawaii after the war in 1946. As Gill told the story twenty years later, he and some of his like-minded fellow veterans made an appointment to meet with Republican Party Chairman Roy Vitousek to explore the possibilities within Hawaii's GOP. "We must have hit him on a bad day," Gill recalled. "He made it very clear that the Republican Party didn't need anybody; they had all the votes anyway and whatever our concerns were, they were of some interest, but not to him. The only way we were going to do anything was to go with some other group, which meant the Democrats." Gill was not the only promising young veteran to receive the cold shoulder from the Republicans when he returned to Hawaii. Spark Matsunaga, who would later serve as a Democratic member of the U.S. House of Representatives and the U.S. Senate, was also rebuffed. The Revolution of 1954 was not simply a victory by the Democrats, it was also a self-inflicted defeat on the part of the Republicans.

Gill had actually signed his Democratic Party card in California, where he did volunteer political work while attending law school. Returning to Hawaii as a young labor lawyer in 1951, he found work with Unity House, the Teamsters local. As Gill recalled in 1976: "A number of Teamsters were old Democrats and they sort of dragged me in. . . . The group . . . probably revolved around the Heen family—Ernest Heen and John Akau, who was very close to them at that point, and a number of others who were probably classed as more of the independent Democrats."

The elections of 1952 provided little excitement for the Democratic Party. They achieved minor gains in the territorial house of representatives, narrowing the Republican majority from 21–9 to 19–11. In the territorial senate the Republican majority dropped from 9–6 to 8–7, as the result of a 4-4 split of the eight seats contested. Democratic Party veteran Judge Delbert Metzger made a good showing against Joe Farrington in the delegate's race, losing by only 9,303 votes.

Johnny Wilson faced an unexpected challenge in the Democratic mayoral primary. Frank Fasi, who had pledged that if he were selected a member of the Democratic National Committee he would not run for public office in 1952, changed his mind at the last minute—under bizarre circumstances. At an August dinner in Wilson's honor, Fasi had pledged his support to the aging mayor. On the night of the deadline for filing, however, Frank Fasi experienced what he called "a miracle." When a scheduled flight he was taking to the mainland was delayed, Fasi interpreted the event as a sign from God that he should run for mayor. His nomination papers were already signed—by some other miracle, no doubt. Fasi filed them minutes before the deadline. Having apparently used up all of his miracles, Fasi was defeated by Wilson in the 4 October primary by a margin of 15,693 to 12,221. But Fasi would be back. It would take him sixteen years to get there, but in 1968 Frank Fasi would finally become mayor of the City and County of Honolulu. In 1952, however, Johnny Wilson went on to defeat his Republican opponent, Neal Blaisdell, by the comfortable margin of 46,417 to 39,546. On his home island of Oahu, Jack Burns not only took pleasure in Johnny Wilson's reelection, but in the first-time election of cell gang regular Matsy Takabuki as a member of the board of supervisors. For sixteen years, Takabuki would serve as Jack Burns' eyes, ears, and voice in city hall.

In 1953, Burns directed his attention to Hawaii's battle for statehood. He fully intended to have the Democratic Party identified as the Party most likely to bring statehood to the Islands. Prior to the Democratic National Convention of 1952, Burns wrote to Interior Secretary Oscar Chapman, the potential Democratic presidential candidate with the greatest commitment to Hawaiian statehood, explaining that if Truman did not run for reelection, the Hawaii delegation was his for the asking. "Our delegates [Burns, Kido, and Long] will not be too hard to handle, and while I may not be very good at winning friends, I have had considerable experience in influencing people. . . . I do know that the convention cannot find anyone who better represents the principles of the Democratic Party than yourself." Chapman thanked the leader of

Hawaii's convention delegation, but did not encourage Burns to do anything to advance his candidacy. In the end, the Democratic Party nominated Adlai Stevenson, with the concurrence of the Hawaii delegation. Stevenson, of course, was soundly trounced by Dwight D. Eisenhower in the general election. With the Republican Party in charge of the executive branch of government, Burns would have to turn to Congress for his opportunities to influence the cause of statehood.

While attending the Democratic National Convention in 1952, Jack Burns had made the acquaintance of the only southern Democratic senator who then favored statehood for Hawaii. He was Russell Long of Louisiana, son of the infamous "Kingfish," Huey Long. In October 1953, Burns brought Long to Hawaii to address the territorial Democratic Party Conference. Burns sought to derail the constant, and largely true, Republican Party lament that it was racist southern Democrats who constituted the largest obstacle to Hawaii's dream of statehood. In his introduction of Russell Long to the members of the Party conference, Burns called him a harbinger of "the new progressive look of the Democrats in the South." In fact, Long was an isolated southern congressional voice on the issue of Hawaiian statehood.

The reasons for Long's support of Hawaiian statehood went beyond his unusually progressive views as a southern member of the U.S. Senate. Long was strongly influenced on this issue by a New Orleans businessman named George Lehleitner, one of the most interesting characters in Hawaii's statehood drama. Lehleitner had served in Hawaii during World War II and became convinced that the Islands deserved better than the territorial government and martial law under which they had been governed. Starting in his own backyard after the war had ended, Lehleitner began a one-man crusade on the mainland to bring statehood to Hawaii. He spoke to service clubs, wrote letters to editors of southern newspapers, and talked about Hawaii to anyone who would listen. In 1953 the U.S. House of Representatives voted favorably on statehood for Hawaii for the third time in six years. In that vote, the entire Louisiana delegation had supported the bill. Jack Burns was always quick to acknowledge Lehleitner's role in achieving statehood for Hawaii:

> George Lehleitner is a guy who really deserves a hell of a lot of credit.
> . . . He took [Hawaiian statehood] as a sacred cause and more than

anyone else, among all the Southerners, he really built up a case for just human rights, really, and for statehood. He didn't care who he worked with. . . . He drew no barriers. . . . He'd see anybody, . . . go anyplace. He'd drop anything.

On 12 January 1954, with the prospect of statehood looking very much alive, Jack Burns made a formal request to the Hawaii Statehood Commission for funding to send a bipartisan delegation to lobby for statehood. Four days later he was turned down. The Democratic Party decided to act on its own. Drawing on Party funds, Hawaii's Democrats sent Burns, territorial senator William Heen, and territorial Democratic Central Committee member Arthur K. Trask to the nation's capital. They departed Hawaii during the last week of February.

Burns saw the delegation's task as having two parts: first, to convince Congress to split the Hawaii and Alaska statehood bill into two separate pieces of legislation; and second, to convince the Democrats, who longed to regain control of Congress after the Eisenhower sweep of 1952, that Hawaii's congressional delegation would not be Republican. Burns had even prepared a probable slate of officeholders in the event of statehood: William Heen and Mits Kido for the U.S. Senate; Herbert K. H. Lee and Charles Kauhane for the House of Representatives; and Johnny Wilson for governor of the State of Hawaii. A careful look at the racial and philosophical balance among these possible candidates demonstrates that Party unity was first and foremost in Burns' pragmatic mind.

During his three weeks in Washington, D.C., Burns was talked out of his separate bill strategy for Hawaiian and Alaskan statehood, only to see the combined bill magnify opposition. As it turned out, the House statehood bill of 1953 suffered the same fate as its 1947 and 1950 antecedents and never made it to the floor of the Senate in 1954. Burns would remember this lesson when he guided the statehood bill in 1958 and 1959 as the Territory of Hawaii's last delegate to Congress. Then, he divided the statehood bills for Alaska and Hawaii and allowed Alaska to go first. Having laid to rest the noncontiguity issue, he then came up with a winning southern strategy for Hawaii and carried the day.

For all of his efforts to create unity within the Democratic Party, Jack Burns was not immune from attack from the Party's right wing, even in the historic year of 1954. When the territorial Democratic Convention opened on April Fools' Day, Frank Fasi threatened a walkout over the question of precinct representation. Fasi eventually stayed in his seat, but a faction led by Ernest N. Heen maneuvered to have Burns ousted as chairman of the territorial Democratic Central Committee. By now thoroughly disenchanted, his old friend Chuck Mau even asked Burns to step down in the name of Party unity. But Burns could count and he knew that he had more than enough votes to be reelected Party chairman. Able to keep attacks from the right wing of the Democratic Party under control, the Burns people kept their eye on the main event, the fall campaign.

The political year changed dramatically when, on 19 June 1954, the popular delegate to Congress, Joe Farrington, died of a massive heart attack in Washington, D.C. Both Republicans and Democrats mourned Farrington's passing. He was recognized as a man who had fought valiantly for statehood throughout his decade of service in the nation's capital. Further, his Republicanism had never included the antilabor red-baiting that was so characteristic of the most conservative elements of Hawaii's GOP. Burns, who had taken a terrible drubbing from Farrington in the 1948 delegate's race, had always expressed positive feelings for Farrington, even when they differed on specific issues.

Governor Sam King, who had been appointed to succeed Oren Long after Dwight D. Eisenhower was elected president and took office in 1953, was required by law to call for a special election to replace the delegate to Congress, even though such an election would take place just two months before the October primaries and three months before the November general election. Governor King's initial response was to seek special legislation in Congress to allow him to appoint a successor to Farrington for the balance of his term. His obvious choice would have been Elizabeth Farrington, the former delegate's widow.

Jack Burns was more than willing to have King make such an appointment. Three days after Joe Farrington's death, Burns was quoted in the *Honolulu Advertiser* as saying, "It would be fine recognition of the sincere and loyal efforts of the late delegate." There was a political subtext behind Burns' magnanimous statement, one that was not lost on the Republicans. All other considerations aside, the last thing Burns wanted was to see Elizabeth Farrington's name on a ballot in the special election opposed by any Democrat. He knew that she would win easily on a sympathy vote to complete her husband's almost expired term. Then, if she should chose to run for reelection in the general election, she would be running as an incumbent who was a proven vote-getter. The Republicans saw the same thing and quietly stopped Sam King's request for the power to appoint a successor.

The best strategy for the Democrats at this point would have been to allow Elizabeth Farrington to run unopposed in the special election. Burns, Frank Fasi, and Johnny Wilson all saw it that way, but Tom Gill had other ideas. Having seen Delbert Metzger's surprisingly strong showing against Joe Farrington in 1952, Gill urged Metzger to stand again. Sadly for Judge Metzger, he listened to Gill instead of Burns. The turnout for the 31 July 1954 special election was very light; fewer than half of the registered voters went to the polls. Elizabeth Farrington trounced Delbert Metzger 43,195 to 19,591. With over two-thirds of the vote, Betty Farrington was now not only a proven vote-getter, but she had experienced the intoxicating feeling of success that a merely symbolic victory would never have given her. She was, in short, a player.

In spite of this untimely intrusion, the summer of 1954 had a special feel about it for the Democratic Party of Hawaii. Most of the AJA veterans who had been at school on the mainland were back, including Dan Inouye. In his 1967 autobiography, *Journey to Washington*, Dan Inouye described a meeting at the home of Dan Aoki during that historic summer:

BURNS: Dan, I think it's time for you to run.

INOUYE: Listen, why me? There are other guys who have been around longer, better qualified . . .

BURNS: Because you can win. This is your time.

INOUYE: In the Fourth District?

BURNS: Who was it that made the big speech about going through the motions? Who is it that keeps saying times are changing and that the people want a chance to come out from under fifty-four years of Republican rule? That was you, Dan, and this is your chance to prove you believe it.

While attending George Washington University Law School in Washington, D.C., Dan Inouye had haunted the halls of Congress. Politics was in his blood. As it turned out, Washington was in his blood as well, but in 1954 Inouye turned his efforts back to Hawaii, answering his leader's call.

Another AJA veteran by the name of George Ariyoshi answered the call of Jack Burns in 1954. Like Inouye, Ariyoshi had gone to law school on the mainland. When he graduated from the University of Michigan Law School in 1952, Ariyoshi returned to Hawaii. Unlike Inouye, he had no thoughts of entering politics. But Tom Ebesu, a precinct worker under Matsy Takabuki, identified Ariyoshi as a promising candidate and arranged to introduce him to Jack Burns. The meeting took place in late August, just a few days before the filing deadline. Ariyoshi described that meeting in his 1997 autobiography, *With Obligation to All:*

> In the meeting, Burns asked me a lot of questions about what I saw going on in Hawaii. I told him I did not like the way opportunity was controlled by a select few. I said not everyone was being treated fairly. I said it wasn't how good you were at doing something, but who you knew. I said this problem wasn't limited to the Orientals or any particular racial group. It applied to the Caucasian person as well, because the Big Five controlled Hawaii, and you could only advance if you were "in" with them.
>
> At a certain point in the meeting Jack Burns looked my way and said, "You should run for office."
>
> I thought he was talking to someone else. I turned around to see if there was someone behind me, but no one was there. He fixed me with a look and said, "You should run for office."
>
> My response was, "I'm too young. Nobody knows who I am."
>
> He said, "It's not the age. It's the heart. It's how you feel."

The conclusion of the story of George Ariyoshi's sudden candidacy will give the reader a sense of how polished the Burns organization had become by the summer of 1954. While Ariyoshi was thinking about whether he should answer Burns' call, Tom Ebesu had completed the application and obtained the necessary signatures for Ariyoshi to file. "And so, on the day of the deadline," Ariyoshi concluded, "Tom and I walked in, we filed the nomination papers, and we became a candidate. And I say 'we' became a candidate because he was very much a part of this effort." Indeed, by 1954 Burns had built a political machine in which the largely invisible workers like Dan Aoki and Tom Ebesu were playing roles as important as the candidates. As Dan Aoki said, "We combined forces and filled up an entire ticket in 1954 and, by God, we ended up with the damned majority in 1955!" Win they did. The territorial house of representatives went to the Democrats by a margin of 22 to 8, a gain of eleven seats over 1952. The territorial senate saw five out of seven Democratic candidates win, giving their party a majority of 9 to 6, a critical two-seat gain. The board of supervisors of the City and County of Honolulu saw the Democrats sweep to a 6 to 1 majority, from a 4 to 3 Republican majority in 1952. As Professor Donald Johnson wrote in his 1991 history of the City and County of Honolulu, "If they had had a seventh strong office-seeker on the list, they might have swept the entire board."

The Democrats suffered two disappointments in 1954. The first involved the mayor's race in Honolulu. The disappointment for Burns came during the primary when Frank Fasi defeated Johnny Wilson for the Democratic nomination by 1,102 votes—24,274 to 23,172. Neal Blaisdell, the Republican who eventually won the general election, received only 14,979 votes in the primary election, a sure sign that many Republicans crossed over to the Democratic mayoral primary to assure the defeat of Johnny Wilson. Indeed, the so-called Friends of Frank Fasi distributed a brochure instructing voters on the fine art of ticket-splitting in the primary election. As Donald Johnson pointed out, "Any doubt that the Republicans might have voted in the Democratic race was dispelled by the strong Fasi showing in Kailua, Aina Haina, Manoa, and other normally Republican strongholds."

Burns, who always maintained a good working relationship with Mayor Blaisdell, was perfectly content to see the handsome, popular, part-Hawaiian ex-athlete/ex-coach defeat the irascible spoiler, Frank Fasi, by a margin of 47,704 to 45,240. Fasi discovered that Democrats could cross Party lines, too. In the general election, ILWU Democrats crossed over to punish Frank Fasi, who had been an adverse character witness against Jack Hall in the Smith Act trial. Burns' only regret about Blaisdell was that he was not a Democrat. Dan Aoki ruminated that Blaisdell, like Roy Vitousek before, "should have been a Democrat. They just lacked the fortitude that Mr. Burns had."

If Jack Hall could take some of the credit for the defeat of Frank Fasi, there were many in the Burns camp who felt that Hall should take the blame for the second, and far greater, disappointment in the 1954 elections—Jack Burns' loss to Elizabeth Farrington in the race for

Hawaii's delegate to Congress. In a contest which Burns lost by only 890 votes—69,466 to 68,576—any help from the ILWU would have been enough to push Burns over the top. The biggest problem Burns faced in the contest with Elizabeth Farrington, aside from the residual sympathy she carried into the contest, was money. Mike Tokunaga lamented, "We ran completely out. We figured that we needed about $3,000 to win. . . . Dan [Aoki] and I went down to see Jack Hall. . . . We asked him for the money. He told us there was no use spending money on Jack Burns."

While many of those around Burns wanted to strike out at the ILWU, Burns counseled silence. He knew that attacking the union now would not change the result of this election and that its support would be needed in the future. He would bide his time. Asked about this loss in 1975, Burns responded philosophically:

> Didn't bother me at all, because I was the Party leader. I'm sorry I couldn't get elected, particularly since it turned out [to be] only 890 votes. . . . But I succeeded in my job. My job was to elect the legislature. . . . I never thought I was a good candidate. I'd rather have been a party leader and help put the boys in the spots. . . . I didn't have the baloney. I didn't have all the smiles. I haven't got any jokes. I'm going to talk to you seriously or I'm not going to talk to you.

So ended the year of the Democratic Revolution in Hawaii. It was not the result of a single year's efforts, but the culmination of a decade of striving. It began in 1944 when Burns launched into his own political education, an education he shared so willingly with the next generation. It ended in 1954 with the election of that new generation of political leaders of Hawaii.

E·I·G·H·T

Delegate

FOLLOWING NEAL BLAISDELL'S victory in the 1954 mayor's race, Jack Burns immediately offered his resignation as Honolulu's director of civil defense. In an act of generosity, Blaisdell demurred, telling his friend that he was free to stay. Six months later, under considerable pressure from Governor Sam King, Blaisdell reluctantly reversed himself. On 30 June 1955, Burns found himself without a job. Burns was philosophical, as he had been following his defeat in the 1954 delegate's race when he told his disappointed supporters, "Fifty-six is another election. I'll be back."

King's desire to be rid of Burns may have reflected the difficult time he was having with the new Democratic legislature in 1955, a body heavily peppered with members of Burns' cell gang. Why should the Republicans provide Burns with a paid base from which he could plot their next defeat? Let him sell liquor and real estate in Kailua.

As the new Democratic legislature organized itself in 1955, it turned to its most experienced members for positions of leadership. William Heen was selected as president of the senate; Charles Kauhane got the nod as speaker of the house. The senate was not difficult to organize. As a continuous body, only seven of the fifteen senate seats had been contested in 1954, with the Democrats winning five of them. Thus, there was a significant amount of experience and continuity with which Heen and Senate Majority Leader Herbert K. H. Lee could work. In the house of representatives, on the other hand, only eight of the twenty-two in the Democratic majority had any legislative experience. Speaker Kauhane worked with Dan Inouye on the matter of committee assignments for the younger members. Inouye, clearly the leader of the freshman members, was given the important post of house majority leader. Another promising freshman, Elmer Cravalho of Maui, became vice speaker.

With the lack of experience in the house, the senate found itself in a position to assume leadership in the development of a legislative package. Heen and Lee, who were not members of the Burns group, decided to hire the brilliant but volatile Tom Gill as senate counsel, to assist in drafting legislation. As Gill recalled the situation in 1976:

> We put together . . . seventy, eighty, ninety bills dealing with various phases that we thought were important. . . . I must say that this program was less than beautiful, because it was drafted by amateurs who didn't know what they were doing, including myself. We were saved by Governor King, who decided that any Democratic appearance in 1954 or 1955 was a passing fancy and he was going to take care of it. I think he vetoed seventy-two bills, . . . whereupon we ran on this in 1956 and beat his ass.

Gill's 1976 recollection was only one off—Governor King vetoed seventy-one bills. Of that number, only two were overridden by the legislature, in spite of the Democrats' two-thirds majority in both houses. King recognized that some of the bills were badly drafted and deserved to be vetoed for that reason alone. Others were merely audacious, such as the law that would have exempted ILWU holdings from property taxes. But many of King's vetoes involved core issues from the Democratic Party Platform and King clearly went too far in the protection of the status quo, at least from a political standpoint. As Lawrence Fuchs pointed out:

> He vetoed a large number of tax and spend bills passed by the 1955 Democratic legislature. The governor stopped the bill amending the Workman's Compensation Act, arguing that it was too expensive. In addition, he vetoed a measure which would have abolished the fixed ceiling on the amount of money that could legally be raised by taxes on property. Another bill would have enabled counties to classify land by best use rather than actual use for tax assessments. . . . Realizing that Democratic and labor power was strong on the neighbor islands, King opposed decentralization of government authority. . . . Eight home rule bills were vetoed. . . . The overall record confirmed the opinion of the majority of Hawaii's voters that the Republican Party was tied to the

conservatism of the past and had not yet caught up with the social and economic revolution that was sweeping postwar Hawaii.

At the conclusion of the 1955 legislative session, Chairman John A. Burns praised the Democratic legislature's aggressive efforts to put the Party's Platform into law. He characterized King's vetoes as showing "callous and wanton disregard of the expressed mandate of the people." Support for this view came from veteran political writer Millard Purdy of the *Star-Bulletin*. Purdy devoted a whole page to an analysis of the 1955 legislative session, showing what the Democratic Party had promised, what the legislature had done, and what Governor King had done to thwart it. The case was so persuasive that the Democratic Party photocopied the article and used it as their most effective piece of campaign literature in 1956.

In the period between the 1954 and 1956 elections, Burns devoted most of his political energies to building the Democratic Party at the grassroots level. This took him, on many occasions, to the neighbor islands, where he broadened his personal political base. One of those he met during that period was Ben Menor, a young deputy Hawaii County attorney who had grown up on a Pahoa sugar plantation. Burns saw Menor as a way to broaden the Democratic Party coalition among the Filipino population. Menor, who ultimately became an associate justice on the Hawaii state supreme court, also took a liking to Burns: "I liked him because he was a Democrat. When you grew up on a plantation, everyone except laborers were Republicans. A haole Democrat was unknown. Burns was stern, unsmiling, but you could sense that he had a sincere, genuine interest in those unrepresented in the halls of government. He was a haole you could trust."

Burns also worked to build a better relationship with the ILWU during this period. At a Democratic Party luau on the island of Kauai shortly after the 1954 elections, Burns publicly credited the ILWU with having "brought democracy to the Islands and [having] raised the economic standards of our people." Such talk went down easily on the neighbor islands, but it was a dangerous line to be taking on Oahu, where a vocal minority were still trying to keep the red-scare alive in 1954. It also posed some danger for an advocate of Hawaiian statehood in the nation's capital. Two days after Burns' Kauai remarks, Representative Wesley A. D'Ewart, chairman of the all-important House Interior

Committee (and the committee's counsel, George W. Abbott), questioned Burns about the meaning of his recent remarks in a letter-to-the-editor. Burns, in one of his less heroic statements, backtracked, indicating that his praise of the ILWU was really meant to convey praise for organized labor in general.

As the 1956 elections drew nearer, Burns' praise of the ILWU became less equivocal. In September 1955, Burns pointed out to an ILWU audience that he had been "severely criticized" for his comments that "every living soul in the Territory owes sincere thanks and appreciation to the ILWU which, as an organization, brought political freedom to the Territory." The *Star-Bulletin* chided Burns for his "poor knowledge" of Hawaii's history, pointing to pre–World War II Democrats Lincoln McCandless and Manuel Pacheco as examples of Democratic politicians from the past who exercised their political liberty endlessly, inveighing against the economic and political powers of the Islands. "Of course," the newspaper concluded, "Jack was speaking to an ILWU audience which likes flattery and adulation. And he has his eye on future elections."

Burns did, indeed, have his eye on future elections, but the editors of the *Star-Bulletin* missed the point. Free speech absent power possesses little meaning. By unifying Hawaii's workers and organizing them for political as well as economic activity, the ILWU had given Hawaii's masses the confidence they needed to participate in the political process without fear of reprisal. Burns knew this well. The thousands of plantation workers who carried ILWU membership cards knew it. Their union had done for them what the American Revolution, the U.S. Constitution, and the Bill of Rights had never done—the ILWU had, indeed, made political freedom a reality in their lives as American citizens.

Still, there were those who sought to utilize the issue of communism against the newly successful Democratic Party. In November 1955, Burns appeared on a television program moderated by *Star-Bulletin* reporter Millard Purdy. In the course of the discussion, Burns characterized President Eisenhower as a "captive of big business." Three days later, a letter appeared on the editorial pages of the *Star-Bulletin*. It was signed by "Island Voter," and stated: "It is quite natural that Jack is very anxious to see the Democrats win the next election. Maybe there's a fat job in it for him if they do, but there is just one thing they can't say and that is that Eisenhower is a captive of a communist-dominated labor union, like the Democratic Party is said to be."

But the issue of communism had lost much of its sting, both on the mainland and in the Territory of Hawaii. On the mainland, Joseph McCarthy had been censured by the U.S. Senate and dismissed by the same President Eisenhower as "a pimple on the path of progress." In Hawaii, the "Reluctant Thirty-Nine" had long since been acquitted of the contempt charges brought by the House Un-American Activities Committee and the "Hawaii Seven" were going about their business in total freedom while their Smith Act convictions were going through an appeals process that would ultimately see them reversed by the U.S. Supreme Court. While the issue was not totally dead, it was now generally seen as a tired and desperate attempt by the Republicans to cast doubt upon the new majority Party in Hawaii.

While Burns maintained his image as a Party leader, he was also making some progress as the breadwinner for his family. Having taken out a new mortgage on the family home in Kailua during the 1954 election campaign, he had to. One positive step took place when Burns brought a few investors—including Ernest Murai, Baron Goto, and Wayne Minami—into his small real estate development business. With the acquisition of a small Kailua shopping center, anchored by a Ben Franklin variety store, the business was generating enough cash flow to allow Burns a monthly salary of $250. In 1975, Burns took pleasure in The Burns and Company investors realizing a 500 percent return on their money when the company was liquidated.

Burns loyalists Dan Aoki and Mike Tokunaga also had to contend with the mundane matter of putting food on their families' tables. The Democratic majority briefly considered Dan Aoki for the position of clerk of the territorial house of representatives, but that job went to Jack Burns' brother-in-law, Jimmy Trask, an old-line Democrat who was close to Charles Kauhane. In early 1956, two jobs opened up at the Hawaii Government Employees Association (HGEA). Executive Director Charles Kendall gave them to Aoki and Tokunaga. The HGEA, of course, could always use a direct link to the ruling Party in Hawaii. "I think, politically, it was a perfect setup," Tokunaga later recalled, "because it gave Dan and I a good chance to organize, . . . get involved in union work as well as politics. Charley Kendall—I think some of the time he felt that we were working more for the Democratic Party than the HGEA."

Aoki and Tokunaga devoted most of their political efforts to Party building. They maintained a card file of workers and donors. Between

1954 and 1956, that card file grew from four thousand to twelve thousand names. Among their newest recruits to the Democratic Party was Ed Burns, Jack's brother. Since their resignations from the police department at the end of the war, the two Burns brothers had agreed to disagree on politics. At the urging of Roy Vitousek, Ed had joined the Republican Party in 1945. He had even chaired its campaign committee in 1948. But each Friday he had continued to meet with his older brother's Friday luncheon club. After the Democrats' stunning victory in 1954, Ed Burns told Dan Inouye that he was very impressed with the Platform of the Democratic Party; if they carried through on their promises, he would switch parties. After the appearance of Millard Purdy's scorecard for the 1955 Democratic legislature, Inouye walked into the regular Friday lunch gathering and announced, "Ed, here's your card," extending to the younger Burns brother a Democratic Party membership card. "Okay," Ed replied, "I made you the promise, I'll sign." Ed Burns stayed on board, becoming his brother's first tax director in 1963.

Internecine warfare broke out as the Democrats approached the 1956 elections. At the 1954 territorial Democratic Convention, Tom Gill had engineered passage of a measure that mandated at least four meetings of the territorial Democratic Central Committee each year. Burns had failed to deliver on that requirement. Under growing criticism, Burns prepared a report for the February 1956 meeting of the Central Committee. In this report he stated:

> Your chairman, representing each of you, . . . has made every effort to keep the Party moving forward, to smooth personal differences, to secure the presentation of measures implementing our Platform, and the adoption of bills which . . . best accomplish the designs and intent of the Platform.
>
> Every continuing effort has been made to avoid situations which, if pursued to their normal consequences, would create in the minds of the public an idea of the Democratic Party as a loosely-joined group of *prima donnas* and rugged individualists. . . . Many things which should have been done were not done because this situation exists, and it is, to my mind, most important that we avoid dissension, creating public issues out of disagreements.

In early April, Burns' fight with Gill reached the press, creating exactly the kind of situation Jack Burns had sought to avoid. Prior to the territorial Democratic Convention, Burns announced that he would not be a candidate for reelection to the chairman's post. He advocated the elevation of Bill Richardson from secretary to chairman. Richardson, a Burns loyalist, was totally unacceptable to Gill. In the meantime, Burns was orchestrating a scenario whereby Gill would be ousted as chairman of Oahu County's Central Committee. Burns publicly denied charges that he was trying to unseat Gill, but in a report on the accomplishments of the territorial Central Committee he praised the Democratic county chairmen from the neighbor islands, but pointedly omitted any mention of Gill.

The outcome of this struggle between Jack Burns and Tom Gill was strictly status quo ante bellum. Burns continued to control the territorial Democratic Central Committee through his designated successor as chairman, Bill Richardson. Gill fought off a challenge on the county level from Burns loyalist, Tadao Beppu, a 442nd veteran who would later carve out a successful legislative career for himself.

In 1954, Burns had gotten a late start in his run for delegate to Congress. He did not intend to make the same mistake in 1956. On 22 June 1956, two hundred Democrats gathered to honor Jack Burns and to hear him announce his candidacy. Speakers at the Kewalo Inn affair included Bill Richardson, Ernest Murai, Matsy Takabuki, and William Jarrett. "Billy" Jarrett was a popular part-Hawaiian who had served two terms as delegate to Congress in the 1920s. Dan Inouye served as master of ceremonies for the event. Burns was typically supportive of the rest of the Democrats who would be on the ticket in the fall, but he spoke with a special passion about the necessity of having a Democrat as delegate to Congress. "The people will never attain their highest aspirations," Burns warned, "as long as a Republican occupies that office."

Burns explained to the group that in his first three runs for the position of delegate to Congress—in 1946, 1948, and 1954—he had been a stand-in candidate. However, Burns argued, 1956 was different. "In all humility," Burns asserted, "I am thoroughly and firmly convinced that I have the necessary qualifications and abilities required of the delegate and that this confidence is justified by the record." The record of which he spoke was the way in which he had championed the Democratic Party Platform of 1954 as it related to federal legislation, particularly the Hawaiian Homes Commission Act, vigorous support of statehood, removal of all inequities of federal laws that discriminated against residents of Hawaii, and a fair share of federal tax dollars for the Territory of Hawaii.

Those who had not supported Burns vigorously enough two years earlier, often because they were involved with their own races, vowed to make their leader a winner in 1956. Masao "Pundy" Yokouchi recalled that "by 880 votes we let that guy down. . . . We lost the number one position because we were so concerned about our friends. So, in 1956, . . . most of us devoted our campaigns to Jack Burns."

During the primary campaign, Burns ignored his opponent, a little known attorney named Kenneth Young. Young accused Burns of having been too cozy with the "communist-tainted" ILWU, but red-baiting had little impact on Democrats in 1956. Burns, who had received valuable reports about Elizabeth Farrington's alleged congressional failures from Representative Edith Green, an Oregon Democrat, preferred to focus his attack on the widow of Joseph Farrington who had been twice elected in 1954. Burns criticized Mrs. Farrington for her failure to get Hawaii its fair share from federal programs, particularly the school milk program. He also chided her for her failure to have Hawaii included in the national highways program and for her inability to bring more work to Pearl Harbor's blue-collar workers.

Jack Burns appeared to be running against two candidates in 1956: Elizabeth Farrington and the territory's Republican governor, Samuel Wilder King. Burns told a Kakaako audience that the voters had given the Democrats a mandate in 1954 for a "New Deal" in Hawaii:

> The only reason you didn't get that New Deal is because in Iolani Palace there is a King who is appointed—not elected, not responsible to anybody. If I had been elected delegate two years ago, I tell you right now he [Governor King] would be under a Senate investigation. Nowhere else has a man so disregarded the people—so disregarded their mandate. . . . [Elizabeth Farrington] should have either asked Congress to impeach Sam King or disavow his vetoes of bills passed by the Democratic legislature.

Burns had Mrs. Farrington on the defensive from the beginning of the campaign. And while she had found it comfortable to ride the sympathy votes of 1954 into office, Elizabeth Farrington found out in 1956 that she was not cut out for the role of a toe-to-toe political campaigner. Looking back in 1976, Mrs. Farrington commented, somewhat wistfully,

> I wasn't in there to do a lot of politicking. I didn't want to be a politician. I'd do the job, and I wanted to be reelected, but as far as going

out and organizing like politicians do, I wouldn't have done that. I didn't want to do it that way, that badly. I wasn't there [in Washington, D.C.] to stay or anything like that. I felt that I was there only long enough till we found somebody that was willing to do it. . . . I wanted Hebden Porteus to do it.

Herein lay one of the critical differences between Hawaii's Republicans and Democrats. The Republicans had, for years, depended upon the blessings and support of the economic oligarchy—Merchant Street, as it was frequently referred to—obviating the necessity of a disciplined Party structure. Merchant Street king makers would also pick up the tab. The Republicans had the financial clout to manage their politics on a wholesale basis; the Democrats had to run theirs on a retail basis—a vote at a time. The success of the Burns wing of the Democratic Party hinged upon its ability to tap into two highly disciplined organizations: the ILWU and the 442nd Veterans Club. Their discipline allowed the Burns wing to dominate the Democratic Party and, ultimately, Hawaii's politics.

The unrelenting attacks of Jack Burns caused Elizabeth Farrington to become testy. Increasingly, she took Burns' substantive criticisms personally. Gardiner B. Jones, a political writer for the *Honolulu Advertiser*, attended a joint appearance of the two candidates one week before the general election:

> They were polite and cordial enough, but there was something brittle about it. After all, it was just the other night that Mrs. Farrington put on the spiked shoes and stomped all over Mr. Burns in a rally speech. Yesterday, while Mr. Burns was talking, Mrs. Farrington just sat there, staring at him, her mouth in a straight line. If her gaze had been focused through a magnifying glass, Mr. Burns would have turned into a cinder in a jiffy.

Efforts were made to add a human face to the dour image of Jack Burns during the 1956 campaign. One piece of campaign literature was entitled, "The Woman Behind the Man: The Story of Beatrice Burns." Its cover showed Bea Burns in her wheelchair. Standing behind her, a cigarette in one hand, the other on her shoulder, was a smiling Jack Burns. Their younger son, James Seishiro Burns, stood beside his parents. The brochure told of the manner in which Bea Burns had been struck down by polio as a young mother, of Professor Seishiro Okazaki's role in the difficult pregnancy and birth of his namesake, James Seishiro Burns, and the difficulties her husband had faced raising a family while his wife was confined to a wheelchair. "It was pretty rough," Bea is quoted as saying. "He's been accused of being too grim, but most people don't know how heavy a load he's carried at home all these years."

Another brochure carried the title, "The People Behind Burns," and presented supporters who represented an ethnic cross-section of Hawaii's population: a Portuguese electrician; a Hawaiian small business owner; a Chinese student; a haole housewife; and a Japanese secretary. The brochure also featured Gregg M. Sinclair, president emeritus of the University of Hawaii. Sinclair's statement was given particular prominence:

> I support Jack Burns for Delegate to Congress and I ask my friends to vote for him on November 6, 1956 for the basic reason that he is a Democrat, and the Democrats will control the [U.S.] House of Representatives and the [U.S.] Senate in the next biennium. Jack knows the leaders in the House and Senate and can work with them. . . .
>
> Any citizen who has talked to Jack or heard him speak knows that he is a profound student of government, that he is sincere, able and forceful; and that he will work effectively for the welfare of the people of the Territory.

The intent of this brochure was to show Burns as a man for all of Hawaii's people, to defuse Elizabeth Farrington's assertion that her experience in Washington, D.C., was critical to Hawaii's receiving a fair hearing in the nation's capital, and to reach out to the academic community.

The 1956 campaign was the first time Jack Burns used what turned out to be his most successful campaign tool—the coffee hour. Sitting in small groups with a cup of coffee in his hand, Burns was at his best. This was how he built his cadre of loyal supporters within the Party; why not extend that technique to the voters? In a campaign supporter's living room or over a kitchen table, Burns' rhetoric was stripped of its stridency. What came through, instead, was sincerity, an almost total lack of pretentiousness and genuine personal humility. As Mike Tokunaga put it, "Coffee hours made believers out of people."

Jack Burns' patience with—and praise of—the ILWU finally paid dividends in the 1956 campaign. Perhaps feeling that his lukewarm support of Burns in 1954 had caused his defeat, Jack Hall engineered a formal ILWU endorsement of Burns in 1956. Money followed the endorsement. Mrs. Farrington saw the endorsement as an opportunity. In a joint speaking engagement before the student body of the Punahou School, Burns had told the young audience that he had accepted the ILWU endorsement with pride. Mrs. Farrington, who followed Burns, took him to task, saying, "If I had said today what my opponent said [about the ILWU endorsement], I would not get a single bill through Congress." In a letter to the *Star-Bulletin*, Ernest Murai noted: "The late Delegate Joseph R. Farrington received ILWU support in 1948 elections. (It was in fact the 1946 election.) I don't think it caused him any difficulty as a Delegate." This left Mrs. Farrington with the alternative of silence or an explanation of why her husband had not repudiated his ILWU endorsement.

With ILWU support, and with a virtual lock on the Japanese-American vote—largely because of the aggressive work at the grassroots level by many members of the 442nd Veterans Club—Burns predicted to friends in mid-October that he would defeat his opponent by 10,000 votes in the 6 November election. In a desperate move to overcome what appeared to be a landslide defeat, Elizabeth Farrington grew reckless. At a Maui rally in late October, Mrs. Farrington attempted to poke holes in Burns' well-known record of support for the Japanese community in Hawaii during World War II. Commenting upon Burns' efforts to avoid a large-scale internment of the Japanese during the war, Mrs. Farrington observed, "If he had the power to keep them out, he also had the power to put them in. Let's not forget that." Then she assailed her opponent's patriotism, saying, "Where was Mr. Burns when the blackouts came? He thought it was more important to be here with the police intelligence than out there fighting and dying with these boys. It's a pretty rugged statement, but it is true." It was a strange statement for the wife of a man who had become delegate to Congress in 1942 while the incumbent, Samuel Wilder King, entered the U.S. Navy. It also betrayed a profound lack of understanding of the relationship between Hawaii's Japanese community and her opponent.

Jack Burns could not resist the opportunity to respond to Mrs. Farrington's latest attack, calling it "mud-slinging and name calling." He explained that because he had been 33 years old, with a paralyzed wife and three children to look after, and because his work in internal security with the Honolulu Police Department had been considered essential, he had remained a civilian. Burns added, "I was offered a commission in naval intelligence and turned it down because of my family."

Realizing her blunder, Mrs. Farrington sought to apply damage control by acknowledging Burns' wartime responsibilities. Then she proceeded to put her foot back into her mouth by saying, "But I wonder why Burns should be a hero to young men like Dan Inouye? I think it should be the other way around. It seems to me that Inouye and the boys like him who were out there fighting should be heroes to Burns." What Mrs. Farrington failed to see was that these young AJA veterans were, indeed, heroes in the eyes of Jack Burns. Burns, above all others, had treated them with the dignity and respect they deserved. Mrs. Farrington's attack against the bond between Burns and his AJA supporters turned out to be an inadvertent attack upon the intelligence of one-third of Hawaii's voters.

Statehood, of course, was the ultimate issue in the delegate's race. Burns gave credit to Elizabeth Farrington's deceased husband for his efforts to achieve statehood. Burns asserted that at the time of Joe Farrington's death, "Hawaii was as close to the realization of its fondest hopes as it is possible to be." During Elizabeth Farrington's two years in Congress, Burns continued, Hawaii had moved "further away from statehood than we have been at any time since 1947." The reason, Burns asserted, was Mrs. Farrington's unrelenting and ill-advised attack upon southern members of Congress.

In an effort to emphasize this point, Burns trotted out a 25 June 1956 column by nationally syndicated columnist Drew Pearson. Pearson had quoted Mrs. Farrington as being "jubilant" because a Democratic majority in the House Interior Committee had blocked a Republican attempt to revive the Hawaii statehood bill. Pearson quoted Mrs. Farrington as saying that the Democratic vote against Hawaii would give her an excellent campaign issue. "Was that item published in the *Star-Bulletin*," Burns asked? Normally it would have been, but it was not picked up on that occasion. "Did they ask Drew Pearson to publish a retraction? No. They did not because they could not," Burns asserted. "We have other witnesses who were there and who heard her statement."

When Burns continued to criticize Mrs. Farrington for singling out southern obstructionists as the reason for the failure of statehood to materialize, she fired back: "If my opponent is the great messiah who is going to lead us to the promised land, who is going to lead the Dixiecrats? Neither Roosevelt nor Truman could lead them. President Eisenhower cannot lead them." Burns' response to Mrs. Farrington's comment revealed one of the central features of what would become his "Southern

Strategy" for gaining statehood for Hawaii. "How," Burns asked, "is a person who calls Democrats 'Dixiecrats' going to be able to get anything from a Congress in Washington, which is obviously going to be Democratic?"

On the eve of the 1956 election, Burns appeared on Millard Purdy's television program, "Facts and Focus," once again challenging Mrs. Farrington's assertion that the only thing standing between Hawaii and statehood was southern racism. "Statehood is opposed by many people right here in the Territory," Burns charged, "and it is these people, with contacts in Washington, who have blocked statehood." In fact, both Mrs. Farrington and Jack Burns had a point, but it was disingenuous for either of them to deny that significant opposition to statehood came from both southern Democratic recalcitrance and local Republican opposition.

On Tuesday, 6 November 1956, John A. Burns finally won his first election to public office. His margin proved to be 50 percent greater than the 10,000-vote victory he had predicted. The final count in the Delegate's race was 82,166 for Burns to 66,732 for Farrington. Burns carried every district in the Territory except the predominantly haole Fourth District. Even there, Burns did better than he had in 1954, narrowing Farrington's margin of victory from 6,000 votes to less than 2,000. Burns was not alone in his triumph. The Democrats maintained their two-thirds majority in the territorial house of representatives and extended their 9 to 6 majority in the senate to a whopping 12 to 3 margin. Hawaii's Democrats had consolidated and extended the "Revolution of 1954." As Lawrence Fuchs put it, "For Hawaii, 1956 was what 1936 had been [on the mainland]—endorsement of the New Deal and repudiation of Old Guard policies." The time for Jack Burns to prove himself as a representative of the people of Hawaii had arrived. His political future now depended upon his ability to deliver statehood for the Territory of Hawaii.

N·I·N·E

Statehood

STATEHOOD WAS HARDLY a new issue in Hawaii. In the abortive Treaty of Annexation of 1854, there was a clause expressing the intentions of its nineteenth-century drafters to seek statehood at the earliest possible time. Opposition to statehood also had a long history. Indeed, one of the reasons for the failure of the 1854 treaty was the statehood clause. And although some of the leaders of the overthrow of the Hawaiian monarchy in 1893 may have dreamed of statehood, "they handed over the Islands on the express understanding that statehood was not being contemplated," knowing that a demand for statehood might kill annexation in 1898.

Interest in statehood grew during the period between annexation and the beginning of World War II. In 1940, a plebiscite showed that Hawaii's voters favored statehood by a 2 to 1 margin. Still, the powers in Washington, D.C., and in the Territory of Hawaii showed little inclination to satisfy the voters' wishes. An *Esquire* magazine poll in 1940 showed that only 54 percent of mainland America favored defending Hawaii in the event of an attack. The same poll showed that 73 percent of the American public favored defending Canada in the event of an attack. Clearly, statehood had a long way to go.

World War II ended any legitimate impediment to Hawaiian statehood. The attack on Pearl Harbor and the performance of the 100th Battalion and the 442nd Regimental Combat Team saw to that. By 1946, mainland polls showed that 60 percent of the American public favored statehood for Hawaii. As J. Garner Anthony, the Territory of Hawaii's attorney general during World War II, told a congressional panel in 1950, "Any argument against statehood must be bottomed either upon

disbelief in democracy, self-interest, or ignorance of American history."
Hawaii's voters agreed as they convened a Constitutional Convention in
1950 which produced a framework for state government. It was approved by Hawaii's voters by better than a 3 to 1 margin. By 1954, mainland polls indicated that 78 percent of the American public now favored
statehood for Hawaii.

During the postwar years, those who opposed statehood for Hawaii
had often used the issue of communism as a mask for the real reason for
their opposition. Those fears included racial prejudice, opposition to organized labor, and the fear of an elite that they were losing what John
A. Burns called their "hegemony" over the Hawaiian Islands. By 1956,
the issue of communism was all but dead with regard to Hawaiian statehood, bringing all other issues into clearer focus.

Proof of the passing of the issue of communism came in Hawaii
shortly after the 1956 election, as eight hundred members and guests of
the ILWU met at a dinner honoring Jack Hall. Among the guests was
the Republican Territorial Attorney General Edward N. Sylva, who had
chaired the territorial Department of Public Instruction panel that had
dismissed John and Aiko Reinecke in 1948. He had also served as chairman of the territorial Commission on Subversive Activities. Now, at an
ILWU celebration he said, "There has been too much wall-building between ourselves and the ILWU—and communism." Sylva said that he
was sure that there were many "ex-communists" in the ILWU, "but no
real live communists." For his efforts at conciliation, Sylva was fired by
Governor Samuel Wilder King. But King's days were numbered. Eisenhower soon replaced him with young, moderate Republican attorney,
William F. Quinn. And when Senator James O. Eastland arrived in
Hawaii with a panel from the Senate Internal Security in December
1956, the event was greeted with a collective yawn.

Burns arrived in Washington, D.C., as Hawaii's new delegate to
Congress with a single mission—statehood. He enjoyed a familiarity
with the nation's capital that was unusual for a freshman member of
Congress. As territorial Democratic chairman, Burns had made frequent
trips to Washington, D.C., in the late 1940s and early 1950s. He had
lobbied the Truman administration to replace Governor Ingram Stainback with someone more sympathetic to the Hawaii Democratic Party's
patronage needs. He had spent weeks in the nation's capital in 1949, at
the behest of the ILWU, successfully lobbying against federal interven-

tion in the dock strike. Burns had met many Democratic Party leaders at Truman's 1948 inaugural and as a delegate to the 1952 Democratic National Convention. He had also been a member of a 1954 Democratic Party delegation which went to the nation's capital in support of statehood. In short, Burns knew the players in Washington's Democratic Party establishment.

Jack Burns' sister, Margaret Mary Curtis, described the driving force behind her brother in these terms: "Jack thought he could do anything. He had extreme self-confidence." This self-confidence was perceived by different people in different ways. Those who came to know him well were deeply impressed with his sincerity of purpose and his indefatigable will to succeed. To them he always sought to create a level playing field. To his enemies, Burns was often seen as arrogant and aloof. Some came to see him as a dangerous radical. In Washington, D.C., Delegate Burns earned a reputation as a knowledgeable and determined pragmatist.

Burns had arrived in Washington at a good time for a Democrat. In spite of Eisenhower's landslide victory over Adlai Stevenson in the 1956 presidential election, the Republicans had been unable to recapture control of Congress. As Gregg Sinclair had accurately predicted, Hawaii's delegate to Congress would be working with Democratic majorities in both the House and the Senate. Eager to get started, Burns arrived in the nation's capital in late November 1956. Elizabeth Farrington offered him neither office space nor the files of ongoing delegate business.

Throughout the month of December, while Jack Burns searched for a home for his family, he typed his own letters and watched his correspondence pile up awaiting the assembly of his new staff. While Burns generally believed that his staff should be a reflection of Hawaii's ethnic diversity, his congressional office had a distinctive Japanese-American flavor. The first person he selected was Mary Isa, who had served him so well as his secretary when he was Honolulu's civil defense administrator. As administrative assistant he selected 442nd loyalist Dan Aoki. Seichi "Shadow" Hirai, a law student at George Washington University—Dan Inouye's law school—became a part-time staff member. Jean Sakata, whose husband was a graduate student in Washington, D.C., was another member of the original team. To round out his staff, Burns selected a part-Hawaiian member of a prominent Democratic family, Nobleen Kauhane.

Looking back in 1978, Shadow Hirai remembered that he did "a lot

of research" and "a hell of a lot" of public relations. One of his jobs was
to take visitors around the nation's capital. He also delivered Hawaiian
products—flowers, sugar, and pineapple—to strategic congressional offices. Burns would instruct Hirai, "Don't forget to take some to the old
man's office," referring to House Speaker Sam Rayburn.

The staff had no doubt about its mission. As Dan Aoki recalled,
"Everything Mr. Burns did in Washington . . . was geared toward statehood." Aoki also recalled that Burns heeded Speaker Rayburn's admonition "to be on the floor all the time." Burns made a special point of getting to know the chairman of the House Interior Committee, Clair
Engle of California, and his replacement, Wayne Aspinall of Colorado,
when Engle moved on to the U.S. Senate. Aoki also recalled that Burns
made a special effort "to get to understand the assistants of every congressman and the committee counsel members. . . . These were the people that really counted."

Although the Democrats had a majority in Congress, that was no
guarantee that they would remain united on a vote that involved liberal
issues, including Hawaiian statehood. Neither did the endorsement of
Hawaiian statehood in the Democrats' national Party Platform since
1948 and the Republicans since 1952. A conservative coalition of right-
wing Republicans and southern Democrats was very much alive in the
Eighty-fifth and Eighty-sixth Congresses in which Burns served, and
the conservatives did not favor Hawaiian statehood.

To make things more difficult, the congressional committee system,
which was based upon seniority, gave southern Democrats power far out
of proportion to their numbers. As Representative Dante Fascell of
Florida pointed out, "The chairman ran his committee and no one
looked over his shoulder." Hawaii's ethnic diversity represented an unknown quantity to most southern Democrats. While their own obses-
sive fears centered upon a significant black minority, Hawaii presented
an even more threatening prospect—a society in which the white population was, itself, a minority. Although most southern congressmen had
never experienced any extensive contact with Chinese, Japanese, Filipino, or Polynesian people, they viewed them with suspicion.

Senator J. Strom Thurmond of South Carolina, still a Democrat in
those days, provided what was, perhaps, the most unvarnished expression of southern antistatehood feeling when he declared in a 1959
speech from the floor of the U.S. Senate:

There are many shades and mixtures of heritages in the world, but there are only two extremes. Our society may well be said to be, for the present at least, the exemplification of the maximum development of Western civilization, culture and heritage. At the opposite extreme exists the Eastern heritage, different in every essential—not necessarily inferior, but different as regards the very thought processes within the individuals who comprise the resultant society. As one of the most competent, and certainly the most eloquent, interpreters of the East to the West, Rudyard Kipling felt the bond of love of one for the other; but at the same time, he had the insight to express the impassable difference with the immortal words, "East is East, and West is West, and never the twain shall meet."

True to his campaign statements, Burns refused to categorize southern members of Congress and write them off as certain votes against statehood. As delegate to Congress, Burns sought to build an inclusive view of the South. In a letter to Gregg Sinclair in January 1957, Burns wrote, "I am sure that no section of the country has done as much for Hawaii, her people, and for Statehood for Hawaii as have the people of the South." He cited a number of examples to support this assertion, beginning with the report of Georgian James H. Blount to President Grover Cleveland, in which the 1893 overthrow of the Hawaiian monarchy was denounced as a usurpation of power in which the American forces had acted deplorably. He noted that Alabama Senator J. T. Morgan had proposed—in 1898 during the annexation debate and in 1900 when the Organic Act was being considered—the admission of Hawaii as a state. He pointed to the floor fight waged by "Pitchfork" Ben Tillman of South Carolina to ensure that the new Territory's franchise would be based upon citizenship and education, rather than property.

Moving into more recent times, Burns reminded Sinclair that in 1947 Louisiana Representative Henry Larcade had been the first congressional committee chairman to report out a bill granting statehood to Hawaii. Finally, Burns pointed to Louisiana Senator Russell Long and Florida Senator Spessard Holland for their refusal, in 1954, to append Alaska to the Hawaii statehood bill of that year. Burns was convinced that linking the two would have spelled doom for both.

As selective and contrived as such a recitation may sound, it was central to Burns' so-called Southern Strategy for statehood. He would not alienate the South by calling its elected representatives names. His goal was not to get more votes for statehood—the votes were already there—but to eliminate the procedural delays that angry southern members of Congress could easily create. As Burns closed his letter to Gregg Sinclair, "I am going to see if I cannot work on our 'Southern Brethren.'"

Burns remained convinced that the suspicions of the southern Democrats were fueled by Caucasian residents of Hawaii. Seven months later, in an August 1957 letter to Nelson Doi, Burns lamented:

> I found in the course of getting acquainted that a deliberate attempt had been made to alienate Southern votes. Analyzing this most carefully, I am of the conclusion that one purpose in back of this effort was to build Republican strength in the Islands by equating the so-called minority problem of the South with the minority problem of Hawaii. . . . Several instances of a similar character rather enforce the conclusion that the issue was to be preferred to a [statehood] bill.

And get acquainted he did. Texas Democrat Jim Wright would later recall, "Burns made friends with as many congressmen who had voted against the previous statehood bill as he could." Former Senator and Democratic presidential candidate Eugene McCarthy of Minnesota remembered Burns this way: "Jack knew everybody. He was a very open person. He acted more like a member of Congress than Joe Farrington. Joe was more like an ambassador to Congress from Hawaii. Jack was more aggressive about pushing statehood." Representative Dante Fascell agreed, saying that Burns "was constantly talking to people. I remember him 'walking the floor' of the House all the time." Fascell's colleague, Representative Paul Rogers, also remembered Burns' tenacity, but with an eye to the delegate's low-key style. "Everyone knew Jack was working for statehood," Rogers said, "but he didn't try to assert heavy pressure on you. He just let you know how he felt."

Burns and his staff were crammed into two rooms in the Old House Office Building, but the delegate spent little time there. Burns' constant pursuit of new friends for Hawaii kept him away from the office most days, even when the House of Representatives was not in session. Mary Isa soon learned that it did no good to ask where her boss was going or where he had been. "He spent much of his time waiting to see people," Isa recalled. "He was very patient in that regard." With Burns out, most of the routine work of his office devolved upon Isa and Dan Aoki. Their days were long, often running from 9:00 A.M. until 10:00 P.M. Isa answered much of the mail herself, knowing what her boss would say on various subjects. When they did need to catch the boss, he was hard to track down. "My whole life was spent chasing after him to get him to approve something. It wore me out just trying to keep track of things on his desk."

The Burns staff members were not alone in being left to fend for themselves. Beatrice Burns saw precious little of her husband, except on the run:

> He'd come home at eleven o'clock at night and wouldn't have had din-
> ner. I'd have it ready for him. He'd sit there in his relaxer and eat and
> drink his coffee and watch a live sports show on TV. I'd go to bed. And
> in the morning he'd go to Mass. By then he was a daily communicant.
> He started that when he went to Washington. Saint Thomas Apostle
> was just a block away, so he'd go there before he shaved or anything.
> And while he was there I'd get his breakfast and then he'd come home
> and read the paper while he was eating. [Then he] would shave and
> put on his white shirt. And I'd have everything he needed right on a
> chair by the door and he'd zip out the door.

Bea did see her husband on weekends, and Jack made it a point to take her on a Sunday afternoon drive. Nobleen Kauhane, Mary Isa, and whatever Burns child was in town would often accompany them. "It was nice of him to take me to places I'd never been," Bea remembered. "Besides, Jack seemed to enjoy driving. It relaxed him."

The Sunday afternoon drives offered Bea a respite from the Burns apartment. She was reluctant to prevail on her busy husband and his staff to take her out during the week. "I didn't get out much," she admitted "although I tried to make the Democratic women's meetings. So I brought people to me. We entertained small groups at home."

In spite of what must have been a lonely existence, Bea Burns would look back with pride at her husband's accomplishments in Washington, D.C. "He was held in great, great respect," she recalled, "at a time when he wasn't here [in Hawaii] by everyone. He sat at the Texas table in the House dining room. The Texans liked Jack. Many members would have liked to sit at that Texas table, but few were chosen. Whenever Sam Rayburn saw me, he would stop, shake my hand, and say 'God bless you.' The Texans were courtly. They understood procedures. So did Jack."

Burns did not pursue his Southern Strategy in a vacuum. There were other matters of far greater importance to southern members of Congress. As Bobby Baker, right-hand man to Senate Majority Leader Lyndon

Johnson, recalled, "Since the 1954 Supreme Court decision in *Brown v. Board of Education of Topeka, Kansas,* the South had been in disarray." But Baker agreed with Burns' analysis that the South should not be looked at as a monolith: "Russell Long, Spessard Holland, and George Smathers were neither raving segregationists nor greatly opposed to statehood for Hawaii and Alaska."

The real key to Burns' Southern Strategy was found in Baker's State of Texas. While it can be argued that Texas was a southwestern rather than a southern state, when it came to race, Texas had voted with the "Deep South" for over one hundred years. The congressional delegation from Texas was large, overwhelmingly Democratic, and contained the two most powerful men in Congress: Speaker of the House Sam Rayburn and Senate Majority Leader Lyndon Johnson. Rayburn and Johnson were Texans, but as a result of the power they wielded they had become Texans with a national outlook.

Burns enjoyed particular leverage with the Texans. During the fall of 1944, a battalion of the 141st Infantry Regiment of the 36th "Texas" Division was surrounded by German troops near the small town of Biffontaine, in southern France. Their position appeared to be hopeless. Allied commanders decided to attempt a rescue of the "Lost Battalion," selecting for the task the 442nd Regimental Combat Team. The 442nd took eight hundred casualties in the process of saving three hundred Texans. After the war, the survivors of the "Lost Battalion" thanked the surviving members of the 442nd by making them "honorary citizens of the State of Texas."

Burns made sure that no member of the Texas congressional delegation remained ignorant of this heroic exploit. During his first month in office, Burns wrote to Stanley Watanabe, president of the 442nd Club in Honolulu, asking him for photocopies of the proclamation declaring Hawaii's Japanese-American veterans to be honorary citizens of Texas. He used the material in remarks before the House of Representatives on the occasion of Sam Rayburn's fortieth anniversary in Congress. He used it in letters congratulating newly elected members of Congress from Texas. He persuaded Jim Wright of Texas to use it to answer critics of his pro-statehood position.

In his pursuit of the kingpins of the Texas congressional delegation, Burns first turned his attention to Speaker Rayburn, "Mr. Sam," as he was widely known. Although they looked nothing alike, there was something about Rayburn and Burns that made them kindred spirits. Both used words sparingly. Both had great respect for parliamentary procedure and its dictates. Jim Wright, a future Speaker of the House, noted other similarities between the Speaker and the new delegate from Hawaii: "Both Burns and Rayburn were externally irascible, crotchety old curmudgeons. But in fact, they were both warm and straightforward human beings. Both liked to work with people they could trust. Rayburn was a good judge of others, and he judged Burns a man he could trust."

Rayburn manifested his friendship with Burns in many ways. Burns was frequently included in Rayburn's famous meetings of the "board of education," invitation-only gatherings where Rayburn and his guests would discuss the day's activities in the House of Representatives over generous rations of "bourbon and branch water." Bobby Baker indicated it was at one of these meetings that Burns met Lyndon Johnson, a regular at his mentor's gatherings. "Burns was a teetotaler," Baker remembered, "but he served as a water boy while people sat around and got drunk. He was so kind that when it came time for him to cash a check [i.e., ask for a favor], you couldn't say no."

Any friend of Sam Rayburn's was a friend of Lyndon Johnson. Juanita Roberts, Johnson's personal secretary, explained the relationship between Rayburn and Johnson very succinctly: "Sam Rayburn learned his politics from Sam Johnson [LBJ's father], and he simply reciprocated by helping Sam Johnson's boy." Jack Burns had spent most of the past decade as a mentor to others, and he understood and valued the process. It was now his time to be the student and he chose his mentors wisely. Juanita Roberts recalled the warm friendship that developed between Burns and Johnson. "John Burns was in our office frequently. They laughed together a lot. It was a nice, easy, comfortable relationship. As I recall, Senator Johnson called him 'Johnny.'"

Before the war in Vietnam destroyed his presidency, Lyndon Johnson put together a legislative record unmatched since the early days of the New Deal. LBJ's favorite saying came from the Book of Isaiah: "Come, let us reason together." His art was that of bringing the most disparate interests together and working out legislation they could all agree upon.

A believer in the old saying, "politics is the art of the possible," Johnson had a pragmatic bent that struck a responsive chord in Jack Burns. As Juanita Roberts put it, "Johnson used to say that it was better to have a sandwich than nothing. He argued that it was silly to starve while going after the whole loaf or nothing. The sandwich will give you strength to strive for more."

The lessons Burns learned from Rayburn and Johnson left an indelible impression. He applied them early in the session by adopting a strategy for Hawaiian statehood that was fraught with political danger for himself, but offered what he thought was the best prospect for success. The question was whether Alaska or Hawaii should get the first crack at statehood. Since the strategy of joining Alaskan and Hawaiian statehood had, in the past, simply combined the negatives against both, that strategy was being dropped. The constituency Burns represented felt that the greater population and larger economy of Hawaii should dictate a Hawaii-first policy. In a January 1957 letter to Oren Long, Burns expressed some uneasiness over the question of who should go first. "Some effort seems to be afoot to get the two territories into an argument as to who shall be first," Burns told the former governor. "My approach to this is that we are not concerned with who gets [it] first so long as statehood is given."

In fact, because of the largely unspoken racial resistance to Hawaiian statehood, Alaskan statehood was the easier of the two to achieve. The only real issue Alaska had to overcome was one shared with Hawaii: both territories were noncontiguous with what Alaska called the "lower forty-eight" and Hawaii called "the mainland." Eight months into his first term, Burns wrote to Long, "If nothing more is secured in this Eighty-fifth Congress than the admission of Alaska, I shall feel that my term is an outstanding success, for I am convinced that one will follow the other." This assertion would be put to a test in the second session of the Eighty-fifth Congress in 1958, an election year for Delegate John A. Burns.

During that session, Burns agreed to a strategy to keep the Hawaiian statehood bill bottled up in committee until the Alaska bill had been reported out of committee and passed by the whole House of Representatives. At the urging of the Eisenhower administration, however, the House Subcommittee on Territorial Affairs sent an approved Hawaiian statehood bill to the full committee without Burns' prior knowledge. At this point, the only way Burns could assure that the Hawaiian statehood bill would not reach the floor of the House and be joined to the Alaska statehood bill would be to offer a motion to recommit his own statehood bill. It might be possible for congressional strategists to understand such a move, but it was questionable whether the voters of Hawaii would.

In an act of political courage that Lyndon Johnson hyperbolically compared to Abraham Lincoln's, Burns had the Hawaii statehood bill recommitted. Johnson was not alone in his admiration. Susan Bartlett, wife of Alaska's last delegate to Congress, Bob Bartlett, recalled the situation:

> By 1958 we had the votes for Alaska statehood and the opposing faction decided to do the thing again that had been successful before: tack the Hawaii statehood bill onto the Alaska statehood bill. This, then, would defeat it because the South was against it. But the delegate from Hawaii, Mr. John Burns, refused to allow Hawaii statehood to be tacked to Alaska statehood because he knew that this would defeat the bill. He took this chance of ruining his political career—a great act of bravery.

Burns had to fight off yet another effort to link Hawaiian and Alaskan statehood in 1958. Thinking he was doing a favor for Hawaii, Senate Minority Leader William F. Knowland of California insisted that Hawaii be considered immediately for statehood as a precondition for his support for Alaskan statehood. Knowland did not realize the damage he was doing to Hawaii's chances. Rather than confronting Knowland directly, Burns wrote to Matson Navigation officials in California, urging them to intercede with Senator Knowland. Burns never learned exactly what Matson executives said to him, but Knowland did back off and Alaska became the forty-ninth state.

Immediately after the passage of the Alaska statehood bill, and without any consultation with Burns, Republican Governor William Quinn led a delegation to Washington, D.C., to demand statehood for Hawaii in the waning days of the Eighty-fifth Congress. Delegate Burns was appalled by this ill-timed effort. In a letter to Shigeo Soga on 14 July 1958, Burns described the situation that greeted the Quinn delegation:

> When the delegation arrived in Washington, [Interior] Secretary Fred Seaton was fishing in Canada, President Eisenhower went to Canada for a different reason, Speaker Sam Rayburn was in Texas, [House] Minority Leader Joe Martin was not in Washington. No more than six weeks remained in the session, primaries were going on all the time, campaigns for re-election were taking time and attention. Major legislation remained to be decided before adjournment. No great enthusiasm exhibited itself among the Senators and Representatives. Partisan activity with an eye to the election was increasing and viewed from every possible objective view, the propitious moment did not appear at hand.

Those who feared that Burns' Alaska-first strategy might jeopardize the delegate's chances for reelection failed to take into account the disarray in which the Republican Party found itself in 1958. Old-line Hawaii Republicans were still angry that President Eisenhower had appointed the moderate Bill Quinn as territorial governor. Party leaders seemed perfectly willing to concede the political center to the Democrats. Lawrence S. Gota, the Republican treasurer of the City and County of Honolulu, switched to the Democratic Party in 1958 as did Adrian DeMello, a lifelong Republican, who was seeking reelection to the Honolulu board of supervisors. The Republicans had a very difficult time finding anyone to run against Burns for delegate to Congress. Hebden Porteus, James Kealoha, J. Ballard Atherton, and Wilfred Tsukiyama were all reported as having declined the honor.

The Republicans finally turned to a political novice, Farrant L. Turner, as their standard-bearer. As the former commanding officer of the 100th Battalion, Turner had enjoyed a great deal of popularity among members of the Japanese-American community. The Republicans decided that this was the time to capitalize on that. But as Lawrence Fuchs pointed out in *Hawaii Pono:* "If there was one haole in the Islands more popular among the Japanese than Farrant Turner, it was Jack Burns. Turner was a symbol of the benevolent and open-minded friendship occasionally found in haoles of a bygone era. Burns symbolized the militant repudiation of everything that era stood for." The Japanese-American community may have had great respect for Turner, but they no longer accepted his conservative and paternalistic political views.

The politically inexperienced Turner attacked Burns for his Alaska-first strategy with regard to statehood and dragged out all of the old red-baiting gambits that had been the staple of Republican politicians throughout most of the 1950s. With regard to the first issue, Burns said to the Hawaiian voters, in essence, "Trust me, I know what I am doing. Statehood is on the way." He deplored the irresponsible manner in which the Republicans had sought to interfere with the process in the waning days of the Eighty-fifth Congress—without even consulting Hawaii's delegate to Congress. Fuchs summarized the way in which Burns dealt with the communist issue: "The success of the Democratic Party, he claimed, had killed the communist menace in Hawaii. He pointed to FBI studies showing that although there were 160 Communists the Islands in 1946, there were only thirty-six in 1952, and he maintained that now, in 1958, communism in Hawaii was dead."

On election day, 4 November, Burns was returned to Congress by the voters of Hawaii by the comfortable margin of 81,832 to 67,704—

almost an exact duplicate of his victory in 1956. Clearly, the effort to discredit Burns for his alleged betrayal of statehood for Hawaii had not worked. Democratic majorities were returned to the newly expanded and reapportioned territorial legislature: 16 to 11 in the senate; 33 to 18 in the house of representatives. Momentum had remained with the Democrats even though polls showed that 45 percent to 50 percent of Hawaii's voters thought of themselves as independent. Evidence of voter independence was proven when Republican Mayor Neal Blaisdell was swept back into office, with polls showing that he was just as popular with Democrats as he was with Republicans. Republican Bill Quinn, who had failed in his bid for a territorial senate seat in 1956, was enjoying a 71 percent approval rating for his job as Hawaii's appointed governor, with only 5 percent expressing their disapproval. The Democrats could not afford to be smug, a lesson that would be brought home to Delegate John A. Burns in 1959.

After the election, Burns left nothing to chance with regard to statehood in the next session of Congress. He knew he had Lyndon Johnson's assurances that the Hawaii Statehood Bill would receive early consideration in the Senate. Burns may have had to promise more. Bobby Baker, LBJ's flamboyant right-hand man, asserted in a 12 January 1979 interview with Dan Boylan that it had been through a "deal" he put together that Burns had been able to overcome southern opposition to Hawaiian statehood. As the story goes, after his return to Washington, D.C., in January 1959, Burns went to see Baker to get his advice on strategy for statehood in the Senate. Baker said that he told Burns, "Let me lead you and I'll get it through." Baker then added a warning to Burns that "your people won't like it." Baker asserted that he then told Burns to go see Senator Russell of Georgia and "tell him you've talked to Bobby. Tell him that if he'll get statehood through [and] you are elected to the Senate from Hawaii, you will vote against Rule 22 [the rule closing off debate] in the Senate." Baker continued, saying that Burns had "made the deal with Russell." Baker concluded with the assertion that the real reason Jack Burns did not run for the U.S. Senate in 1959, an office all who knew Burns realized he preferred over the governorship, was because he did not want to carry his commitment to Richard Russell into that high office. Since this story was told four years after Burns had died, there has been no way to check its authenticity. It does possess the attribute of plausibility, however.

To assure consideration by the House of Representatives, Burns had invited Representative Leo W. O'Brien, a New York Democrat and chairman of a special subcommittee of the House Committee on Interior and Insular Affairs, to visit the Islands in late November. O'Brien and two other committee members who favored statehood for Hawaii made "an extensive inquiry" on the subject. Their report, which was submitted in January 1959, was a systematic rebuttal of the arguments of the statehood bill's two "principal antagonists," Senator James Eastland of Mississippi and Representative John Pillion of New York. Eastland echoed J. Strom Thurmond's view that Hawaii's Asian population could not be assimilated into the American population; Pillion charged that the Territory was totally controlled by the ILWU and would, in the event of statehood, be sending "four Soviet agents to take seats in our Congress."

With Lyndon Johnson and Leo O'Brien running interference for him and with Alaskan statehood having removed the issue of noncontiguity, Burns returned to the nation's capital for the Eighty-sixth Congress, satisfied with the 1958 elections in Hawaii and satisfied that prospects for statehood in this session seemed all but certain. He was right. On 11 March 1959, the U.S. Senate passed the Hawaii Statehood Bill by a 76 to 15 margin; the next day it passed the House by a vote of 323 to 89. To Jack Burns and his exhausted staff in Washington, D.C., the final vote was almost anticlimactic, but in Hawaii the response was, as Gavan Daws described it, enthusiastic:

> The news reached the Islands within minutes. It was a pleasant spring morning in Honolulu, and no one felt like working. Offices and stores emptied out, the streets filled up, the bells of all the churches rang, civil defense sirens wailed (a take cover signal, oddly enough), a lot of beer was drunk, and an American flag with fifty stars flew over Hawaii for the first time.

One of Burns' first acts following the passage of the statehood bill was to send contributions to Saint Anthony's Church in Kailua and the Immaculate Conception Shrine in Washington, D.C. To the latter he wrote, "Enclosed herewith is a contribution in expression of heartfelt appreciation to Almighty God for many favors—particularly Hawaii statehood. The contribution is made in the name of Mrs. Anne Florida Burns, deceased August 18, 1958, whose intercession I sought."

T·E·N

False Start

FOR FIVE MONTHS in 1959—from the final congressional passage of the Hawaii Statehood Bill on 12 March to Admission Day on 21 August—politics held center stage in Hawaii. On 27 June the voters expressed their approval of statehood by a 17 to 1 margin. Out of Hawaii's 244 electoral precincts, only one—the tiny island of Niihau, which was privately owned by the Robinson family and almost entirely populated by Hawaiians—voted against statehood. The question of who would govern the new state and who would be sent to Washington, D.C., to represent the people of Hawaii was more closely contested. The Republicans saw this moment as an opportunity to reclaim their political dominance. The Democrats expected a reaffirmation of their hard-won majority status. At this crucial moment John A. Burns hesitated, a lapse for which he and his Party would pay a significant price.

As early as Christmas 1958, John A. Burns, Jr. told his mother that he believed that his father would run for governor of the State of Hawaii, rather than run for the U.S. Senate. Bea Burns, who had by now grown comfortable in Washington, D.C., later recalled her response to her son: "'Oh, no! Why would he do that?' I was horrified. A run for the Senate would have been so easy and convenient. Our kids were all on the mainland. The people in Washington expected him to run for the Senate."

As early as two weeks after the passage of the statehood bill, it was clear that Burns was wrestling with the question of which office he should run for. In a letter to author and friend James Michener on 28 March, Burns wrote, "As you point out, it can be said that I am entitled to stand for the Senate. Considered from every personal standpoint, I should stand for election to the Senate. There is involved in this a great deal more benefit to me personally than the well informed realize." But Burns recognized the concerns that were being expressed by those who were urging him to run for governor. He put it this way in his letter to Michener:

> It is not important that I can stand for governor and be elected. It is important that the governor be one who is well acquainted with the history and traditions of Hawaii; that he be one who has an ingrained knowledge of the mores of our people; that he be deeply knowledgeable as to our form of government and possess a real awareness of its fundamentals and principles; that he be a man of character, integrity and decision; that he have an understanding of the economic and social institutions by which we live; and that he have . . . a sense as to horizons of the future and how to attain them.

In short, Burns was saying that Bill Quinn, who had come to Hawaii after World War II, should not be the State's first governor and that Burns himself might be the only Democrat capable of defeating him.

In the midst of this indecision, Jack Burns celebrated his 50th birthday with his family in the nation's capital. On 30 March, Bea Burns baked her husband a chocolate cake with chocolate icing, "because that is Jack's favorite and his mother had always made a chocolate cake for him for his birthday." Bea omitted the fifty candles, saying that so many "might be a fire hazard." Burns looked his 50 years—and more. His hairline had receded, and that hair which remained had turned snowy white. Twenty-eight months as Hawaii's delegate to Congress—and many missed lunches—had caused his face to thin. He presented a somewhat haggard appearance. Twenty years later, in an interview on what would have been her husband's 70th birthday, Bea Burns recalled, "Jack aged when he was delegate, not while he was governor."

In this surpassing moment of his political career, many Democrats awaited Burns' triumphal return to Hawaii. They waited in vain. And while Burns remained in Washington, D.C., Governor Bill Quinn presided over the celebration and prepared his campaign to become Hawaii's first elected governor. There was no doubt about his intentions. On the other hand, not even Jack Burns' political intimates were sure which way their leader would jump. Burns actually felt that he was better suited to become a member of the U.S. Senate than he was to be governor of the State of Hawaii. Others felt the same way. "I always thought

Jack Burns should have been in the U.S. Senate," *Honolulu Star-Bulletin* reporter Doug Boswell reflected. "He was gregarious. He liked to get around and talk to people. He didn't like being chained to a desk." In part, Burns' hesitation may have been the result of what so many were telling him—that any office he wanted from the voters of Hawaii was his. But this failed to take into account how important his presence in Hawaii was to the Democratic Party organization. Crucial decisions had to be made, and the Party adjudicator was not there when he was sorely needed.

If Jack Burns was unsure of which direction he should go, Jack Hall was not. The regional director of the ILWU and one of the new State's major power brokers, Hall made it absolutely clear that he wanted Jack Burns to be the next inhabitant of Washington Place, the governor's mansion. In a letter to Jeff Kibre, an ILWU representative in Washington, D.C., Hall wrote:

> We all feel very strongly here that Jack Burns should run. . . . No other Democrat can be elected and even if he could, the importance of the governorship for this first term outweighs all considerations. My God, just the opportunity to clean up the judiciary, let alone the police commission, university regents, Department of Public Instruction, etc., is sufficient reason for electing a real liberal to the top state post.

Hall undoubtedly expected to have some input into the five hundred appointees the new governor would be able to make.

From the beginning of the process, Burns seemed to be waiting for a draft. From Washington, D.C., he wrote what now appear to have been some rather disingenuous letters to friends in Hawaii. To Herbert Isonaga he wrote: "Herbert, my very real ambition is to be the last *delegate*. I have no real driving ambition beyond that. As I have been in the past, I will remain to be of service to the people where, in the judgment of those like yourself, I may be able to do the most good." And to Morris T. Takushi he wrote: "I do not know where the information came from that I am running for governor. As you know, I don't make up my mind on those things—such decisions are in the hands of people like yourself and others who have to do the work in raising the money and getting the voters out to vote."

In addition to his indecision, Burns was creating problems by trying to micro-manage certain aspects of the Democratic Party's campaign strategy from a distance of five thousand miles. One concern he had was about the ethnic makeup of the Democratic Party ticket. On 20 March he wrote to Bob Dodge, saying, "A ticket composed entirely of AJAs would find itself totally defeated." He went on to suggest a list of candidates that manifested the kind of ethnic diversity he favored: for U.S. Senator, Judge William Heen, Chinese-Hawaiian; for the other U.S. Senate seat or governor, ex-Governor Oren Long or himself, haoles; for U.S. House of Representatives, Dan Inouye, AJA; and for lieutenant governor, Mits Kido, AJA.

The names did, indeed, suggest a fair amount of ethnic balance, but they also suggested age. With the exception of Inouye, this was an older group. Heen and Long were in their 60s; Kido and Burns were in their 50s. In 1959, the pride of the Democratic Party, and most of its energy, lay with its younger members. It was questionable whether they, or their supporters, would be willing to wait while the Old Guard rewarded itself with most of the choice positions. And while Burns was attempting to construct a ticket by remote control and decide exactly which slot he wanted for himself, the Islands were rife with rumors of what he and dozens of other potential candidates might do in this most important political race in Hawaii's history.

According to Dan Aoki, the person who had the decisive influence upon Burns' entering the governor's race was not a Democrat, but a Republican; not a politician, but a businessman—the president of American Factors, Inc. (Amfac), Henry A. Walker, Jr. About three weeks after the final congressional vote on statehood, Walker, writing as president of the Honolulu Chamber of Commerce, sent Burns a wire which said, in a paraphrase by Aoki, "Mr. Burns, run for the U.S. Senate and we'll support you; and if you run for governor, we're gonna fight you all the way." When he read that telegram, Aoki said, Burns stepped up to the challenge and declared, "I'm running for governor."

By early April, Aoki was writing cautiously to friends in Hawaii about the situation. To Paul Tokunaga, Aoki speculated, "Under the present circumstances—don't quote me—I'm afraid he is going to be forced to be our candidate for the Governor of Hawaii."

Other fears were circulating in Hawaii. Publicist Ed Sheehan wrote to Burns about something he had heard on the street:

> Something that concerns me is a rumor I hear about your addressing the ILWU convention [in Seattle] on your way back. . . . If I may pre-

sume to say this: I honestly think you would be supplying your enemies with the only piece of ammunition they would have against you
in the coming elections. . . . I've always been a great admirer of your
honest approach to labor, and your great courage in taking a firm stand,
. . . but why hand the Republicans a big club at a time like this?

Burns tried to allay Sheehan's fears, pointing out that Senator Warren
Magnuson of the State of Washington would also be addressing the
ILWU convention in Seattle. He also insisted that Hawaii must "thank
the ILWU" for their role in statehood. It was the ILWU, Burns wrote,
that started "a great rank and file movement . . . which the returning veterans implemented."

While Sheehan agreed with the sentiments Burns was expressing,
he believed that having Burns say this in public could be a major political blunder. In addition to the usual anti-ILWU feeling in the Islands,
there was a strong backlash resulting from the union's successful 128-
day sugar strike in 1958. It may have been called the "Aloha strike" by
the ILWU, but many Island residents had been adversely affected by the
union's action and others were developing a gnawing feeling that the
ILWU was becoming too great a power in Hawaii. Sheehan feared that
there were many who might respond positively to the Republican suggestion that the ILWU should not be allowed to take over Hawaii's politics as well as its economy.

On 8 April, Burns flew to Seattle. The following day he addressed
the ILWU convention. In his introduction, Jack Hall praised Burns for
his legislative strategy of separating the Alaska and Hawaii statehood
bills. He added that the ILWU would actively support Jack Burns for
any office he should seek in the coming election, "whether it be Governor or Senator."

Burns delivered a speech to the ILWU delegates that was almost entirely devoted to the subject of statehood for Hawaii. In the thirteen-
page text of the speech, there was one short paragraph in which he
praised the union:

As we analyze the situation in Hawaii and . . . give proper credit where
credit is due, I am going to make a statement that I have made before
in Hawaii: that the foundations of democracy in Hawaii were laid by
the ILWU! Because they freed the working man of the plantation, at
that time some 27,000 people, from the economic and the political
control of management; because they enabled them to realize that they

had dignity, that they were citizens who had a right to their own opinions and a right to participate in such little government as we had. They created the climate that could allow others and themselves to develop a freer society than that which we had.

The Honolulu newspapers featured the statement praising the ILWU in their coverage of his speech, but it was greeted as old news. After all, Burns had been saying the same thing for years. The Republican Party would find better use for the speech later in the campaign.

At this point, Burns made the move that probably cost him his own election and threw his Party into greater confusion than that which had existed before. Rather than going from Seattle to Honolulu, Burns headed back to Washington, D.C., claiming that there were legislative matters he must attend to before returning to the Islands. He also told Dan Inouye, privately, that he would not be returning before his son, James Seishiro Burns, had graduated from Saint Benedict's College in Atchison, Kansas, on 27 May. He had promised Bea that he would attend and he could not disappoint her.

By late April, Burns sensed that things were going badly in Hawaii and sent Dan Aoki back to talk with fellow Democrats. Aoki found a political mess. It had all started when Frank Fasi announced his candidacy for the U.S. Senate. Dan Inouye, without consulting Burns, had followed suit. Then Burns' anointed candidates, Heen and Long, entered the contest. That put four Democrats in the race for two seats in the U.S. Senate. Then Patsy Mink had filed for the seat in the U.S. House of Representatives, the spot Burns had in mind for Inouye. Mits Kido, Burns' choice for lieutenant governor, was facing three Democratic challengers: Spark Matsunaga, Richard Kageyama, and Frank Serrao. Through Aoki, Burns was able to get Dan Inouye to change and run for the House, a switch that embittered Patsy Mink, who had not announced for the House seat until after Inouye appeared to have committed himself to run for the Senate. As far as the other Senate race was concerned, Burns had no influence over the maverick Frank Fasi. In the lieutenant governor's race, Burns had no leverage with an independent Spark Matsunaga, Kido's chief competition.

While Burns remained on the mainland, his staff sought to develop the public relations aspect of the impending governor's race. In their candidate, they had a man who had little use for the process. Burns' attitude was well expressed in some fatherly advice about job hunting to his son, Jim, shortly before his college graduation:

> May I suggest for your consideration that attitude and personality are a very real part of any job performance. As a matter of fact, the personality factor is sometimes the whole criteria (sic) of a person's ability to do a job. This is most unfortunate. It does have its place, but real ability and satisfactory performance of requirements, even the minute ones, with intelligence and effort are the ones on which the ledger of the Almighty keeps record.

Jack Burns knew how to play the game, but it bothered him mightily that he could not simply be judged on his performance. It made him a difficult candidate to manage.

Finally, on 6 June 1959, Jack Burns arrived in Honolulu with Bea and their daughter, Mary Beth. They had crossed the Pacific on the *Matsonia*, losing another precious week of time. Over one thousand well-wishers met the Burns family at the pier. A motorcade carried the delegate and his family through downtown Honolulu. That night, Burns gave a half-hour "Report to the People" on KGMB-TV. The campaign had finally started.

An April Lou Harris poll showed Bill Quinn with a 65 percent to 35 percent lead over Burns in the governor's race. Joe Miller, who had been borrowed from the AFL-CIO's Council on Political Education (COPE), analyzed Burns' political base and encouraged the candidate to concentrate upon maximizing the Japanese and Filipino vote. Both groups were notoriously unreliable bloc voters, Miller pointed out, and must be actively cultivated right to the end of the campaign. Miller also pleaded with Dan Aoki about the role of the ILWU in the campaign:

> Jack Hall and the ILWU [must remain] silent in the campaign. *This must be done!* . . . I know Hall and [the] ILWU have their egos, but it is much more important for them to sublimate them to Jack's success [Jack Burns, that is]. They will be much better off with Jack [Burns] as governor and if keeping silent helps attain that goal, then they should be more than willing to do it.

With no real challenge in the 27 June primary, Burns used the three weeks between his arrival and the primary election to get himself into trouble with other Democratic candidates. Burns' active support of Bill

Heen for the U.S. Senate, Dan Inouye for the U.S. House of Representatives, and Mits Kido for lieutenant governor had created bad feelings among their opponents and those who supported them. Their lack of enthusiastic support for Burns in the general election was damaging to Burns. As Mike Tokunaga recalled years later: "Sparky Matsunaga got mad at us. Patsy Mink was mad at us, and Frank Fasi was mad at us. We had too many people against us, ... so in the general [election] there was a backlash."

Burns faced another problem in the general election—a very popular opponent. In addition to the advantage of incumbency, Bill Quinn was young—37 years old—and handsome; he was a graduate of Harvard Law School; he had an attractive family; and he possessed a fine tenor voice, which he used effectively at many a campaign luau. Quinn also had a campaign issue that had captured the imagination of many native Hawaiian voters—he called it "The Second Mahele." The so-called Great Mahele of 1848, of course, had been the foundation of private property in Hawaii for 111 years. The Second Mahele was designed to redress the injustices done to the Hawaiian people so long ago. To make it acceptable to his Republican supporters, land distributions under Quinn's Second Mahele would be made from the new State's large inventory of land, not at the expense of any private land owner. Thus, Bill Quinn had stolen the traditionally Democratic issue of land reform.

Bill Quinn and the Republicans stole another issue from Burns and the Democrats—ethnic diversity. With Frank Fasi having defeated Bill Heen in the 27 June primary, the Democrats presented three haoles for the three top statewide offices—Burns for governor, Fasi and Long for the U.S. Senate. Mits Kido, lieutenant governor, and Dan Inouye, U.S. Representative, both AJAs, rounded out the Democratic nominees for top five spots. By contrast, the Republicans had Bill Quinn, a haole, at the top of the ticket; James Kealoha, an Hawaiian, at lieutenant governor; Hiram Fong, Chinese, and Wilfred Tsukiyama, AJA, running for the U.S. Senate; and Charles Silva, Portuguese, running for the U.S. House of Representatives. Thus, the Republicans had five ethnic groups represented in the top five contests while the Democrats had only two. Burns had once again been trumped on what he thought of as a core Democratic issue.

Only in the last two weeks of the campaign did Burns abandon an appeal to voter gratitude for his having brought statehood for a discussion of more substantive issues. At that point, he looked to the 1952 Democratic Party Platform for inspiration. Burns called for a $17 million cut in personal income taxes, with the loss in state revenue to be recovered by equalizing real property taxes on large land holdings. Like Quinn, Burns called for land reform. He called for reform in the administration of the Hawaiian Homes Commission, affordable housing, and a $25 million home purchase loan fund.

Burns also called for expanding opportunities for higher education so that all deserving students could attend college. He spelled out the need for a statewide economic development plan. In sum, Burns was expressing his conviction that his administration would provide a government "that represents all our people on an equal basis." In the final days of the campaign, Burns was even reaching out for Republican votes, asserting that his appointments would be made on the basis of qualifications, "regardless of Party affiliation."

The ILWU albatross became a heavier burden for Burns as the campaign progressed. William Ewing, managing editor of the *Honolulu Star-Bulletin*, captured the essence of the issue, as the Republicans used it, in his election eve television attack upon Burns:

> It's very simple. By his own statement, the ILWU has supported Burns from the day he entered public life. The ILWU made him what he is today. He would never have got there without the support of the ILWU and, of course, Harry Bridges. He is their boy. Up to now, Burns has never had the means of returning the favor. But he will, if elected, with nearly 500 appointments to make. Anybody who thinks the ILWU doesn't expect to be paid off is simply naive. . . .
> Ask anybody who has been around the Legislature during the last few sessions, who was the most ubiquitous, most conspicuous lobbyist there. The odds are he'll answer, "The ILWU representative." If Jack Burns occupies the Governor's office, he [the ILWU representative] will be there, too.

Ewing closed with a reference to Burns' Seattle speech before the ILWU, about Burns' assertion that the ILWU had brought democracy to Hawaii. "I know something about the ILWU," Ewing said. "It is a fine union for getting benefits for its members, but economic democracy is the kind of democracy they have in Russia. The ILWU had no more to do with bringing political democracy to Hawaii than I had, maybe not as much." It is unlikely that many understood the Marxist distinction between economic and political democracy, but many had a feeling about the potential for too much control in the hands of a powerful union, especially with memories of the 1958 sugar strike so fresh in their minds.

The irony of the ILWU albatross is that the union became so preoccupied with defeating Frank Fasi, their old red-baiting nemesis, that they failed to give Jack Burns the kind of support they had promised him. In addition, ILWU support of Hiram Fong for the U.S. Senate carried with it the suggestion that voting for a Republican candidate for governor might be acceptable. Jack Hall's assumption that Burns could not lose undoubtedly resulted in a less vigorous effort in his behalf than might otherwise have been mounted.

Burns' increasing identification with the ILWU had another unexpected consequence—it split the labor vote. The AFL-CIO's local Committee on Political Education voted 48 to 47 to support Bill Quinn for governor. A 27 July editorial in *Hana Uwila*, a monthly publication of the International Brotherhood of Electrical Workers (IBEW), explained the AFL-CIO position:

> The first governor of our new state will set the pattern of legislative behavior for many years to come. There will be judges and commissioners to appoint as well as directors of the many departments. . . .
>
> Imagine, if you can, a government in which all of these offices are filled by hatchetmen of the ILWU. In view of the plans which Harry Bridges and Jimmy Hoffa have for Hawaii, is that not a frightening thought? Doesn't it seem obvious that we would be cutting our own throats by putting Burns into office?

The reference to Hoffa was related to efforts by the Teamster boss and Harry Bridges of the ILWU to carve up Hawaii in such a way that the two unions would not have to compete with one another for members and jurisdiction. From their standpoint, the effort was to avoid the divide and conquer strategy that had been used so successfully by Hawaii's employers over the years. To many it appeared to have more sinister implications. When Jack Burns refused to comment upon the proposed agreement between the two unions, the 16 July 1959 issue of the *Honolulu Star-Bulletin* ran individual pictures of Burns, Bridges, Hoffa, and ILWU Secretary-Treasurer Louis Goldblatt across the top of the page, with the headline: "Burns Silent on Star-Bulletin Bids for

Statement on Bridges and Hoffa." The implication, which was totally false, was that Burns was somehow involved in the deal. Bud Smyser said years later, "I think it was demagoguery the way we presented it. I think those pictures disturbed a lot of the staff, myself included. . . . I don't apologize for many of the things we've done over the years, but that would be one I'd apologize for."

To realize how badly an election can be misjudged by someone who was in a good position to make an educated guess about the outcome, the 1959 election eve predictions of Jack Hall provide an illustration. The regional director of the ILWU predicted that Burns would defeat Quinn for governor by 15,000 votes; Kido would beat Kealoa for lieutenant governor by 3,000 to 5,000 votes; Fong would prevail over Fasi in their Senate race by 5,000 votes; Long would triumph over Tsukiyama in the other senate race by 15,000 votes and Inouye would crush Silva in the race for the house of representatives by 20,000 votes. In fact, Quinn beat Burns by 4,138 votes; Kealoha swamped Kido by 15,596 votes; Fong defeated Fasi by 9,514 votes; Long edged out Tsukiyama by 4,577 votes; and Inouye buried Silva by more than 60,000 votes. Not only had the Republicans captured three of the five top statewide offices, but they had regained control of the new state senate as well.

Hall was not the only one to miscalculate. In an effort to help out his friend, novelist James Michener bought a half-hour of television to plug Jack Burns' candidacy. To add clout to his own endorsement, Michener invited his Kahala neighbor, the nationally known political writer, William Lederer, to appear with him. To Michener's surprise and horror, Lederer proceeded to tell the television audience that he felt Quinn to be the better qualified of the two candidates for governor. "That son-of-a-bitch," Michener bitterly recalled, "endorsing Quinn statewide on my money!"

The most critical miscalculations in the 1959 elections, however, must be laid at the feet of the leader of the Democratic Party in Hawaii, John A. Burns. He clearly failed to think things through until it was too late. When disaster struck, Burns uncharacteristically turned on those closest to him, blaming them for his defeat. Four months after the election, Michener wrote an opinion piece for the *Honolulu Star-Bulletin* called, "How to Lose an Election." Michener listed several reasons why the Democrats had lost: their appearance of overconfidence; Burns' late return to Hawaii; the ethnic imbalance of the ticket; and the lack of Party organization. "The way the candidates were chosen for major offices," Michener declared, "was a disgrace. The lack of communication between major candidates was pitiful."

Michener went on to criticize the Democratic Party for its failure to utilize professional public relations experts, estimating that the Republicans had employed roughly forty publicists to the Democrat's one. That one, Joe Miller, had arrived late and left the Islands ten days before election day. Money, of course, is always a factor in any election and in 1959 Bill Quinn outspent Burns by better than 2 to 1. Quinn reported expenditures of $55,228; Burns only $21,492. "But if you are really determined to lose an election," Michener intoned, "the best single way is to allow major splits to tear your Party apart without making any serious attempts to heal them."

As if all of this were not enough, a disheartened Jack Burns headed back to Washington, D.C., where even more indignity awaited him. Initially, he had declined to go, saying that he could not afford it and that he was, after all, only a lame duck. Burns finally relented because he saw that he could be helpful to Dan Inouye, who was about to become the first Japanese-American ever to become a member of the House of Representatives. He knew that he could arrange some useful introductions for his protégé. John A. Burns, Hawaii's last delegate to Congress, also enjoyed a series of testimonials from his colleagues of the past thirty-one months in a ceremony that ended the first session of the Eighty-fifth Congress on 20 August 1959.

The following day, President Dwight D. Eisenhower signed the Hawaii Statehood Proclamation at the White House. Present at the ceremony were Vice President Richard M. Nixon; the last secretary of the Territory of Hawaii, Edward Johnson, who was representing Governor Bill Quinn; chairman of the Hawaii Statehood Commission, Lorrin Thurston; Interior Secretary Fred Seaton; Speaker of the House Sam Rayburn; Senator-elect Oren Long; and Representative-elect Dan Inouye. In his final indignity for 1959, a year that had started with such promise, Delegate John A. Burns had not even been invited.

When Sam Rayburn heard that Burns had not been included among the honored guests at the White House ceremony, he responded, "In that case, I won't go myself. No one has done more to achieve statehood for Hawaii than Jack Burns and no one has a better right to be present at the Proclamation signing. . . . Well, if they're counting Jack Burns out, they can count me out also." Upon hearing of Rayburn's gesture, Jack Burns visited his House mentor and said, "I appreciate your friendly support, Mr. Speaker, but forget about me. I can stand the snub. . . . In the interest of Hawaii and its people—and for my sake—I am asking you to go to the White House on this occasion."

Drew Pearson, in his nationally syndicated column, "Washington Merry-Go-Round," wrote that when offered one of the souvenir signing pens by President Eisenhower, Rayburn declined it. Dan Inouye was reported to have leaned over to the Speaker and said, "Mr. Speaker, maybe Jack Burns would like that pen." Rayburn agreed, saying to President Eisenhower, "I'll take that pen after all. I'd like to give it to Jack Burns." After the ceremony, Rayburn turned to Fred Seaton and said, "I don't know who is responsible, and I'm not blaming you personally, but this was inexcusable and pretty small, if you ask me. The White House deliberately ignored the man who had the most right to be here today."

E·L·E·V·E·N

Governor

FOR THE SECOND TIME in a moment of triumph, John A. Burns had experienced a bitter personal defeat. His 1954 loss to Elizabeth Farrington may have been caused by a powerful sympathy vote for the widow of Delegate Joseph Farrington; but Burns' failure to control his Party during the special election lent Mrs. Farrington a winner's mantle, thus contributing to his defeat in the fall. Once again, Burns' failure to take charge of his Party after the statehood vote in March resulted in his defeat in July 1959. Burns had used the 1954–1956 period to mount an organizational effort in behalf of his Party. In 1956, he was rewarded for his efforts by being elected Hawaii's delegate to Congress. The question in 1959 was whether Burns would once again turn defeat into victory in 1962. As Burns returned from his humiliation in the nation's capital at the end of the summer of 1959, many doubted that he could.

Jack Burns returned to Hawaii from Washington, D.C., with many decisions to be made. He had no job. His prospects for a patronage position appeared slim, with the White House, Iolani Palace, (the state capitol) and Honolulu Hale (the city hall) all in Republican hands. On election night, Governor Bill Quinn had magnanimously commented to the press, "I think the State of Hawaii is going to have to make good use very quickly of the outstanding services of Mr. Jack Burns." When asked if this statement constituted a job offer, Quinn quickly backtracked. Eventually, Quinn appointed Burns to a planning committee for the recently authorized East-West Center.

This nonpaying position was a small morsel, indeed, for the man from whom Lyndon Johnson had borrowed the idea of the East-West Center. When University of Hawaii Professor Murray Turnbull became the first director of the East-West Center, he wrote a four-page, single-spaced letter to Lyndon Johnson, asking the Senate Majority how he should proceed with the job. According to Dan Aoki, Turnbull received a four-sentence reply from Bobby Baker, in behalf of his boss, which went roughly like this: "Thank you for your letter. . . . The man that really created the East-West Center is in your backyard. His name is John Burns. Please contact him." Burns was never happy that Bill Quinn had "given" the East-West Center to the university. Had Burns been elected governor in 1959, Aoki contended, the East-West Center would "very definitely" have been a separate institution.

As they had in 1954, those close to Burns took his 1959 defeat personally. Ben Menor, Burns' Big Island coordinator, took the loss particularly hard. Burns had needed a large neighbor island vote to offset Quinn's advantage on Oahu, but he had carried the Island of Hawaii by only 250 votes. "I wanted a 2,000 to 2,500 margin," Menor recalled, "but the presence of Hawaii Mayor Kealoha on the Republican ticket and Quinn's Second Mahele hurt Burns." Menor thought the ILWU issue had also damaged the Burns candidacy: "Independents and business-people were bothered by Burns' ties to the ILWU."

In an effort to reinvigorate "the old man," a crowd of Burns supporters gathered at the 442nd club house for a dinner to honor their leader. Over two hundred of those present pledged to donate $2 per month to allow Burns to direct his efforts to a victory in the 1962 governor's race. The funds were used, primarily, to allow Burns to travel throughout the new State to help rebuild the Democratic Party organization, which had deteriorated during his three years in Washington. The funds were collected and administered by city councilman, Burns loyalist, and accountant Herman Lemke. To Burns, this vote of confidence constituted a mandate. As Burns recalled in 1962, "It was the first definite decision made that I would run again."

Although the decision to run in 1962 had been made, Jack Burns was decidedly at loose ends. He maintained a small office in downtown Honolulu with the voluntary assistance of Sally Sheehan. Mary Isa had remained in Washington, D.C., as Senator Oren Long's office manager. In a letter to Sheehan, she offered some tips on how to deal with Burns' peculiar work habits:

> On the office procedure, I usually knew how JB would, or should, answer his mail. This really isn't hard to do. Like he used to say, just put

yourself in his shoes, and if you [were] him, what would you say? So, just type an answer for his signature that way. Your main difficulty [will] be in getting him to come in regularly to the office, pick up a pen and sign his name on the letter. I called it like pulling teeth. And [about] his snoozing at his desk, if I were you, I would not stand for it. What's he got so much to do these days that he can't have a good night's sleep?

Never, never (just plain folly to do so) leave the letters he receives on his desk for him to do something about. If you can do it, do it. That was how I used to work when he was Delegate—and how I grayed and wrinkled almost overnight.

Sally Sheehan, like her husband a professional publicist, did her best to keep Burns in the public eye. She arranged for a series of short broadcasts for radio station KPOA. They were not very effective. Those who did tune in heard Burns talking too fast and bogged down in the details of esoteric subjects such as a foreign trade zone or how to create a more equitable system of taxation. The average listener couldn't change the station quickly enough.

Burns filled these footloose days much as he had in the late 1940s and early 1950s, talking politics in coffee shops and luncheonettes all over town, to all who would listen. One who listened was Richard Kosaki, a recently minted Ph.D. in political science who was working half-time at the Legislative Reference Bureau, the other half at the University of Hawaii. "I sometimes lunched with Burns between 1959 and 1962," Kosaki remembered. "We usually ate saimin at Sekiya's Restaurant. He'd sit there, smoking cigarettes and drinking coffee. Burns was for the minority, the underdog, social justice. Publicly, his social conscience didn't show up as much as it did privately."

In November 1959, the Republicans organized a statehood celebration to coincide with Thanksgiving. They invited a congressional delegation from Washington, D.C., to attend, but as Eisenhower had done on Admission Day, Jack Burns was not invited. Mike Mansfield, the Democratic senator from Montana, told the Honolulu Stadium crowd, "Without Jack Burns, neither Alaska nor Hawaii would be states today." New York Representative Leo O'Brien, who had worked closely with Burns on the Hawaii Statehood Bill, called the Republican snub of Burns "disgraceful" and "completely fantastic."

As 1959 drew to a close, Jack Burns remained a politician without a job or prospects. His income had been reduced from his $22,500 congressional salary to the $4,500 he received as manager of Burns and Company. John, Jr. and Jim were on the mainland, but Mary Beth, who had completed college, was living at home. She contributed a portion of her teaching salary to help with family expenses. Fortunately, the debts Burns had incurred during the 1954 and 1956 campaigns had been paid off during his years in Congress. New debts would mount during the 1959–1962 hiatus, but all would eventually be paid by a generally frugal Jack Burns.

In 1975, Dan Aoki talked about another source of income Jack Burns had during that lean period: "So one day I says, 'Hey Jack' . . . the story around town is that you're a bandit on the golf course. You better take it easy, eh?' He says, 'Oh, somebody's got to pay the bills.' And I might say he was down to a 6 handicap and used to play a great round of golf."

Aoki remembered that Burns especially liked to team up with son Jim, who was an outstanding golfer in his own right. On one occasion, when the two were teamed up against another pair, young Jim found himself on the eighteenth hole with a ten-foot putt to make for the match. After he sank it, his proud father beamed at him and said, "Jim, what kind of golf [clubs] do you want to buy?" Jim was delighted, but as they walked back to the clubhouse he started to think. Then he asked his father, "Hey, Pop, how much would it have cost you if I had missed that putt?" Jack smiled and said, "Oh, $150." Jim was speechless. For Jack Burns, many of his happiest—and perhaps most profitable—hours during the 1959–1962 period were spent on the Mid-Pacific Country Club golf course in Lanikai.

Aoki, who was also out of a job after the election, found his old position waiting for him at the Hawaii Government Employees Association (HGEA), working with his friend Mike Tokunaga. As union organizers, Aoki and Tokunaga once again worked both sides of the street, building relationships that would serve their real boss, Jack Burns. To the HGEA leadership, this was not a case of moonlighting. For them it was a sound investment.

The presidential election of 1960 took Jack Burns back to Washington, D.C., at the request of his friend and mentor, Lyndon Johnson. Burns carried the title "National Representative" of the Johnson for President committee. In January, Burns took up residence at the Carroll Arms Hotel, where he spent much of the next six months. Lyndon Johnson faced an uphill fight against John F. Kennedy, Hubert Humphrey, and

Stuart Symington, all of whom had long been announced candidates for the Democratic nomination for president of the United States. Johnson chose an insider's strategy, remaining close to his work in the nation's capital, attempting to cash the many political IOUs he had accumulated over the years.

From Washington, Burns maintained a keen interest in the activities of the new state legislature through extensive correspondence with his political friends in the Islands. But when he came back to Hawaii for the Democratic Party's 1960 State Convention, he had national politics on his mind. He wanted to be elected as one of the Party's delegates to the Democratic National Convention in Los Angeles. In that vote, Dan Inouye was the leading vote-getter with 469 votes; Burns finished a close second with 456 votes; and attorney David McClung received 350 votes. At the Los Angeles Convention, Dan Inouye deferred to his mentor and Burns served as the chairman of the Hawaii delegation.

Immediately after the state Democratic Convention, Burns hit the campaign trail for Lyndon Johnson. Burns visited Alaska, Arizona, California, Colorado, Idaho, Indiana, Montana, New Mexico, Nevada, Oregon, Utah, Washington, and Wyoming in behalf of LBJ. It was a futile quest. For the first time in American politics, a candidate had captured enough delegates in the primary elections to have a virtual lock on his Party's nomination. Burns arranged to have Dan Inouye give a seconding speech for Johnson's nomination, but nothing would stand in the way of John F. Kennedy's first ballot victory in Los Angeles. With the result a foregone conclusion, no effort was made by Burns to hold the Hawaii delegation for Johnson. The result was a four-way split: three and one-half votes for Lyndon Johnson; two votes for Adlai Stevenson; one vote for John F. Kennedy; and one-half vote for Stuart Symington. Hawaii's Johnson supporters took some small measure of comfort in the selection of Lyndon Johnson as Kennedy's running-mate.

Following the Democratic National Convention, Burns returned to the Islands and turned his attention to Hawaii. Frank Fasi was once again seeking to become the mayor of the City and County of Honolulu. Bob Dodge, the Democratic Party insider who had been the principal architect of the landmark 1952 Democratic Party Platform and of the new city charter, was running against Fasi in the Democratic primary. Burns, still smarting over the difficulty his 1959 endorsements had caused him, refused to take a public stand in the primary contest. If there had been any chance for Dodge to defeat Fasi, Burns might have sup-

ported him, but that was not in the cards. Although Burns was a philosophical idealist, he was a political realist. Dodge, not widely known outside the Party, was easily defeated by Fasi in the Democratic primary.

Burns was now faced with Frank Fasi's demand that he endorse the
Democratic Party's nominee against the popular Republican mayor,
Neal Blaisdell. The most Fasi could get out of Burns was a cryptic, "I
have never supported Mr. Blaisdell, and never voted for him." Although
Burns' lieutenants Dan Aoki and Mike Tokunaga worked actively in the
Fasi campaign, Jack Burns limited himself to speaking for the entire
Democratic ticket. Burns' reluctance to support Fasi was based on their
past conflict and the good working relationship his intimates, supervisors
Matsy Takabuki and Herman Lemke, enjoyed with Neal Blaisdell. And,
as he had with Dodge, Burns studiously avoided any close identification
with a certain loser. In the general election, Blaisdell rolled over Fasi.

In the 1960 presidential race, John F. Kennedy defeated Richard M.
Nixon by less than 120,000 votes. Hawaii mirrored the closeness of the
national vote, with Kennedy edging out Nixon by only 115 votes. Ironically, Nixon did so well in Hawaii because the ILWU wanted to punish Kennedy for a deal he had made with the AFL-CIO at the expense
of the ILWU and the Teamsters. Burns, of course, was clearly identified
with both the ILWU and Lyndon Johnson. Although the Kennedy
people were glad to have had Johnson on their side during the presidential race, the new vice president would find himself with little power
and influence in an administration filled with people who personally dis-
liked and mistrusted the former Majority Leader. Among other things,
Johnson found that he had little influence over patronage.

Patronage was what Jack Burns sought in 1961. He not only needed
a job, he needed a launching pad for his 1962 campaign to unseat Bill
Quinn. Burns went to Washington, D.C., hat in hand, to present his case
to Lyndon Johnson. As he wrote to Bobby Baker: "[Putting it] bluntly,
I need to have recognition by the new administration—the higher the
office the better. The alternative is my remaining an unemployed politician. Thus, I must seek the service of my leader as I did in Statehood and
in the East-West Center." Burns reminded his friend that Johnson had
failed to respond to his late October plea for help in Hawaii: "About ten
days before the election of November 8, 1960 I told you that LBJ could
turn Hawaii Democratic.... The fact is that LBJ could have won it had
he appeared. JFK could not as I earlier told Ted [Kennedy] when he was
here. The same intuition tells me that recognition [for me] is needed."

Burns had two highly visible positions in mind. He would like to be made assistant secretary of state for far eastern affairs or director of the East-West Center. There was a condition to the East-West Center post. As he told Mary Isa, "I would [accept the position] if the director would be able to operate as he should—not under the present circumstances where he would be subordinate to the president of the university." This was a demand that would have to be approved by Governor Bill Quinn, which was not a likely proposition. When U. Alexis Johnson, the highly respected foreign service professional, was named assistant secretary of state for far eastern affairs, Mary Isa reported, "I went into tears." She expressed frustration at her new boss, Senator Oren Long, "the guy who could really have taken it into his hands and gotten the job for Jack. Instead, this guy just sits on his hands in his comfortable office and 'awaits developments.' Boy, if only I didn't need my job so bad."

In 1961, as in 1951 when Jack pushed his appointment as territorial governor, Oren Long owed his position, in large part, to Jack Burns. On both occasions, Long had failed to go to bat for Burns on matters of patronage. Long preferred to think of himself as a statesman who had answered a call to service, rather than a politician who had actively sought the positions to which he had been elevated. Jack Burns came to think of Long as a man who didn't understand what it meant to be a team player.

The Kennedy administration did come up with three job offers for Burns: director of territories in the Interior Department; high commissioner of the trust territories; and U.S. customs collector in Honolulu. None of these positions promised to give Burns the visibility he felt he needed. He would challenge Quinn as a private citizen. He did have two things going for him—many friends and lots of time. Unlike 1959, this time he would use both wisely.

Burns got a big assist in 1962 in the form of Republican Party disunity. Lieutenant Governor Jimmy Kealoha, who had outpolled Bill Quinn in the 1959 election, wanted very much to be governor. "There was petty bickering between us from day one," Quinn later recalled, "and all the way through the life of the administration." Even capturing control of the state senate proved to be a Pyrrhic victory for Quinn. As he recalled: "We put a great deal of effort into preparing our legislative program for the 1960 session. It was composed of twenty major pieces of legislation. It was a Republican program with integrity, and my own senate destroyed it. It lost all identity. It was a tragedy. They even 'dinged' two of my cabinet selections."

Quinn had himself to blame for many of his problems. His first mistake was that he failed to meet the patronage demands of those who had elected him. As he saw it, looking back in 1980:

> Had I used those 550 jobs politically, Bill Quinn could have been Governor forever. But you talk about "Camelot," we were really idealistic. We were torn between building a political empire and starting the state out as it ought to have been done. We chose the latter. Call it naive and stupid, if you will. I must take responsibility for not building the Republican Party or a Quinn machine.

Idealism was not Quinn's only failing. He and his publicists had also oversold the Second Mahele program. The idea of selling state lands at $50 per acre found rough going with Democrats and Republicans alike. The Republicans opposed it on principle; some Democrats opposed it on principle while others simply would not allow a Republican governor to take credit for such a massive program of land distribution.

While Quinn's troubles mounted, Burns was quietly building his organization, playing golf, and staying out of factional fights within the Democratic Party. In early 1961, Hawaii's Democratic Party chairman, Bill Richardson, appointed state Representative Robert Oshiro to head a committee to study the electoral failure of 1959 and to make recommendations for 1962. Oshiro would have a profound impact upon the remainder of the political career of John A. Burns.

A 37-year-old Wahiawa lawyer, Oshiro had come to Democratic Party politics relatively late. One of the youngest members of the 442nd, Oshiro was a significant beneficiary of the G.I. Bill. He finally returned from the mainland in 1953 with a law degree from Duke University, the same law school that had produced Richard Nixon. In spite of his educational credentials, Oshiro, whose family had come from the Okinawa prefecture of Japan, found himself blocked from joining any of the larger downtown law firms. He decided to set up a one-man shop in his hometown of Wahiawa. There Oshiro learned politics from Earl Sturdyvin, a Colorado-born saloon keeper who, at the behest of Oahu County Committee Chairman Tom Gill, set out to organize the town for the Democratic Party.

Oshiro first met Burns in 1956, at a Democratic Party rally at Wahiawa's Fred Wright Park. Burns surprised Oshiro by greeting him with the words, "Hi, I understand you're a darn good lawyer for Ben Franklin." The reference was to Oshiro's having examined some lease documents for the Ben Franklin store in the Burns and Company commercial building in Kailua. Other than that, all Oshiro remembered about his first meeting with Burns was that "he stood tall and straight. He minced no words, very straight, very simple, and to the point."

Two years later, in the fall of 1958, Oshiro was surprised to receive a call from Mike Tokunaga. At Burns' behest, Tokunaga asked Oshiro if he would be interested in serving as clerk of the territorial house of representatives during the 1959 legislative session. Oshiro accepted and another Burns lieutenant was in place. When news of statehood hit Hawaii, Oshiro was on the floor of the house chamber in Iolani Palace. Looking back in 1977, Oshiro recalled that moment: "That news was so electrifying that I had goosepimples. I wanted to cry. . . . Right then and there I made a decision. I'm going to run [for the state legislature] because I wanted to share and participate in laying the foundation for the new state." Oshiro won a seat in the new house of representatives in 1959. His pleasure was dampened, however, by the defeat of Jack Burns. Oshiro later recalled sending a letter to Burns in which he said, "If I could reverse the situation, I would give up my seat for you to be there as chief executive."

Burns and Oshiro got to know each other better in 1960, when Burns was in Washington, D.C., working on the Johnson campaign and Oshiro had come to the nation's capital to testify before a committee chaired by Alaska Senator Bob Bartlett. They got off to a bad start when, at a chance breakfast together at the Carroll Arms Hotel, Oshiro told Burns: "You should not have lost the '59 election. You're to blame for the loss." Before Oshiro had a chance to explain his thinking, Burns "exploded. . . . That's when I found out he had a temper." After the storm clouds had passed, Oshiro found a very different Jack Burns. "He was very helpful for me," Oshiro recalled. "He coached me on how to testify before a Senate committee. He made calls to various people that I wanted to see. He opened many doors for me. He was very, very helpful."

In 1961, Robert Oshiro had the opportunity to return the favor; his committee was very helpful in Burns' bid to become governor of the State of Hawaii. State Democratic Chairman Bill Richardson, who had appointed Oshiro to chair the committee, saw something new in Oshiro's approach to politics, something the Democratic Party badly needed. Oshiro was, Richardson said, "a big statistics man. . . . He had a whole room just for statistics and he had charts and all that. Bob was always that way, he knew every answer politically [and] never let anything go that might become important. . . . The old politician kept everything in his head."

Oshiro sent out questionnaires, took polls, and interviewed people incessantly. His first interview was with Jack Burns, who had invited him to his home for dinner. The visit left Oshiro with a lasting impression:

> The house was unkempt, it showed he didn't have any money. I'll never forget [it] because when I went into the house, it was a small house. . . . The yard was unkempt, terrible. He was in his old dungarees. . . . It wasn't negative; it wasn't positive. It told me [that] here was a man who was delegate to Congress, here's a man who was in [that] top political post and apparently he didn't make money on it. [My visit confirmed] all the stories about him, that . . . [he was] broke.

Another thing Oshiro noticed during his visit was that all of the counters in the kitchen had been lowered to wheelchair height. In spite of the squalid appearance of the house and yard, "there was a lavish dinner [and], to my surprise, Mrs. Burns cooked it all from a wheelchair."

From his interview, Oshiro learned that, contrary to rumor, Jack Burns was not simply coasting into the 1962 elections:

> He was devoting a great deal of time to people. . . . You have to understand Jack Burns' style of politics. His campaigning would be . . . to have golf with a certain person and . . . get his input. . . . This is how he developed loyal, trusted friends. He's on a one-to-one basis . . . where he doesn't take anyone for granted, and if it takes ten hours, he's going to spend ten hours with that guy. That's what he was doing.

In addition to his interview, Oshiro had Burns fill out a questionnaire, just like all the others who wanted to be players in the Democratic Party. One of the responses on Jack Burns' questionnaire that caught Oshiro's attention dealt with the respondent's occupation. Burns was the only person who completed one of the questionnaires to write, simply, "politician."

Whatever Burns was doing, it seemed to be working. In November 1961, with the election still a year away, Dan Tuttle, a University of Hawaii political science professor who had accurately predicted Burns' 1959 defeat, reported his most recent numbers for the 1962 governor's race. They showed Burns with 51.4 percent of the voters, Quinn with 42.7 percent. The remaining 5.9 percent was spread out among Tom Gill, Richard Sharpless, Herbert K. H. Lee, and Jimmy Kealoha.

While Oshiro sought to put together a slate of candidates that would avoid major intra-Party conflict in the primaries and support the top of the ticket, Burns continued to build his own personal campaign. In doing so, Burns decided to use a strategy at which he had always excelled—meeting one-on-one or in small groups over a cup of coffee. Dan Aoki and Mike Tokunaga handled the logistics of Burns' coffee hours.

One key group with whom Burns had never done well was the faculty at the University of Hawaii. Many professors held Burns in disdain because of his lack of formal education and because of his weakness as a public speaker. At an early Burns coffee hour with a group of university professors, Ralph Miwa, an associate professor of political science, became a convert. Miwa came away from the meeting "convinced . . . that this guy was [an] unalloyed, natural-born Jeffersonian in his thinking about American political processes." Soon a group of university faculty was meeting regularly with Burns at the home of Terry Ihara, a professor in the university's School of Education and a 442nd veteran who was a close friend of Aoki and Tokunaga. For those who were willing to listen, Burns made an excellent impression. "In my book," Miwa declared, "if you define an intellectual as a guy who's willing to discuss, to debate, to look at the issues and argue the merit of issues, . . . [Burns] was more of an intellectual . . . than 90 percent of the people I knew at the Manoa campus."

As 1962 began, Robert Oshiro's admonition that the Party should make its decisions about who was going to run for what office in such a way that expensive and bitter primary contests could be avoided was about to be put to its first test. The top of the ticket presented no problem. The Party's fact-finding committee had cast twelve of its sixteen votes for Jack Burns for governor. Oren Long received two votes, Richard Sharpless and Herbert K. H. Lee each received one. The overwhelming consensus was that Burns should be allowed to select his own running mate.

Jack Burns had learned from the Republican's 1959 success and decided that his choice for the office of lieutenant governor should be at least part-Hawaiian. Ernest Kai, Herman Lemke, and Bill Richardson made Burns' short-list. Burns disqualified Kai because of his 1951 refusal to consult with Burns on patronage if appointed territorial governor by Harry S Truman. Lemke, as it turned out, showed no interest in leaving city and county government. Burns readily accepted Lemke's decision because he knew the value of having Lemke and Takabuki as city council allies. This left Bill Richardson who, despite his wife's plea that he leave politics, agreed to be Burns' running mate. His agreement, however, was contingent upon an understanding that, at the end of Burns' first term, Richardson would be named to the state supreme court. With Richardson running for lieutenant governor, Robert Oshiro became state Democratic Party chairman.

A problem arose when Senator Oren Long started looking for support for his reelection to the U.S. Senate. The U.S. Senate being a continuous body, in the 1959 elections one senator was elected for a three-year term, the other for a six-year term. Hiram Fong, of course, had won the six-year term; Long's seat would be contested in the 1962 elections. In 1959, when Long was selected as the Democratic candidate for the three-year term, it was with the understanding that he would step aside at the end of that term. It was this understanding that had led Dan Inouye to withdraw his candidacy for the U.S. Senate and run for the House of Representatives. Making Long adhere to Party discipline would be an early test of Robert Oshiro's recommended Democratic Party strategy. With Mike Tokunaga orchestrating the whole process, Long soon found out that there was little support for his candidacy. As Tokunaga observed, "Wherever [Long] went, most of the people agreed that it was Dan Inouye's turn to run. . . . Even the unions . . . agreed that it was Dan Inouye's turn to run." Long went quietly into his second political retirement with Party discipline still intact.

Frank Fasi, as usual, caused his share of mischief—and more. The Democratic Party leaders, with Burns' approval, had decided that Tom Gill would be their candidate to take Inouye's seat in the U.S. House of Representatives. Burns, who always appreciated Gill's ability, if not his personality, thought that having Tom Gill five thousand miles from Honolulu was not without merit. When Fasi announced that he was going to jump into the race against Gill, the Party organization went to work. When the ILWU endorsed the prickly Gill, no friend to the union, Fasi's defeat was sealed. As a result of the 1960 census, Hawaii had picked up a second seat in the U.S. House of Representatives. The Democratic Party's Fact-Finding Committee had selected Herbert K. H. Lee as their favored candidate for that spot. In a lapse of Party discipline that created no major uproar, Lee was opposed—and defeated—by the independent Spark Matsunaga.

On Sunday afternoon, 12 August 1962, Jack Burns formally announced his candidacy for governor before a crowd of 1,400 Democrats under a tent on the Pali Golf Course. Burns said little that was new. He simply reiterated themes he had been espousing for a decade. After telling those assembled that he felt that he was the man best qualified "to foster a climate favorable to the maximum development of the tremendous potentialities of these people of Hawaii—potentialities as yet untapped," Burns went on the attack against Bill Quinn. Burns said it was time to end "a long honeymoon of *'maheles,'* of pie-in-the-sky surveys as substitutes for action, of an everything-is-rosy fairy tale. It is time we got off cloud nine and started toward 'the second milestone of statehood' for our people." As he had in the past, Burns continued to characterize the Republican leadership as oligarchic, asking whether the rights of Hawaii's citizens "should continue to be blighted by the antiquated economic-political, self-appointed ruling group which too long has dominated Hawaii."

With the platitudes out of the way, Burns became more substantive. First he attacked the Quinn administration for failing to enforce an equitable tax system in Hawaii. He also faulted the governor for not enforcing the State's anti-trust laws, which were designed to give Hawaii "an open and competitive economy." Burns also charged that the Republican failure to respond to demands for home rule on the neighbor islands proved that they "do not believe in the people, do not trust them, do not in reality believe them safe repositories of the public interest."

On the positive side, Burns spelled out a number of initiatives he intended to advance as governor of the State of Hawaii. First, he proposed the creation of an International Trade Center, an International House, and an International Merchandise Mart. Burns also called for the continued improvement of the University of Hawaii, including the addition of professional graduate schools, particularly in law and medicine. He wanted the university to be "an institution second to none." Burns also advocated a community college system that "would provide post high-school training for students learning special trades and for older citizens whose jobs had been displaced by technological changes and required new skills." Finally, Burns urged scrutiny of the state's land policies, admitting that the subject was complicated and that it demanded fairness to both existing landowners and those who were landless.

Burns concluded with a plea for action:

There is an urgency to all of this. The danger of being bypassed is one. But there is another. Are we providing the opportunities for our young people to make a living in Hawaii? Is our economy expanding fast enough to provide the jobs their education and abilities qualify them for? You all know the answer to this. Our young people are leaving us. They leave the neighbor islands and do not return. They leave Oahu for the bigger wages and lower expenses of the Mainland. And what price must we pay for the misdirected energies of those who stay here to face the discouragement of limited opportunities?

Many who saw Jack Burns give his announcement speech at the Pali Golf Course were amazed—not by what he said, but by his demeanor as he said it. Burns had taken the advice James Michener had given to him after the 1959 debacle and hired a California public relations consultant by the name of Robert Alderman. In 1980, Alderman recalled that in his first meeting with Burns, he told the candidate that he would require three things of him: "First, listen to me and take my advice. Second, wear out two or three pair of shoes; get around and meet people, shake their hands. Third, you're an austere type of person. You've got to learn to smile."

Burns had much to smile about after the 3 October primary elections. Facing token resistance from maverick Honolulu attorney Hyman Greenstein, Burns prevailed by a vote of 71,648 to 7,871—nearly a 10 to 1 margin. Bill Quinn had a much tougher time in the Republican primary, defeating his disaffected lieutenant governor Jimmy Kealoha by a 44,095 to 33,277 margin. Bill Richardson, Burns' chosen running-mate, won a close contest in the lieutenant governor's race against Ernest Kai, defeating him by a vote of 37,883 to 36,913—less than 1,000 votes. Dan Inouye, who had come to be the Democratic Party's perennial vote leader, moved easily into the general election in the U.S. Senate race as did Tom Gill and Spark Matsunaga in their bids for the U.S. House of Representatives. Burns had four of his five first choices going into the general election, and Spark Matsunaga turned out to be a considerable asset to the Democratic Party ticket. He may have been independent, but he was no Frank Fasi.

With Burns comfortably ahead of Quinn, there appeared to be only one roadblock standing between Burns and his election as governor. The Republicans were demanding a debate between the candidates. Thinking that the Harvard-trained Quinn would destroy this graduate of St. Louis High School, the Republicans pushed hard. A seemingly unconcerned Jack Burns agreed to the debate. His closest advisers were less sanguine. On the eve of the confrontation, the Burns camp put together a panel to test their man. Burns reluctantly agreed to meet with them. Arriving half-an-hour late for the trial run, Burns strode into the room and said, "All right fellas, let's go. All you guys are Quinn. I'm Burns. Let's debate." As Dan Aoki described the scene that followed, "He went right down the line, boom, boom, boom, boom, boom, boom. After he answered everybody he says, 'Any corrections to be made? Any strategy you want to lay out?'" There was none. Burns had been impressive, but the question remained: How would he be under the pressure of a televised debate?

Quinn's supporters thought they had the answer: their man would demolish Burns. They, too, prepared their candidate for the debate. "Quinn had an incredibly fine mind," Roger Coryell, Quinn's press secretary remembered. "He'd put the information into his computer mind. When we asked him something that he didn't have an answer to, staff was right there to get it for him. That convinced us, I think, that we were really going to whip Jack Burns in the debate on the basis of the obvious grasp of the government and facts of the state administration that Quinn had and Burns didn't have."

The next day, 2 November 1962—the day before the general election—they got their answer. Burns took the offensive on the first question and Quinn never regained his balance. Neither candidate made any serious blunders, which meant that Burns had won. The only real question had been whether Burns could hold his own against the governor. Clearly he had. Even Quinn partisans only gave their man a "split-decision" in their recap. The Republican *Honolulu Star-Bulletin* headline on election day read: "Quinn Given Edge in Lackluster Debate." The polls told a different story, with Burns winning the governor's race by 33,000 votes. Richardson, Inouye, Gill, and Matsunaga all joined Burns in a Democratic sweep. Most had predicted a Democratic victory, but few had expected such a landslide. Jack Burns had once again played the Phoenix, rising out of the ashes of defeat to a glorious victory.

PART IV

The Making of a Consensus
(1962–1975)

T·W·E·L·V·E

Getting Started

FEW KNEW THE NEW GOVERNOR better than Monsignor Charles A. Kekumano. The future Catholic priest first "knew of" Jack Burns when the two were students at St. Louis School. "I was a small kid at the time," Kekumano remembered, "but the little kids were always aware of the big kids." They first met in the 1940s, when Burns attended classes on the Church's position on labor that were taught by one of Kekumano's seminary instructors.

In July 1954, Kekumano returned to Hawaii from Catholic University in Washington, D.C., with his doctorate in theology—just in time for the Democratic Party takeover of the territorial legislature. Kekumano reestablished his acquaintance with Burns; soon he became the Democratic politician's monthly confessor. "I was his confessor, but I was more his pastor and his friend," said Kekumano. "Burns took God into account all his life and always considered God and his wishes before acting."

Central to Burns' religious faith was the Catholic Mass. "He turned to God daily," said Kekumano. "He derived tremendous moral and spiritual strength from the age-old Church ritual of turning to God through the Mass. He did so in his early life and throughout his mature years"— every morning of every day of his life in elective office.

Kekumano found Burns "very human. He never gave the impression of being all-wise. By character he always listened and said very little. He rarely ever expatiated at great length on anything. He would take what you had to say; he would grunt; say, 'Well, fine,' then evaluate it and do what he could on his own. But he would act quietly. You never knew what he would do, but you knew he would act. He would never, ever condescend to help. He did so in a brotherly fashion. By nature, he was always encouraging."

Kekumano considered Burns a most uncommon politician: "Politically, he was never a wheeler-dealer in the Machiavellian sense. He had strong convictions, and he could convey his own thinking without sermonettes. For him the basics were clear, and they were equally clear to those around him. From advisers to department heads, those around him understood him, thus you got a sense of team action in his administration."

In the weeks bridging the end of 1962 and beginning of 1963, the newly elected governor went about building his team, beginning with his personal staff. Mary Isa became his first appointment. Burns' longtime secretary had returned to Hawaii in the fall of 1962 to help in the final stages of the campaign. Oren Long's impending retirement from the U.S. Senate had freed Isa to leave Washington, D.C. Although her appointment as the governor's secretary was no surprise, Isa learned about it in the newspaper.

Dan Aoki also took his accustomed place—chief of staff—in Burns' gubernatorial office. Having worked as Delegate Burns' administrative assistant in Washington, D.C., Aoki could quickly assume that role for the governor. Joining Isa and Aoki in Burns' inner office were *Honolulu Star-Bulletin* reporter Don Horio, as press secretary; a young Harvard-trained Hawaiian who had just lost in a race for the state house of representatives, Kekoa Kaapu, as administrative assistant; and Burns' old friend and Friday lunch club companion Bill Norwood, in the cabinet-level position of director of administration. Norwood's primary responsibility was to act as Burns' legislative liaison. Another Burns intimate, Mike Tokunaga, remained one of Burns' ever-present operatives. While Tokunaga's official title was deputy director in the comptroller's office, in fact he acted as another administrative assistant to the governor—and alter ego to Aoki. While Aoki could be tough and abrasive, Tokunaga maintained a calmer, softer mien. Both were totally devoted to "the old man."

With the efficient management of his office assured, Burns turned his attention to the selection of his cabinet. Dan Aoki recalled that a group that included himself, Jack Burns, Ed Burns, Bill Richardson, Mike Tokunaga, Matsy Takabuki, Mits Kido, Ernest Murai—and others on an occasional basis—carried on a "talent search" at Takabuki's home, "night after night." Aoki also remembered that Burns did everything he could to assure that his cabinet would be both highly qualified and reflective of the ethnic diversity of Hawaii's population. Political considerations were important, but secondary.

For director of the state Department of Transportation, Burns selected Fujio Matsuda, a son of Japanese plantation workers, graduate of McKinley High School, member of the 442nd Regimental Combat Team, and a G.I. Bill-trained engineer who had earned a Ph.D. at the Massachusetts Institute of Technology. Matsuda was "nonpolitical," but had voted for Bill Quinn for governor in both the 1959 and 1962 elections. When Burns asked Matsuda to serve as state director of transportation, Matsuda protested that he had no experience in the field. Burns assured him that his degree from MIT and his chairmanship of the Civil Engineering Department at the University of Hawaii constituted sufficient credentials.

Matsuda recalled later that, as he was leaving Burns' office, the governor-elect called to him and said, "Oh, by the way, not that it matters, but what's your politics?" When Matsuda responded that he was "an independent," Burns said, "Good, I was afraid you might be a Republican! . . . Don't worry about politics, I'm the politician. You do the best job you can." After ten years as Hawaii's director of transportation, "Fudge" Matsuda would become the first non-Caucasian president of the University of Hawaii.

For attorney general, Burns turned to Bert Kobayashi, another Japanese-American. In his pursuit of Kobayashi, Burns demonstrated his single-mindedness. A graduate of Harvard Law School, Kobayashi was a past president of the Hawaii Bar Association. His law firm included a young state senator named George Ariyoshi and the soon-to-be appointed director of the state Department of Labor, Alfred Laureta. Although Kobayashi was interested in politics, he had no intention of becoming personally involved. With four children—and an equal number of nephews for whom he was financially responsible—Kobayashi felt that he could not afford the "luxury" of public office.

Kobayashi turned down Burns' telephone offer of the attorney general's position. The governor then summoned him to his office, where he showed Kobayashi a list of those who were actively seeking the position. "Governor," Kobayashi noted, "there are so many good ones here, why don't you select one of them?"

"No way," Burns shot back. "I want you. I know you."

"Governor," Kobayashi rejoined, "I don't know you." Burns proceeded to detail cases Kobayashi had handled in the past. Burns had clearly done his homework. In an effort to close the deal, Burns reminded Kobayashi of a chance meeting they once had: "I had a long talk with you, even though you don't remember, on the steps of Kapahulu Japanese School . . . and I got a deep insight [into] your basic philosophies. So, no matter what you say, I'm telling you that you've got to become the attorney general."

Kobayashi fell back on his plea of financial hardship. "Governor," he asked, "how am I going to make ends meet when the attorney general's paycheck is not even one-fifth of what I'm earning [now]?" Lapsing into pidgin-English, Burns replied, "I no can help. That's your problem." Kobayashi finally agreed to join the Burns team for a two-year stint; he remained as Burns' attorney general for eight years, then moved to the state supreme court.

Burns made Sidney I. Hashimoto the third AJA member of his cabinet when he appointed him director of the Department of Treasury and Regulation. Like Fujio Matsuda—and Dan Inouye—Hashimoto was a graduate of McKinley High School and a member of the 442nd. A University of Hawaii graduate, Hashimoto earned his law degree from New York University, served as assistant public prosecutor and deputy city and county attorney, and came highly recommended by Burns' closest ally on the city council, Matsy Takabuki. Hashimoto also had some legislative experience, having been elected to the territorial house of representatives in 1958.

For his director of economic development, Burns tapped Dr. Shelley Mark, a Chinese-born Ph.D. in economics from the University of Washington. Burns had come to know Mark when the University of Hawaii economics professor did a stint at the Legislative Reference Bureau. Mark had helped Burns to draft a speech on Hawaii's role as a meeting place for Pacific Rim nations—a persistent theme of Burns' three terms as governor. Mark was also one of the university professors Burns had been meeting with since his 1959 defeat by Bill Quinn.

Businessman Andrew Ing, a University of Hawaii graduate with a Harvard M.B.A., became Burns' first budget director. Although he did not know Burns well at the time of his appointment, Ing was close to one of Burns' principal contacts in the Chinese community, Clarence Ching. When Ing protested that he did not have any direct experience that would prepare him for the position of budget director, Burns told him not to worry. "The job simply called for common sense and an understanding that the State must maintain financial stability."

William Among, who was named director of social services, was a

trusted friend of the governor's from his years with the Honolulu Police
Department. Among, another graduate of the University of Hawaii, was
of Chinese-Hawaiian ancestry. At the time of his appointment to Burns'
cabinet, Among was serving as business administrator for Maluhia Hospital, the state convalescent hospital in Kamehameha Heights.

For director of personnel services, Burns selected a Maui-born, Por-
tuguese-Hawaiian wife of a Samoan, Edna Tavares Taufaasau. The sister of federal judge Nils Tavares, Taufaasau had sought the position in
her own behalf. At the time of her application, she was serving as director of the central board of examiners in the Pacific area for the U.S. Civil
Service Commission. Another University of Hawaii graduate, Taufaasau
had been with the Civil Service Commission since 1938. She came well
qualified for the post; her ethnicity proved to be an added bonus for the
governor.

For state comptroller, Burns turned to Val Marciel, a man who could
claim Hawaiian, Portuguese, English, and French blood. In Marciel,
Burns was also recognizing a man with thirty-five years of public service
as a territorial and state employee. Like Burns, Marciel had attended the
University of Hawaii briefly in the early 1930s, but financial difficulties
had precluded his continuation. Also like Burns, Marciel was a charter
member of the Mid-Pacific Country Club and the Kailua Lions Club.

For adjutant general, Burns turned to insurance executive Robert L.
Stevenson. A graduate of St. Louis School and the University of Hawaii,
Stevenson had served for twenty-six years in the Hawaii National
Guard. He retired at the rank of colonel in 1957, when he was passed
over for promotion to brigadier. With Burns' appointment, Stevenson
attained the rank of major general in the Hawaii National Guard. A
highly decorated hero during World War II, Stevenson was serving as
vice president-secretary of First Insurance Company of Hawaii at the
time of his appointment.

Burns looked in the mirror in search of his director of the Department of Taxation; there he found his brother, Ed Burns. The governor
considered the director of taxation a critical position because of his intended strategy for land reform, which focused on the taxation of land
at its "highest and best use." For this, he needed somebody he could trust
completely and who understood real estate appraisal. Ed Burns fulfilled
both requirements. The younger of the two Burns brothers was also well
known and respected by his former Republican colleagues.

Announcing his brother's nomination on Inauguration Day, Governor Burns said, "While I do not particularly like to bring a relative into my administration, my brother Ed has outstanding qualifications as an administrator and as one of Hawaii's prominent appraisers, which will be invaluable to my administration." Perhaps the Kennedy brothers had paved the way two years earlier, for no editorial criticism of Ed Burns' appointment appeared in the local papers.

For the position of director of health, Burns reappointed Dr. Leo Bernstein, who had served during Bill Quinn's administration. Two other haole holdovers were actually named by boards which were appointed by the governor. One was R. Burl Yarberry, who continued in his cabinet level post of superintendent of education. The other was Dr. Thomas H. Hamilton, who had been appointed, but had not yet assumed his new responsibilities, as president of the University of Hawaii.

Three more board-appointed cabinet-level posts were left unfilled until 1963, when University of Hawaii Professor of Animal Nutrition Kenneth K. Otagaki became chairman of the board of agriculture; Abraham Piianaia, a well-known leader within the Hawaiian community, became chairman of the Hawaiian Homes Commission; and Jim Ferry, a Kailua realtor and Mid-Pac golfing companion, was named as chairman of the board of land and natural resources. In selecting Ferry, as with his brother, Burns wanted a someone whose personal loyalty was beyond question and whose knowledge of Hawaii's real estate values was sound.

A quick look at the fifteen individuals selected by Burns, not including holdovers Bernstein, Yarberry, and Hamilton, is revealing. Four of the fifteen were of Japanese ancestry; four were Caucasian; four were part-Hawaiian (two Hawaiian-Chinese and two Hawaiian-Portuguese); two were Chinese; and one was Filipino. As Bud Smyser, managing editor of the *Honolulu Star-Bulletin,* said, "Racially, the cabinet has an even better balance than the much-envied Democratic state ticket in November." While the cabinet reflected Hawaii's ethnic diversity, it had an additional local element to it. Six of the fifteen were graduates of the University of Hawaii and three were members of the university faculty. Never in the history of the Territory or State of Hawaii had a governor's cabinet known such local representation and ethnic balance.

No one cried political cronyism in regard to Burns' cabinet, although it might have been suspected in the cases of his brother and close friends Bill Norwood, Val Marciel, and Jim Ferry. Burns dispensed so few political favors through his cabinet selections because so many of Burns' political associates now held elective office themselves: Bill Richardson was lieutenant governor; Dan Inouye was in the U.S. Senate; Mits Kido, Nadao Yoshinaga, Sakae Takahashi, and George Ariyoshi were all in the state senate; Toshio Serizawa, Elmer Cravalho, Robert Oshiro, David McClung, and Tadao Beppu were in the state house of representatives; Masato Doi, Herman Lemke, and Matsy Takabuki were on the Honolulu City Council. Burns' entrance into the governor's office was not a beginning, but a continuation of a massive transfer of political power that had begun eight years earlier, when the Democrats took control of the legislature in 1954.

On 3 December 1962, while still in the process of selecting his cabinet, John A. Burns was inaugurated as Hawaii's first Democratic governor. For the first time since Hawaii began to practice a semblance of self-government under the Organic Act of 1900, both the executive and legislative branches of government were under the control of the Democratic Party, a dominance that would soon enough be reflected in the state judiciary.

An article in the *Wall Street Journal* shortly after Burns' election had depicted the new governor of Hawaii as "a radical," and spoke of the fears of the economic establishment in the State. The article raised the question, "What manner of man is this who has just been elected Governor of the nation's newest state?" Another contemporary East Coast voice was finding out. In a letter to a friend, Tom Hamilton, the president of the University of Hawaii and former head of the multicampus State University of New York, described his first meeting with Hawaii's new governor:

In August of 1962, I accepted the presidency of the University of Hawaii. However, in New York, I still had the responsibility for presenting that budget to the Legislature. Thus, I could not assume full-time duties until January 1, 1963. . . .

This was the Fall of a political campaign, and a Governor was being elected. Before the election I steered clear of both candidates on my trips. . . . [The day after the election in November], in my office in Albany, I received a call from Hawaii. . . . Hawaii had elected, I was told, John A. Burns as Governor.

It seemed that my caller was able to restrain his enthusiasm with considerable ease. Furthermore, my informant continued, the new Governor was a Jacksonian. Obviously, the word "Jacksonian" distressed my caller quite a bit. . . . I simply made a mental note to make certain my hob-nailed boots were shined for the Inaugural Ball and remind Ginny not to be surprised if punch were served in washtubs on the lawns of Washington Place. . . .

My next trip to Hawaii was in mid-December. Now, I said, I should talk with the new Governor. And so a breakfast was arranged. I was to be picked up by the Governor's driver at seven a.m. . . . A little before seven, a limousine pulled into the drive [of the Moana Hotel], flags-a-flying. The driver was a thin-faced, ruddy complexioned man with a wisp of white hair that kept falling toward the eye. "By George," I thought, "Where have I seen a picture of this chauffeur?"

A hand was extended, and the driver said, "I'm Jack Burns. The driver was busy."

"Shades of Nelson Rockefeller!" I thought. "Hamilton, you are in a new state."

We proceeded to that little breakfast room in Washington Place . . . and talked. Man did we talk! And about what did we talk? Not the University, not the state of the economy, nor what I was going to do first; we discussed political philosophy.

Finally, I glanced at my watch. It was 11:40 [A.M.]. Having a luncheon date, I excused myself. My luncheon companions were still a bit long in the face. How, one asked, had I spent my morning? When I told them, the questions came fast. "How," they asked, "will he operate?" I replied as follows:

"One does not judge a human being on the basis of one conversation, even a long one. But two things seem clear to me. First, rightly or wrongly, he sees what has happened as the successful culmination of a peaceful revolution. He is not about to preside over its failure. Second, he is not a Jacksonian. He is a Jeffersonian. And there is a world of difference." Turns out I was right on both counts.

Although the president of the University of Hawaii was considered a member of the cabinet when Burns was elected, Tom Hamilton quickly, and wisely, persuaded the governor of the incompatibility of this arrangement. Hamilton and Burns agreed that the university president would attend meetings of the cabinet, but only as an observer. In his effort to keep the university out of politics, Hamilton had also balked at Burns' request that all members of the university's board of regents proffer a "courtesy resignation," which would allow him to appoint his own board. When Regent Herb Cornuelle asked Hamilton what he thought the board should do about Burns' request, Hamilton responded: "The purpose of having regents' terms so that they do not coincide with that of a governor is to minimize political control of education. . . . If you all resign, you should find yourself a new boy [president], because you will have admitted you have politicized the university."

Within two weeks of Burns' election, Chinn Ho, president of Capital Investment Company, and his attorney, City Councilman Matsy Takabuki, were in New York to discuss a business loan with representatives of Chase Manhattan Bank. They decided to use their presence in the nation's financial capital to soften the impression among New York bankers that John A. Burns was the "radical" the *Wall Street Journal* had painted him to be. Takabuki later recalled telling Chase Manhattan executives, "As far as land and fiscal policy [are concerned], . . . I'm convinced that you will find him to be more conservative than the prior governor, the Republican governor."

Ho and Takabuki gave the same assurances to Ed Palmer, senior vice president and head of First National City Bank's Western Regional Office. They asked Palmer, the man who had arranged the financing for Chinn Ho's Ilikai project, if he would help to arrange a meeting for Burns with representatives of various Wall Street firms. Palmer agreed. Upon his return to Hawaii, Takabuki met with Burns, telling him, "At the first opportunity, I think it's very important that you meet with people out there who are going to be the guys that [are] going to make the decisions about buying bonds . . . and giving loans to the State of Hawaii for its growth and development." In early 1963, while Burns was on a trip to Florida, Palmer arranged such a meeting. Burns went to New York and left the bankers he met convinced that he was, indeed, no radical.

Democratic Party Chairman Robert Oshiro led a similar effort in Hawaii:

> I made it very clear during the 1962 campaign, that the Democratic Party cannot become a Party of substance unless we communicate across the street. And that is when I began talking to these executives of Merchant Street: Hawaii Telephone, Hawaiian Electric, telling them our perspective, what we are looking for. . . . I would deliberately set up opportunities for these people to meet the Governor.

Governor Burns' first inaugural message carried no hint that he was a radical. In this speech, Burns made six pledges. First, "To secure for the people of Hawaii fair and equitable taxation." Second, "a thriving business and industrial community, . . . our only means of providing employment of youth, of providing a maximum expression of their precious talents for the good of all." In this statement, Burns was not advocating "business as usual." In a bow to small business, the governor called for "the discipline of open competition [to] best insure services and fair prices to us all."

Third, Burns made the pledge which had given him the "radical" label in the first place, reiterating his determination to force landowners to use their lands for "the fullest and best use for all the people of Hawaii. I am pledged to eradicate a practice which allows unproductive land to aggravate our land shortage, to inflate land prices, to avoid paying its share of the cost of government when all the while its value is increased by improvements wrought on productive land." Trying to assuage the fears that such a statement might evoke, Burns added that his land policies aimed at increasing "productivity," not at "vindictiveness."

If his third point sounded a bit Jacksonian, his fourth point was straight from Thomas Jefferson: "I have subscribed to that philosophy of government which would place at the local level those powers of self-government not better reserved to a higher level." Burns had campaigned hard on the charge that the Republicans did not trust the people of Hawaii to make their own decisions. The result, for generations, had been the rule of all the Islands by a small, appointed elite from Honolulu. Home rule issues would be in the forefront of the governor's 1963 legislative program.

Burns' fifth point occupied almost as much space in his address as the other five combined. The governor spoke expansively of his dream of Hawaii becoming "a center for stimulating greater exchanges between the people of the Pacific Basin, for providing services which would facilitate that exchange and attract the future Pacific trader to come to Hawaii for negotiations. For Hawaii is at the hub of the great wheel of the Pacific." Delegate Burns had sold this vision to Lyndon Johnson in the creation of the East-West Center. Burns based his faith in such a future not only on the central physical location of the Hawaiian Islands, but even more on the nature of the inheritance the State's multiethnic population had received from the Hawaiian people:

> Embodied in our people is the very blood of the Pacific peoples, the understanding of their peoples, the understanding of their cultures, a

feel for their needs. In the harmonious blending of peoples through understanding and trust, we have no peers. Although, through the long history of immigration to these shores the Hawaiian people became outnumbered, they still conquered all with their warmth, their generosity, their spirit of aloha, of brotherhood. They have given to all our people the potentiality of becoming the greatest ambassadors on the face of the earth.

Such sentiments came easily and naturally to Jack Burns. He had grown up in the midst of Kalihi's multiethnic population, sharing play and meals, good times and bad, with people from many different backgrounds. As a cop he had been exposed to all of Hawaii's people on the most basic level and had, in the war years and after, become their champion. He believed in all of them—Hawaiian, Japanese, Chinese, Filipino, Korean—and in their ability to contribute to a world larger than the confines of their island home. "Let us welcome this challenge," Burns implored, "confident in our own potentialities and in our ability to meet each new obstacle with wisdom and courage. Let us not be timid."

Burns' final pledge related to his Pacific theme: "As we move into our East-West role, our educational institutions must anticipate and play a leading part in the development of our evolving opportunities. We must insure that in the controversy of child versus money, the child comes first." The preceding sentence was the most frequently quoted from governor Burns' first inaugural—and it was his own. The draft speech did not include it. Burns penciled it in. He knew that if Hawaii's children were to lead, they must acquire an education equal to the challenges of a technological world and sufficient to overcome the psychological barriers inbred by more than a century of plantation paternalism.

As he neared the end of his speech, Burns sought to soothe those who feared he was a radical and to temper the feelings of those who hoped he was. He told the Iolani Palace crowd—estimated to number nine thousand—that "in bringing change, we must exercise due restraint." To those who feared the new governor would run the State into debt, Burns assured, "It will be my aim to raise no more revenue than will be necessary to promote these goals for which the people have expressed their desire."

The press responded cautiously to Burns' brief inaugural address. The *Honolulu Star-Bulletin* editorialized: "Many of the programs Governor Burns outlined might have been taken from the radio scripts of his predecessor. . . . One would find it difficult, from the inaugural address alone, to learn precisely what course the new Governor intends to set."

As Governor Burns prepared his legislative package, the house of representatives and senate organized themselves. The house, with a 40 to 11 Democratic margin, had little trouble in selecting Elmer Cravalho of Maui to continue as Speaker. The senate, however, in spite of a 15 to 10 Democratic margin, had a harder time getting organized. Neighbor island senators were disproportionately represented, and they chose to throw their weight around. Their eventual election of Nelson Doi of the Big Island as president of the senate proved a momentary victory, but it left behind feelings of resentment.

Governor Burns' state of the State message, on 21 February 1963, began with a note of fiscal alarm. "In the past statehood boom," he began, "our tax income was greater than our requirements. . . . Taxes on individuals and businesses were cut back. Substantial amounts of current income were used to finance capital improvements." The governor warned that by fiscal year 1965, the operating budget would be in deficit, "even if no improvements or new programs are authorized."

To back up his concerns, the governor explained that during the "boom years" of 1959 and 1960, personal income in Hawaii had grown by 12 percent per year. In 1961, that figure had dropped to 7 percent and by 1962, income growth had fallen to a mere 3 percent. Employment, which had expanded by nearly 24,000 workers from 1959 to 1960, grew by a "modest" 3,500 from 1960 to 1961. From 1961 to 1962, Burns told the joint session, employment had actually declined by 3,000 jobs. Unemployment had gone from 3 percent in 1959 to 4.5 percent in 1962. The result of all of this was that general fund tax revenues, which had increased by $9 million in fiscal year 1960 and $10 million in fiscal year 1961, were down by $500,000 in fiscal year 1962.

To close the anticipated gap between revenue and expenditures, Burns reiterated his intention to reform the tax assessment system. But the Democratic majority saw land reform as more than a way to enhance tax revenues and force nonproductive land into use. The legislature saw tax reform as a matter of simple justice and, in 1963, introduced three major bills on the subject. Burns, recognizing that the legislature would be introducing such measures, indicated that he would prefer to utilize existing statutory tools to address the current situation.

Burns' first legislative requests were tame and organizational in nature. He asked that the state Departments of Agriculture and Land and

Natural Resources be headed by directors appointed by the governor, rather than by boards that were appointed by the governor. The directors were to be members of the governor's cabinet. Burns also called for the merger of the Planning and Research Department with the Department of Economic Development. This arrangement, he asserted, "would provide a more orderly and efficient arrangement under which the economist, the researcher and the planner could work in close coordination." The name of the new sphere of duty would be the Department of Planning and Economic Development.

To bolster the economy, Burns called for the creation of a Foreign Trade Zone on Sand Island. He estimated the cost to the State to be a modest $30,000 to $40,000 per year. His plans for the University of Hawaii were more ambitious. Burns thought the university should serve as a magnet for what he called "think industries." He pointed to ongoing efforts in solar research on Maui, oceanography on Oahu, and the Pacific Missile Range on Kauai as examples of the kind of ventures Hawaii could attract with the aid of a strong university. Burns also made his first pitch for the completion of the medical school, which now bears his name, with both M.D. and Ph.D. degree programs. "The time is at hand," he said, "to lift our vision."

Burns next turned to "the disproportionate concentration of population and economic activity on Oahu," saying that it had "created a serious imbalance in our economy. . . . Our immediate need is to provide a variety of low-cost recreational and vacation facilities [for] . . . our Neighbor Islands." As a part of this effort, Burns gave his endorsement to legislative plans for an interisland transportation system. One of the legacies of the Burns era was the rapid development of the neighbor islands as tourist destinations. It was always near the top of his list of objectives.

Consistent with his wish to develop the neighbor islands, the governor believed that they should enjoy home rule. Burns introduced measures that would give the counties the right to appeal property assessments and remove the "ceiling" which then limited the rate at which counties could tax real property. This was something of a subterfuge, as Burns also intended to cut the disproportionate share of general excise tax then allocated to the neighbor islands. What he was offering with one hand, he intended to take away with the other. What he was suggesting, however, was certainly more rational than the system he was seeking to reform.

In the field of education, Burns called for the popular election of the state's school board and for a system of community colleges. While this was a nod in the direction of home rule, it fell far short of creating a decentralized educational system with autonomous school districts for each county. At this point, Burns had the view that the Manoa Campus of the University of Hawaii would eventually focus upon upper division and graduate work, leaving the first two years of instruction to the community colleges. He was not the first to conceive of such a system—or the last to see it fade away in the empire-building proclivities of state universities. Governor Burns also recommended a law school to go along with the proposed medical school.

Finally, Burns proposed a measure that would require each Party's candidates for governor and lieutenant governor to run together, as a team, in the general election. Had he been able to look ahead to 1966, he might have proposed that they run as a team in the primary election as well. The bill also stipulated that the lieutenant governor serve as the presiding officer of the state senate, as the U.S. Constitution does with the vice president, giving that office constitutional responsibility beyond the running of statewide elections.

The *Honolulu Star-Bulletin* was more positive in its characterization of Burns' first state of the State message than it had been in its assessment of his first inaugural address:

> He meets the challenge of shrinking tax income by proposing austerity budgets and by deferring capital improvements that can wait. . . . This is in sharp contrast to the national trend toward greater imbalance in budgets and tax-cutting at a time when deficits are piling up.
>
> His policies toward land reform are far less radical than those of some other members of his party—and urges that the Legislature move with deliberation in this area. Wait until the new assessment policies have had a chance to perform, and then act, is his counsel. It is good counsel.

Thus, the team was in place and a program had been presented to the state legislature. The stage was now set for the real beginning of the first term of Governor John A. Burns.

T·H·I·R·T·E·E·N

First Term

LAND REFORM WAS THE hottest issue of the 1963 legislative session. Lawmakers considered three different measures, before the Democratic majority finally settled on the Maryland Land Bill. The Maryland Land Bill took into account that most homeowners in Hawaii lived on leased land—people owned the improvements on the land, but not the land itself. This unique form of home ownership went back to the time of the Great Mahele of 1848, the division of land in Hawaii which created private property in the Western sense. Tragically, the division resulted in the transfer of most of the land into the hands of a very few people or entities. As Lawrence Fuchs pointed out:

> In 1959, the new state government owned 32 percent of all the land in Hawaii; the federal government nearly 8 percent; the Hawaiian Homes Commission 2.5 percent; and twelve private landholders owned 30 percent. . . . The biggest private owner was a charitable trust, the Bishop estate, whose 363,000 acres was more than the area possessed by the next two largest owners combined, Richard S. Smart, owner of the huge Parker Ranch on the Big Island, and the Damon estate. In all, twelve large private landholders—actually only eleven, since the Robinson family owned two estates—controlled 52 percent of all the private lands in Hawaii in the year of statehood. . . . The Bishop and Campbell estates owned 40 percent of the private land on Oahu, and over one-fourth of the entire island.

The Maryland Land Bill required large landowners who leased land to homeowners in Hawaii to agree to sell the land to the homeowner at "fair market value," providing the home had been owned for at least five years. As appealing as this sounded, Governor Burns had withheld his support of the legislation. The new governor was simply not prepared to take on the major owners of leased land—particularly the politically sensitive Bishop Estate, whose property represented the bulk of the endowment of the Kamehameha Schools.

Burns also feared that the Maryland Land Bill posed a serious constitutional problem. If the Fourteenth Amendment extended the constitutional prohibition against impairment of the obligation of contract, it would have rendered the five-year holding period in the Maryland Land Bill unconstitutional. Thus, leasehold conversion would be applicable only at the end of the term of the lease, creating two classes of homeowners in Hawaii—those with leaseholds eligible for conversion and those that were not. The result would have been serious inequities in the housing market.

While the Maryland Land Bill cruised through the house of representatives, it faced tougher going in the senate. Its two forceful Democratic opponents in the senate were described by George Cooper and Gavan Daws in their 1985 study, *Land and Power in Hawaii:*

> One of these was Harry M. Field from Maui, a part-Hawaiian sympathetic to the Bishop Estate, a major lessor whose lands amounted to a kind of surviving Hawaiian patrimony. The other was Mitsuyuki Kido, the senator-developer who, in 1959, had supported a bill to raise the pay of Bishop Estate trustees at the same time he was negotiating a co-venture with the Estate to develop 520 acres of its land in Heeia, Oahu.

With ten Republicans and two Democrats against the Maryland Land Bill, it fell to Senator George Ariyoshi to break a 12 to 12 deadlock. Ariyoshi had hesitated to commit himself earlier, but he finally voted against the bill for constitutional reasons. In his 1997 biography, *With Obligation to All,* Ariyoshi described the reaction to his tie-breaking vote:

> The criticism was thunderous. I had to wonder if my career in politics was over. In the process, I learned that Governor Burns actually agreed with my vote. He called and said he was pleased to see me take the position I had. He said it required courage to stand up for what I felt strongly about, and furthermore that I had saved him the trouble of vetoing the bill.

In their opposition to the Maryland Bill, Republican Senators Yasutaka Fukushima and William "Doc" Hill sounded like 1990s advocates of Hawaiian sovereignty. Fukushima told his senate colleagues, "I was brought up in an atmosphere that the lands of the Hawaiians should belong to the indigenous group." Hill sounded even more emphatic: "It would be a shame and disgrace for us here, who are really foreigners in Hawaii, to take from the Hawaiians what is justly theirs." Buck Buchwach, managing editor of the *Honolulu Advertiser*, reported ninety spectators witnessed the final senate debate on the Maryland Land Bill, forty of whom were Hawaiians wearing red ribbons symbolizing opposition to the measure. Representative Tom Gill was quoted from Washington, D.C., saying, "The failure of the Maryland Land Bill in the State Senate interposes another delay in our inevitable movement toward economic democracy in Hawaii."

Governor Burns got most of what he wanted from the 1963 legislature. Lawmakers passed his whole package of home rule legislation. Legislators also approved the structural changes the governor proposed for the Departments of Agriculture, Land, and Natural Resources and the Hawaii Homes Commission and agreed to merge the Departments of Planning and Economic Development, as requested.

Burns also received legislative approval of the election laws which he felt would reform the two-party system in Hawaii: the election of the governor and lieutenant governor as a team in the general election; voter registration under the control of each county clerk; and the closed primary, which ended the mischief of cross-over voting. The legislature also appropriated $75,000 to begin planning for the governor's much-coveted Foreign Trade Zone and, despite a tight budget, education was given the favored position he had requested. All in all, the new governor had much to be pleased about. The *Honolulu Star-Bulletin* called it "a good session," commenting that "much of the arrogance that accompanied the Democratic victory of 1954 has vanished as the years and political realities have brought maturity to the brash young men."

New York Times reporter Lawrence E. Davies found approval of Burns and the Democratic legislature among Hawaii's business leaders as well as its editorial writers. "They warily grant that Governor John A. Burns has been 'less radical' than they had feared," wrote Davies. "Some who bitterly opposed him say he has done a creditable job so far." As proof of Burns' conservatism, Davies cited the governor's signature on a personal history bill that required state employees to disclose whether they had ever been members of the Communist Party.

The accomplishments of Burns' first legislative session may have required humility and a moderating of positions, but they also required hard work. By the end of his first legislative session, Jack Burns had fallen into a long daily routine that he would follow through much of his governorship. He would rise early to make daily 7:00 A.M. Mass at the Catholic Cathedral on Fort Street Mall. He would then return to Washington Place for breakfast. It was at the Washington Place breakfast table that his workday began. "I would say that nine days out of ten he would have someone there for breakfast, somebody he needed to talk to . . . it could be a newspaper reporter, one of his cabinet members, a businessman," Bea Burns remembered. When the whole cabinet gathered for breakfast in Washington Place's small breakfast nook, "people ricocheted off the walls it was so crowded."

Honolulu Advertiser editor George Chaplin became a frequent Burns breakfast companion at Washington Place. "He'd be sitting there, usually with the *Advertiser* in front of him, and kind of grunt at you when you came in," Chaplin remembered. "Small talk was not his strong point. And then the scrambled eggs would come out, and he liked a lot of ketchup on his eggs. . . . Then he'd sit there and either keep reading the paper while we were eating or the phone would ring or he'd call or something and change his schedule. Sooner or later the ice was broken and it usually developed into an animated conversation running over all kinds of things. . . . But he was never, really, that much of a social animal. Very reserved man. . . . Jack didn't care for small talk. He wanted to talk about the meat of a problem and the substance, although he'd get into a little gossip now and then, which was a little bit of fun and you'd think . . . out of character for him, but it was never vicious gossip."

In his office on the second floor of Iolani Palace, secretary Mary Isa took charge of his day. Theirs was a long and complex relationship. "He gave you responsibility and allowed you to carry it out," she remembered three years after Burns' death, "which caused you to work harder to live up to his expectations. He was not a paperwork man. He wore me out trying to keep track of things on his desk. I claimed he lost things, and he claimed I lost them—endlessly." Such arguments resulted in Burns' nickname for Isa, "Miss Spitfire."

Isa often found herself frustrated by Burns. "He had poor working habits," she observed. "He would call me or other staff or department heads at 10:00 or 11:00 P.M. at home about something he wanted to get said right then and there before he forgot about it." His lack of attention to paperwork and his tendency to let off steam at Isa and administrative assistant Dan Aoki sometimes became difficult to bear. At one point during Burns' governorship, Isa drafted a letter of resignation— just as she had once before in Washington, D.C. But just as she had in Washington, she tore it up. "I knew that I was serving alongside a man who was doing great things for Hawaii, and I felt a commitment to the man and to the 'cause.'

"Part of his problem was his need to talk to people. He had a marvelous sense of the grass roots. He would stop and talk to people on his way to church or to the Capitol. And his door was always open to department heads and legislators. It was my job to keep people moving along." Because of this "need to talk to people," traffic jams often developed in Burns' outer office. When Isa would stick her head in his inner office to remind Burns of someone waiting to see him, he would often respond: "He can wait." "He felt that a person would sit and wait to see him as long as necessary if his business was really important."

Burns worked a long day at the Capitol, "in the beginning from 9:00 A.M. to 10:00 P.M. I frequently took work to him at Washington Place"—where Bea Burns watched it pile up. "He used to work at home. . . . He didn't have much time to do paperwork in the office. (There) it was either interviews or phone calls. So all his paperwork was at home. The breakfast room looked like it had been shot at and missed. . . . And even the State dining room had papers lined up there that we didn't dare touch. . . . Then his bedroom was another big, fat mess because he had papers all over there."

In his second state of the State address, on 19 February 1964, Burns had a list of good numbers to report: an increase of 2,500 jobs in 1963 (versus a loss of 2,500 jobs in 1962); $268 million in construction in 1963, up slightly from the previous year; a rise in personal income from $1.59 billion in 1962 to $1.66 billion in 1963; a 5 percent increase in diversified manufacturing; and sugar prices at their highest level in forty years.

But the governor indicated that he felt the Islands' economic future did not lay with sugar: "From both a short and long term point of view . . . tourism shows the greatest promise of sustained growth." The tourist industry, Burns reported, had brought $170 million into the economy in 1963 (versus $154 million in 1962). More than 427,000 tourists had visited the Islands in 1963 (versus 365,000 in 1962). Hawaii had hosted forty-four conventions in 1963 (versus eleven in 1962).

Experts, Burns told the assembled lawmakers, were expecting 475,000 visitors to Hawaii in 1964. The governor thought that number would exceed 500,000. Experts also saw a need for 10,000 to 15,000 new hotel rooms in Hawaii by 1968. The governor thought the number would be closer to 20,000. Burns confidently predicted that the ratio of new jobs in the construction industry to new hotel rooms would be 2 to 1. While critics complained that tourism was creating a new plantation economy, with too many menial, low-paying jobs, Burns disagreed. Instead, he touted tourism as a "recession-proof" industry, citing Hawaii's growth of tourism during the national recessions of 1953–1954, 1957–1958, and 1960.

Returning to one of his favorite themes, Burns commented on his 1963 trips to Japan on behalf of the Hawaii Visitor's Bureau, to Europe "in the interest of trade and economic development," and to Korea, as an official representative of President Johnson. These experiences, Burns said, convinced him that Hawaii had a pivotal role to play in "world affairs, particularly in the Pacific area. There appear to be opportunities for our political experience and the talents and attitudes of our multi-racial people to have a constructive effect in countries seeking the stability and harmony which we have developed in this mid-Pacific Island State."

Burns also spoke glowingly of recent developments in science and education. He boasted of the growing stature of the University of Hawaii and the East-West Center; the new Geophysics building at Manoa; the solar observatory at the tip of Haleakala, involving the Universities of Hawaii and Michigan and the Smithsonian Institution; the $2.5 million improvement of NASA's space tracking station on Kauai; the $4 million expansion of the Pacific Missile Range's satellite tracking station at South Point on the Big Island; oceanographic research that the university was beginning at Kewalo Basin and Makapuu; and cooperative efforts being made with the U.S. Bureau of Commercial Fisheries aboard the university's research vessel, *Townsend Cromwell*. "Centuries ago," Burns intoned, "the Western World revolved around the Mediterranean. In the last century, the Atlantic has provided the major trading patterns linking nations together. Now we are in the Pacific Era. We must know our ocean, what's in it and what surrounds it."

"The tragic assassination of President John F. Kennedy" in November 1963 would also affect Hawaii. In his address, Burns spoke about what Lyndon Johnson's presidency could mean for the State: "Hawaii's faith in and loyalty to our new President are second to that of no other State in the Union. I am equally convinced," Burns said of his friend and mentor, "that never before . . . have we had a President more aware of the needs and potential of Hawaii, or more dedicated to programs through which our destiny can be achieved." Clearly, a Burns administration in Hawaii would have a stronger voice in Washington, D.C., with Johnson as president than it had had with Kennedy.

Burns expressed particular pleasure with President Johnson's December 1963 signature on a bill to return Sand Island to the State of Hawaii, thus clearing "the way for us to move ahead with plans for the creation of a Foreign Trade Zone in Honolulu Harbor." He also cited the return of Pier 39 and twenty acres of "backup area" adjoining the harbor; forty-two acres of "prime industrial land in the Fort Shafter Heights area"; and another forty-six acres at Bellows Air Force Station on Windward Oahu, including one mile of beachfront.

But the State had problems. The Burns administration went into the 1964 budget session confronting a $10 million revenue shortfall. The governor sought to cover the deficit by going back to two beneficiaries of his 1963 legislative efforts—the neighbor islands and the University of Hawaii. The night before the budget session began, the governor had gone on television to explain to the public that the neighbor islands received a far greater share of tax revenues than their population justified. Burns had used a chart to make his point:

County	% of State Population	% of Tax Revenues Received
Honolulu	80%	55%
Hawaii	9%	20%
Maui	7%	15%
Kauai	4%	10%

Burns pointed out that new taxing powers had been granted to the neighbor island counties by the 1963 session of the state legislature. He also promised that the State would continue to provide diminishing subsidies until the less populous counties could "achieve a more independent fiscal status."

Burns reiterated his 1963 projection of a five- or six-year period during which state revenues would fall short of expenditures. He cut back his expenditure projection from $180 million to $174.4 million and his revenue projection from $177 million to $165.5 million. He pointed out that although Hawaii's economy was expected to grow at a rate of 4.6 percent for fiscal year 1965, this good news was tempered by state revenue projections of only 3.2 percent growth during the same period and state expenditure projections of 3.8 percent growth.

The disparity between the growth of state revenues and expenditures, Burns explained, was due to the expansion of state government. "Workers in State and County functions in Hawaii," Burns reported, "have increased from 17,000 ten years ago to 25,000 in 1963." The governor then compared the cost of other state governments to Hawaii's. His most telling point was that the annual per capita cost of administering state government in Hawaii was $20, compared to a $12 national average. "Are the people of these Islands," Burns asked, "getting their money's worth?"

Burns promised that his administration would work harder and smarter, but he also asked a question about tax fairness: "Our real property taxes are the lowest in the nation, the closest being found in the states in the South where property rights are paramount to human rights. Our property taxes," Burns asserted, "were originally conceived in the same vein." Burns assured the legislators that his new appraisal system was in place and would bring appraisals into a more realistic relationship with market values. Burns then turned to the centerpiece of his brand of land reform:

> Land is being assessed at "highest and best use," as provided by law. . . .
> Larger holdings will not receive special treatment, as has been the case
> in the past. . . . It is hoped that the result will be a more equitable dis-
> tribution of real property and its taxes so that homeowners are carry-
> ing no more than their fair share, and large land owners will be influ-
> enced to make more land available for homesite ownership in fee, as
> well as for other uses.

Burns did not fare as well in the 1964 budget session as he had in the 1963 session. His biggest disappointment on the funding side was the legislature's failure to approve his request for $1 million for his Foreign Trade Zone on Sand Island. *Honolulu Advertiser* managing editor Buck Buchwach reported, however, that the legislature "did juggle the funds and came up with $683,000 unspent for Waimanalo development in last year's appropriations they may use to get started on the zone." The governor also came up against the unwillingness of neighbor island senators to approve reallocation of state excise taxes in a manner more representative of Hawaii's population. Their refusal to do so became more than a budgetary question when, on 26 March 1964, two days before the budget session came to a close, the U.S. Supreme Court issued its "one-man-one-vote" decision in *Baker v. Carr*. The decision said that states could not follow the federal model in the apportionment of members to the upper houses of state legislatures. In other words, the state senate would have to reflect the state's population in the same way as the state house of representatives. When, on 15 June 1964, the U.S. Supreme Court applied the principles of *Baker v. Carr* to the states of Virginia, Colorado, Delaware, Alabama, New York, and Maryland, Governor Burns decided to act.

On 16 July 1964, Burns called the state legislature into a special session, to commence on 23 July, to reapportion the state senate. The charts below show the *Baker v. Carr* implications for Hawaii. The figures appeared in the *Sunday Star-Bulletin & Advertiser* three days before the beginning of the budget session, showing that the *Baker v. Carr* decision was not unexpected.

Senate Representation, Population and Voter Registration

County (% of Senate)	Civilian Population (% of State)	Registered Voters (% of State)
Honolulu (40%)	513,500 (79.1%)	164,300 (74.1%)
Hawaii (28%)	62,300 (9.6%)	27,200 (12.3%)
Maui (20%)	45,500 (7.0%)	18,300 (8.3%)
Kauai (12%)	28,100 (4.3%)	11,800 (5.3%)

Senate Representation Options

County	1962 Election	By Population	By Voter Registration
Honolulu	10	20	19
Hawaii	7	2	3
Maui	5	2	2
Kauai	3	1	1

Immediately, the state senate confronted a provision in the Hawaii state Constitution intended to protect the rights of the neighbor islands. It provided that any change in apportionment required "a majority vote from a majority of the State's counties," making it theoretically possible for 2.5 percent of the State's population (just over 15,000 voters from Maui and Kauai) to nullify any legislative effort at reapportionment.

The plan Jack Burns presented to the special session went beyond the minimum required to meet *Baker v. Carr* standards. He also wanted an interim plan that would go into effect for the 1964 primary elections, less than three months away. Burns' plan sought to set the size of the house and senate at their current levels—fifty-one members of the house and twenty-five members in the senate; delete the proviso that a candidate reside in the district he or she sought to represent; establish single-member districts for both the house and the senate; and establish that the apportionment be based upon the decennial census, which included aliens and military in the State. Burns' proposal proved a recipe for stalemate, although the simplest plan would have met intense opposition from the neighbor islands—and the ILWU. The special session ended after thirty futile days of argument.

Neighbor island legislators denounced Burns for having called the special session in such haste. Maui senator Nadao Yoshinaga said, "The blame is on one man alone and that is the Governor of the State of Hawaii." Big Island Republican senator "Doc" Hill, charged: "I've never seen a blunder as great as was made in the calling of this session." Within less than six months, the governor's critics would have good reason to eat their words. Perhaps Governor Burns would have been less forceful in handling the issue had he been facing reelection in 1964. Many of the legislators were, however, and they did not relish the free-for-all which would have accompanied a hastily redrawn political map.

The highlight of the 1964 election season was Tom Gill's challenge of Hiram Fong for his seat in the U.S. Senate. In the primary, Gill easily defeated Nadao Yoshinaga, garnering almost 40,000 votes more than Fong in the newly closed Party primary. The Democrats waited until the November general election to cross over to vote for the popular Hiram Fong. In the general election, with President Lyndon Johnson carrying the State of Hawaii with 78.7 percent of the vote over Republican challenger Barry Goldwater, Fong defeated Gill by 14,000 votes, having overcome a 16-point mid-August deficit in the polls (Gill 50%; Fong 34%; undecided 16%).

In other top contests, Democrats Spark Matsunaga and Patsy Mink breezed to victory in their races for the U.S. House of Representatives. In the Hawaii state legislature, the Democrats picked up a seat in the senate; likewise, the Republicans picked up one seat in the house of representatives. Another popular Republican vote-getter, Mayor Neal Blaisdell, joined Fong in the winner's circle. Both Blaisdell and Fong were backed by the ILWU. The political landscape after the 1964 elections could be described as status quo ante bellum.

But the Democrats did have a problem; Gill had relinquished his seat in the U.S. House of Representatives in an effort to defeat Fong for the U.S. Senate. Patsy Mink had won Gill's old seat, leaving Gill—a young, smart, ambitious politician—without a job. Burns decided to make Tom Gill the director of Hawaii's Office of Economic Opportunity. As a member of Congress, Gill had worked on the legislation which created the OEO. He knew the law and he knew his way around the nation's capital. It was a logical and gracious appointment, and Gill did an excellent job as Hawaii's OEO director. But ten years later, Burns loyalist Dan Aoki still bristled: "What did he do? Organize a political organization right under Governor Burns' nose."

On 17 February 1965, the Hawaii state legislature convened in general session. That same day, a three-judge federal district court panel ruled that Hawaii must redistrict its state senate in compliance with *Baker v. Carr.* The three-judge panel also invalidated that portion of the Hawaii state Constitution which would have made it possible for a small minority of voters from the neighbor islands to exercise a virtual veto over senate reapportionment. The federal court next ruled that this reapportionment must be done on a timetable set forth by them, ruling that on or before:

1. 1 August 1965, there must be a plebiscite in which the voters of the State of Hawaii determined whether or not to hold a Constitutional Convention on the subject of reapportionment.
2. 15 September 1965, delegates to the Convention (if held) must be elected.
3. 15 October 1965, the Constitutional Convention (if held) must open.
4. 15 January 1966, there must be another plebiscite to ratify the work of the Constitutional Convention (if held).

Failure of the legislature to act or of the voters to call for a Constitutional Convention would result in a court-ordered reapportionment plan. Furthermore, the federal court ordered, action on reapportionment must precede any other business of the state legislature.

If ever a governor had the right to say, "I told you so," Jack Burns had it in February 1965. But the governor refused to gloat. In his 1965 state of the State address, Burns did not even mention the matter of reapportionment. When questioned about this omission by the press, Burns said simply, "The court took a fairly firm position on that, didn't it? There's nothing left for me to add." In the twenty-minute message he did deliver to the joint session, once again Burns emphasized tourism, foreign trade, education, governmental reorganization, and tax reform.

Kazuhisa Abe, the Big Island senator who had replaced Nelson Doi as president of the senate, protested the federal court order on reapportionment. "The court has no right to say it should be the first order of business. I think it's an unreasonable interference with the legislative function." Abe's protestations notwithstanding, the legislature immediately petitioned the court to allow them to prepare a reapportionment plan themselves, in lieu of holding a Constitutional Convention. The federal court approved their petition on 9 March 1965. On 14 April, the legislature submitted their plan, which called for six state senators to be elected from four districts on the neighbor islands and nineteen senators to be elected from two districts on Oahu. Two weeks later, the federal court rejected the legislature's plan on the following grounds:

> This court finds that the present multi-member district scheme of senatorial reapportionment resulted, in material part at least, from gerrymandering . . . [and] does not meet the test of equality of representation set down by our Supreme Court. Circuitous or expensive as it may be, the route . . . of a constitutional convention must be followed.

On 21 May 1965, the U.S. Supreme Court granted the Hawaii state legislature the right to complete its legislative session, pending the outcome of their appeal of the federal district court's 28 April decision.

Another eleven months passed before the U.S. Supreme Court accepted a modified version of the legislature's proposal as an interim plan for Hawaii's 1966 elections. The court allowed multimember districts, "unless it can be shown that multi-member districts have been drawn to minimize or cancel out the voting strength of racial or political elements of the voting population." But the court insisted on eight districts rather than six—three on the neighbor islands and five on Oahu. The original plan of the state legislature had included two senatorial districts on Oahu, one with ten and the other with nine senators; the Supreme Court allowed no more than four members in any multimember district. While an interim plan was now in place for the 1966 elections, the Supreme Court instructed the state legislature to prepare an amendment to the Hawaii state Constitution containing "the pertinent provisions of the interim plan to be submitted to the people for approval at the [1966] election."

While this dramatic shift in power from the neighbor islands to Oahu was taking place, the Burns administration continued to press its agenda. Commenting on Burns' style at the conclusion of the extended and overshadowed 1965 general session, Dan Tuttle, a University of Hawaii political science professor, wrote:

> Eschewing the spotlight as an aggressive gubernatorial leader, the Governor, it should be noted, chose instead to work deftly and firmly behind the scenes in order to help guide the "Educational Legislature" to a successful conclusion, reapportionment problems notwithstanding. . . . If, indeed, House Speaker Cravalho and Senator Nadao Yoshinaga were directors of the 1965 production, Governor Burns was the ever attentive producer. . . . In short, the man named Burns still delights in reflected rather than direct glory.

The relationship between Burns and the state legislatures of the 1960s was close, almost symbiotic. Jack Kellner reported on state government for radio station KHVH and later for television station KGMB in the 1960s: "The legislature was made up of the 1954 revolutionaries," Kellner remembered. "Oh, there was the Nelson Doi bunch, Walter Heen's bunch, Najo Yoshinaga's bunch, Larry Kuriyama's bunch; they had their differences. But they'd all gone through a period of history together."

It was a particularly dramatic period of history—one they had shared with Jack Burns. According to Kellner, "Burns was much more than the titular leader of the Democratic Party. You constantly heard legislators asking, 'What does the old man want?' His desires were given consideration at the legislature and at party conventions as well."

In 1966, Governor John A. Burns and most of his legislative friends were going back to the voters of Hawaii for their first report card. Burns would be forced to do it while fighting off attacks from within his own party, as well as those from Republicans. It would be a painful year for the governor, but one in which he would emerge victorious and from which he would learn much.

A Case of the Hives

WHILE JACK BURNS SPENT his first term as governor bringing new people and a new philosophy into Iolani Palace, Bea Burns spent her first term as First Lady settling into Washington Place—and leaving her mark on it. "I didn't look forward to moving into Washington Place," she remembered. "I thought it would be proscribed. I thought I wouldn't be free, that none of us would be. . . . I just felt it would narrow the scope. Instead of that, it enlarged it. I was happily surprised. I didn't do anything outstanding there . . . but whatever I did was more effective because I was there. I had more clout." Her husband gave it to her. "Jack . . . turned Washington Place over to me, he said, 'That's your *kuleana.*'"

Bea had always loved growing things, but she found the gardens at Washington Place "in very bad shape." At her husband's suggestion, she called in members of Outdoor Circle and several other organizations, fed them lunch, and showed them the sorry state of the grounds. They came up with a landscaping plan, but Washington Place had only a single gardener to implement it. "There was nobody on weekends or holidays or if somebody got sick . . . so Jack used to come home at eleven o'clock and go out and turn the sprinklers on."

So Bea went after more help, and this time she knew the drill. She put on two lunches, one for the members of the senate Ways and Means Committee, the other for the members of the house Finance Committee. "Before lunch I took them all around the grounds and through the house and I explained and they said, 'Why didn't you tell us before?'" Bea soon had four gardeners and a maintenance staff. By the time she left Washington Place in 1974, a crew of twenty-three were taking care of the grounds of the governor's mansion, the Capitol, and the Judiciary. Washington Place had a cook as well, so for the first time in her life

Bea was relieved of the responsibility of preparing meals. But the greatest freedom of Washington Place came with the governor's limousine: "I had transportation, which I'd never had before. That made it great." It wasn't always great for the security people who drove the cars. Burns himself was an ex-cop whose job had taken him up and down every highway on Oahu. Bea hadn't driven since stricken with polio in 1935. "The security men used to say, 'If you're drivin' Papa, he'll tell you exactly where to go. But if you drive Mama and trust her directions, you'll end up in Kahuku every time.'"

Jack Burns himself appeared very much in the driver's seat as he entered the 1966 election year. As he pointed out in his state of the State message to a joint session of the Hawaii state legislature on 16 February:

- More than 600,000 visitors came to Hawaii in 1965 (versus 365,000 in 1962, the year before he claimed the governor's chair).
- Tourism added $260 million to Hawaii's economy in 1965 (versus $154 million in 1962).
- The University of Hawaii budget for fiscal year 1967 was set at $42 million (versus $14.6 million in 1962), with less than half coming from Hawaii tax dollars.
- The student population was up by 42 percent since 1962, while state support was up by only 29.4 percent.
- Public school enrollment was up by 6.5 percent since 1963, while support per student had risen by 32.8 percent.
- While the state's population had grown by 10.4 percent since 1963, general fund support for public libraries had increased by 57.2 percent.
- Since December 1962, Burns had made official visits to Japan, Taiwan, the Philippines, Okinawa, Vietnam, New Zealand, and British Columbia.
- During the same period, the East-West Center had established programs in Thailand, Pakistan, the Ryukyus, Samoa, and Micronesia.
- The legislature had gone into its 1964 session looking at a $10 million revenue shortfall. In fiscal 1966, a $6.3 million surplus was anticipated.

Such impressive statistics helped to provide Jack Burns with the first good press of his political career. The intimacy of Iolani Palace undoubtedly contributed as well. "Before the new Capitol was built, the reporters used to sit on the back steps of the Palace," *Honolulu Star-Bulletin* political writer Doug Boswell remembered. "From there you could see Washington Place. Burns would come out of Washington Place and walk down Miller Street toward the Palace. Often he would sit down on the steps with the reporters and talk. He'd also come down to the press room in the Palace basement to talk. He'd stay for forty-five minutes or so, chewing the fat."

The *Star-Bulletin*'s Tom Coffman remembered evening meetings with Burns as well: "At *pau hana* time the reporters would sit out on the back stairs of the Palace. The minah birds gathered in the trees. The evening light. Jack would come out, have a couple of cigarettes, and talk off the record. Larry McManus [of the rival *Advertiser*] entitled his political column 'The Back Stairs of the Palace.'" According to Bea Burns, the resulting good treatment in the press "scared the pie out of Jack. He thought he'd done something wrong."

Given his choice, Burns would have preferred to run for reelection with his current lieutenant governor, the popular Bill Richardson. But in 1962 Burns had promised Richardson a seat on the supreme court at the end of one term as lieutenant governor. The matter came to a head on 18 December 1965, when Chief Justice Wilfred C. Tsukiyama announced his intention to resign. As Doug Boswell of the *Honolulu Star-Bulletin* observed that day, "Richardson was regarded as the likely choice of Governor John A. Burns to succeed Tsukiyama on the high court."

Had he wanted it, Bill Richardson could have written his own political ticket at the beginning of 1966—lieutenant governor from 1966 to 1970; governor in 1970. When Burns put it to him, Richardson replied, "Well, I'd rather be chief justice at this point." Burns responded, "What about Amy [Richardson's wife]?" Richardson's reply was, "Jack, you've got to ask her yourself." Remembering the difficulty he had convincing Amy Richardson that her husband should run for lieutenant governor in 1962, Burns was not optimistic. When he did ask, his lack of optimism proved to be justified. "I've always given you a straight answer," Amy Richardson responded. "Chief justice."

Had Burns known what was in store for him, he might have fought harder to keep Richardson as his lieutenant governor. But with Richardson leaving office before the end of his term, the governor still had an opportunity to place his second choice for the post in a position to run as an incumbent. In 1965, the state legislature had passed a law providing for succession to the office of lieutenant governor, should it become vacant. The first person in line was the president of the senate, but Kazuhisa Abe took himself out of contention the day of Tsukiyama's resignation. That suited Burns because the person second in line was the Speaker of the House, Elmer Cravalho. As early as 18 December 1965, in the same article in which he identified Richardson as Burns' probable choice for the next chief justice, Doug Boswell wrote that Burns "reportedly believes the post would groom Cravalho for a shot at the governorship in 1970." Although Boswell reported that "Cravalho is reported to have told Burns that he would not accept," Burns had reason to believe that he could change the Speaker's mind.

In Cravalho's own words, he and the governor got along very well:

> I felt free to walk up any time, and he would walk down anytime, and just drop in casually, especially sometimes late in the afternoon. . . . He'd come from upstairs and we'd sit on the steps of Iolani Palace, you know, and just sit and talk. And sometimes he'd take me to have dinner at Washington Place. Jack was a very Spartan man, very common and very simple—in his food, his tastes, in his table. And it was a pleasure. He never put on the dog. . . . It was a very, very good relationship.

By the time of Richardson's official appointment to the supreme court, on 25 February 1966, the press was again speculating that Cravalho would be Burns' running mate in the fall. As the *Honolulu Advertiser* wrote the very next day, "The Richardson appointment also sets in motion a chain of political developments that could affect the leadership of Hawaii for another decade. . . . By almost all reliable reports, it's just a matter of time until Cravalho moves up following Richardson's confirmation in mid-March."

Eleven years later, Cravalho admitted that he created confusion over whether he would agree to become Richardson's replacement. "There isn't a soul . . . who can ever say that I ever told him 'yes,' I would, . . . but at the same time, I never said 'no,' during the preliminary discussions. . . . So, in that sense, by my silence, I believe I misled the governor to believe that it would be 'yes.'" According to Cravalho, it was Burns' unwillingness to be specific about the job that made him hesitate. He recalled asking the Governor: "What do you want me to do as lieutenant governor? I ask you for nothing, no patronage, no nothing. You just tell me." Burns responded,

"Well, Mr. Speaker, we'll work it out." When Cravalho repeated that he would not take the position without a specific job description, Burns is reported to have said, "Go home to Maui and think about it."

Elmer Cravalho went home to Maui for the weekend to "think about it" and to talk with friends. His friends were unanimous in urging him to take the lieutenant governorship. When Cravalho returned from Maui, he carried two letters—one was an acceptance letter and the other a letter of rejection. When Burns persisted with his "we'll work it out" approach to a job description, Cravalho pulled out the rejection letter and walked it downstairs to the waiting press. The following day, Burns spent another hour trying to convince Cravalho to change his mind, but to no avail. At the end of the meeting, Cravalho told the press, "I finally convinced him I could be more valuable in the legislative branch than in the executive." To cloud the air even more, an enigmatic Cravalho added, "If I accept now, it would close the door to other Democratic candidates and I don't want that to happen. My declining now, however, doesn't preclude my running for the post later this year."

Many have speculated about Cravalho's unwillingness to accept the State's second spot and, perhaps eventually, the governorship itself. He would later offer excuses: "I don't like the pomp, the ceremony, the trappings of office," and "I didn't want to be in a position of being tracked . . . or committed for a period of eight years." Ultimately, personal considerations made a return to Maui more attractive to Cravalho than exposing himself to the rigors and scrutiny of statewide politics. As it turned out, Cravalho resigned as Speaker of the House the next year and returned to Maui, where he served as mayor from 1967 to 1979.

Burns still had one more acceptable constitutional officer whom he would welcome as both lieutenant governor and as a running mate in the fall election—Attorney General Bert Kobayashi, who stood next in line of succession for the remainder of Richardson's term. But in a letter dated 5 April 1966, Kobayashi added to the confusion by declining the office while saying that he was "giving serious thought to possibly running for the position of Lieutenant Governor during the . . . coming elections." That decision, Kobayashi wrote, "will require considerable self-appraisal and a series of probing discussions. . . . [But] because I wish to be fair to any and all prospective candidates for the Lieutenant Governorship, I respectfully decline to take advantage of the succession law."

In 1980, Bert Kobayashi made it clear that he never intended to run for lieutenant governor: "No way. I love politics, but no. I had resolved never to run. So what does [Burns] do, the rascal? Comes over to my house and tries to prevail upon my wife until about 1:30 in the morning to see whether through my wife he can convince me to run for office. My wife's answer was just very simple: 'It's up to Daddy.'" The probable explanation for Cravalho's and Kobayashi's keeping their options open to run for lieutenant governor is that they were trying to help the governor forestall his worst nightmare—a Gill candidacy for the second spot.

On 13 April 1966, Governor Burns finally resolved his short-term problem, announcing that Andrew Ing, state director of budget and finance and fourth in the line of succession to the lieutenant governor's office, would complete Richardson's term. Ing had no ambition to run for the office of lieutenant governor in the fall elections, now less than six months away. A Harvard M.B.A., Ing was interested in business and finance, not politics. He served Governor Burns and the State of Hawaii out of a sense of responsibility, at considerable financial sacrifice to himself and his family. After his brief term as lieutenant governor, Ing returned to Budget and Finance.

That out of the way, Burns faced his long-term problem. Having been turned down by Richardson, Cravalho, and Kobayashi, he had to find a running mate who had not already made his political commitments for the year. While pondering that question, Tom Gill came to his office to pay a courtesy call. Gill's opening gambit was characteristically abrasive: "Do you think you'd get hives if I was your lieutenant governor?" Gill followed this up by asking the governor if he thought he could work with him. "The big question," Burns corrected Gill, "is whether you can work for me? Because there is only one decision-maker around here, in the final analysis. It's not a Burns–Gill administration, it's a Burns administration." As Gill recalled the meeting, "He made it very clear that he'd prefer somebody else."

Why would Tom Gill want to run for lieutenant governor when the man he would have to work with most intimately clearly did not want him around? Looking back ten years later, Gill explained: "I didn't want to run for Congress again, because after all Patsy [Mink] had [won] the seat I left open [in 1964]. It seemed like bad cricket. . . . So the lieutenant governor spot was open . . . and it seemed to me this was a good thing to do. At least I thought I could do all right at it." What Gill did not say in his 1976 interview, but readily acknowledged in 1993, was that he saw the lieutenant governorship as a stepping stone to the governorship in 1970. He added that he did not expect Burns to run for a third term in 1970.

Over the weekend of 21–22 May 1966, both political parties held their state conventions. Most observers expected the highlight of the Republican Convention to be the announcement by Honolulu Mayor Neal Blaisdell that he would seek the governorship in 1966. But, in a dramatic statement to the assembled delegates, Blaisdell announced that he would not oppose Burns for governor. In his history, *The City and County of Honolulu,* Professor Donald D. Johnson of the University of Hawaii wrote:

> For some city and state workers, such a campaign would have created a painful division of loyalties, for many had supported both Blaisdell for Mayor and Burns for Governor. Furthermore, department heads and others in the city structure stood to lose their non-civil service posts if a change of Mayor took place. Angel Maehara and other political advisors close to Blaisdell therefore argued against the change, contending that the Republicans were merely trying to use the Mayor to strengthen their ticket, which was undoubtedly true. Political writer Doug Boswell made two contemporaneous points about Blaisdell's decision not to run for Governor. First, he noted that "political observers at the [Republican] convention Saturday were struck by the image of a Blaisdell organization which operates in isolation, outside of the Republican stream." Second, Boswell speculated that those mainstream Republicans who wanted Blaisdell to "anchor" the Republican ticket were "ignoring the possibility that Blaisdell himself might suffer a defeat."

At age 63, Blaisdell was in the middle of his fourth term as Honolulu's mayor. Two years later, in 1968, Blaisdell retired rather than endure another electoral contest against the ever-present Frank Fasi. Herman Lemke, who chaired the Honolulu City Council at the time, later opined that Blaisdell left public office because of family pressure. As Lemke speculated, "I guess he said, 'The hell with it.'" There was speculation that Burns had kept Blaisdell out of the 1966 governor's race by promising that he would make him a trustee of the Bishop Estate. Lemke said that he had no personal knowledge of such a deal, but he did say that Blaisdell was disappointed when he was passed over as a Bishop Estate trustee in 1968 in favor of Burns loyalist Hung Wo Ching. The governor, of course, could not guarantee an appointment to the board of the Bishop Estate. While Burns undoubtedly had significant influence over individual members of the supreme court, the ultimate appointment was theirs to make.

Following Blaisdell's announcement that he would not run for governor in 1966, Burns issued a warning to the five hundred Democratic delegates who had gathered for their convention at the Ilikai: "Now that the Republicans have lost their strongest candidate, we must guard against complacency. The party that goes cocksure into a campaign often gets knocked off." The big news from the Democratic Convention was that the Party had apparently come to grips with the lieutenant governor's race. As Doug Boswell reported, "sources said the decision, if it is adhered to, means that Governor John A. Burns and his political lieutenants will make no overt attempt to deny the nomination to former Congressman Thomas P. Gill."

On 9 June, the public got the first glimpse of a political project that Governor Burns had been working on when Larry McManus wrote an article for the *Honolulu Advertiser* under the headline, "Kamaaina 'Defects' to Demos." The story described the political metamorphosis of Kenneth F. Brown, scion of one of the State's best known Hawaiian families. Burns had first met Brown at the Waialae Country Club, where Burns was offered a courtesy membership after he became governor in 1963. Brown was the club president and a respectable golfer. He and Burns developed a quick liking for one another both on and off the golf course. Looking back in 1978, Kenny Brown said of Burns, "I'm convinced that he's the most intelligent man I have ever known." This was quite a tribute from a man who had been educated at Punahou, Hotchkiss, and Princeton.

As their friendship developed, Burns named Brown to stage the Canada Cup matches at Kaanapali, Maui, in November 1964. Brown impressed Burns with his handling of the prestigious international golfing event. Brown had other attributes that appealed to the governor. Most important, he was part-Hawaiian, a nephew of the well-known sportsman and Republican politician, Francis Ii Brown. His grandfather had been John Ii, one of the first Hawaiians to read and write English. Ii had become a teacher, historian, superintendent of schools, and member of the Kingdom of Hawaii's house of representatives, house of nobles, and supreme court. Burns hoped that, as his lieutenant governor, Brown could provide that link with the Hawaiian community that he had lost with Bill Richardson's departure.

Governor Burns was also attracted to an almost endless list of public organizations with which Kenny Brown was associated, including: director, Queen's Hospital; chairman, Hawaiian Open Golf Tournament; president, Navy League of Hawaii; president, Waialae Country Club; director, Francis Ii Brown Golf Club; chairman, Honolulu Development Agency; director, Prince Kuhio Hawaiian Civic Club; member, Mayor's Stadium Commission; director, Ulu Mau Village; and president, Hawaiian Professional Corporation. Brown's business interests were equally impressive. In addition to his own architecture firm, Brown was chairman and president of Pacific Savings & Loan and a director of Amfac; Hawaiian Airlines; Pacific Network, Inc.; Island Holidays, Inc.; Leeward Oahu T.V. Network; Central Alarm Company; Hawaiian Network, Inc.; Olohana Corp.; and Ainamalu Corp.

But Brown, the developer and owner of the Holiday Isle Hotel—a $4.5 million, 286-room hotel then under construction at the corner of Kalakawa and Lewers in Waikiki—was hardly typical of Burns' political associates. Most didn't even know who he was. When Mike Tokunaga, Burns long-time lieutenant, first heard the news from Matsy Takabuki in a phone call, his response was, "Who's he?" Hiroshi "Scrub" Tanaka, the governor's principal political loyalist on the Big Island, remembered having made the same response. When Tanaka called a Hilo meeting of his Big Island contacts, thirty-three showed up, with some coming from as far away as Kona. When Tanaka asked those assembled how many knew who Kenny Brown was, "only two" could identify Burns' choice for lieutenant governor. "So right there," Tanaka recalled, "I knew our work was cut out for us."

When Gill was asked his reaction to the possibility of Brown entering the lieutenant governor's race, his cheerful response was, "Welcome in. The water's fine. . . . [The Brown campaign] will be well loaded . . . with Republican money, trying to beat me." Ten years later, his response was less generous: "That was a dumb thing," Gill said of Burns' effort to promote Brown as his running mate. "They couldn't get up any enthusiasm for Brown. . . . They couldn't sell him in the boonies [rural Hawaii]."

Gill had reason to feel confident. On 21 July, the day after Brown's announcement that he was changing his Party registration to the Democratic Party, the *Honolulu Advertiser* released a poll they had taken in mid-May of 301 Oahu Democrats, asking them who they favored for lieutenant governor. Tom Gill had received 142 votes, followed by City

Council Chairman Herman Lemke, 50; City Councilman Frank Fasi, 48; and Attorney General Bert Kobayashi, 37. Kenny Brown, of course, had not announced his membership in the Democratic Party when the poll was taken, much less announced that he might be a candidate for lieutenant governor.

On 31 July, Tom Gill and Kenny Brown shared the platform at the statewide convention of 125 members of the Young Democrats of Hawaii. Gill warned those assembled: "There's a danger that if we stretch our political tent so far as to include too many of the 'Big Mules' they are liable to crowd and trample a lot of our traditional Democratic donkeys. If that should happen, we will not only lose our vote base, but we will lose our identity as a Party." The *Honolulu Advertiser* reported that the positive response to Gill's remarks was roughly twice that accorded to Brown for his tribute to Governor Burns.

By 5 August, when Tom Gill made his formal announcement that he was running for lieutenant governor, he was ignoring Brown. He now took on the role of the team player, telling those assembled, "Jack [Burns] and I can produce great things for our people and our State." Gill even tried to carve out a logical role for himself as Burns' lieutenant governor. Pointing out that roughly one-fifth of the State's $57 million operating budget came from the federal government, Gill emphasized how much his past experience—in Congress and with the Office of Economic Opportunity—would help the governor. It seemed to make sense—at least on the face of it.

But nothing seemed to make much sense to Governor Burns in the summer of 1966. He had made the same mistake he made in 1959, when he felt that the State of Hawaii should have rewarded him with the governorship. He had worked so hard and achieved so much that the logic of events should, in his mind, make itself clear to the voters. As Burns told Doug Boswell, "I figure when you do a good job, people will know about it." Burns felt that the voters should not only reelect him governor, but they should allow him to choose his own lieutenant governor. And nothing made less sense to him than having Gill as his running-mate. By now the issue had become so emotional that it clouded the governor's judgment and nearly cost him the election.

Like an inexperienced swimmer caught in a riptide, Burns continued to resist the inevitable. At an August political coffee at the home of University of Hawaii professor A. Leonard Diamond, the governor said that he preferred Kenny Brown over Tom Gill for lieutenant governor for the following reason, which was reported in the *Honolulu Star-Bulletin:* "When the Governor leaves the State, the Lieutenant Governor becomes acting Governor, with real power. In another state, when this situation arose, the acting Governor called the legislature into special session to investigate the Attorney General." Burns added that he would feel comfortable leaving Hawaii with Kenny Brown to back him up and, by inference, that he would not feel comfortable leaving Tom Gill behind.

In the same issue of the *Star-Bulletin,* an appeal for Party unity by Gill to a group of Kauai Democrats was reported. Gill said:

> We won in 1962 with a wide base of support among labor, small business and the great mass of independent voters. . . . Jack Burns and I can produce this same unity in 1966. Between the two of us, we will probably marshal the support of all organized labor in this state. Between the two of us, we can keep in the Democratic fold the often disparate elements of small business, the housewife, the independent white collar workers and the intellectual community.

Yet another story on 20 August revealed that the executive committee of the AFL-CIO's Council on Public Education (COPE) had voted 3–2 against endorsing Governor Burns in the Democratic primary, citing the bad treatment Burns had given Gill as the reason for the negative vote. Two weeks later, at the AFL-CIO's statewide meeting of COPE, representing some thirty thousand workers, Tom Gill rose to calm the troubled waters. He told those assembled:

> I am deeply appreciative of the warm and strong support so many of you have given to my candidacy. I also am aware of your puzzlement and anxiety over the support my opponent [Kenny Brown] has received from certain groups both within and without the Democratic Party. I know that some of you have expressed indignation at the position of the governor in this matter. But I hope you will not allow this concern to blind you. . . .
>
> No political party can run without a head. The leader of our Party in this election is Governor Burns. I support him for reelection. I will support him after the election.

Art Rutledge spoke after Gill. He reminded the delegates that he had been a member of the screening committee that had voted against Burns' endorsement. Rutledge then announced that he would support the endorsement of a Burns–Gill team, emphasizing that he had never opposed Burns as governor. The crusty union leader ended with a quip aimed at a potential Burns–Brown ticket: "There's no sense in having the governor and lieutenant governor both out playing golf." Governor Burns later appeared to accept COPE's endorsement, but made no mention of either Tom Gill or the lieutenant governor's race.

While the AFL-CIO was swallowing hard and endorsing Burns, the rival ILWU was telling its members to "close ranks" and defeat Tom Gill in the primary. Jack Hall, executive director of the ILWU, told his union members that a lieutenant governor should be "willing to submerge himself to the administration. If the candidate [Gill] is critical, he should run for governor, not lieutenant governor." Jack Hall still had not forgiven Tom Gill for running against Hiram Fong for the U.S. Senate in 1964. The ILWU had endorsed Gill for the U.S. House of Representatives in 1962 and was prepared to do so again in 1964. But when Gill announced that he would run for Fong's seat, the ILWU had gotten behind the candidacy of Nadao Yoshinaga in the Democratic primary. While the ILWU found it difficult to generate enthusiasm for Kenny Brown, the union's leaders were quick to denounce Tom Gill.

In his frustration, Governor Burns was making the support of Kenny Brown a matter of personal loyalty among his friends. Elmer Cravalho made a public statement that a Burns–Gill ticket might well lose to the anticipated Republican ticket of Randolph Crossley and Dr. George Mills. Burns publicly agreed with Cravalho's assessment. In the face of this kind of pronouncement, Tom Gill continued to sound like the ultimate team player. Walter Johnson, the former chairman of the history department at the University of Chicago, editor of the papers of Adlai Stevenson, and distinguished professor of history at the University of Hawaii, spoke of Tom Gill at a rally at Heeia Lookout, comparing him to the great statesman he had known so well:

> Like Adlai Stevenson, Tom Gill has a fundamental belief in reason, the possibility of progress, basic optimism, and intellectual curiosity. Again, like Stevenson, Tom Gill is not an aggressive Madison Avenue manufactured type, but instead he is a decent, thoughtful human being who is willing to speak out in an independent fashion.

With one week to go in the primary campaign, Governor Burns left Hawaii for Africa. He went to represent President Lyndon Johnson at the nationhood ceremonies for two small states that had been carved out

of South Africa: Botswana and Lesotho. The ostensible reason for sending the governor of Hawaii was that Botswana was Hawaii's antipode—
that point which is on the exact opposite side of the planet. With him,
Governor Burns took Alfred Laureta, the state director of labor and Dr.
James Robinson, director of Operation Crossroads Africa. On his departure, Burns told the press: "I deeply regret only the coincidence that
I must be out of the State at a time when I should be here to give all
the support I can to the man who must be our next lieutenant governor,
Kenneth F. Brown."

Burns did not leave his campaign staff empty-handed. He had made
nine one-minute television spots. They presented Burns at his worst: a
stiff, unsmiling complainer saying that he needed "a partner, not a competitor; a constructive deputy, not a constant critic." Burns attacked
Gill's campaign literature, which he called "misleading" in its implication that Burns wanted Gill for his lieutenant governor. "This is not
true," a strident Burns protested. "Mr. Gill knows it is not true. He knew
it long before he announced his candidacy."

In his 1973 book, *Catch a Wave*, reporter Tom Coffman wrote about
how Burns learned the results of the 1966 primary election:

> The primary was on Saturday [1 October]. Very early Sunday a *Star-
> Bulletin* editor placed a call to Burns in Botswana. The telephone op-
> erator didn't know how to route the call, so the editor suggested she
> go through Europe to Cape Town. Finally, she made the connection.
>   "How did the election come out?" Burns asked from the other side
> of the world.
>   The Governor was told that he had won, but that Gill had beaten
> Brown.
>   Burns asked, "How many votes did I get?"
>   The answer was 86,000.
>   "How many did Gill get?"
>   The answer was 90,900.
>   There was a long pause, finally broken by a question from the
> editor.
>   Burns interrupted, "Would you give me those figures again?"

The Honolulu press got it right. The *Sunday Star-Bulletin & Advertiser* pointed out on its editorial pages that Gill's victory over Brown
"proved again that political popularity is rarely transferable." Of Burns,

Inouye, and Cravalho, all of whom had campaigned for Kenny Brown, the paper wrote:

> Individually, their following is considerable. Collectively, it is massive. But the vote showed (a) that their supporters could not be assigned to someone else and that (b) the attempt to do so was resented by a substantial number of those who went to the polls.
>
> Tom Gill . . . never doubted his victory. The Establishment's opposition to him cast him as something of an underdog, a role which he willingly and productively accepted.
>
> He never rocked the boat; he never fought back. . . . His campaign was "cool." He was not his usual astringent self.

The *Honolulu Star-Bulletin* pinpointed the beginning of the downward spiral for the Burns organization when it wrote: "In retrospect, things began to go wrong from the Governor's standpoint from the moment Elmer Cravalho turned down the vacancy in the Lieutenant Governorship six months ago and Humpty Dumpty never really got put back together again."

Honolulu's two rival union leaders were quick to agree upon a strategy for the general election. Jack Hall, the ILWU chief, warned, "The people had better stick to the Democratic side because everything done by the administration to build a stable economy may go down the drain." Art Rutledge, head of the AFL-CIO's Unity House, came to the same conclusion, but from a vastly different perspective: "Tom Gill has been elected to a partnership in running the Government. Burns has got to make this clear now, the quicker the better."

The ink was still wet on the primary election returns when the Republican standard-bearer for governor, Randolph Crossley, began to throw Governor Burns' primary campaign back at him. "The Governor has made it clear," Crossley intoned, "that he cannot work with Mr. Gill. How can Governor Burns now turn around and say that he can work with him? I don't think the public is that gullible." In Crossley, Burns faced a formidable opponent. Coming to Hawaii in 1928 to start an advertising firm, Crossley at various times was a rancher, pineapple grower, flower wholesaler, contractor, trading stamp dealer, and owner of a savings and loan association.

Crossley first entered public life in 1943, serving a single term in the territorial house of representatives from Kauai. From 1947 to 1949 he was a member of the Public Utilities Commission. In 1950 he was a delegate from Kauai to the Constitutional Convention. And from 1950 to 1953, Crossley served as chairman of the territorial Republican Party. In 1953, Crossley stood on the brink of political success. As Lawrence Fuchs explained it:

> Crossley, whose personal and business counsel was Herbert Brownell, the chief strategist in the Eisenhower camp, was promised the governorship shortly after the General's election. After four visits to the White House, the appointment was all but announced. Eisenhower assured Crossley that the gubernatorial commission was ready for signature, and all that remained was for Brownell and Crossley to work out the mechanics of the announcement. If Crossley preferred, the announcement could be made right from the White House. Crossley preferred to have Delegate Joseph Farrington tell of his appointment, since he had been feuding with Farrington, . . . a Taft man, and he hoped that the feud would end once the decision was made. Crossley sold his pineapple interests [on Kauai] and waited for an announcement that never came.

Crossley's effort to reach out to Farrington and the Taft wing of Hawaii's Republican Party backfired and gave his opponents time to mount a campaign for Samuel Wilder King as Hawaii's new territorial governor. Ultimately, it was Eisenhower's promise to Senator Robert A. Taft that the Ohio conservative would have a fair share of the patronage in exchange for his support in the general election that sealed Crossley's fate.

Randy Crossley responded to his disappointment by resigning as Hawaii's territorial Republican Party chairman and moving to Oahu, where he embarked upon a new and even more prosperous phase of his business career. Had he remained active in Republican Party politics, Crossley might well have become governor of the territory instead of Bill Quinn after Eisenhower's election to a second term, but that was not to be. Crossley did reenter Hawaii politics after statehood, serving as a state senator from the Island of Oahu from 1959 to 1964. When Neal Blaisdell took himself out of the 1966 governor's race, Crossley jumped into the breach. For his running-mate, Crossley chose the popular part-Hawaiian physician, Dr. George Mills.

As Burns' absence from Hawaii grew longer, rumors began to fly. Those who knew Burns best feared that the governor might take Kenny Brown's defeat hard. As Brown later recalled, "They persuaded me to go to New York to meet him when he arrived back from Botswana. . . . So I was waiting there in the airport . . . as he walked out." Brown remembered Burns' first words: "I never thought I'd see you here," the surprised governor told him. Brown recalled that Burns was "kind of discouraged," but mostly mad, "really pissed off," and that "he didn't want to go home." According to Brown, what bothered Burns most was that his own people had not given him the support he deserved. Brown agreed, but with less rancor than Burns: "I don't believe that the whole Burns organization ever got fully into my campaign. You know, they were going through the motions. . . . And when Burns said, 'Work!' they worked. But if you're already convinced that you're going to lose, you can't work that well. Like . . . Punahou playing Notre Dame—no way."

While Hawaii awaited the governor's return, Burns remained elusive. First, he went to Washington, D.C., to consult with Dan Inouye. Then Burns and Brown "hid out at the Burlingame [California] Country Club for about four days. . . . We played golf every day, smoked cigars, and talked philosophy. And that was it." Burns finally called Matsy Takabuki and asked him to fly to California and fill him in on the Hawaii scene on the way back. Takabuki found a Jack Burns who was close to saying, "I don't give a damn whether I get elected or not." Takabuki told his friend, "Look, Jack, there's a hell of a lot of things that have yet to be done. You can't give this away. All these years we worked for it. Not only you, we worked for it. And I think you owe this obligation to the people. . . . Look, there's a greater thing than merely Jack Burns. . . . Cripes, you can't give up, Jack. What the hell!"

After an absence of two weeks, Jack Burns returned to Hawaii—a little more than three weeks before the general election. Tom Gill remembered the governor's arrival bitterly. Gill's offer to go to the mainland to meet with Burns had been spurned and his suggestion that he board the plane for a brief chat before the governor disembarked was similarly dismissed. In the end, when Burns finally got off the plane, he gave Tom Gill a cursory handshake, posed for a quick picture with Gill and Brown, and ran into the camera and microphone of Bob Jones, news anchor for Channel 9. As Gill described it, "Jones stuck a mike under his nose and said something about, 'Well, I guess you don't like Gill for your running mate.'" Burns' reported response was, "I'm happy to have any Democrat as my running mate. Anyone the people select." With that, Burns got into a waiting car and was gone. As Gill recalled it ten years later, "If they'd planned it for weeks, they couldn't have done any worse. . . . [Burns] did an awful job, with an incredible amount of help from his stupid henchmen."

Five days later, on 15 October, Governor Burns finally stepped forward with his first real endorsement of Tom Gill. Speaking to more than sixty Democratic candidates at the auditorium of the Hawaiian Electric Company, Burns delivered what was reported in the *Honolulu Star-Bulletin* as "a fighting speech." Harry Albright, chairman of the Democratic Campaign Committee, was ecstatic: "It was one of the biggest ovations I have ever heard from a group of candidates. The response was terrific." More than anything, it was an expression of the collective relief that the governor had finally pulled himself together for the final three weeks of the campaign.

Bea Burns also hit the political hustings. She joined Lois Gill for a day of campaigning on Kauai. "I was struck by Lois's intelligence," she remembered. "She was nice gal and very bright. She campaigned on the issues; she had them down pat. I spoke about the man, my husband."

While Burns was away, Randolph Crossley had been doing more than trying to exploit the Burns–Gill split in the Democratic Party. He had also come up with an issue that resonated with many of Hawaii's voters. "The first piece of legislation we will present," Crossley told an audience, "will be to eliminate the four percent [state excise] tax on food." He also promised that he would get rid of this regressive tax on medicine and medical care. "Why," Crossley asked the voters, "should you have to pay a tax to be sick?" When the Democrats pressed Crossley about how the $20 million to $25 million in lost revenue would be made up, the challenger produced a last-minute "recoupment plan," which Burns called "a collection of outdated figures and very few facts." It was a complicated issue and few voters were capable of evaluating the figures just one week before the election. Still, Crossley had struck a responsive chord with his attack on what amounted to a sales tax on such essentials as food, medicine, and medical care.

Considering the closeness of the election, the endorsement of the Burns–Gill ticket in the *Sunday Star-Bulletin & Advertiser* of 30 October 1966 might well have made the difference. The facts and figures contained in the endorsement echoed those from Governor Burns' 1966 state of the State message. The paper's conclusion was:

> In brief, Hawaii is enjoying more prosperity than ever before in its history. . . In relations between management and labor, the Burns ad-

ministration has made its services effectively available in seeking to avert strikes in major industries. . . . In taxation, the Burns adminis-tration has brought about more equitable assessments. . . . At Pier 39, a Foreign Trade Zone has been established . . . and in short order has doubled in size. . . . The State has been successful in getting back 1,200 acres of Federal land in the last two years.

The endorsement went on to praise the Burns administration for its con-tributions in education, ocean sciences, the Governor's Advisory Coun-cil on Science and Industry, tourism, and ethical standards. They also praised the Democratic Party for presenting as its candidate for lieu-tenant governor "a more mature" Tom Gill.

The result, nine days later, was a squeaker. Burns and Gill received 108,840 votes to 104,324 for Crossley and Mills. Over 87 percent of the State's registered voters had gone to the polls, a remarkable turnout in a nonpresidential election year. After the polls closed on Tuesday, 8 No-vember, Jack Burns could not be found. It turned out that he was driving around the island of Oahu—alone. When he showed up the next day he said, by way of explanation, "I'm a loner. There are times when I'd rather be alone, and last night was one of them." Larry McManus, *Advertiser* political writer, had found Burns at Washington Place with Bert Kobayashi and Matsy Takabuki. "If Burns was elated by his vic-tory," McManus observed, "his weariness well concealed it. He was terse and taciturn." It was a fitting conclusion to a difficult year.

F·I·F·T·E·E·N

Second Term

JACK BURNS MEANT IT when he told Tom Gill that there would be no Burns–Gill administration. The new lieutenant governor learned quickly that he was not in the "partnership" Art Rutledge had proclaimed in October 1966. Any chance that partnership might have had ended with Gill's very first public exposure as lieutenant governor.

Even before the general election in November 1966, Burns had asked Gill to investigate the rapid rise of food prices in Hawaii. Burns was looking for something to blunt Randolph Crossley's attack on his administration for the state excise tax on food. Gill turned this campaign assignment into his first job as lieutenant governor. In a revealing reminiscence, Tom Gill discussed his approach to the matter:

> We put together a pretty good committee and held quite a few hearings. I guess we got more publicity out of it than I should have. And we released the report to the legislature and to the media at the same time. But I guess I made a tactical error. I should have given it to [Burns] first, even though he said nothing about it.

The 177-page food price report Gill released on 15 March 1967 was an outstanding analysis of the subject—thorough, analytical, and based upon significant community participation. But it was received by the public as a powerful statement by Tom Gill rather than an initiative of the Burns administration.

Few doubted that a contest between the two men had begun. When Burns and Gill were inaugurated on 5 December 1966, neither mentioned the other in his inaugural message. In his speech, Burns looked forward to a continuation of the progress his administration had made

230

during his first term, focusing upon familiar themes: education; full employment; the development of new industries, "in particular, those oriented to ocean sciences"; preservation of Hawaii's natural beauty; the creation of new recreational opportunities; and, finally, the theme of Pan-Pacific leadership, announcing a joint state-federal Pacific Conference on the Problems of Urban Growth for May 1967.

Gill's inaugural address contrasted markedly. He sounded like a man who had just been elected with a mandate to clean up the mess he had inherited from his defeated opponent:

> We can no longer escape a serious and broad assault on the wildly proliferating problems of urban life. Pollution of our air and water, traffic snarls, . . . shrinking recreation areas, and the seeming futility of the present planning mechanism—all of these and more run like cancer through our metropolitan complex.

Gill then continued with words that seemed to be aimed directly at Governor Burns and those whom he would refer to as the governor's "alarming friends" in 1970: "We have no room for conflicts of interest, undisclosed and secretly pursued; we have no use for those who view public office as the road to private gain."

While Gill made no specific accusations, his friends from the AFL-CIO Council on Political Education (COPE) were raising serious questions about a land deal that had been consummated by a company called Ethereal, Inc. COPE charged that Ethereal had purchased land from the Oahu Sugar Company in Waipahu in 1965 which included a private park—Hans L'Orange Park—that had been maintained by the company for many years for the benefit of its employees and other residents in the area. During the 1966 session of the legislature, COPE charged, Senator Nadao Yoshinaga, Ethereal's vice president, had introduced a bill allocating $105,000 for the State to acquire the park, money that would go directly into the pockets of Yoshinaga and three other Burns loyalists who were principals in Ethereal: Masao "Pundy" Yokouchi, president of Ethereal and Burns-appointed chairman of the Hawaii Foundation on Culture and the Arts; Seichi "Shadow" Hirai, treasurer of Ethereal and clerk of the senate; and John Ushijima, state senator from the Big Island. The charges hung like a cloud over the impending organization of the Hawaii state senate.

On the surface, the state senate in 1967 looked very much like the

1966 senate. The Democrats still enjoyed a two-thirds majority, the Republicans having reduced the Democratic majority by only one, from 16 to 9 to 15 to 10. The change, however, was far more than the one-seat difference would suggest. That change was geographic. With reapportionment, the state senate had gone from a 15 to 10 neighbor island majority to a 19 to 6 Oahu majority. In the 1966 elections, Oahu members of the state house of representatives had scrambled to move over to the senate, resulting in a decidedly different roster of senators. Governor Burns' influence in the state senate declined, since his greatest strength came from the neighbor islands—yet another by-product of reapportionment. The man who gained the most from this change in geographic distribution was Tom Gill.

When the fifteen senate Democrats attempted to organize themselves, they found themselves split into two factions—the Burns faction, led by Nadao Yoshinaga who had moved from Maui to Oahu as a result of reapportionment, and the Gill faction, led by Nelson Doi from the Big Island. Each group had seven members. The tiebreaker was George Ariyoshi, who sought to play the role of peacemaker. None of his efforts to resolve the impasse before the legislative session began proved successful and as the 1967 legislative session convened, the majority Party was still unable to organize itself. The struggle became so bitter that David McClung, a member of the Gill faction, even suggested that Republican Hebden Porteus be elected senate president

Once the senate had convened, the Doi forces attempted a bold move when they tried to replace Burns loyalist Shadow Hirai, the popular clerk of the senate. When it became clear, however, that Hirai had the votes necessary to retain his position, the Doi faction quickly backed off. The attempt to have Hirai removed was ill advised, and not quickly forgotten—or forgiven. The Republicans, who were in a position to engage in some serious mischief, instead allowed the Democrats to continue to embarrass themselves. Republican William H. "Doc" Hill, the dean of the state senate, commented on the Democratic confusion: "In the thirty-nine years since I became a legislator, I have seen skullduggery and may have been mixed up in some myself, but I've never seen anything like this."

On the second day of the legislative session, in his state of the State message, Burns made no mention of the division within the Democratic Party. Instead, he offered an expanded version of his recent inaugural address. The governor also proudly announced that the state government had ended the 1966 fiscal year with a surplus of $12.8 million and expected to end the 1967 fiscal year with a $7 million surplus. "The economic outlook is not as clear-cut as it appeared when we met here a year ago," Burns told the joint session, "although most signs point to continued prosperity and high productivity."

As the senate's organizational struggle continued, Burns' people leaked the name of Kazuhisa Abe, former Big Island senate president, as a potential candidate for the state supreme court. Burns wanted to reward Abe for having declined the lieutenant governorship in 1966, for having stepped aside in the senate race when it was clear that there were too many neighbor island incumbents fighting for a smaller number of seats, and for having supported Kenneth Brown's candidacy in the primary contest against Gill. The Gill forces were incensed by Abe's reward. As Doug Boswell wrote: "The two men [Burns and Gill] are enveloped in a capsule of bitterness which points toward a crisis for the Democrats in the primary election of 1970. . . . Many Democrats believe Burns now has no choice but to run for a third term in 1970 as a means of blocking Gill's drive for the State's top elective post."

On 24 February, the senate finally organized itself. The compromise candidate for senate president—the spot Doi had sought—was John Hulten, a member of the Burns wing of the Party who was best known for his advocacy of a state-operated interisland ferry. Ways and Means— the post coveted by Yoshinaga—went to Vincent Yano, a member of the Gill wing of the Party. In an appointment that would later prove useful to Burns, John Ushijima became chairman of the Judiciary Committee. With three appointments to the supreme court coming up during the session, control of the Judiciary Committee would be crucial to the success of the governor's appointments.

One month into the legislative session, Governor Burns decided he needed a legislative liaison, a role Bill Richardson had frequently played for him as lieutenant governor. Gill had suggested the post for himself, but Burns ignored the suggestion. Instead, he decided to use Myron "Pinky" Thompson who had been appointed to the cabinet-level post of director of administration. Thompson filled the position which had been vacated by Bill Norwood in July 1966 when he became the high commissioner of the trust territory of the Pacific. Tom Gill's first reaction to Thompson's appointment was positive:

I thought he was a very good appointment and looked forward to working with him. . . . We had a good relationship because he'd been a social worker with the Liliuokalani Trust and I got to know him in the OEO program. He's a very square guy. And we did a few things. And one day he came over, sort of hang-dog expression on his face, and I asked, "Pinky, what's eating you?"

And he said . . . something along this line: "Well, I don't know how to say this, but if you could assure me that you will never run against Burns, I think we will be able to do a lot of work together."

And so I told him, "Look, I'm not running against anybody at the moment, but I don't see how I'm supposed to commit for the rest of my life in this type of situation. I don't think you really want me to do that, do you?"

"Well," he said, "there are difficulties." What he was saying, of course, was that the whole gang of hoodlums over there wanted to make sure that I never challenged Burns. And the only way that I could become effective was to become one of the spare parts, which I wasn't about to do. So, I didn't see much of Pinky after that.

Myron Thompson ended up filling much of the role a compatible lieutenant governor might have occupied. Kenneth Brown also helped, signing on as an unpaid special assistant to Burns. Brown served in the governor's office for two years, before winning a seat in the state senate in 1968.

Jack and Bea Burns gained some respite from the legislative wars at the National Governors Conference in Washington, D.C. On 18 March, Burns gathered with his fellow governors for an all-day briefing from President Lyndon Johnson and various cabinet members. Bea, meanwhile, joined Lady Bird Johnson and the other state First Ladies for a beautification bus ride. Lady Bird took them to a tree-planting ceremony at a place called Gravelly Point on the Virginia side of the Potomac River.

There fifty-four flowering dogwood trees, one for each state and territory, awaited planting by the First Ladies. The temperature stood at twenty-nine degrees and rain had turned Gravelly Point into a muddy sinkhole. Despite the conditions, "Bea insisted on going and when we reached the site, away she went through the mud in her wheelchair. She didn't shovel much, but she was the most determined participant," Mrs. Johnson remembered.

That evening the governors went to the White House for dinner.

Mrs. Johnson stood in the receiving line beside the president, graciously shaking hands and remembering sadly the number of governors—and friends—no longer there. She did, however, express pleasure at seeing "John Connally (Texas) . . . the handsomest man in the room . . . and Jack Burns who looks like a poet."

The Gill forces felt good about the 1967 legislative session. They finally got a watered-down version of the Maryland Land Bill passed. Governor Burns allowed it to become law, but he never enforced it. He continued to feel that zoning and tax measures were a better road to land reform. The Gill forces also wrote into law a new code of ethics for state employees; the bill established a State Ethics Commission to enforce the code. They also passed a law creating a state ombudsman, the first such position in the United States. Gill's food price study helped to establish milk price controls at the producer level.

Home rule had its day in the 1967 state legislature as well. A new transit law made it possible for the counties to operate mass transit systems. At issue was the desire of the City and County of Honolulu to purchase Honolulu Rapid Transit, which was foundering as a private company. Emphasizing just how centralized authority was in the State of Hawaii, Maui County needed special legislation in order to hold a special election to replace the deceased chairman (now mayor) of the Maui County board of supervisors, Eddie Tam.

Less than three weeks after the end of the legislative session, Elmer Cravalho resigned his post of Speaker of the State House of Representatives to run for the office of mayor on his home island of Maui. In an ironic ceremony, his fellow representatives presented Cravalho with a silver plate bearing the names of all members of the third state legislature. It had been prepared in anticipation of his departure in 1966 to become lieutenant governor. Governor Burns, who desperately wished that Cravalho had received his gift as originally planned, praised his friend as a great Speaker of the House, comparing him with his friend from the U.S. House of Representatives, Sam Rayburn.

If Governor Burns lamented the loss of Elmer Cravalho, he drew pleasure from the appointment and confirmation of three new members of the state supreme court. On 9 May, Burns had officially appointed Democrats Kazuhisa Abe and Bernard Levinson, along with Republican Masaji Marumoto, to positions as associate justices. Judiciary chairman John Ushijima deftly managed their approval by the senate. Not everybody liked the appointments. The AFL-CIO was still kicking about Abe's nomination and the *Honolulu Star-Bulletin* saw the whole process as tainted, editorializing that "the political spoils system reaches now even into the courts."

Hawaii, of course, was not immune to events elsewhere in the world. The war in Vietnam had a powerful positive impact on Hawaii's economy and an equally powerful negative impact on its social fabric. Governor Burns had been a constant supporter of Lyndon Johnson's policy in Vietnam from the time of the Gulf of Tonkin Resolution in 1964 through the escalation which began in 1965. In 1967, the war in Vietnam would claim one of his favorite public servants, University of Hawaii President Tom Hamilton. The events which led to Hamilton's resignation, after almost five years of unprecedented growth at the university, revolved around Assistant Professor of Political Science Oliver Lee.

Lee, a part-Chinese, part-German naturalized citizen of the United States, began teaching at the University of Hawaii in 1963. His credentials included a B.A. from Harvard University, an M.A. and Ph.D. from the University of Chicago, an eighteen-month stint in the U.S. Army Reserve as a strategic intelligence analyst, four years of teaching at the University of Maryland, and a brief stay at the Library of Congress where he was a Far Eastern analyst. His vita was impressive, but reports on his teaching were mixed and he had little scholarly production to recommend him as a tenured member of the faculty.

After his arrival on the Manoa campus, Lee gravitated to the Vietnam protest movement and became an outspoken critic of U.S. policy in Asia. By the spring of 1967, the Waikiki Lions Club had made it a club project to have Lee exposed and fired from his teaching post. On at least two occasions, Tom Hamilton came to Oliver Lee's defense, saying that Lee's First Amendment rights were not limited by his membership on the faculty. At the end of the 1965–1966 academic year, Oliver Lee was denied tenure and was, in the spring of 1967, teaching on a probationary basis. As the pressure mounted from the community, the Political Science Department rallied around Lee and issued a recommendation in favor of tenure. Lee's teaching and scholarly production had not improved in any discernible way, but his academic colleagues did not want to appear to have yielded to public pressure.

On 29 May 1967, Oliver Lee received a letter from W. Todd Furniss, dean of the College of Arts and Sciences, notifying him of the fa-

vorable tenure recommendation of his department and informing him
that while "there can be no guarantee of tenure, . . . your probationary
period will be completed on June 30, 1968, and that tenure, if granted,
will be effective July 1, 1968." In other words, if you don't make any
serious mistakes, tenure will be yours in another year.

Four days after the letter of intent was written, a campus organization called the Student Partisan Alliance (SPA) issued a statement,
intended for military personnel, "encouraging desertion, disposing and
destroying of weapons, eliminating officers and non-coms in action, ra-
diomen exposing unit positions, divulging classified information to
prostitutes, black-market dealers, etc." Oliver Lee served as the faculty
adviser for the SPA. Lee had used a University of Hawaii mimeograph
machine to duplicate the statement, which was nothing less than a call
to treason. Lee admitted that he had read the statement before its distribution, but claimed that he had not specifically approved it. It was
later revealed that Lee had advised the students that "while they were
taking some risks of prosecution and conviction, the risks were not too
great." The reason Lee gave for this confidence was that the document
had mentioned only "the exploitative systems of North America and Europe," and had not, specifically, named the U.S. government as a target.

The public outcry against Oliver Lee was deafening. On 5 June, acting on the recommendation of Dean Furniss, President Hamilton
announced that Lee's letter of intent had been withdrawn and that he
would be terminated immediately. The lines were quickly drawn and the
University of Hawaii settled in for a long battle. On 28 June, the board
of regents voted to support Hamilton's decision, saying: "To tell a group
of students to issue a potentially seditious statement [and] that they were
'basically legally in the clear' is tantamount to encouragement, rather
than the word of caution the Regents would have expected from a
mature and responsible faculty member who has assumed the duty of
advising students."

Lee mounted his defense. He took his case not only to the university's faculty senate, but to the American Association of University Professors, arguing that he had not received "due process" before his firing.
In December, when the faculty senate told President Hamilton that to
fire Oliver Lee he would have to start the process over again—and this
time to give him the due process which was his right—Hamilton resigned. "I have spent a great deal of energy protecting academic freedom

and academic due process," Hamilton told the press. "I regret none of it, but it is time for someone to stand up for academic responsibility, and I do so now."

Now the public cried out to save Tom Hamilton. Lieutenant Governor Tom Gill characterized Hamilton's resignation as "a grievous blow." Mayor Neal Blaisdell was "shocked and dismayed." The faculty senate unanimously requested that Hamilton remain in the presidency. The *Honolulu Star-Bulletin* reported that "Governor John A. Burns could not be reached for comment." Labor leader Art Rutledge called upon "the Governor of the State, [the] representative of the people, [to] discuss the matter with Hamilton and ask him to stay."

The governor maintained a maddening silence. When asked whether Burns had ever discussed the Oliver Lee case with him, Hamilton recalled:

> Whenever I was about to take a step in these negotiations, I would go down and tell Jack Burns, because I realized that there were some political overtones about it. And he'd simply sit down with me and he'd say, "Okay, Boss, you do it." I suppose he called everybody "Boss," and I would leave. I don't recall him ever calling me on this matter. . . . He played, at least as far as I'm concerned, no role in it.

Burns' role in the Oliver Lee case was consistent with his policy of noninterference with those to whom he had delegated responsibility.

In 1979 Tom Hamilton admitted that "I might have handled it differently, but you can't live in the past. You do what you think is right at the time and live with the consequences." For Hamilton, the consequences were that after completing a lame-duck year as president of the University of Hawaii he accepted the presidency of the Hawaii Visitor's Bureau. For the university there were at least two major consequences of the Oliver Lee case: first, the university had sacrificed a highly regarded president for a lightly regarded teacher and scholar. Second, the faculty principle of due process had been upheld.

The Oliver Lee case finally ended on 11 April 1969, when the board of regents voted 5–2 to reinstate the controversial political science professor, "without tenure, on probation," for one year. Lee accepted the regents' offer when Acting President Richard Takasaki assured Lee that he would receive tenure in April 1970. Governor Burns' public reaction to the regents' ruling revealed none of his feelings about the case itself:

The action taken by the Regents should provide the means for resolving the issue so that all of us—the administration, the faculty, the students and each citizen of the State can concentrate on making positive contributions to the growth and development of our university.

It is my hope that the search for a new president can now be expeditiously concluded.

In fact, the greatest motivation for the conclusion of the Oliver Lee case was that the two leading candidates for the position of president of the University of Hawaii—Wytze Gorter, dean of the Graduate Division, and Harlan Cleveland, U.S. ambassador to NATO—had indicated that they would not accept the post as long as the Lee case remained unresolved. Cleveland, who was chosen for the position, assumed his responsibilities at the beginning of the 1969–1970 academic year. By 1975, he was gone. Thirty years later, Oliver Lee remains a tenured associate professor at the University of Hawaii.

While Governor Burns said nothing publicly about the Oliver Lee case, he remained a vocal supporter of Lyndon Johnson's policy in Vietnam. In his state of the State message on 23 February 1968, two months after Hamilton's resignation, Burns told the joint session of the state legislature that he would skip the routine discussion of money matters to address "grave problems in Hawaii and in the Pacific region." Burns turned first to the issue which had given rise to the Oliver Lee case— the war in Vietnam:

> To this date, Hawaii counts 125 of her young citizens dead in this war and hundreds injured. And for a minority in our community, there is the added dimension of a troubled conscience concerning all wars and this war in particular. This minority deserves our attention and respect.

That much acknowledged, the governor continued:

> Freedom! This is what the war in Vietnam is about today. . . . We who live here today must never forget, in our peace, in our comfort, and in our prosperity, that the war is not a world away; it is next door. It is our urgent concern. . . . Hawaii has a special, a particular role, in helping to shape the national policy in this regard.

The second "grave development" to which the governor addressed himself was the changing character of the rapidly growing population of the State of Hawaii and the question of how this new population would be received in the "Aloha" State:

> There is a danger that some in Hawaii may not welcome these new-comers with open arms, open doors and open hearts, but instead will exhibit an attitude entirely alien to the spirit of Aloha.
>
> Provincialism must never get a foothold on these Islands. None of us owns Hawaii. It was passed on to us by others. We, too, have only a transitory claim to this Paradise. Only the Hawaiian people can rightfully claim it as their own, and it was the Hawaiian people who—with supreme generosity—risked all they possessed in welcoming Caucasians, Chinese, Japanese, Filipinos, Koreans, Puerto Ricans and others to their Islands. . . .
>
> No wave of visitors to Hawaii has been more welcome than the military men, their wives, children, sweethearts and other relatives who have come here under the military Rest and Recuperation program. There were 123,000 of these guests in Hawaii last year. . . . "We will be back someday," they say again and again, and we pray that this may be so.

During his 1968 state of the State message, Burns made no mention of the coming Constitutional Convention, popularly known as Con-Con. As a part of its 1966 reapportionment decision, the U.S. Supreme Court had required the State of Hawaii to ask the voters if they would like to have a Constitutional Convention to discuss reapportionment—and any other aspects of the state Constitution they might wish to examine. Hawaii's voters had been quick to say "yes," by a margin of nearly 2 to 1 (119,097 to 62,120). Knowing that a Constitutional Convention could open "Pandora's Box," the governor was not enthusiastic about the enterprise. His vain hope was that the delegates would limit themselves to the questions of reapportionment and raising the State's obviously outmoded debt ceiling of $60 million.

When they finally convened in mid-July, the 82 delegates submitted 110 constitutional amendments for consideration. They included everything from reapportionment to unicameralism; from raising the debt limit to lowering the voting age; from extending judicial terms to limiting the number of terms the governor could serve. By the time they adjourned on 24 September, after seventy-two days of deliberation, twenty-three measures had been approved for presentation to the voters in the general election of 5 November 1968.

In the general election, the voters rejected only one of the twenty-three ballot measures with which they were presented—the lowering of the voting age from 20 to 18 years old. The new apportionment affected the house of representatives much more than the senate. The senate, having been reapportioned by the U.S. Supreme Court in 1966, required only minor changes. In the house, Oahu picked up another two seats and now held thirty-eight of the fifty-one seats. In addition, house districts were made smaller with a maximum of two or three members per district. Prior to this, four members were common in a single house district—the Republican Fifteenth District had six. The purpose of the exercise was to make certain that areas such as Manoa for the Democrats and Kahala for the Republicans were not disproportionately represented in the state house of representatives. The newly drawn districts were to go into effect for the election of 1970.

Another constitutional amendment that was approved by the voters was a measure that ended the state senate's status as a "continuous body" (i.e., one in which only half of the members were up for reelection every two years). Now all senators would be elected in the biennial election in which a governor was not being selected. To achieve this, those senators elected in 1970 would serve two-year terms, with all senate seats up for grabs in 1972 and every four years thereafter.

The voters also approved a measure that would dispense with the alternation of longer general sessions of the state legislature with shorter budget sessions. Judicial appointments were lengthened from six to ten years for the circuit court and from six years to seven on the supreme court. The recently enacted state code of ethics was incorporated into the state Constitution. Collective bargaining for public employees was assured. The State of Hawaii, generally credited with having one of the most progressive state Constitutions in the United States, had made incremental changes to its frame of government.

The 1968 political season proved to be less kind to the governor. But the drama came not from state politics, but from the local politics of the City and County of Honolulu. It started on 30 June, when Edwin P. Murray, a trustee of the Bishop Estate, died at the age of 80. One month later, Mayor Neal Blaisdell announced that he would not run for reelection after fourteen years in office. Everyone assumed that the mayor was simply clearing the decks for his appointment as a trustee of the Bishop Estate. When asked about this, his comment was: "I do not believe it is proper for me to comment on this, inasmuch as the decision rests with the supreme court, except to say that I would consider an invitation to serve as a Bishop Estate trustee a great honor, a privilege, and an opportunity to continue to serve our community." When asked about his health, the 65-year-old, part-Hawaiian former star athlete and coach replied, "My health is excellent. I did 300 push-ups this morning before breakfast."

One month later, on 30 August, Blaisdell's dream of becoming a Bishop Estate trustee was shattered when the Burns-appointed supreme court tapped Hung Wo Ching for the position. Ching, who was a member of one of Hawaii's most powerful Chinese families, was well known as a Burns fund-raiser and a close personal friend of the chief justice. Few questioned his qualifications. Born in Honolulu, the 56-year-old businessman had attended Royal School, McKinley High School, and the University of Hawaii. He held a bachelor's degree from Utah State University and a doctorate in economics and marketing from Cornell University. He had also done graduate work at the Harvard Business School. The *Honolulu Advertiser* characterized his career as one in which a local product had risen from a "shoeshine boy to become Chairman of the Board of Aloha Airlines"—and a member of the boards of Alexander & Baldwin, Bank of Hawaii, and the Hawaiian Telephone Company. Hawaiian church leader Abraham Akaka told reporters that he was "pleased" with the appointment.

Five days after Ching's appointment had been announced, on 4 September, Neal Blaisdell announced that he would run for the U.S. House of Representatives against Democrat Spark Matsunaga. When asked whether Ching's appointment to the board of the Bishop Estate had been a factor in his late announcement for the house seat, Blaisdell bristled. "Absolutely not! I had no reason to believe that I was the favorite son. . . . I was hopeful, because I thought I could do an effective job. But the appointment had absolutely no influence on my decision to make this race." Still, the suspicion lingered that Blaisdell had been made a promise that was not kept.

In a 1993 interview, Bill Richardson confirmed Blaisdell's assertion that no deal had been struck between him and Burns—or anyone else. Richardson was emphatic in characterizing Burns' posture on such matters: "No deals, absolutely no deals." The former chief justice said, "Burns may have talked with us about some of our appointments after they were made, but there was never an attempt to influence the decision-making process of the supreme court."

In the general election, after an ill-prepared, lackluster campaign, Neal Blaisdell took a terrible drubbing; Spark Matsunaga received 125,007 votes to 60,862 for Blaisdell. Unlike his friend Jack Burns, however, Neal Blaisdell enjoyed a full life after his political career ended. As Donald Johnson pointed out in his history of the City and County of Honolulu:

> Retired from politics, Neal Blaisdell became an executive for Western Airlines, traveling and enjoying a host of friends he had made both in Honolulu and abroad. His vigorous good health prevailed until a fatal stroke suddenly ended his life, just a day short of his seventy-third birthday on November 5, 1975 [seven months after the death of John A. Burns]. All Honolulu mourned the passing of a capable, devoted leader, who had served the city and county well and earned its respect and gratitude.

Jack Burns had lost a good friend at city hall, and Blaisdell's withdrawal had allowed Frank Fasi to realize his sixteen-year-old dream of becoming Honolulu's mayor. Fasi withstood a challenge from Burns loyalist Herman Lemke in the Democratic primary, which also eliminated a friendly face on the city council. If that wasn't bad enough, the governor's other close ally on the council, Matsy Takabuki, lost the seat he had held on that body since 1952. For Takabuki, losing came as a blessing: "On election night, when it became apparent that I had lost, Jack Burns called me to express his deep regrets. 'Jack, please don't worry,' I said to him. 'I'm glad it's over. I'm not going to lose any sleep over this. I have no regrets. I'm going to bed!'" There was one more Burns casualty in the 1968 elections: James Seishiro Burns, the governor's youngest son, finished eighth in a field of eight in his first—and last—run for the state house of representatives from Windward Oahu.

Jack Burns faced two more significant personnel changes at the dawning of 1969. After heading the state Department of Taxation for six years, the governor's younger brother was leaving. Ed Burns had presided over the Burns administration's preferred method of land reform, the taxation of land on the basis of its "highest and best use." This new method of appraising real estate for tax purposes had provided a strong disincentive to holding fallow land for speculative purposes and had spawned, for better and for worse, a dramatic increase in real estate development. At a testimonial dinner for his brother, Jack Burns said, "He has been *the* outstanding administrator in our government. The Tax

Department is a model for other departments." Continuity in the department was assured when Ralph Kondo, Ed Burns' deputy since 1965, assumed his position.

The other significant personnel change in 1969 took place five thousand miles away from Hawaii, when Richard M. Nixon replaced Lyndon B. Johnson as president of the United States. Burns felt that Johnson had been leading the United States into the "Pacific Era," and that with Nixon the country's orientation would turn toward Europe. Burns did not foresee that Nixon would prosecute the war in Vietnam as vigorously as Johnson had and that Nixon would begin normalizing the United States' relations with the People's Republic of China. But Burns did know that his special access to the office of the president of the United States had ended and he feared for the East-West Center under a Nixon–Agnew administration. After all, he told Helen Altonn of the *Honolulu Star-Bulletin,* the Eisenhower–Nixon administration had been "absolutely opposed to it." Burns also worried—correctly—about the Peace Corps Training Center on the Big Island. "We had the first contract for the Peace Corps," Burns pointed out. "Will the new administration even continue the Peace Corps to Pacific nations? I have heard nothing from the President-elect."

The 1969 legislative session opened with the most memorable speech John A. Burns ever made—his so-called inferiority of the spirit speech. The governor brushed off the more mundane aspects of state business with three short lines: "The theme is prudent spending. The tone is one of caution. The policy is pay-as-we-go." Moving into his main theme, Burns criticized those who "would close down again the doors we have opened and are determined to keep open." Burns acknowledged problems with housing, labor shortages, environmental decay, lagging public services, education, crime, and land use, saying, "All these continue to warrant our fullest attention today, [but] they are neither new nor insoluble."

Burns asked the members in joint session, and the public beyond, to stretch their minds and hearts, invoking the memory of explorers Cook, Vancouver, and Kotzebue, "the wisdom of Kamehameha and the Hawaiian people," the goodness of Father Damien, "the yearnings of the great Sun Yat-sen ... [and] Syngman Rhee, living in Hawaii, ... and the courage of Admiral Chester Nimitz . . . [who] helped to restore the Pacific and Asian regions a measure of freedom." Burns also invoked the memory of "the countless thousands of Island men of many races" who had provided a new vision of Hawaii's future out of the ashes of World War II. "Hawaii has become the young, throbbing Heart of the Pacific, . . . an example of the vibrant life at its best and an inspiration to millions."

The governor then drove to the core of his message:

> To be perfectly candid, I sense among certain elements of our community—particularly those who are descended from our immigrant plantation workers—a subtle "inferiority of the spirit," which is totally unwarranted and which becomes for them a social and psychological handicap in life.
>
> You who have grown up with me here in these Islands and who remember the pre–World War II climate know full well what I mean. You know, too, that there should be no basis for this feeling. On the contrary, our people are equal to [or] in my judgment, superior to their counterparts anywhere. They should be proud, and we should be proud, of their ethnic roots, of the riches and treasures of their Pacific and Asian cultures.
>
> I submit further that they should be given every opportunity—even in our public school system—to learn more about their own rich past. . . . Hawaii's history, in its every facet, should be a matter of general knowledge to all our people. . . . The contributions to our society of the Chings and Lums [Chinese], the Cravalhos and the Henriques [Portuguese], the Kahanamokus and the Kealohas [Hawaiian], the Samsons and the Menors [Filipino], the Kims and the Ahns [Korean], the Cooks and the Judds [Caucasian]—their stories—and thousands of other stories like them—are an integral part of Hawaii's real history. . . .
>
> Let us clearly understand that diversity and division are not the same. In diversity there can be unity. In division, there is schism. . . . "What is past is prologue. Study the past." These words of advice from Shakespeare are inscribed [on the front of] the National Archives in Washington. We would [do] well to take them to heart here today, lest the past be lost forever and with it our children's future.

The lawmakers listened intently to Burns' philosophical words—words that called for a state of mind rather than a plan of action. The press was listening, too, but often with a sense of frustration. Gerry Keir listened to Burns' 1969 state of the State address as a political writer for the *Honolulu Advertiser.* Looking back in 1982, Keir remarked that "Burns always maintained a dreamy vision of Hawaii and the Pacific. His state of the State addresses become increasingly metaphysical. It was tough for a reporter. In terms of legislative programs, he had little left.

But he had something to say and he kept on saying it: 'You're not second-class citizens.'"

That was, of course, the message of his life. His wife understood that better than anyone. "I've always said, 'If you'd skin him, he's not a haole,'" she said. "As governor, I think the main thing for him was to erase that 'subtle inferiority of the spirit' he talked about. When children visited the office, he'd ask them what they wanted to be. If they said something that didn't aim very high, he would ask them why they didn't want to be governor or senator or president of a company."

During the 1969 legislative session, Burns lost only the third member of his original cabinet when he appointed Attorney General Bert Kobayashi to a long-promised seat on the state supreme court. The governor said that he agreed to Kobayashi's move with "mixed feelings," calling him "the strong right arm of this administration since I first took office." Burns' first choice for a new attorney general was his old friend, Matsy Takabuki. "Fortunately," Takabuki recalled, "I was able to persuade the governor that I could be more helpful to his administration as an outsider than as an insider." For his second choice, Burns once again opted for continuity, appointing Kobayashi's deputy attorney General Bert Kanbara.

On 15 March 1969, Burns attended the dedication of Hawaii's new Capitol. For the previous three years, he had served as a sidewalk construction foreman on his morning walks to work from Washington Place. With its volcanic chambers, open-air roof, and sixteen-foot koa doors, the Capitol captured in concrete, wood, and tile much of the aspiration Burns tried to instill in Hawaii's people. "It should give you a spiritual or emotional pick-up," he told *Star-Bulletin* writer Helen Altonn during a 1967 tour of the construction site. "Symbolically, it has included the spirit of the future, not only of Hawaii, but of the entire Pacific, the Orient and the Occident—both the eastern and western civilizations." Late in the construction process, Burns demanded raising the building's roof—at considerable public expense.

The 1969 legislative session itself proved to be a lackluster affair, ending with a dramatic public relations setback for Governor Burns. Magic Island, a land reclamation development project next to Ala Moana Park, had been kicking around since the 1950s. As Tom Coffman pointed out in *Catch a Wave*, "By the time Burns had become Governor in 1963, a peninsula of thirty-five acres had been built off the Waikiki end of Ala Moana Park and . . . he halted further land-fills." In

1969, Burns actively lobbied for a Magic Island development bill. The bill would have allowed Dillingham Corporation to fill substantial new sections of the reef off Ala Moana Park in order to build luxury condominiums. Many saw the development as the destruction of the last local beach between Diamond Head and Ewa Beach. The bill appeared moribund until a last-minute blitz by the Burns forces, Dillingham lobbyists, and the ILWU's Eddie DeMello pushed it through.

Burns defended his action by saying that he was trying to keep the construction industry vital. Tom Gill delighted in the whole episode. As Coffman wrote, "Gill was in a confident mood. He made a critical decision. In June, shortly after the legislature adjourned, Gill leaked a poll to the press, showing a lead over Burns of ten percentage points among Democratic voters." Burns, ever the realist, quickly distanced himself from the Magic Island project. The existing thirty-five-acre peninsula was converted into a public park, "in time for Burns to plant a ceremonial tree by the ocean before November 1970."

During the last two years of his second term, Governor Burns faced the most difficult decision of his public life—the repeal of Hawaii's hundred-year-old law against abortion. During the 1969 session of the legislature, Representative George W. T. Loo introduced an abortion bill in the house. It was based on a model law supported by the American Medical Association. The legislation would have restricted abortions to a licensed hospital, when certified by two licensed physicians, for any one of four reasons: (1) to preserve the mother's physical or mental health; (2) for an unmarried girl, 16 years old or younger; (3) in cases of rape or incest; (4) where the child was almost certain to be born with a grave physical or mental defect.

Loo's bill easily passed in the house of representatives. It would have passed in the senate as well had it not been for Senator Vincent Yano. Yano, a 48-year-old father of ten, who had been raised as a Roman Catholic, said he needed time to study the bill before reporting it out of the senate Public Health Committee to the full senate. Many assumed that Yano's hesitation was a Roman Catholic's reaction to the issue of abortion. They were wrong.

On 14 September 1969, before a meeting of the Honolulu chapter of the American Association of University Women, Yano revealed the true reason for his opposition to the Loo bill. "That bill," Yano charged, "does not meet the problem. In the eight states that have it, studies have shown that the legal abortions have not increased, nor have the number of illegal abortions decreased." Yano's solution was a new law that had only two conditions:

1. All abortions must be performed by a licensed physician in a hospital, or under conditions approved by the Hawaii Medical Association.
2. No abortion shall be performed after the viability of the fetus to live outside the womb, except in cases where the Hawaii Medical Association has certified a probable birth defect.

The *Honolulu Star-Bulletin,* in a feature called "Speak Up," gave the paper's readers a chance to express themselves on the issue. More than 1,500 questionnaires were returned. The results were published on 7 November 1969. Those who favored the Yano plan numbered 1,355; those who favored the Loo plan numbered 86; those who opposed the repeal of the existing abortion law numbered 66. The *Star-Bulletin,* responding to Roman Catholic bishop John Scanlan's characterization of abortion as "an erosion of morality," editorialized: "Until it can be proved without scientific doubt that life begins at conception, there can be no justifiable reason for the State to refuse [to allow] non-Catholics to live by their own moral convictions."

As the 1970 legislative session opened, the *Star-Bulletin* did a more scientific sampling of Hawaii's public opinion on the issue of abortion. The sample was made up of 450 individuals who were at least 20 years old and eligible to vote. They were asked: "Do you agree with the State Senate proposal to repeal the law which now prohibits abortion? The bill would make abortions legal." In other words, do you agree with the concept of abortion upon demand? The response was: 54 percent agreed; 32.8 percent disagreed; 12.3 percent undecided.

U.S. Senator Dan Inouye gave an early rendition of the classic prochoice position when he spoke in support of the abortion bill at Honolulu Community College. Inouye asserted that the question "should be left to the conscience and determination of each woman, in consultation with her physician. . . . It is my sole desire that every child brought into this world should be loved and wanted. We can ask no less for our children."

At the urging of Representative Loo, the senate bill was amended to include a ninety-day residency requirement to avoid the prospect of Hawaii becoming to abortions what Nevada was to divorces. Loo wanted no "abortion-tours" to Hawaii. With that change the Yano bill was approved in the senate by a 15 to 9 margin and in the house by a 31 to 20 vote. Governor Burns now had ten working days to sign the bill, veto it, or allow it to become law without his signature.

The question, of course, was how a deeply committed Roman Catholic governor would respond to what was clearly one of the burning moral issues of our time. Everyone wanted to know. *Honolulu Advertiser* reporter Gerry Keir spent a long afternoon trying to discern Burns' intentions: "The abortion bill was sitting on his desk. Several times in the course of the interview I was certain that 1) he was going to veto it, that 2) he was going to sign it, and that 3) he was going to let it pass without his signature. He left me, as he often did, batting the side of my head over what he'd said."

State Senator John Hulten, a devout Catholic himself, batted himself aside the head as well—in frustration with Burns. Hulten and Burns had talked often about their religion, and Hulten spent an hour on the phone with Burns pleading with him to veto the abortion bill. "He argued that if he vetoed, the legislature was likely to come up with a worse bill," Hulten remembered. "He said he had to represent *all* the people. I pointed out that government exists to protect the helpless and that the most helpless is the unborn fetus. Burns didn't seem racked by the problem. He didn't seem bothered. He'd rationalized his decision. A veto might not have accomplished anything; it might have been overridden. But I argued that he should have shown his principle." Aside from conversations with Hulten and a few others, Burns kept his own counsel. In the end, he allowed the bill to become law without his signature. It immediately became the most progressive abortion law in the nation. In a written message to the people of Hawaii, the governor explained his decision:

I have declined to sign this bill after much study and soul-searching; after receiving competent advice from Island and national specialists in law, medicine, theology, human rights and public affairs, and after sincere prayer to that Creator named in our nation's Declaration of Independence as the Source of our unalienable rights to life, liberty and the pursuit of happiness.

When a citizen is elected Governor, . . . he must never let his private political and religious convictions unduly influence his judgment as Governor of ALL the people. . . . In the recent debates and public controversy over proposed abortion law changes in our State, I have been subjected to pleadings, warnings, even threats from many sources, including clergymen and lay members of my own Roman Catholic Church. . . .

I have always abhorred the idea of abortion, I believe it a gravely sinful act. . . . The personal experiences Mrs. Burns and I have had in raising our family have additionally strengthened my convictions on abortion. . . . While I do have strong personal views as to the morality of abortions, I cannot permit these views to influence my official actions as chief executive of this State. . . . The executive's veto power should be exercised mainly where there is a clear conflict of views as to the effect of a policy against the best interests of all the people of this State, where legislation does not adhere to the end desired, is contrary to other law, is patently in error, or unconstitutional. The limitations of the office of the Governor should be respected. It is not the function of the chief executive to legislate; it is his function to administer the law.

Jack Burns discussed the abortion bill at great length with his youngest son, by then a 33-year-old former "miracle baby," James Seishiro Burns. It was only through the indomitable faith and determination of Bea and John Burns that Jim Burns had been born at all. The doctors had recommended an abortion—to save the mother's life. James S. Burns, now the chief judge of the state of Hawaii's intermediate court of appeals, remembered his father's abortion decision as "the best example of how he had mellowed in later years."

Jim Burns sought to play a role in his father's decision: "I lobbied, personally, with him not to veto it. . . . [It was] a question of imposing one's religious beliefs upon the community. And I think he tried to separate himself—Jack Burns, the individual Catholic—from Jack Burns, the governor of the people of the State of Hawaii. When asked in 1976 whether the abortion bill had been his father's "toughest political decision," Jim Burns replied without hesitation, "Yes, there's no doubt about it. He agonized over that more than anything I could think of."

Burns' decision to allow the abortion bill to become law without his signature took the matter out of the 1970 election campaign debate. Had Burns vetoed the bill, it may well have become an issue in his contest against Tom Gill. Gill had quietly expressed himself in favor of the abortion bill, but generally kept a low profile on the issue. But if abortion was not an issue in the 1970 governor's race, practically everything else that took place in the State during that critical year was. It was a year to remember.

Inauguration Day 1962. Jack Burns marches out of Iolani Palace for the Royal Bandstand to give his inaugural address. Bea looks on.

The governor, his lady, and his three grown children: (*top row*) Jack, Jr., a Woodrow Wilson scholar and crack Washington researcher and speech writer; Jim, a lawyer and eventually chief judge of Hawaii's intermediate court of appeals; (*bottom row center*) daughter Mary Beth who today is a practicing clinical psychologist; beside Mary Beth, Jim's first wife Lynette.

Attorney General Bert Kobayashi, who—besides his official duties—played a critical role in settling a number of labor disputes.

Brother Edward Burns, who as tax director put into practice Burns' promise of taxing land at its "highest and best use."

Fujio "Fudge" Matsuda, the director of transportation, who oversaw much of the highway and airport building that accompanied Hawaii's explosive growth in the 1960s.

Tom Hamilton, the president of the University of Hawaii, who enjoyed Burns' trust and support in building the University—but who resigned over the Oliver Lee case.

Jack Burns and the legislature understood each other. Here he talks with three in-fluential law-makers: Senator Kazuhisa Abe, State Representative Howard Miyake, and House Speaker Elmer Cravalho.

Burns enjoyed an easy relationship with Honolulu's Republican mayor, Neal Blaisdell.

Jack Burns doing what he loved to do best. He was a member of Lanikai's Mid-Pacific Country Club and while as governor played every Wednesday afternoon at the Waialae Country Club.

Father Kekumano and Burns in front of the Catholic Cathedral on Fort Street, where Governor Burns was a daily communicant.

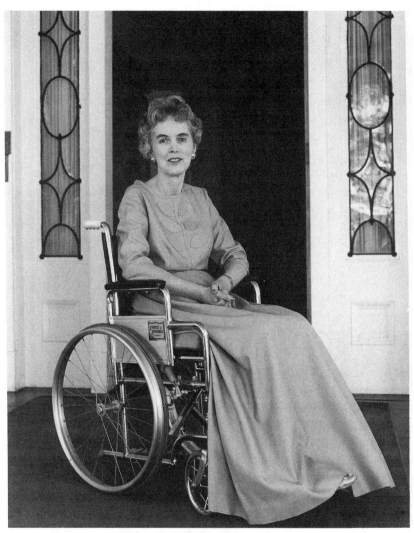

Bea Burns found life in Washington Place "liberating."

The governor with Queen Elizabeth II during her visit to Hawaii.

Bea with the Queen Mother.

From left to right: Lady Bird Johnson, Patricia Sharp (wife of Admiral Ulysses S. Grant Sharp), President Lyndon B. Johnson, Governor Burns, Bea Burns, and Jim Burns.

Burns congratulates the State's new chief justice of the supreme court, Bill Richardson, in 1966.

Richardson's appointment turned 1966 into a wild political year when Burns attempted to name newcomer Democrat Kenneth Brown as his running mate.

Tom Gill won the nomination, but as this photo made clear, they were not comfortable with one another.

Burns took great pride in the construction of the State's new Capitol. He played sidewalk construction boss throughout its construction, 1967–1969.

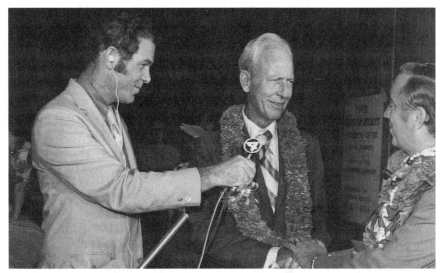

Burns is being greeted by Senate President David McClung on election night in 1970 as channel 4 reporter Byron Baker captures the moment for his interview.

The 1970 Democratic Party ticket: Burns and Senator George Ariyoshi.

On election night Bea celebrates with the campaign's architect, former state
Representative Robert Oshiro.

Burns surveys the construction of his retirement home in the hills above Waimea, Hawaii, with Kenneth Brown's wife Joan.

S·I·X·T·E·E·N

Catching a Wave

GOVERNOR BURNS ENTERED the 1970 election year on the defensive. Polls showed him more than 20 percent behind Tom Gill. Critics particularly attacked his stewardship of Hawaii's most precious resource, its environment. In his 22 January state of the State message, Burns enlisted the support of the State's lawmakers, asserting that they, as partners in the accomplishments of the past seven years, were also being attacked:

> I am constrained to describe as the height of presumption any allega-
> tion that you have ignored environmental concerns in the past. From
> the outset of this administration, I have found the legislative branch
> completely receptive and understanding of our environmental needs.
> How else could we, for instance, achieve acquisition of Kahana Valley
> for a regional park at a cost in excess of $5 million? How else could we
> have established Hanauma Bay as a marine conservation area? How
> else the countless number of other projects in our environmental pro-
> gram of recent years? We need make no apology for the past.

Everyone knew whose "presumptuous allegations" had angered the governor. Burns was clearly directing his ire at Lieutenant Governor Gill who, having been excluded—or having excluded himself in the governor's view—from meaningful participation in the Burns administration, had become a one-man speaker's bureau. Unlike many of his environmentalist critics, Governor Burns sought to balance the needs of the economy with any threat to the environment. As he said in his state of the State message, "It should be remembered that the key ingredient in any environment is man himself. If a man is hungry, ill-housed, under-educated or poorly treated in his society, what service is it to him that

267

his environment remains in its pristine natural state?" Burns sought to keep the economy growing, fine-tuning environmental problems as they became apparent. Gill, on the other hand, feared that these problems would be impossible to manage if they were not anticipated and planned for in advance. It was a fundamental philosophical difference.

In 1970, Burns attacked one of the most troublesome problems of Hawaii's poststatehood prosperity—housing. In August 1969, Burns had appointed a panel to study the State's housing problems. That beginning led to The Governor's Conference on Housing, which was held 9–13 February 1970. The agenda was heavily salted with mainland housing experts. The conference began with two days at the Royal Hawaiian Hotel in Waikiki. Then the conferees hit the road, spending one day each on Kauai, Maui, and the Big Island.

The keynote speaker was Howard R. Maskof of the National Corporation for Housing Partnerships. Maskof told those assembled that 19 percent of all U.S. housing was substandard, that vacancy rates for rentals throughout the country were dropping below the amount needed for mobility, and that U.S. housing needs over the next ten years amounted to 26 million new units. He pointed out that the current annual rate of 1 million to 1.3 million units per year was less than half of that required to meet the nation's housing needs. In other words, Hawaii was not alone. The rest of the conference was devoted to ways to achieve quality, low-cost housing.

Gill was not impressed with The Governor's Conference on Housing. Indeed, he thought it dangerous:

> No conference ever solved a traffic problem, cleaned up a cubic inch of air or water, or built a single house. Yet, if attended by sufficient media coverage and general publicity, it can give the impression of movement. Nothing really happens, but an image is created. Weeks or months later, when the problem still persists, as it will, the public remembers vaguely the image of action, but sees no results. And the cynicism about government deepens. . . . Less of our effort should go into creating the illusion of action and more into the hard, grubby work of wrestling with the perverse details of the problems which threaten to overpower us.

On 25 February, Bill Cook, the governor's special assistant for urban affairs, unveiled a $32.4 million housing bill before Senator Vincent Yano's Public Health, Welfare and Housing Committee. As the bill moved through the legislature, it developed a life of its own. The public relations drive to pass the housing bill included Hawaii's first state housing fair, an event that opened on 9 May and traveled throughout the Islands before summer's end. On 12 May, in the longest session of the eleven-year history of Hawaii's state legislature, a $100 million omnibus housing bill was passed—more than three times the governor's request two and one-half months earlier.

Gill was in a tough spot. The omnibus housing bill was decidedly more than the "illusion of action" he had spoken of at the time of The Governor's Conference on Housing. To support the Burns administration's housing efforts would undermine one of his most important issues in the coming campaign. But, if Gill chose to criticize the governor's efforts, he risked being seen as more interested in his own political future than the needs of the people of Hawaii. Gill chose the latter risk. In March, even before the housing bill had been passed, Gill told the house Committee on Consumer Protection and Housing: "You can pump all the money you want into it and you're going to get nothing . . . as long as [the people of Hawaii] are restricted by the current market mechanism . . . and it pays to sell at the highest price the traffic will bear."

Gill favored the creation of a second market to be controlled by the state and county governments. Dwellings would be available by lot, not bid, and resale would be controlled in such a way that speculation would be avoided. Gill also favored mixed-price housing projects, which would avoid the creation of economic housing ghettos—for the rich or for the poor. He called for greater density of housing in order to create more open space for parks. He argued that these housing clusters should be built near transportation corridors and joined by mass transit, thus removing automobiles from Oahu's choked streets and highways.

Then, to downplay the efforts of the governor and the legislature to pass a housing bill, Gill asserted in an April speech that "the mechanism for allowing the State to go into massive housing development has been on the books for ten years. It was passed by the Legislature in 1959. I wrote the law. But it has not been used." Gill sought a utopian solution to a practical problem. Had Gill's complete vision been adopted at that time, Oahu might be a better place. But politics, as the more pragmatic Burns well knew, is "the art of the possible." Gill's approach to housing appealed to the intellectual community at the University of Hawaii, but it did not connect with the public at large, who cherished the American dream of the single family dwelling with two cars in every garage—or carport in Hawaii—and a wide open highway. And if the highway wasn't open, the solution was to build more highways.

At the opening of the state housing fair on 9 May, the governor sought to isolate those who criticized his housing program: "I'm told that there are those in Hawaii who have labeled efforts to solve the housing problem as 'Mission Impossible.' I do not agree with this pessimistic view. There are twenty-eight builders participating in this housing fair who do not agree. The State Legislature does not agree, nor do the Mayors and Councils of these Islands." Clearly, something had to be done. According to the Federal Housing Administration (FHA), new homes in Hawaii were selling for almost 60 percent above the national average; used homes for more than 90 percent above the national average. In Hawaii, the price of land—when it could be bought—made up over 40 percent of the price of a home; on the mainland, that figure was 20 percent.

In 1970, the Burns administration undertook another effort to demonstrate the governor's interest in planning Hawaii's future. From 5 August through 8 August, The Governor's Conference on the Year 2000 held center stage in Honolulu. The keynote speaker at the opening dinner at the Ilikai Hotel was Arthur C. Clarke, scientist, writer, and co-author of the film *2001: A Space Odyssey*. Clarke had little to say about Hawaii, but he definitely had star quality.

In an astute move, Burns asked George Chaplin to chair the conference. Chaplin had come to Hawaii in 1958 as the editor of the *Honolulu Advertiser* and had succeeded in taking that archconservative morning daily to journalistic respectability and an editorial position somewhat to the left of its rival, the afternoon daily *Honolulu Star-Bulletin*. The conference made something of a star out of a University of Hawaii political science professor with a "Prince Valiant" haircut, futurist Jim Dator. It also produced a book containing the best efforts of a "Task Force" of 250 members.

On 9 July, when Tom Gill had officially announced that he would run for the Democratic nomination for governor, he asserted that he had been "excluded from all major decisions, given no assignments, . . . [and] on occasion not even been informed by staff when the Governor left town." Alluding to his 1967 visit from Myron Thompson, Gill told his audience, "I was early given to understand that I could not work within the administration unless I pledged not to run for Governor in 1970." He called Burns "a very decent human being and a personally honest man," but went on to say that Burns was the captive of "some of the most alarming friends . . . [who are] doing too well to risk the uncertain winds of change." Gill concluded:

> There is strong evidence that, up until my nomination as Lieutenant Governor in 1966, Jack [Burns] had no intention of running for a third term. He told some of his friends that two terms was enough. But after the primary election of 1966, all this suddenly changed. There was an intruder in the house! . . . I doubt very much if his associates would [now] let him retire.

Responding to reporters, Burns acknowledged that he had, indeed, expressed himself in favor of a two-term limit before the Constitutional Convention of 1968. The amendment, however, was not adopted by the delegates. "Since they didn't think that way," Burns reasoned, "I've got a different obligation. As long as the good Lord gives me health and the voters want me, I'm here." When asked what he thought of Gill's announcement that he would oppose Burns in the Democratic primary, the governor replied, "It's a free country."

When Gill made his formal announcement, Burns was still six weeks away from his own declaration that he would be a candidate, but nobody doubted it was coming. When Bea Burns was asked in 1976 how her husband had broached the subject of a third term with her, the response was revealing: "He didn't. Bob Oshiro did. Everybody knew that I didn't want him to run again." Her response to Oshiro was typical of the governor's wife: "It's Jack's decision. . . . You know how I feel. If Jack wants to do it, okay." Asked if her husband had really wanted to run, Mrs. Burns replied, "No, [but] he felt the alternative was devastating. He didn't want to be governor. . . . He only did this because of what he felt was needed for Hawaii, and he felt that if he didn't do it, they wouldn't get [it] done."

Jack Burns' brother, Ed, was as opposed to a third term as his sister-in-law—and just as much out of the loop:

> I was sorry to see him agree to run again from a personal standpoint. I felt he'd done his job. It was up to somebody else to carry on. And if Tom Gill got in, . . . so what? The shape of things weren't going to change that much, because Tom Gill or Frank Fasi or anybody else was going to have a hell of a time with the state legislature. . . . So that didn't bother me. . . . I was against his wanting to run again, [but I] never told him directly—I didn't have the opportunity to. I let it be

known to Matsy [Takabuki] and others that I felt he shouldn't run again. . . . This was a decision that he got talked into, and I think he had some regrets as time went by, especially when he became ill the first time.

James S. Burns, the governor's youngest son, an attorney in his mid-30s at the time, confirmed the obvious: "Had not Tom Gill been the guy running, he would probably not have run. . . . But here's a man who worked most of his adult life to bring Hawaii to its position in 1970, and I think he could see that his successor might well destroy most of the things that he worked to achieve." Jack Burns was not about to turn the State of Hawaii over to Tom Gill. Instead, he turned himself over to Robert Oshiro.

In 1968 Oshiro stepped down as state chairman of the Democratic Party. His intention was to devote all his energies to Governor Burns' reelection campaign. He also sought to bring Senator David McClung into the Party's leadership, as the new state chairman, thus broadening the base of the Burns coalition. Just months earlier, McClung had sided with the Gill faction in the senate organizational struggle. Now he was fully committed to the reelection of John A. Burns.

In anticipation of the 1970 governor's race, Oshiro hired Lennen and Newell Pacific, a public relations firm, to run the media side of the campaign. More important, Oshiro went back to the grassroots that Jack Burns had worked so well before the 1962 election. Only this time it was Oshiro, not the candidate, who was drinking the coffee. As he described the strategy in 1977:

> What I tried to do was to go back to the basic believers and re-instill and re-kindle their dedication to Jack Burns, . . . to revitalize this rev-olutionary zeal that they had in the forties or the fifties or whatever, and make them proud of what Jack had done. And I think the great-est strength of the 1970 campaign . . . pivoted around a belief in a man and [that] man's commitment to Hawaii's people.

In 1969 and 1970, Oshiro attended coffee hours "four—five nights a week." He went wherever he could gather a few people to listen to him. Meeting with three or four people was not unusual. "I've gone to (cof-fees) with as few as two," he recalled. "But those small groups . . . pick up numbers."

To top it off, at the start Oshiro was doing this for a man who might not be willing to run again. "He was supportive of what I was doing, spiritually," Oshiro recalled. "Physically, he was very reluctant." Burns would remind his friend, "Bob, I'm no 52-year-old, you know. . . . You do what you want, but don't get me involved to the extent that I'm going to be running around with you."

As far as money, the universal lubricant of politics, was concerned, Oshiro had a real problem in 1969: "I didn't have a candidate. All I had was the possibility of a candidate. And yet I knew I needed money for the 1970 campaign. So what I did was to get the public relations firm to prepare a brochure for me and we called it 'The Prospectus Brochure.' The primary purpose of the brochure was to just let . . . the business community know that when [they were] ready to help in anyone's campaign, keep us in mind. I didn't ask for a nickel . . . in that brochure." Yet the business community sent him more than $150,000.

Oshiro was quick to point out that, generally speaking, he never handled the money in any campaign. He left that to the money men like Clarence Ching and Matsy Takabuki. "We never had . . . a formal campaign structure," Oshiro continued, "and this is very important. All we had were volunteers who said 'Look, I'll go money,' and help us raise money. . . . I don't have any direct knowledge of this," Oshiro said, "but on the basis of the varied conversations I've had with people after the fact and during the period, [the] bulk of the money came from contractors, engineers, developers, [and] architects, if you want to categorize them." When asked whether having Tom Gill as an opponent made it easier to raise money for the 1970 campaign than it would have been against another candidate, Oshiro's quick response was, "Yes, my answer would be 'yes' to that question."

In 1970, the Burns campaign needed lots of money because Oshiro and Lennen and Newell were preparing a media campaign unprecedented in Hawaii's political history. That media campaign has been well documented in Tom Coffman's campaign study, *Catch a Wave*. On 12 May, the day the 1970 legislative session ended, six weeks of television spots began, featuring the legislative achievements of the Burns administration and asking the viewers to "think about it." Lennen and Newell Pacific's advertising executives felt Burns' achievements had largely been kept a secret; they needed to inform the public of his many accomplishments.

The "think about it" series had a subtheme. Countering the strident presentation by Tom Gill about all the problems in Hawaii, the Burns commercials showed Hawaii in its best light, with beautiful scenery and happy people of many races. A mellow voice would then ask the viewers, "Hawaii isn't such a bad place to live, is it?" The Burns campaign asked the people of Hawaii to look at their State in a positive way.

The media people also sought to humanize their often austere candidate. They did so with a thirty-minute, award-winning film called *To Catch a Wave*. The film has often been referred to as slick, but that is the wrong word for it. It was professional. The public relations people knew that Burns was at his best one-on-one. They would make a film where thousands of viewers had a chance to be with the governor of Hawaii one-on-one. It was because the film was so true to Burns' personality that it was so effective.

But while the film was effective, it was a mistake to say that the film had won the election for him, as Coffman's book *Catch a Wave* implied. In the end, Burns' victory came more as a result of Oshiro's grassroots work and the fortuitous selection of his running-mate.

Unlike 1966, in 1970 the governor weighed the political ramifications of who his running-mate would be more carefully. In the decade following 1960, the haole population of the Islands had risen from 32 percent to a reported 38.8 percent, while the Japanese-American population had dropped from 32.2 percent to 28.3 percent. While this would seem to have mitigated against an AJA candidate for lieutenant governor, the Burns campaign recognized that the AJAs represented 45.8 percent of all registered Democrats, while haoles represented only 20 percent. With this in mind, they turned to a politician who had never been closely associated with either the Burns or the Gill factions of the Democratic Party and one who had never lost an election—state senator George Ariyoshi.

Burns had recruited George Ariyoshi to run for public office in 1954, but Ariyoshi had never become a part of the governor's inner circle. Ariyoshi was, therefore, surprised when he was approached by several people who were speaking in behalf of Governor Burns, "in 1969, between Christmas and New Year's . . . about running for Lieutenant Governor." One of them was Ariyoshi's former law partner and Burns' attorney general for most of his first two terms, state supreme court justice Bert Kobayashi. When Ariyoshi asked how Governor Burns felt about his running, he was told, "You'll get a call from him." That call led to a breakfast meeting at Washington Place. There, according to Ariyoshi, Burns told him that "he wasn't thinking so much about who would run with him in 1970, but who would succeed him in 1974." Ariyoshi's response was, "Governor, I'm having a hard time thinking about 1970. Please don't ask me about 1974." Burns countered, saying, "Okay, as long as you don't say no for now."

Ariyoshi did not fit the typical mold of the AJA politician. He was not a product of a plantation family; his father, a Japanese seaman, had jumped ship in Honolulu in 1919 and had worked at a variety of mostly urban enterprises over the years. His mother ran a small saimin shop in Palama until she was able to open her own Smith Street Cafe. Ariyoshi was too young to have been in the 100th or 442nd, having graduated—president of his senior class—from McKinley High School in 1943. After a year at the University of Hawaii, Ariyoshi was drafted and served as an interpreter for the U.S. Army in Japan during the early days of the military occupation following World War II.

When he got out of the Army in 1947, Ariyoshi followed in the footsteps of many veterans and used the G.I. Bill as his ticket to complete college—at Michigan State—and then go to law school at the University of Michigan. In 1952, at the age of 26, Ariyoshi returned to Hawaii and began to practice law. He came face to face with what he felt was an unacceptable level of racial prejudice. It was when he expressed this feeling to John A. Burns in 1954, that he was convinced that he should run for public office. Thus began a political career that had lasted for sixteen years. In 1969, Ariyoshi had decided to serve one more term in the state senate and then to retire in 1974 to pursue his first love—law. That, of course, was before he received his telephone call from Governor Burns.

To catch the momentum of the highly productive 1970 legislative session, George Ariyoshi decided to announce his candidacy on 18 May. Burns knew that in Ariyoshi he had found a man willing to play a subordinate role and to be a team player, but he did not realize the powerful message his running mate would bring to the campaign. On 8 July he found out. At a $100 a plate fund-raiser at the Hilton Hawaiian Village, Ariyoshi delivered what came to be known as his *"Okaga sama de"* speech.

"I am what I am because of you," George Ariyoshi told those who had come to honor him and support his candidacy. He went on to tell what it was like to rise out of the slums of Honolulu; he talked of his early desire to be a lawyer and of his father's pledge to give "the shirt off his back" to make it come true; he spoke of his homeroom teacher at Central Intermediate School, Mrs. Margaret Hamada, who had given so freely of her time to help him overcome a speech impediment; he told how Governor John A. Burns had encouraged him to go into public life to make things better for others; he spoke directly to his children, telling them how lucky they were to live in Hawaii, "where government places its emphasis on people and human dignity, where your education and your enjoyment of life is given such high priority, where there is equality of opportunity, and where you can dream, and dreams become real if we work for them."

Ariyoshi pointed out than Hawaii had not always been this way, that there had been a tremendous change in recent years. "If any man in Hawaii is to be given credit for this change," Ariyoshi concluded, "it is your present Governor, our dear friend, John A. Burns." The standing ovation Ariyoshi received was loud, sustained, and heart-felt. No one ever called George Ariyoshi a great speaker, but he had given the speech of his life on this night; he would give this speech, or a variant of it, for the rest of the 1970 campaign. In the meantime, Tom Gill's choice for lieutenant governor, Big Island Judge Nelson Doi, had taken himself out of the race. Gill would have Vincent Yano as a late and reluctant running mate.

On 14 August, John A. Burns officially announced that he would be a candidate for the Democratic nomination for governor of the State of Hawaii. He had reason to feel optimistic. The 20 percent deficit to Tom Gill with which he had begun the year was dwindling rapidly. In a poll taken on 12 and 13 August by the *Honolulu Star-Bulletin*, Gill had 46.6 percent of the vote; Burns had 38.9 percent; and 14.5 percent remained undecided. Gill's lead was in single digits and the momentum was moving in the governor's direction. Then a serious stormcloud threatened the governor's long anticipated formal announcement.

On the same day Burns announced his candidacy, *Honolulu Star-Bulletin* political writer Buck Donham revealed that Shiro Nishimura, a former member of the State Land Use Commission who had been appointed by Governor Burns, had voted to redistrict ninety-two acres of agricultural land to urban use. The land in question was part of a 137-acre parcel owned by Hui O Kauai, a partnership in which Nishimura had a 10 percent interest. As it turned out, Hui O Kauai made a $575,000 gain in less than one year. Based on a sale price of $900,000 and a purchase price of $325,000, it computed to a gain of 277 percent in one year. Based upon a down payment of only $22,500 it computed to a one-year gain of 2,555 percent. Here was Tom Gill's "Exhibit A" among those he referred to as Governor Burns' "alarming friends." In his defense, Nishimura pointed out that his vote had been in favor of all changes proposed at the close of a five-year review and that he had not— and would not have—voted upon a measure involving his land only.

The day after the *Star-Bulletin* story broke, Governor Burns flew to Japan to open Hawaii's highly successful Expo 70 exhibit. When he returned, Burns sought to deflect the Nishimura case by announcing that he was expanding his investigation of any conflicts of interest to include "all sensitive boards and commissions" in the State. He was doing so, he said, because "I believe recent stories may have prompted some people to lose faith in the many dedicated, honest, and hard-working people who are unselfishly giving their time and effort on State boards and commissions." Then, in an interesting tactic, the governor praised the *Star-Bulletin* for its efforts in the Nishimura case. "This kind of reporting," Burns said, "keeps the government on its toes."

As a matter of fact, it led to another Burns initiative just four days after his return from Japan. On 26 August, as the primary campaign was about to go into its final month, Governor Burns announced that Bill Cook would be his special assistant for housing as well as urban affairs. Cook, a former reporter and public relations man, became a voting member of the newly empowered Hawaii Housing Authority. He would be the governor's point man in the implementation of the Omnibus Housing Act of 1970. Cook had originally come to Burns' attention through his friends on the Honolulu City Council, where he had been successful in drafting a successful $237,000 Model Cities grant proposal for the City and County of Honolulu. At this critical point in the campaign, he impressed many as a man of action. "Even while the rules and regulations are being drafted," Cook told the press, "we're in negotiations with the private sector for development of 15,000 to 20,000 units. We expect to have signed agreements . . . before the end of the year."

By this time, Cook had become one of Governor Burns' principal offensive weapons aimed at challenger Gill. Indeed, the day before Governor Burns had returned from Japan, Cook had told the press: "There are those who would have us believe that the blame for the high cost of housing rests with greedy developers, home builders and landlords. It would be ridiculous for me to suggest that everyone in the home-building industry is simon pure, but it would be an equally ridiculous generality to suggest that all are greedy profit-takers." Cook concluded by saying that the Governor's Committee on Housing "refused to believe" that the basic problem was greed. "So, instead of making demagogic utterances—none of which would produce a single house—they shaped what I believe, and what many Federal officials believe, to be the most progressive State housing legislation in America."

Concerned over the possible effects of the Nishimura revelations, the Burns campaign organization had its internal polling specialist, Rick Egged, do a sampling of opinion. Egged found that fewer than 50 percent of the voters were even aware of the Nishimura case and, of those who did know, only 7 percent blamed Burns for it. In a second poll, taken on 10 September, 72 percent of all voters polled said that Gill was unjustified in his attacks against Burns. More important for the primary election, while four-of-ten haole voters felt that Gill was justified, only one in twenty AJA voters thought so—in a year when AJA voters constituted 45.8 percent of all registered Democrats in Hawaii.

Next, Daniel Inouye, the most successful politician in Hawaii since Johah Kuhio, came home to fight for his mentor. Inouye went right after those who were trying to characterize the Burns administration as corrupt. "When I see my dear friend and political father being attacked," Inouye said in his resonant voice, "I get mad." Inouye pointed out that Governor Burns had made more than 1,600 appointments of department heads, commission members, and board members since 1962. "Even assuming [Nishimura was] guilty of conflict of interest, my response is, 'Thank God we've got a clean government.' This is a false issue."

Inouye then moved from Burns' perceived vulnerability to his real strength—and Tom Gill's perceived vulnerability—asserting, "It's refreshing to have someone who can bring us together at a time when we have polarization all around us." Inouye concluded by saying that Governor Burns had only "one political weakness that I have tried to correct. He refuses to correct it, though. That weakness is that he won't blow his own horn; he won't brag about himself; he won't tell you what his administration has done for the State of Hawaii. So we have to say it for him."

And say it they did. As August ended, with the wind seemingly behind Governor Burns' sails, the first television airing of *To Catch a Wave* took place. It ran nine times before the 3 October primary. Its message was powerful in its simplicity. It showed Governor Burns more as the "Great White Father" than the "Great Stone Face." Many of those who opposed Burns, particularly the university crowd, failed to appreciate the power of the film. They were particularly bemused by one line by the governor, "Any damn fool can take a stand." To them it was an admission of the governor's unwillingness to take difficult positions. To his constituency, and particularly the Japanese community, it was an affirmation of his role as a consensus builder.

Another element of Burns' momentum was organized labor's effort to reelect Burns and to defeat Gill. Burns had endorsements from the ILWU; the Hawaii Government Employees Association (HGEA); and, in a reversal of Tom Gill's former lock on the AFL-CIO, Walter Kupau's State Federation of Labor. Gill, a labor lawyer himself, still had many friends within the ranks of labor. He could always count on his old friend Art Rutledge and his Unity House unions, several AFL-CIO affiliates, the United Public Workers (UPW), and the Hawaii State Teacher's Association (HSTA). According to Charles Turner, *Honolulu Advertiser* labor writer, all of this translated into a 2 to 1 margin for Burns from the ranks of organized labor.

The campaign ended with Gill clearly on the defensive, criticizing Burns at every opportunity for the money he was spending on the campaign. Gill made repeated demands for a public debate, all of which were studiously ignored by the Burns camp. For his part, the governor seemed to grow more serene as the campaign progressed, earning the title given to him in one of his own newspaper ads: "The Quiet Man of Washington Place."

On election day his serenity was rewarded with an 82,036 to 68,719 victory over Gill, completing a 30-point swing from the beginning of the year. George Ariyoshi earned an equally impressive victory with 79,806 votes for lieutenant governor compared with 39,372 for Vincent Yano, Gill's choice, and 25,115 for City Councilman Charles Campbell.

One of the significant statistics of the campaign was voter turnout. On Oahu, the seat of Gill's strength, only 68.9 percent of the registered voters cast a ballot. The neighbor islands, where Burns enjoyed overwhelming support, voted at much higher rates: Hawaii, 75.6 percent; Maui, 81.4 percent; and Kauai, 84.3 percent. The ILWU had once again delivered for Burns. In a tight Republican primary race for governor, Samuel P. King edged out Hebden Porteus by a vote of 20,428 to 17,800.

Conservative David Watumull played the spoiler with 3,202 votes. King's running mate was Ralph Kiyosaki, who was best known for his service as superintendent of the state Department of Education.

Before going to his headquarters on election night, Jack Burns made two hospital visits: first, he went to see State Senator Nadao Yoshinaga who, that afternoon, had suffered a serious heart attack when confronted by a shark while swimming at Ewa Beach; second, he visited the architect of his 1970 victory, Robert Oshiro, who had been hospitalized in a state of exhaustion two days before the primary election. His doctors later determined that he had contracted hepatitis while campaigning for Governor Burns on Maui.

After the primary election, the general election was anticlimactic. The Republicans knew that their only chance for success was a divided Democratic Party. To this end, much of Sam King's campaign sounded like warmed-over Gill material. Hoping to avert opposition from Gill, Jack Burns and George Ariyoshi visited Gill a week after the primary election. Their meeting resulted in an "Open Letter to the People of Hawaii," which appeared in newspapers throughout the State on 16 October.

This letter, which was later portrayed by some as the price Jack Burns paid for Tom Gill's silence during the general election campaign, was so general that it could be interpreted by different people in different ways. Looking back six years later, Gill interpreted it as having encompassed "most of the stuff that we [meaning the Gill people] had run on in '70 . . . and '66, but which Burns had never paid any attention to, and of course didn't pay attention to after the election, either. But he ran it. I thought it was kind of funny. . . . I said something to the effect that this was a good program, and I certainly appreciated the interest that he had in it, and everybody knew that both of us were lying like hell." The purpose of the letter, of course, was not to reconcile the political philosophies of Jack Burns and Tom Gill, but to give the appearance of unity in the Democratic Party.

Sam King's campaign differed from Tom Gill's on one issue—law and order. A tragic event made it the paramount issue in the final days of the general election campaign. On Thursday evening, 23 October, at approximately 11:00 P.M., Democratic state Senator Larry Kuriyama was shot and killed in the garage of his Aiea Heights home after coming home from a political meeting. Just minutes before he was shot, Kuriyama had been with Governor Burns. While he had supported Gill during the primary, Kuriyama had closed ranks behind the governor for the general election.

Kuriyama's murder, which has never been solved, shocked the community. Foolishly, Sam King decided to try to get some political mileage out of it. Taking the line from *To Catch a Wave*, "Any damn fool can take a stand," King was quoted in the Sunday paper as saying, "If the governor had taken a stand on organized crime, Senator Kuriyama could well be alive today." It was a heartless and irresponsible thing for King to say and it shocked friend and foe alike. Those who remembered Sam King's vigorous red-baiting in the 1950s were not surprised. He had proven his instinct for the jugular before, and even in the face of almost universal criticism, King refused to back away from his statement.

Tom Coffman reported that an unpublished poll, taken after Kuriyama's death, rejected the notion that Burns was in any way responsible for the tragic event. Women rejected King's charges by a 3 to 1 margin; men by a 4 to 1 margin. When Republican Fred Rolfing read King's statement in the Sunday paper, his reaction was, "There goes the election." Art Woolaway, another prominent Republican, had a similar reaction, saying, "This is going to cost him the ball game." A common refrain heard in the days after King's statement was, "I was thinking about voting for him, but not now."

In the absence of a Tom Gill-led "Democrats for King" drive, Sam King never did have a realistic chance to defeat Governor Burns in the general election, even if he hadn't made the egregious Kuriyama gaff. The one thing the Kuriyama episode may have done was to heighten interest in what had otherwise been a rather dull contest. As it turned out, on 3 November 1970, 85 percent of all registered voters in the State of Hawaii went to the polls. They gave Governor John A. Burns and Senator George R. Ariyoshi a stunning 16-point victory—137, 812 (58%) to 101, 249 (42%). Burns and Ariyoshi had, indeed, caught a powerful wave of voter sentiment. They had managed to channel that sentiment, both positive and negative, in the primary and in the general elections in such a way as to produce a model of how to approach electoral politics in Hawaii.

Governor John A. Burns delivered his third inaugural address on 7 December. Reviewing the performance of the Burns administration for the past eight years, he ticked off a list of accomplishments they had sought to achieve:

A more equitable system of taxation. To develop conditions for full employment in an economy not only of expanding wealth, but of expanding opportunity. A system of universal education that would make opportunity for genuine self-development more meaningful for all our youth. To preserve and enhance our natural beauty and to make it ever more accessible to our people. To preserve and enrich our diverse cultural inheritance. To actively pursue those activities which would ensure our rightful place in the Pacific Community of Nations. In sum, we sought those changes that have effectively led to openness in all aspects of our social, economic and political life.

In his conclusion, Governor Burns called Hawaii, "the envy of the world." But he also observed, "Success inevitably breeds new challenges; the rainbow's end is, as it should be, elusive and forever ahead of us."

End of the Rainbow

IF A STRANGER TO HAWAII had asked Tom Gill and George Ariyoshi what it was like to be lieutenant governor of the State of Hawaii, he or she would have probably assumed from their answers that they had served under different governors. Tom Gill would have told a story of being denied participation in the administration of a man whose motto was "my way or the highway." George Ariyoshi would have a different story to tell. In 1979, he reminisced about his relationship with Jack Burns:

> Even before the general election, during the primary election, Jack Burns and I started to do a lot of things together. Every night we would go our separate ways [on the campaign trail, but] we always got together at Washington Place before I went home and we'd talk about what happened during the day.
>
> And during the period just before the general election, we started to talk about the things that would happen after the election. And I remember so clearly Jack Burns telling me, . . . "George, I don't want you to lose your individuality. I want you to remain creative, I want you to come up with ideas and suggestions. If you feel anything, let's sit down and talk." And the only thing he would say is that once a decision is made, we all pull together.

Therein lay the different experiences of Gill and Ariyoshi as lieutenant governor. Jack Burns saw himself as the captain of a team, and he liked to work with team players. Burns allowed a man's own light to shine and took pride in the accomplishments of others—as long as they remained loyal to the team. Dan Inouye was a perfect example. Burns never resented Inouye's leading the ticket on election day, because he felt they were working together in a common cause. From that day in the

283

early 1950s when Dan Aoki and Matsy Takabuki asked Gill to join the Burns team—when Gill responded "Why don't you join *my* team?"—it was clear to those who shared Burns' vision for Hawaii that Gill was no team player. While Ariyoshi was not a part of the Burns inner circle during the early years, Burns recognized in him the qualities of courage, loyalty, and modesty that he liked. When George Ariyoshi finally became a part of the inner circle in 1970, he discovered all the benefits of team membership. As lieutenant governor, Ariyoshi remembered:

> He used to call me and ask me whether I was free for lunch and I would go out to lunch with him. After that, we would just walk back to the office and he'd ask me if I could stay. . . . And we used to spend hours and hours, sometimes ten hours a day. . . . [Then] we would go from [the state Capitol] to Washington Place and have dinner. . .
>
> And I really came to the conclusion that he wanted to get me exposed to the job of being governor. I had a chance to sit through his conferences. . . . I really felt that I went through a tremendous training period watching him address problems.

Ariyoshi was no mere "fly on the wall." As he pointed out in his autobiography, "Right after the 1970 election, [Burns] made me the head of his cabinet. I called all of his cabinet meetings, and I worked closely with the departments."

Bea Burns confirmed the closeness of the relationship between her husband and Ariyoshi. "He liked him," she recalled. "We all did. But as a lieutenant governor, it was a joy to have somebody [Jack] could trust and that he felt would forward the goals of the administration." Ariyoshi recalled Bea Burns saying to him, on more than one occasion, "George, you don't know how good it is to see Governor Burns so relaxed on so many of his trips."

Ariyoshi later talked about how Burns' trust in him was translated into responsibility. He recalled that between Tom Gill and Tony Hodges, an environmentalist who ran an interesting—if quixotic—campaign for the U.S. Senate in 1970, environmental activism had become a real force in Hawaii. Environmentalists were particularly critical of the sugarcane processing plants on the Hamakua coast of the Big Island. These mills discharged their waste product, called bagasse, directly into the ocean. When Ariyoshi spoke with Burns in the spring of 1971 about the conflict between the economic and environmental consequences of this practice, the governor told him, "Why don't you take a look at that and come back with a recommendation."

Ariyoshi consulted with the owner of the mills in question, C. Brewer & Company. C. Brewer had been ordered to clean up its water pollution problems in its Big Island operations within six months. The company wanted thirty months to institute a solution that would not only solve the environmental problem, but would provide a new source of energy by converting bagasse into electricity. Although he was aware that he could be charged with having arranged a sweetheart deal with C. Brewer, Ariyoshi recommended the company be given the extra time it had requested. In spite of criticism from environmentalists, Burns repeated a remark he had made to many subordinates to whom he had delegated responsibility over the years, "You're the boss."

Three years later, in June 1974, Acting Governor George R. Ariyoshi spoke at the dedication of the Hilo Coast Processing Company's $9 million power plant, a facility designed to be run on sugarcane waste. On that day, Ariyoshi recalled the events of the spring of 1971: "One thing stood out clearly in my mind. . . . The immediate compliance with pollution control regulations would surely mean the closure of Hilo-Hamakua sugar mills—the death of an industry as the price for our natural environment." The theme of balancing long-term solutions with complex problems was one that Governor Burns had expressed many times. In Ariyoshi, he found someone who shared this approach.

Ariyoshi used this approach again when Burns named him chair of the Kohala Task Force in the summer of 1971. In early March, Castle & Cooke had announced that they would phase out Kohala Sugar Company at the end of the 1973 grinding season. Along with Ariyoshi, Burns named Big Island Mayor Shunichi Kimura, Big Island Planning Director John Farias, State Planning Director Shelley Mark, State Agriculture Board Chairman Fred Erskine, and State Board of Land and Natural Resources Chairman Sunao Kido to a task force. Burns charged the members of the task force to come up with a long-term solution to a complex set of problems. One year later, on 5 June 1972, while Governor Burns was attending the National Governors' Conference in Houston, Texas, Acting Governor George Ariyoshi signed a $4.5 million appropriations bill which would begin the work of rebuilding the economy of the Big Island's North Kohala district.

On the same day, Ariyoshi vetoed seven bills that had been passed by the state legislature at the end of the 1972 session. He said that the governor had discussed the measures with him before leaving for the Governor's Conference, "but he left the decision entirely up to me." It would be hard to imagine Burns giving Tom Gill such responsibility, but George Ariyoshi was clearly being offered the opportunity to emerge from the large shadow cast by Jack Burns.

In the early 1970s, the Burns administration faced a dramatically changing economy and some new challenges. On 22 July 1971, Edward Y. Hirata, building superintendent for the City and County of Honolulu, announced that Oahu construction had dropped a dramatic 43 percent during the previous fiscal year. Building permits issued in 1969–1970 had amounted to $457 million; in 1970–1971, building permits were valued at $263 million.

Hawaii's economy had been on a roll since statehood. Between 1960 and 1971, major industry employment had expanded from 228,050 to 344,300. Per capita income had grown from $2,335 to $4,797. The State's population had increased from 632,772 to 737,559. While such statistics seemed to indicate a robust economy, other numbers from the same period gave cause for concern. While the annual value of sugar production had risen from $127 million to $210 million, mechanization had decreased the number of employees in the sugar industry from 13,500 to 9,851. Tourism had grown from a $131 million industry, serving 296,517 visitors, to a $645 million industry, serving 1.8 million visitors, raising the specter of "the new plantation economy." The military portion of the State's economy had grown from $373 million to $721.8 million, largely due to the war in Vietnam.

As early as January 1971 in his budget message to the state legislature, Burns had issued a warning:

> General thinking among the experts is that the growth rate of Hawaii's economy is tapering off and the growth rate over the next several years is expected to approach more normal patterns. It may be untimely that a leveling of the economy should occur at a time when fixed commitments incurred by the State are steadily mounting.

Burns' fiscal conservatism—and the discretionary powers the governor of Hawaii then enjoyed—kept the fiscal year 1973 deficit down to only $8.8 million. *Honolulu Advertiser* political writer Doug Boswell reported in October 1973 that this relatively happy outcome was the result of "a tight clamp on State spending [and] a renewal of the State's economic strength. . . . While Burns has chopped more than $83 million in three years, collective bargaining by government employees has added more than $30 million in new costs."

One of the features of the poststatehood economic boom had been labor peace. This, too, changed during Governor Burns' third term. On 1 July 1971, the first manifestation of labor problems came from the West Coast as 15,000 ILWU longshoremen went on strike, closing twenty-four ports. Many in the Hawaii business community feared a re-run of 1949 and called on President Richard Nixon to invoke the Taft-Hartley Act's eighty-day cooling-off period. Governor Burns said little publicly, but appointed a Governor's Emergency Committee on Business and Industry—chaired by economist Wesley Hillendahl—to monitor the effects of the strike. Burns himself worked behind the scenes to get the ILWU and the Pacific Maritime Association back to the bargaining table.

Mayor Frank Fasi loudly criticized the governor for everything from his failure to back up the business community's call for a Taft-Hartley injunction to his unwillingness to put the State of Hawaii into the shipping business. On 19 August a statement came from the governor's office, saying, "If Mr. Fasi paid as much attention to municipal affairs as he does to telling others what to do, this City might possibly be in better shape. Unlike the Mayor, the Governor is more concerned with getting things done, rather than with sounding off." Asked for his personal comment on the statement, the governor simply said that it was "unauthorized."

Governor Burns recognized that the consequences of the strike did not begin to approach the dimensions of the 1949 strike and that it would only be resolved when the union and the employers got back to serious bargaining. On 8 October, after one hundred days, President Nixon did invoke a Taft-Hartley injunction—out of concern for the West Coast states of California, Oregon, and Washington more than any concern for Hawaii. When the injunction expired on Christmas Day, the ILWU postponed the continuation of the strike until 17 January 1972. Harry Bridges needed extra time to continue negotiations with Teamster President Frank Fitzsimmons about a merger of the two unions. The unlikely marriage of the seventy thousand-member ILWU with the two-million member Teamsters Union was never consummated, but it kept Harry Bridges busy until the employers were willing to go back to the bargaining table.

On 17 January, the West Coast dock workers struck anew with

threats from Bridges that the strike "could well include our Hawaii ports and even our union in the British Columbia area." By the end of January, longshoremen in British Columbia were out and it was reported that Harry Bridges was seeking to make contact with dock workers on the west coast of Mexico. By this time, it looked as though Hawaii was going to be awash in labor difficulties. On 2 February 1972, *Honolulu Advertiser* labor writer Charles Turner outlined a series of six potential strikes involving close to thirty thousand workers from longshoremen to schoolteachers to refuse workers.

One by one, the labor disputes of 1972 were resolved at the bargaining table. Even the 134-day West Coast longshoremen's strike finally ended on 19 February, only to have two short encores in Hawaii—in July for forty-eight hours and in October for sixty hours. Governor Burns was concerned enough about the ILWU's July stopwork demonstration to skip the Democratic National Convention in Miami and to become personally involved in the resolution of the dispute. In October, when Hawaii's first dock strike since 1949 looked imminent, Burns asked his friend Bert Kobayashi to serve as a mediator. Kobayashi, then an associate justice on the state supreme court, had successfully mediated several labor disputes for Governor Burns when he was state attorney general. He did so again on this occasion.

Contrary to rumors that he had abdicated, the first two years of his third term were busy times for Jack Burns. Besides a slowing economy and labor strife, political issues also arose. The first political controversy began on 17 June 1972 with the supreme court's appointment of "Matsy" Takabuki as a trustee of the Bishop Estate. Since by 1972 all the members of the supreme court were Burns appointees, many felt the choice of Takabuki had been dictated by the governor. Burns vehemently denied it.

Don Horio, the governor's press secretary, released a statement on 21 June: "When the appointment was announced last week, the Governor said he had complete faith and confidence in the judgment of the Supreme Court in this appointment." Associate Supreme Court Justice Masaji Marumoto spoke out, responding to an editorial in the *Hawaii Tribune-Herald* which charged that Governor Burns had "directed" the Takabuki appointment: "In the four years that I have served on the bench after having been appointed by Governor Burns in 1967, I have yet to see an instance where the Governor made even an attempt to influence or interfere with the prerogatives of the judiciary." The best the press could get out of the governor himself was, "When it comes to matters of the judiciary, I stay out."

In his 1998 memoir, Matsy Takabuki wrote of the first time he knew of any move to have him appointed to the board of the Bishop Estate:

> One morning in 1972, the governor invited me to breakfast. . . . He mentioned that a search was going on for someone to fill a trustee position at the Bishop Estate. I said that I had not given any thought about the trusteeship and he would be foolish to think about someone like me. I promised him that I would make a list of people he might recommend and would get back to him later. I went back to my business without giving the matter any more thought.

Shortly after his meeting with Burns, Takabuki received a phone call from Chief Justice Bill Richardson, asking him to meet with Richardson and Associate Justice Bert Kobayashi. Takabuki recalled that when he got to Kobayashi's Manoa Valley home he was told that he was

> the only person the whole court could agree upon to appoint as trustee of the Bishop Estate. I was incredulous and asked whether they had considered the possible reaction of the Hawaiian community. I was a nisei, I reminded them, a fact that would not sit well with Hawaiians. Every one of my enemies would yell "politics," knowing of my relationship with the Supreme Court and the Governor.
>
> I tried to persuade them to reconsider.

Clearly, Burns had spoken with either Bill Richardson, Bert Kobayashi, or both about Takabuki's appointment. Given his respect for the separation of powers, it is unlikely that Burns pressured Richardson and Kobayashi to make Takabuki a trustee. All four men had known and trusted each other for a long time. To the two who served on the court and the governor, Takabuki's business acumen made him an obvious choice.

Another point needs to be made: Matsy Takabuki made both a personal and financial sacrifice to join the board of the Bishop Estate. In 1972, trustees collected nowhere near the million-dollar salaries of the 1990s. As a matter of fact, Takabuki was instructed to sever his business relationship with Chinn Ho to avoid "the appearance of conflict of interest." In 1972, when he protested to Bert Kobayashi that he would be making a sacrifice to accept the appointment, he was told, "Don't tell me about the financial sacrifice you will be making. Remember the sermon you and the governor gave me about public service? You knew I was making a big financial sacrifice when I became attorney general." Takabuki had no counter for that point, so he prepared to assume his new responsibilities at the Bishop Estate.

But Takabuki had predicted correctly the reaction of the Hawaiian community to his appointment. The Reverend Abraham Akaka, who had welcomed non-Hawaiian Hung Wo Ching's 1968 appointment, called the nomination of Matsy Takabuki "a dark and disappointing day for many of our native Hawaiian people. We felt like strangers and foreigners in our own homeland." As Matsy Takabuki recalled:

> The bells of Kawaiahao Church rang as Hawaiians marched around the statue of King Kamehameha protesting my appointment. The church was made available as a place for Hawaiian leaders to meet and plan their resistance. They filed suit in court to invalidate the appointment; many of my old political adversaries joined this litigation as lawyers.

In an interview with Tomi Knaefler of the *Honolulu Star-Bulletin*, Dr. Alan Howard, a former Bishop Museum anthropologist who by 1972 was professor of anthropology at the University of Hawaii, made what turned out to be a prescient observation:

> The Takabuki protest symbolizes the Hawaiians' first battle cry to legitimize their ethnic identity. If they fail to gain it through this route, they have no choice but to express themselves through conflict—politically and militantly. At heart, the Hawaiian movement is no different than the blacks' fight for ethnic identity. The protest points up the myth of Hawaii's melting pot concept, which, in fact, is a boiling pot of suppressed racial differences long denied political airing. The melting pot illusion simply must go. The damage it has done is to blur ethnic diversity and to allow the Anglo culture to dominate.

Howard was referring, of course, to what has become the Hawaiian renaissance and the Hawaiian sovereignty movement.

Neither was consistent with Jack Burns' view of Hawaii. While he had great respect for the cultural heritage of Hawaii, he worked for a Hawaii whose citizens, including Hawaiians, would look more to those things that united them as human beings rather than to those that separated them as members of different racial and ethnic groups. In his

1969 "inferiority of the spirit" speech, Burns had extolled "the contributions to our society of the Chings and Lums, the Cravalhos and Henriques, the Kahanamokus and the Kealohas, the Samsons and the Menors, the Kims and the Ahns, the Cooks and the Judds." Burns would have warmed more to the idea of Hawaiian society as a "stir-fry" than a "melting pot," but he would have chafed at the idea of racial and ethnic separatism, regardless of the flag it rallied around. Indeed, Jack Burns thought of himself as being Hawaiian; and to him, being Hawaiian was not a question of blood, but a state of mind and heart.

The Takabuki appointment gave Burns' two least-favorite Democrats a chance to take a few shots at him. Tom Gill prophesied that the appointment would "nail down control for the present power elite in a very real way. It is as though we have returned to a quarter century ago." In the inaugural issue of *Honolulu News*, a short-lived political tabloid listing Frank Fasi as editor, Takabuki's appointment was laid at the feet of Governor Burns. The story, written by Fasi retainer Brian Casey, also dredged up the charge that Bill Richardson and Burns had "double-crossed" Neal Blaisdell in 1968 by not living up to their agreement to appoint Blaisdell a trustee of the Bishop Estate in exchange for his withdrawal from the 1968 governor's race.

The part-Hawaiian Chief Justice Bill Richardson took a great deal of abuse for the Takabuki appointment, even from members of his own family. But Richardson refused to back away from the appointment. Takabuki, too, could have withdrawn his name, but as he told Richardson and Bert Kobayashi, "I would not resign as long as you people want me to stay on, but any time you want me to withdraw, just let me know." The appointment had become a matter of principle and a test of wills, and Richardson and Takabuki stood firm.

A group of twelve attorneys, including Gill and Sam King, pressed the legal challenge to Takabuki's appointment. They asked the circuit court to invalidate Takabuki's appointment on the grounds that the state supreme court did not have appointive power, that being an executive prerogative; and that the hearings at which candidates were considered should have been held in public. On 27 July, Judge Yasutaka Fukushima rejected both points and held that the appointment was valid, citing a 1917 decision of the Hawaii supreme court and the 9th circuit court of appeals which upheld the validity of the provisions of the will of Bernice Pauahi Bishop, including the manner of selection of trustees.

On 27 July 1972, Matsuo Takabuki was vested as a trustee of the

Bishop Estate. In his acceptance speech, Takabuki quoted Abraham Lincoln: "I do the best I know, the very best I can, and I mean to keep right on doing so until the end. If the end brings me out all right, what is said against me will not amount to anything. If the end brings me out wrong, ten angels swearing I was right would make no difference." As it turned out, he did not need the angels.

Matsy Takabuki enhanced an already substantial reputation as a financial expert during the twenty-two years he served as a trustee of the Bishop Estate. Based upon an interview with trustees Richard Lyman and Atherton Richards, the estimated value of the Bishop Estate in 1971 was $400 million; the annual income was a meager $5 million, for a return of roughly 1.25 percent. In 1971, about 5,000 Hawaiians and part-Hawaiians were being served by the beneficiary of these funds, the Kamehameha Schools. On 30 June 1992, the Bishop Estate conservatively estimated its assets at $1.37 billion, with an annual income of $170 million. In 1992, the Kamehameha Schools served an estimated 40,000 young Hawaiians and part-Hawaiians.

From the beginning of his third term, Burns attempted to prepare the way for Ariyoshi to replace him. In all probability, Tom Gill would make another run for the governorship in 1974. While this bothered Burns, it did not bother him nearly as much as the possible candidacy of Frank Fasi. Jim Burns defined his father's feelings about the two men as "the difference between political animosity and personal animosity." While the thought of Tom Gill as governor made Jack Burns uncomfortable, the thought of Frank Fasi made Burns sound as if he might run for a fourth term. "I'm doing my job," Burns told the press, "as if I were going to run for reelection, just as I always have." Dan Aoki publicly echoed his chief's thought. "We're not closing the door. He's not a lame-duck governor." Burns and those around him were convinced that the best way to derail a Fasi run for the governorship in 1974 was to defeat him in his 1972 bid for reelection as mayor of Honolulu.

As the election year of 1972 began, Tom Coffman of the *Honolulu Star-Bulletin* assessed Fasi's prospects for reelection: "At age 51, Frank Fasi has never been in better shape for a campaign. In this campaign, for once in his life, Fasi will have the upper hand. He is the smart bet. He has money, a much expanded organization and a record as an activist mayor." On the other hand, Coffman continued, "Honolulu still crawls with his enemies. . . . To name only a few: Governor John A. Burns; numerous legislators; councilmen; entrepreneurs; most of the Democratic Party apparatus; the union giants; and the editorial voices of the newspapers and two of the three TV stations." Coffman concluded with the unthinkable: "If Fasi cannot be upset in 1972, he will be a prime contender for Governor in 1974."

To Burns and his political intimates, Walter Heen, the heir apparent to the Heen political dynasty, looked like an early Democratic prospect to challenge Fasi. But after Lennen and Newell Pacific came up with some disappointing poll results, Heen pulled out. Political neophyte Cecil Heftel looked like a possible prospect after his strong U.S. Senate race against Hiram Fong in 1970, but he was too independent of the regular Democratic Party and he seemed more interested in a place in the State's congressional delegation. As 1972 opened, Fasi's only known opponent was Kekoa Kaapu—on his way to becoming a professional candidate who was taken seriously by no one.

In April Tom Coffman reported rumors that "Burns people" had approached Tom Gill about running against Fasi. Governor Burns told Coffman that he knew nothing about it, but added that "any such talk may be possible." When Gill was asked about the rumors, he played it close to the vest, responding, "Nobody has said anything to me directly, [but] my primary interest does not lie in that direction." In 1976, Gill confirmed that he had been approached. He was not flattered. To him it seemed clear that the Burns people were simply trying to use him. "So I . . . told them the election would cost them two million bucks; one million to beat Fasi and the other million to beat them [in 1974]. That stopped all the speculation. There was no further contact."

In 1972, the Burns wing remained very much in control of the regular Democratic Party organization. On 14 March, a strong turnout at precinct elections guaranteed the Burns forces two-thirds of the seats at the state Democratic Convention a week later, thus assuring the Burns–Ariyoshi wing of the Party control until the crucial gubernatorial election year of 1974. It also gave them the power to name the Democratic Party's delegation to the Party's 1972 National Convention. Burns people claimed sixteen of the twenty positions—controlling fourteen of the sixteen votes—on Hawaii's delegation. This particularly irritated U.S. Representative Patsy Mink, who was limited to one-half vote.

Mrs. Mink and "Coalition '72," the Gill wing of the Party without the active participation of Gill himself, protested the heavy-handed approach taken in delegate selection by the Burns wing of the Party, to no avail. Governor Burns' son, Jim, led the move to limit Mink's role in the Democratic delegation. Many in the Democratic Party's inner circle sensed that Representative Mink was out of touch with Island politics. As Jim Burns put it, "Apparently she has been spending too much time in Oregon, Paris, and elsewhere." Jim Burns' reference to Oregon and Paris had to do with Patsy Mink's whimsical entry into the Democratic presidential primary in Oregon—where she finished far down the list with 2 percent of the vote—and Mink's quixotic attempt to end the war in Vietnam through personal diplomacy at the Paris Peace talks.

As the campaign wore on, mainstream Democrats finally found a candidate to run against Frank Fasi—Mason Altiery, a television newsman turned state senator. In a last-ditch effort to bolster Altiery's campaign, Governor Burns endorsed him. The Burns organization sent letters to all of Burns' supporters from the 1970 campaign; the governor made a few campaign appearances with Altiery; and Burns precinct workers organized a door-to-door effort in behalf of the candidate. But it was all for naught. Frank Fasi won the Democratic primary with 52 percent of the vote; Mason Altiery was second with 31 percent; and Kekoa Kaapu was a distant third with 16 percent. Frank Fasi, who boasted that he had beaten "the syndicate," would face Republican D. G. "Andy" Anderson in a rerun of their 1968 race.

After the primary, reporters asked Governor Burns if he would support Frank Fasi in the general election. His response was, "I am a Democrat. . . . I don't support Republicans against Democrats." Others close to Burns were less cautious. Senate President and Party Chairman David McClung said he would find it "impossible" to support Fasi. Senate Majority Leader Donald D. F. Ching was simply quoted as saying, "I'd rather do without a mayor." A "Democrats for Andy" organization quickly came into being. While Burns did not take a public role in the organization, several of his high-ranking administration members did: Fujio Matsuda, state transportation director; Robert Gilkey, deputy director of the Labor Department; and Mike Tokunaga, deputy comptroller. Don Horio, the governor's press secretary, worked "behind closed doors" with "Democrats for Andy." And they almost pulled it off.

On 7 November, while Hawaii was giving Richard Nixon a 67,000 margin in his reelection bid over George McGovern in the presidential race, Frank Fasi defeated Andy Anderson for mayor of Honolulu by a

vote of 110,548 to 102,953—in a race that was much closer than anticipated. Gerry Keir's analysis of the election returns reveals just how
strange an election it was. In ten of the eleven normally Democratic districts on Oahu, Anderson ran well ahead of the Republican Party's congressional candidates, Diana Hansen and Fred Rolfing. Anderson, however, barely carried his own Kaneohe-to-Kahuku district and lost to Fasi
in Republican Kailua—Governor Burns' district.

As 1972 waned, Governor Burns was visibly slowing down. While
he continued to attend daily Mass, Burns would often remain at Washington Place until noon, doing paperwork. Not until afternoon did he
cross Beretania Street to his fifth-floor Capitol office for his "public cal-
endar." He was back at Washington Place each evening by 6:00 P.M. or
7:00 P.M. Certain rituals also defined his week. Wednesday afternoons
he was driven to the Waialae Country Club for a round of golf and a
nineteenth hole game of cards, and late Friday afternoons he went to the
Nikko Sanatorium, where Hachiro Okazaki would give him his weekly
massage. The noon hour on Fridays belonged to his Friday lunch club;
then there was his weekly Lions Club meeting. He delegated increasing
responsibility to Lieutenant Governor Ariyoshi, particularly when it
came to social obligations.

On 30 March, Burns' 64th birthday, the governor had been cheered
like a distance runner on his victory lap. Seven hundred loyal Democrats
paid $100 a plate to honor their leader and to hear keynote speakers Sen-
ator Henry "Scoop" Jackson of Washington and Democratic National
Chairman Robert Strauss of Texas extol the virtues of Jack Burns. By
summer, the *Honolulu Advertiser* was writing about the governor's Big
Island *pau hana* (retirement) home "on the slopes of the Kohala Mountains, overlooking the ranch country town of Kamuela, the plains of
Waimea and two of Burns' favorite golf courses, Mauna Kea and
Waikaloa."

Burns would never live in that home; he would never get the *pau
hana* years he deserved. On a spring day in 1973, Governor Burns
lunched with George Ariyoshi. On their return to the governor's office,
Burns grasped his abdomen and told Ariyoshi that he had a pain in his
stomach. Ariyoshi urged him to have it checked; Burns assured him that
he would, "later on." The pain persisted. A cough nagged him throughout the summer and early fall of 1973. Bea thought he might have lung
cancer. Then he complained of a severe pain in his leg. When Bea urged

him to see a physician, Jack brushed her off: "Oh, we'll take care of it. Okazaki [his massage therapist] and I'll take care of it."

Bea's concern grew. On Friday, 12 October, she finally asked family physician Clarence Chang to bring an internist to Washington Place. At 7:15 P.M., when Jack returned from his weekly visit to Okazaki, Dr. Chang, internist Bernard Fong, and Kenny Brown greeted him. Seeing Chang, Burns asked, "What are you doing here?" Chang said nothing, but pointed a thumb at Bea. Reluctantly, Burns submitted himself to Fong's examination and agreed to have x-rays the following week. On 17 October, the governor was admitted to Saint Francis Hospital for what was termed "treatment of an upper respiratory infection." On 22 October, he underwent surgery for cancer of the colon. On that day, George Ariyoshi became acting governor of the State of Hawaii. This time, it was not temporary.

While the governor endured a succession of five separate surgeries, George Ariyoshi ran the State and tried to demonstrate that he deserved to be governor in his own right. The biggest challenge Ariyoshi faced during the last thirteen months of the term was posed by the shortages resulting from the Arab oil embargo, called by the Arab oil-producing countries to punish the United States, Western Europe, and Japan for their support of Israel in the 1973 Arab-Israeli War.

At first, Ariyoshi appeared indecisive. Then he instituted mandatory gasoline restrictions—GASPLAN. Slowly, the long lines and short tempers gave way to odd–even gasoline service, depending on whether your license plate ended with an odd or an even number. The plans included restrictions against topping off, which required gas stations to make sure your gas gauge showed no more than one-quarter of a tank of gasoline in the automobile. All in all, Ariyoshi had made the best out of a bad situation.

On 11 April 1974, Governor Burns delivered his first public address since his surgery of the preceding October. The occasion was the last day of the legislative session. Reporters dubbed his speech the "Aloha Address." Burns assured the legislators and others in attendance that, "God willing," he would complete his term, concluding with these moving words:

> With no regrets, with an unclouded conscience, and with the knowledge that we have done our best with our limited abilities, I shall leave this office in due time; I shall leave it enriched with countless new and

cherished friendships, with nothing but warm memories of the years of mutual toil toward noble ends, and with a deep and abiding love for the people in whose cause we have sought a life of public service. *Mahalo* and God bless you all.

Phil Mayer of the *Honolulu Star-Bulletin* described the scene that followed: "Burns, who fought off a fever Wednesday night, gave way to tears several times when legislators praised him after his speech. But he was smiling broadly after the tributes while he went through the House chamber shaking hands."

Ten days after Burns' "Aloha Address," on 21 April 1974, Robert Oshiro called George Ariyoshi and made an appointment to see him in five days. "I met with George," Oshiro told reporter Doug Boswell, "and agreed to get on with the management of his campaign. But, of course, I had to make it clear that I had to have a free hand." Asked if he had taken over the management of Ariyoshi's campaign at the request of Governor Burns, Oshiro replied, "No, not Burns. . . . A sick man wouldn't ask another sick man to undertake that kind of job." Still not fully recovered from the hepatitis he had contracted during the 1970 election campaign, Oshiro, by his own calculations, had taken on a difficult task for the Burns wing of the Democratic Party:

> Ariyoshi showed only 18% support in the polls. In the months before April, the major question in my mind was whether it would be McClung or Ariyoshi. . . . The inevitable conclusion was that McClung was not electable. I was convinced that George was the best candidate, not especially in terms of articulateness or some of the other dimensions by which we measure our people, but in terms of character.

Along with Oshiro came Dan Aoki and Don Horio. George Ariyoshi's 1974 campaign had begun in earnest.

Governor Burns himself made no public statement about the Democratic primary contest for governor. Later in the spring, Jack Burns received a visit from Tom Gill. As Gill recalled it:

> It was pleasant enough. I don't have any hard personal feelings with the guy and I don't think he shows too many himself. . . . He was having breakfast. . . . [I] sat there at the round table with him for half-an-hour. He talked in his usual elliptical fashion about nothing much. I tried to make the point . . . that from my best measurements . . . I was

the one that could beat Fasi and I didn't think at that point that
Ariyoshi could. . . . Not that he loved me more, but that he liked Frank
[Fasi] less. He allowed that he was having trouble with one of his boys,
and McClung had been around trying to cash his chips and he was in
kind of a dilemma. He kept talking in circles, the way he usually does,
and that was the end of that.

To a significant degree, Jack Burns created the McClung problem
all by himself. McClung had entered the race early because, like Gill,
he thought Ariyoshi could not win. When it became clear that the
McClung campaign was going nowhere, Jim Burns went to see David
McClung. As Jim Burns recalled it, McClung said, "If your father tells
me 'no,' I'll get out." When Jim Burns went to his father to discuss
McClung's offer, the response he got was, "Oh, that damn fool, he won't
listen to me." Much to Jim Burns' frustration, his father would not de-
finitively tell McClung not to run. In words reminiscent of Gill's, Jim
Burns pointed to his father's unwillingness to be more direct: "He would
come at you obliquely. He just kind of painted a great picture, and if you
had any brains in your head, you'd see what the picture was all about.
Apparently, Dave chose not to see the picture that he was drawing and
chose to take refuge in the fact that my father didn't say 'get out,' and
continued on."

On 2 July 1974, Acting Governor George Ariyoshi moved into the
governor's office at the State Capitol. Still clinging to hope, or the appearance of it, Don Horio told the press: "It simply means that he
[Ariyoshi] can function more efficiently from the Governor's office because all the State's business funnels through here. . . . There is still only
one Governor. Ariyoshi is only acting in behalf of the Governor until
the Governor fully recovers."

On 6 August, Jack Burns signed the nomination papers for George
Ariyoshi's candidacy for Governor of the State of Hawaii, an act seen by
many as an endorsement. Don Horio challenged that characterization
of Burns' act, saying that it was "a courtesy he was happy to extend. . . .
He'd do it for McClung, too." Still, Burns remained unwilling to make
an all-out public commitment to George Ariyoshi in the Democratic
primary campaign. It was a dangerous hesitation, for if Ariyoshi and
McClung were to split the vote of the Burns wing of the Party, it could
well open the door for Fasi or Gill to win the primary. As primary day

approached, it looked like a three-horse race: Tom Gill, Frank Fasi, or George Ariyoshi. Take your pick.

On 6 October, George Ariyoshi captured the Democratic Party nomination for governor of the State of Hawaii with 71,060 votes—36 percent of the vote; Frank Fasi finished second with 61,831 votes—32 percent of the vote; Tom Gill finished third with 59,123 votes—30 percent of the vote; and David McClung, who never did get the message, received a meager 3,495 votes—2 percent of the vote. Although Fasi had let the ticket on Oahu, beating Ariyoshi by 308 votes and Gill by 884 votes, the neighbor islands once again gave the Burns organization their overwhelming support. While McClung had not played the role of spoiler, what about Tom Gill and Frank Fasi? If one of them had chosen not to run, George Ariyoshi's chances for victory might well have been dashed.

The headline on Doug Boswell's *Honolulu Star-Bulletin* election analysis read:

"A Victory for Jack Burns." Boswell wrote:

> The perception of Fasi as invincible began to dim several weeks ago with public opinion polls reflecting a slide from a high of 37% of the Democratic vote to about 30% two weeks before the election. . . . For Burns, . . . the fruits of victory were doubly palatable. The primary closed the door—perhaps with finality—to two old Democratic foes, Thomas P. Gill and Frank F. Fasi.

Boswell was only half right. Over the next twenty years, Frank Fasi would knock on the door of Washington Place four more times—in 1978, 1982, 1994, and even in 1998, when he was roundly trounced in the Republican primary by Maui Mayor Linda Lingle.

In the latter days of the primary campaign, as his strength grew, George Ariyoshi sought to give his quiet support in the lieutenant governor's race to a political neophyte, Daniel Akaka, a younger brother of the venerable minister of the Kawaiahao Church, Abraham Akaka. Like Governor Burns, he was leery of an all-AJA ticket and knew the benefit of having a part-Hawaiian as his running-mate. Nelson Doi, however, was too well known and too widely respected for his work in the state legislature and on the state bench for Akaka to threaten him seriously. Doi received 92,613 votes to Akaka's 77,162. Former City Council Chairman Herman Lemke received 19,511. Akaka might have had a chance had Lemke, another part-Hawaiian Burns loyalist, stayed out of the race. Lemke's political career was over, but Akaka would go on to win a seat in the U.S. House of Representatives in 1976 and eventually to a place in the U.S. Senate.

In the general election, two AJA attorneys—Ariyoshi and Doi—faced two haole millionaire businessmen—Randolph Crossley and Ben Dillingham. It was as if a thoroughly demoralized Republican Party had asked its members, "Who has enough money to go out and take a drubbing for the Grand Old Party?" Crossley and Dillingham had the money and they took the drubbing, but their loss was not as big as expected. In the lowest voter turnout since statehood, Ariyoshi and Doi won by a vote of 136,262 to 113,388. A total of 22,895 voters left their ballots unmarked for governor and lieutenant governor. Over 54,000 citizens who had voted for a Democratic gubernatorial candidate on 6 October chose not to vote, or to vote Republican on 6 November. A candle, not a torch, had been passed. It would be up to George Ariyoshi to keep the flame alive. He did, for twelve years, retiring after three terms as governor of the State of Hawaii with his record of never having lost an election still intact.

On 18 November, Governor Burns entered the hospital once again with a high fever, suffering from an abscess in his lower abdomen. Two days later he underwent his fifth surgery in the past thirteen months. Governor Burns was still in the hospital on 2 December when his wife of forty-three years supervised her own move back to the family home in Kailua, and when, on the following day, George Ariyoshi was inaugurated as the third governor of the State of Hawaii. With Burns in his hospital room at the time of the inauguration were two long-time friends, Dan Aoki and Bob Oshiro. Beatrice Burns, attended by her son Jim, represented the governor at the inauguration. A fourth person was in the hospital room. *Honolulu Star-Bulletin* reporter Tomi Knaefler had been given permission by Governor Burns to join the three men in his fourth-floor room at Saint Francis Hospital. She described the scene as they watched the inauguration on television: "It was when Ariyoshi was officially declared governor of the State of Hawaii that emotions shot to a peak. Burns uttered a quiet cry. He and Oshiro clasped their hands tightly together. Oshiro said, 'Well, Governor, welcome back to private life.'"

After the ceremony, a gruff-sounding Jack Burns tossed a hand in the direction of the television and said, "Let's turn that noisy thing off." In the process, his eye came to rest on a picture of his newest grandson, a physically handicapped child of 3. Young Nori had been adopted by the governor's daughter, Mary Beth, the previous spring from the Holy Family Home in Osaka, Japan. The child was, as Mary Beth put it, "the light in Grandpa's eye." Now, on this day of days, Grandpa Burns looked at the picture of Nori and said proudly, "There's the samurai. He's a real Kabuki actor, that kid."

To the very end, John A. Burns kept on fighting. "He never admitted he was going to die," Bea remembered. "In fact, he told his sister Helen one day that he was going to lick cancer just like he had licked everything else." His faith undoubtedly lent him hope. Throughout his illness, he continued to take daily communion, a priest coming to him when he could no longer make it to church. He never gave in to his cancer until it finally took him on the afternoon of 6 April 1975, just six days after his 66th birthday, bringing an end to what can rightfully be called "The Burns Years" in Hawaii's history.

Burns at his desk in Washington Place during his third term.

E·P·I·L·O·G·U·E

The Burns Years

WHEN IS AN HISTORIAN justified in attaching the name of a single individual to a significant period of years, as we have attached the name of
John A. Burns to the years from 1945 to 1975? In the case of Jack Burns,
it wasn't because he was a brilliant and charismatic politician. After all,
he lost four of his first six elections. He was capable of terrible political
miscalculations: as in 1959, when he failed to come back to Hawaii from
Washington, D.C., to fight for an office he thought should be his by
merely claiming it; and again in 1966, when he thought he should be
able to choose his own lieutenant governor without consulting other
Party leaders. But Burns paid attention and he learned from his mistakes. In 1962, he avoided the aloofness that had cost him so dearly in
1959 and won a stunning victory; and in 1970, he avoided the divisive-
ness that had almost resulted in his defeat in 1966 to win the most impressive victory of his political career.

But the central feature of Burns' success over the years, and the historical reason why those years can properly bear his name, was the coalition he worked so hard to build and sustain during that period he occupied center stage in Hawaii's changing political scene. That Burns did
not occupy center stage in a conspicuous manner does not mean that he
was not there. His dogged fight for what he saw as social justice in
Hawaii was often lonely and frequently painful. But he hung in there,
true to his belief in equal opportunity for all of those who had been
locked out for the first half of the twentieth century. As novelist James
Michener put it, "Jack kept it together in those bad years; only he."

The working press who covered Burns over the years acknowledged
his role as a crusader for social justice. Doug Boswell, who went to Iolani
Palace in 1964 to cover state government for the *Honolulu Star-Bulletin*

303

and stayed for the next twenty years, placed Burns at the head of Hawaii's gubernatorial pack. "His achievement was not in terms of legislation, but in the spirit of things he achieved," Boswell contends. "He strove to change the ethnic balance of the State, and he succeeded. He wanted to involve everyone in the State, to make them all coequal; and to a significant degree he did. He wanted to see Americans of Japanese ancestry in responsible positions in both the public and private sectors, and they are. And he encouraged Merchant Street to bring *all* people into the ongoing picture of Hawaii. Burns did a great deal to establish the climate we enjoy in contemporary Hawaii."

As a cub reporter for KGMB-TV news, Bambi Weil covered politics from 1970 through the end of Burns' administration. Ultimately, Weil left journalism for law school, and eventually a state judgeship. Predictably, Weil found Burns' greatest accomplishments in the legal area: allowing the abortion bill to become law and the Burn's-appointed supreme court led by Chief Justice William Richardson. "It was an activist court in the best tradition of the United States Supreme Court under Chief Justice Earl Warren."

But the press differed markedly in their overall assessments of Burns' contribution. Byron Baker covered state government for both print and electronic media from 1966 to 1973. Baker grudgingly acknowledged Burns' importance "as a symbol of changes that occurred, but as an individual governor measured against other governors, he was not so outstanding." Baker faulted Burns for "his terrible habit of procrastinating" and for his championing a University of Hawaii medical school—"another expensive toy"—among other things. Former Associated Press and *Star-Bulletin* reporter Buck Donham was equally harsh, criticizing Burns for his belief in "growth for growth's sake," for his "overdependence on tourism" as Hawaii's economic base, and for allowing his "administration to be shut to outsiders."

Tom Coffman's views probably represented best those of the younger generation of reporters who covered Burns. Coffman credited Burns with "two clear ideas: racial equality and educational and economic opportunity. Burns could get into people's guts on those great issues. After that, he wasn't so crystal clear." Indeed, in Coffman's estimation little of relevance happened during Burns' administration: "His first term was the one that mattered; thereafter it was downhill. The governor had the power, but as the years went on he had the power not to act but just to be."

But "those great issues," racial equality and educational and economic opportunity, have been associated with every great political and moral leader in the American pantheon: Thomas Jefferson, Andrew Jackson, Abraham Lincoln, Theodore and Franklin Roosevelt, and Martin Luther King all achieved their stature primarily as champions of human equality. Many of Burns' critics during his political career shared his egalitarian sentiments, critics like Tom Gill, Frank Fasi, and Vince Esposito; but he had become identified with them, particularly in the minds of Hawaii's Americans of Japanese ancestry, earlier than anyone else—before the bombs had dropped on Pearl Harbor. When his critics scored him on environmental issues or corruption in his administration, they were playing minor keys compared to the tune of equality Burns had played so early, so long, and so well.

The single, most significant part of the transformation that took place in Hawaii during "The Burns Years" was the rise of Hawaii's Japanese-American community from its subservient role to a position of leadership in the community. It is not accidental that a non-Japanese individual was central to this dramatic emergence. It is likely that without this outsider's leadership, the Japanese-American community might easily have fallen into factionalism, which could have diminished their collective power. As Shunichi Kimura, the young lawyer—and Gill supporter—who as mayor guided the Big Island through much of the tumultuous 1960s, said of Burns:

Burns was like a magnet. He was the one guy we could all relate to. He didn't have the normal attributes of a political leader, but it was the belief that he had which drew people to him. He was the one major guy who drew people together. He was the guy for *that* time. He did it in such a way that it did not cause a wrenching in the community— by consensus. Burns was granite in his beliefs. When bombarded by criticisms, he quietly kept working. He held hands with business leaders, so as not to drive them out.

Matsy Takabuki, who played a unique role in John A. Burns' life, spoke of his friend's hold on the young Japanese-American veterans of World War II:

Burns did much to ameliorate the wartime hysteria against our families and friends. For that reason, the 442nd made John Burns an honorary member.

Initially, I wondered whether Burns was for real. I suspected that we were being used by him. And to be quite honest, we considered how we could use him. However, as I got to know him, I recognized that he spoke from his heart. What he said he was trying to do was not just rhetoric. He deeply believed in his vision of equality. . . .

Jack Burns . . . kept telling us, . . . "Do not be ashamed of who you are. Talk about your war record. You guys deserved it. You have proven that you are Americans. You earned this honor under fire."

U.S. Senator Daniel Inouye, the man who still unabashedly refers to Burns as his "political father," was the central figure among the Japanese-American veterans who sat at Burns' feet to learn the ABCs of Democratic Party politics. When Burns died, Inouye said of his mentor:

They called John Burns "Stone Face." He seldom smiled. His physical bearing made him appear ramrod and inflexible. He was never an inspiring orator. And he had many enemies. Yet, without question, he will go down as one of Hawaii's greatest political leaders, if not *the* greatest. In years to come, political scientists, sociologists, economists, historians and all other students of government and politics in Hawaii will certainly have much to say about Burns' great political success— and much to learn from it.

University of Hawaii political scientist and former director of the Legislative Reference Bureau Norm Meller watched Burns from 1947 until the end of his life. He credits Burns with enjoying "tremendous loyalty from the young Japanese. He felt at ease with them." Meller compares Burns to the genro in Japanese culture, the elder statesman: "He was both activist and genro, their advisor. Unconsciously, he took the place of the oldster. Too often we forget the youth of the AJAs following World War II."

Others, like Malcolm McNaughton, president of Castle & Cooke throughout most of the 1960s and 1970s, held a less exalted view of Burns' contribution to Hawaii's history. In 1983, McNaughton said:

I think the Democrats and the Burns situation was about like the famed congressman from Texas . . . who pointed to a log going down the Mississippi River and says, "See that log going down there? It's just covered with [ants]. And those [ants] think they're steering that log, and it's just going down the river [on its own]." That's what I think of

Burns and his administration. They've taken credit for everything and I think it was all going to happen [anyway]. I don't think Quinn would have done anything different.

There is something to be said for McNaughton's brand of economic determinism. First Hawaiian Bank's chief economist, Thomas K. Hitch, in a book published in 1991, shortly after his death, spoke of the years from 1959 to 1973 as "the boom years." In his work entitled *Islands in Transition,* Hitch discussed the relationship between the growth of Hawaii's population and its economy. During the 1950s, Hawaii's population grew by 132,983 (26.6%). During the 1960s it grew by another 137,141 (21.7%), standing at 769,913 in 1970. But the truly striking figures are those which show the growth of the State's economy. From 1958 to 1973, while the population was growing at an annual rate of roughly 2 percent, the economy was growing at an annual rate of nearly 7 percent. As Hitch pointed out, from 1949 to 1958 the economy grew at an annual rate of just under 4 percent; from 1973 to 1988 it grew at an annual rate of about 3 percent.

In other words, John A. Burns had the good fortune to serve as governor of the State of Hawaii at a very favorable time. That 5 percent differential between population growth and economic growth in those years created an economic environment in which many things were possible that were not possible either before or after that period of time. Was Governor Burns responsible for those rates of economic growth, or as Malcolm McNaughton said, would Bill Quinn have done just as well? It is impossible to answer that question with any degree of certainty.

This, of course, leads to the question of whether the times make the man, or the man makes the times. Was Herbert Hoover responsible for the Great Depression, or was it the excess of the Roaring Twenties along with the crippling effects of chronic agricultural problems and protective tariffs? Was Franklin D. Roosevelt's New Deal responsible for the recovery or was it the economic benefits of the United States becoming the "Arsenal of Democracy"? Was Jimmy Carter the cause of the inflation of the late 1970s and early 1980s, or was he the victim of an economy run into hyperinflation by the "guns and butter" combination of Lyndon B. Johnson's prosecution of the war in Vietnam while trying to pay for his Great Society programs on the domestic front—not to mention the Arab oil embargo? Was Ronald Reagan responsible for the prosperity of the

1980s, or was that prosperity the result of deficit spending which tripled
the national debt? Was George Bush responsible for the economic re-
cession that led to his defeat in 1992, or was that simply the cyclical pre-
cursor to the prosperity that resulted in Bill Clinton's reelection in the
1996? To bring the subject back to Hawaii and to the present, is Governor Ben Cayetano responsible for the economic doldrums in which the
State presently finds itself, or is he the victim of the excesses of Hawaii's
economy in the 1980s and Japan's prolonged economic woes?

One conclusion is that there are no simple answers to complex problems. Another conclusion is that no man—or woman—can be completely responsible for the times in which he or she governs. But there
are political figures who leave such an imprint upon their times that future generations look back to them as a yardstick. Like him or not,
Franklin D. Roosevelt was such a man. For generations, Democratic
Party politics continued to be defined in the New Deal terms he established when he was president of the United States. And like him or not,
Ronald Reagan was also such a man. The conservative wing of the Republican Party is still looking back to a yardstick which was established
during what they like to call "The Reagan Years." On the international
scene, Margaret Thatcher's drive toward privatization in the United
Kingdom has left her personal imprint upon the British political and
economic landscape ever since.

Jack Burns was such a man in Hawaii. The coalition he did so much
to build as Party leader, delegate to Congress, and governor took control
of Hawaii's legislature in 1954, of its congressional delegation in 1956,
and of its executive in 1962—and held on to all three ever since. At
century's end the Burns coalition of labor and Americans of Japanese
ancestry is almost a half-century old. It is longer-lived than Franklin
Roosevelt's New Deal coalition, and it has elected the country's first
Japanese-American governor, its first Hawaiian governor, and its first
Filipino governor. The Burns coalition elected the country's first Japanese-
American and Polynesian members of the U.S. House of Representatives and its first Japanese-American and Polynesian U.S. senators.

Echoes of the old Burns coalition could still be heard in Ben
Cayetano's defeat of Linda Lingle in the 1998 governor's race. The eth-
nic-labor coalition that Burns put together from 1945 to 1975 still had
enough staying power to enable the Democratic Cayetano—a candidate
from the smallest and lightest voting ethnic group in the State—to with-

stand a powerful challenge from the Republican Lingle. Although Ben Cayetano is too young to have been close to Burns, he still clings to his vision of public service by virtue of an appointment he received from Governor Burns to a state commission.

But the memory fades in the face of new generations for whom John A. Burns is nothing more than a name on some buildings on the Manoa campus of the University of Hawaii or an airport on the Kona Coast of the Big Island. As historians, it is our responsibility to point out why the period in which John A. Burns cast his long shadow over the political life of Hawaii truly deserves to be called "The Burns Years." We hope this work has done that.

NOTES

In these notes, the John A. Burns Oral History Project has been abbreviated as JABOHP. Page numbers are from the transcripts of the tapes. Tape numbers are shown only when more than one tape was reviewed on a single day. The tapes and transcripts are housed in the Hawaii Collection of the Hamilton Library at the University of Hawaii.

Frequently cited newspapers are cited in the following way: HA = *Honolulu Advertiser;* HSB = *Honolulu Star-Bulletin;* SSA = *Sunday Star-Bulletin & Advertiser.*

Quotations from the *Journal of the House of Representatives,* State of Hawaii, are cited as: Hawaii, *House Journal,* followed by date and page number.

In references which extend over a single paragraph, an opening and closing excerpt is cited. Citations from the author's text are set off by < >; direct quotations are set off by " " marks.

Prologue—Death of a Leader

Page

3   "He was a mid-Pacific Jacksonian": SSA, 6 June 1975, p. B2.

4   "In all his work": HSB, 9 April 1975, p. A1.

4   "At the cemetery": HSB, 9 April 1975, p. A6.

Chapter One—Youth

8   father "rode a white horse": Edward Burns, interview with Dan Boylan, 12 February 1979, from author's notes.

9   "went out with other women": Lawrence Fuchs, "A Complicated Man": *Hawai'i Pono* author Lawrence Fuch's 7 November 1958 interview with Delegate John Burns, *Hawaii Observer,* 24 November 1976, p. 17.

9   She "put the fear of God in Harry Burns": Edward Burns, interview with Dan Boylan, 12 February 1979, from author's notes.

10   "The Church became her substitute": Sheenagh Burns, "Jack Burns: A Daughter's Portrait," *The Hawaiian Journal of History* 24 (1990): 165. Sheenagh Burns is Bea and Jack Burns' second child and only daughter. They christened her Mary Elizabeth, but she had her name legally changed in adulthood. Ms. Burns holds a Ph.D. in clinical psychology, and her "A Daughter's Portrait" offers a fascinating interpretation of the motivations behind Jack Burns' career.

10   "Don't come near, or I'll blast this thing": Edward Burns, interview with Dan Boylan, 12 February 1979, from author's notes.

10   "Every evening, after the children had gone to bed": Beatrice Burns, interview with Dan Boylan, 30 March 1979, from author's notes.

10–11   "Mother was always in charge": Margaret Mary [Burns] Curtis, interview with Dan Boylan, 16 March 1982, from author's notes.

11   "I was spoiled": John A. Burns, JABOHP, 2 January 1975, p. 4.

11   "We were living in Waikiki": Edward Burns, JABOHP, 30 April 1975, p. 15.

12   "I don't know how I could be so selfish": John A. Burns, JABOHP, 2 January 1975, p. 5.

12   "I still drank like hell": John A. Burns, JABOHP, 2 January 1975, p. 6.

12–13   "a little bit of a problem": John A. Burns, JABOHP, 2 January 1975, p. 8.

13   "He'd come home drunk": Margaret Mary [Burns] Curtis, interview with Dan Boylan, 27 July 1979, from author's notes.

13   "I'll show you how to manage your money": Margaret Mary [Burns] Curtis, interview with Dan Boylan, 27 July 1979, from author's notes.

13   "just barely" made it to graduation: John A. Burns, JABOHP, 2 January 1975, p. 13.

13   "Jackie is one of those crazy army boys": *Ka Lamaku,* St. Louis high school year book, spring 1930.

14   "It just amazed me": John A. Burns, JABOHP, 2 January 1975, pp. 13–14.

15   "nothing else was available": Beatrice Burns, JABOHP, 11 February 1976, p. 1.

15   "I think his integrity came out": Beatrice Burns, JABOHP, 11 February 1976, p. 2.

15   "It's all right," the priest reassured her: Margaret Mary [Burns]
         Curtis, interview with Dan Boylan, 16 March 1982, from author's
         notes.

16   "Tell your father I'll come up there": John A. Burns, JABOHP,
         2 January 1975, p. 19.

16   "a lazy hunk": Beatrice Burns, JABOHP, 11 February 1976, p. 6.

17   "a pretty good guard": Elmer Leehman, interview with Dan Boy-
         lan, 6 June 1982, from author's notes.

17   "He was never at home": Beatrice Burns, JABOHP, 11 February
         1976, p. 8.

Chapter Two—Policeman

19   When Chief Gabrielson looked: application for employment
         for the Honolulu Police Department, John A. Burns police file,
         Archives of Hawaii.

19   "We were delighted because of the higher income": Beatrice
         Burns, JABOHP, 11 February 1976, p. 8.

19   "A quiet but effective street cop": Leon Strauss, interview with
         Dan Boylan, 6 February 1979, from author's notes.

20   "And I thought . . . if I cry I'll die": Beatrice Burns, JABOHP,
         11 February 1976, pp. 12–13.

21   "Officer J. A. Burns . . . smells of liquor": accident report dated
         14 December 1935, Archives of Hawaii.

21–22   "Dear Mrs. Burns": William A. Gabrielson, letter to Flo Burns
         dated 18 December 1935, John A. Burns police file, Archives of
         Hawaii.

22   "He expected as much of me": Beatrice Burns, JABOHP, 11 Feb-
         ruary 1976, p. 17.

22   Ozaki "did all sorts of horrible things": Beatrice Burns, JABOHP,
         11 February 1976, p. 16.

23   "Jack had a . . . keen and probing mind": Leon Strauss, interview
         with Dan Boylan, 6 February 1979, from author's notes.

23   "In the whole time": John A. Burns, JABOHP, 16 January 1975,
         p. 5.

23   "There were never any broken bones": Mary Beth [Burns] Staats,
         interview with Dan Boylan, 17 July 1979, from author's notes.

24   "He was very strict with himself": Mary Beth [Burns] Staats, in-
         terview with Dan Boylan, 17 July 1979, from author's notes.

24   "He was too strict": Beatrice Burns, JABOHP, 11 February 1976,
         p. 32.

24   "Jack, Jr., hardly got a sentence out": Mary Beth [Burns] Staats, interview with Dan Boylan, 17 July 1979, from author's notes.

24   "Jim was in charge of everything": Mary Beth [Burns] Staats, interview with Dan Boylan, 17 July 1979, from author's notes.

25   "You think I'm mad": Mary Beth [Burns] Staats, interview with Dan Boylan, 17 July 1979, from author's notes.

25   "Come dance with me, bug": Mary Beth [Burns] Staats, interview with Dan Boylan, 17 July 1979, from author's notes.

25   "At times he acts as if he were in a trance": Don J. Hays, 1937 fitness report, John A. Burns police file, Archives of Hawaii.

25   "I was at the top of the [promotion] list": John A. Burns, JABOHP, 16 January 1975, p. 6.

25–26   Women who came to Hawaii to engage in prostitution: Edward Rohrbough, unpublished manuscript, no pagination, Archives of Hawaii.

26   "If you want civil rights, go back to the mainland": John A. Burns, JABOHP, 16 January 1975, p. 17.

27   "I was only nice to you because I had to be": John A. Burns, JABOHP, 16 January 1975, p. 17.

27   "[Burns] had so much on the Chief": Edward Burns, undated memo, John A. Burns police file, Archives of Hawaii.

Chapter Three—Loyalty

29   "Supposing . . . that the Japanese": Senate Committee on Immigration and Naturalization, *Immigration to Hawaii*, testimony of Walter F. Dillingham, [AU: Need no. of Congress session] Cong., 1st sess., 1921, p. 100.

29   "Never lose sight of the real issue": Gavan Daws, *Shoal of Time* (Honolulu: University of Hawaii Press, 1968), p. 305.

30   In 1938, approximately 150,000 people of Japanese ancestry: Thomas D. Murphy, *Ambassadors in Arms* (Honolulu: University of Hawaii Press, 1954), p. 23.

30   By 1941, the Japanese and Japanese-American population had risen: Dennis Ogawa, "A War of Race," lecture presented at the University of Hawaii, 8 July 1992.

31   "We received information that Hachiro Yamamoto": John A. Burns, JABOHP, 16 January 1975, p. 6.

31   "The investigations . . . were done discreetly": Kanemi Kanazawa, interview with Dan Boylan, 15 July 1982, from author's notes.

31   "The high-powered mainland FBI": Kanemi Kanazawa, interview with Dan Boylan, 15 July 1982, from author's notes.

32	From "I pledge myself to support" through "Because the major defendant is Navy intelligence": John A. Burns, JABOHP, 16 January 1975, pp. 9–11.
33–34	"Why Attack the People of Hawaii?": HSB, 18 November 1941, p. 8.
35	"asking for a change in the nationality act": John A. Burns, JABOHP, 14 January 1975, tape 4, p. 10.
35	"I don't want to get involved in politics": John A. Burns, JABOHP, 10 January 1975, tape 3, p. 2.
35	"I don't care," Burns barked: John A. Burns, JABOHP, 10 January 1975, tape 3, p. 3.
36	"Close the door" through "give me names": John A. Burns, JABOHP, 16 January 1975, p. 8.
36	By the evening of 8 December: Murphy, *Ambassadors in Arms*, p. 23.
37	"If two of us voted yes": John A. Burns, JABOHP, 29 January 1975, tape 4, p. 3.
37	"The total . . . was 1,444": Lawrence H. Fuchs, *Hawaii Pono* (Honolulu: Bess Press, 1961), p. 303.
37	This was a far cry from . . . the West Coast: Murphy, *Ambassadors in Arms*, p. 1.
38	Burns himself encouraged the closure of Shinto shrines: Rohrbough, unpublished manuscript, no pagination.
38	"I knew a lot of this stuff was silly": Rohrbough, unpublished manuscript, no pagination.
39	"In Wisconsin the weather was frigid": Daws, *Shoal of Times*, p. 349.
39	"Open to distrust because of their racial origin": Daws, *Shoal of Time*, p. 350.
40	"Okay, Uncle Sam has kicked you": John A. Burns, JABOHP, 14 January 1975, tape 4, p. 13.
40	60 percent of Hawaii's fighting forces . . . 80 percent of the Territory's casualties: Fuchs, *Hawaii Pono*, p. 306.
40	"The highest aspiration of our boys": Daws, *Shoal of Time*, p. 351.

Chapter Four—Peace

63	"This is a democracy": Dr. Ernest Murai, JABOHP, 8 July 1975, p. 15.
63–64	Most plantation managers were pleased to cooperate: Rohrbough, unpublished manuscript, no pagination.

64–65　　　"My first impression of him": Dr. Ernest Murai, JABOHP, 8 July 1975, p. 14.

65　　　　　"The first time I met him": Mitsuyuki Kido, JABOHP, 31 July 1975, p. 14.

65　　　　　"I didn't like him": Jack Kawano, JABOHP, 21 August 1975, p. 19.

65　　　　　"I remember many times": Jack Kawano, JABOHP, 21 August 1975, p. 19.

65　　　　　"He was not primarily concerned for the Japanese": Dr. Ernest Murai, JABOHP, 8 July 1975, pp. 16–17.

65　　　　　"After we got a little acquainted": Jack Kawano, JABOHP, 21 August 1975, pp. 19–20.

65–66　　　"My God, I forgot my children!": Dr. Ernest Murai, JABOHP, 8 July 1975, p. 18.

66　　　　　"We told the military . . . you give us five hundred guys": John A. Burns, JABOHP, 14 January 1975, tape 4, p. 11.

66　　　　　"What triggered me into politics": Mitsuyuki Kido, JABOHP, 31 July 1975, p. 11.

67　　　　　"It was through his auspices": Chuck Mau, JABOHP, 21 September 1975, tape 1, p. 24.

67　　　　　The GOP majority in the House: official tabulation—territorial election, Tuesday, 11 November 1944, Archives of Hawaii.

68　　　　　With only nine hundred members at the beginning of 1944: Fuchs, *Hawaii Pono,* p. 357.

69　　　　　"The Democratic Party . . . was made up of": Mitsuyuki Kido, JABOHP, 31 July 1975, p. 24.

70　　　　　"When I found out they had dumped Sumner": Edward Burns, JABOHP, 12 February 1979, p. 20.

70　　　　　"After the '45 session": John A. Burns, JABOHP, 16 January 1975, tape 5, p. 6.

70　　　　　"Cash on hand $500": John A. Burns, application to transfer liquor license, August 1945, John A. Burns Police File, Archives of Hawaii.

71　　　　　"I knew labor belonged in the ranks": John A. Burns, JABOHP, 10 January 1975, tape 3, p. 6.

71　　　　　"[Stainback] filled ten of the top thirteen positions": Fuchs, *Hawaii Pono,* p. 310.

71　　　　　"Stainback took the flat position": John A. Burns, JABOHP, 16 January 1975, tape 5, p. 8.

71–72 "He let the store go": Beatrice Burns, JABOHP, 11 February 1976, pp. 21–23.

72 "The chair announced that he had the proxies": John A. Burns, JABOHP, 16 January 1975, tape 5, p. 7.

73 "The Democratic precincts they used to have": Dr. Ernest Murai, JABOHP, 8 July 1975, pp. 35–36.

74 "John A. Burns, a member of the Oahu County": HSB, 28 August 1946, p. 4.

74 Burns finished dead last: official tabulation—city and county primary election, Saturday, 5 October 1946, Archives of Hawaii.

74 "You may think it strange": T. G. S. Walker, letter to Harry Shigemitsu, 6 September 1946, Archives of Hawaii.

75 Kido's 10,619 votes placed him first: official tabulation—territorial election, Tuesday, 5 November 1946, Archives of Hawaii.

75 "He was stiff": Mitsuyuki Kido, JABOHP, 31 July 1975, p. 31.

75 "Jack was never a good speaker": Chuck Mau, JABOHP, 21 September 1975, tape 1, p. 26.

76 Burns "always spoke about the principles": Mitsuyuki Kido, JABOHP, 31 July 1975, p. 30.

76 "It took a lot of courage": Chuck Mau, JABOHP, 21 September 1975, tape 1, pp. 25–26.

76 "He had determination": Jack Kawano, JABOHP, 21 August 1975, p. 30.

76 "I can recall him appearing": A. A. Smyser, JABOHP, 25 June 1975, pp. 1–3.

77 Farrington . . . received 45,765 votes: official tabulation—territorial election, Tuesday, 5 November 1946, Archives of Hawaii.

Chapter Five—Emerging Leadership

78 "In a one-for-one relationship [Jack] was charming": A. A. Smyser, JABOHP, 25 June 1975, p. 4.

79 "I'm Jack Burns. I want to talk politics": Toshio Serizawa, JABOHP, 28 July 1979, pp. 14–17.

79–80 "We knew that we wanted the young people": Chuck Mau, JABOHP, 21 September 1975, tape 1, p. 30.

80 "A lot of them stayed here": O. Vincent Esposito, JABOHP, 12 June 1975, p. 8.

81 "The difference between them": Senator Daniel K. Inouye, with

Lawrence Elliott, *Journey to Washington* (Englewood Cliffs, N.J.: Prentice-Hall, 1967), p. 209.

81   "Do you think you can win?": Inouye, *Journey to Washington*, p. 211.

82–83   "We want a government run by and for the people": HA, 19 September 1946, p. 1.

83   Lindsley Austin, who "was so incensed": Sanford Zalburg, *A Spark is Struck!* (Honolulu: University of Hawaii Press, 1979), p. 165.

83   what [Stainback] called the "plan for the communists": HSB, 12 November 1947, p. 1.

83   The final dismissal of John and Aiko Reinecke: For a full account of the Reinecke case, see Thomas Michael Holmes, "The Reinecke Case: A Study in Administrative Injustice," *Hawaii Bar Journal* (Fall 1976).

84   Hawaii was caught up in the . . . "McCarthy Era": For a brief discussion of the McCarthy Era on the mainland and a complete discussion of that phenomenon in Hawaii, see T. Michael Holmes, *The Specter of Communism in Hawaii* (Honolulu: University of Hawaii Press, 1994).

85   "We are moving politically": Zalburg, *A Spark is Struck!*, p. 223.

85   "Our union has always followed a program of independent political action": Zalburg, *A Spark is Struck!*, p. 230.

85–86   "We don't question the motives": HA, 26 March 1948, p. 6.

87   "If I am defeated by Delegate Farrington": HA, 29 August 1948, p. 1.

87   Burns defeated Victoria Holt: official tabulation—territorial primary election, Saturday, 2 October 1948, Archives of Hawaii.

87   "My decision to run is based entirely upon": HA, 3 September 1948, p. 1.

87   Farrington . . . won . . . 49,128 to 23,703: official tabulation—territorial primary election, Saturday, 2 October 1948, Archives of Hawaii.

87   "I haven't a chance of a snowball in Hades": HA, 19 October 1948, p. 5.

87   "I don't *appear* to have a chance": HA, 20 October 1948, p. 5.

88   Farrington had trounced him by a vote of 75,725 to 24,920: official tabulation—territorial election, 2 November 1948, Archives of Hawaii.

88   Farrington carried 163 of the Territory's 168 precincts: HSB, 11 November 1948, p. 3.

88	"I know of no one to whom I would rather lose": HSB, 5 November 1948, p. 8.
88	In the 1948 elections, the Republican Party had won: HSB, 8 November 1948, p. 9.
88–89	"The era of selfishness and unfettered greed": HSB, 5 November 1948, p. 9.

Chapter Six—Roadblocks

90	"The Big Five called it a political strike": Ann Fagan Ginger and David Christiano, eds., *The Cold War Against Labor* (Berkeley: Meiklejohn Civil Liberties Institute, 1987), p. 461.
91	Jack Hall asked Burns to go to Washington, D.C.: Zalburg, *A Spark is Struck!* pp. 265–267.
92	"I couldn't talk to MacKeller worth five cents": John A. Burns, JABOHP, 24 January 1975, p. 18.
93	"to counteract the false statements": HA, 23 March 1950, p. 9.
94	"Further attendance at the Constitutional Convention": HSB, 26 March 1950, p. 1.
94	"Kageyama has struck a foul blow": HA, 11 April 1950, p. 2.
94	"Lau Ah Chew . . . is not my kind of Democrat." HA, 24 April 1950, p. 8.
94	Silva's decision to plead the Fifth: HA, 21 April 1950, p. 2.
95–96	Ernest Heen and Harold Rice led ninety-one delegates: *Honolulu Record,* 1 May 1950, p. 10.
96	"This is the new Democratic Party": *Honolulu Record,* 1 May 1950, p. 10.
96	"To Whom It May Concern": HA, 21 July 1950, p. 8.
97	Inouye jumped into the contest: HA, 12 May 1950, p. 1.
97	"They are going to have one hell of a time": HA, 14 May 1950, p. 1.
97	"No one is authorized to solicit or accept funds": HA, 6 June 1950, p. 10.
97	Sterling's efforts were to no avail: HA, 13 July 1950, p. 12.
98	Wilson won . . . by a margin of 15,608 to 10,058: HSB, 9 October 1950, p. 12.
98–99	"We were practical": Mitsuyuki Kido, JABOHP, 31 July 1975, tape 2, p. 11.

99   "A development of this kind": HA, 1 May 1950, p. 10.

100   The appointment . . . aroused . . . "stiff opposition": HSB, 8 March 1951, p. 5.

100   "long residence on the island of Oahu": Johnny Wilson, as quoted in Bob Krauss, *Johnny Wilson: First Hawaiian Democrat* (Honolulu: University of Hawaii Press, 1994), p. 324.

100   Burns asked for twenty-four hours: John A. Burns, JABOHP, 24 January 1975, p. 19.

101   Long revealed that the best he could do for Burns: Mitsuyuki Kido, JABOHP, 31 July 1975, tape 2, pp. 12–15.

101   Justice Hugo Black asserted: Holmes, *The Specter of Communism in Hawaii*, p. 176.

102   "They used the Communist Party": Zalburg, *A Spark is Stuck!*, pp. 199–200.

103   "I think it's time . . . to go to Washington": Chuck Mau, JABOHP, 21 September 1975, tape 2, p. 23.

104   "to advocate and teach the duty": *United States v. Fujimoto et al.* (Criminal No. 10,495–1952-53), p. 81. For a full account of Kawano's testimony before HUAC in Washington, D.C., and a thorough account of the Smith Act trial, see Holmes, *The Specter of Communism in Hawaii*, chaps. 15–17.

104   "I told the counsel for the FBI": John A. Burns, JABOHP, 29 January 1975, tape 9, p. 12.

Chapter Seven—Revolution

110   "They had sections . . . where only the haole used to stay": Dan Aoki, JABOHP, 25 March 1975, p. 2.

112   "The young Japanese adored Burns": James Michener, interview with Dan Boylan, 19 July 1983, from author's notes.

112   "My contemporaries were all brought up": Daniel Inouye, JABOHP, 6 August 1975, p. 12.

113   Burns "was not a very talkative fellow": Daniel Inouye, JABOHP, 6 August 1975, p. 13.

115   "tail end of the struggle": Dan Aoki, JABOHP, 25 March 1975, pp. 5–6.

115   "We would have had no qualms": Dan Aoki, JABOHP, 25 March 1975, p. 12.

115   Fasi "had been calling us Communists": Mitsuyuki Kido, JABOHP, 31 July 1975, p. 2.

115   "Why get into a pissing contest": Dan Aoki, JABOHP, 25 March 1975, p. 11.

115–116   "Frank has always been Frank": Tom Gill, JABOHP, 7 November 1976, p. 85.

116   "How about you guys joining me": Dan Aoki, JABOHP, 25 March 1975, p. 14.

116   "he's at least an honest man": Dan Aoki, JABOHP, 25 March 1975, p. 13.

117   "I was left out in the cold": Chuck Mau, JABOHP, 21 September 1975, tape 2, p. 18.

117–118   "We believe that the people of Hawaii": *Platform of the Territorial Democratic Party, 1952*, Archives of Hawaii.

118   "a more active position in the leadership": HA, 10 May 1952, p. 5.

118   "To hell with legalisms, Burns is our man": William Richardson, secretary, *Minutes of the Territorial Democratic Central Committee*, 24 May 1952, Archives of Hawaii.

118–119   "Nothing has caused the Party more trouble": John A. Burns, letter to the Democratic County Committees, 23 June 1952, Archives of Hawaii.

119   "We must have hit him on a bad day": Tom Gill, JABOHP, 7 November 1976, p. 4.

119   "A number of Teamsters were old Democrats": Tom Gill, JABOHP, 7 November 1976, p. 7.

119   The elections of 1952 provided little excitement: comparison of official tabulations—territorial elections of Tuesday, 7 November 1950 and Tuesday, 4 November 1952, Archives of Hawaii.

120   Judge Delbert Metzger made a good showing: official tabulation—territorial elections, Tuesday, 4 November 1952, Archives of Hawaii.

120   Fasi was defeated by Wilson: official tabulation—city and county [of Honolulu], primary election, Saturday, 4 October 1952, Archives of Hawaii.

120   Wilson went on to defeat . . . Blaisdell: official tabulation—city and county [of Honolulu], general election, Tuesday, 4 November 1952, Archives of Hawaii.

120   "Our delegates [Burns, Kido, and Long] will not be too hard to handle": John A. Burns, letter to Oscar Chapman, 8 May 1952, Archives of Hawaii.

121   "new progressive look of the Democrats in the South": HSB, 24 September 1953, p. 4.

121–122   "George Lehleitner is a guy": John A. Burns, interview by Helen Altonn, HSB, 20 August 1974, p. 2.

123   "It would be fine recognition": HA, 23 June 1954, p. 1.

124   Elizabeth Farrington trounced Delbert Metzger: official tabulation—territorial special election, 31 July 1954, Archives of Hawaii.

124   "Burns: Dan, I think it's time for you to run": Inouye, *Journey to Washington*, pp. 242–243.

125   "Burns asked me a lot questions": George Ariyoshi, *With Obligation to All* (Honolulu: The Malama Foundation, 1997), pp. 38–39.

125   "And so, on the day of the deadline": George Ariyoshi, JABOHP, 26 July 1979, p. 10.

125–126   "We combined forces and filled up an entire ticket": Dan Aoki, JABOHP, 31 May 1977, p. 17.

126   And win they did: official tabulation—territorial elections, Tuesday, 2 November 1954, Archives of Hawaii.

126   "they might have swept the entire board": Donald D. Johnson, *The City and County of Honolulu* (Honolulu: University of Hawaii Press, 1994), p. 222.

126   Frank Fasi defeated Johnny Wilson: official tabulation—city and county [of Honolulu] primary election, Saturday, 2 October 1954, Archives of Hawaii.

126   the fine art of ticket splitting: Zalburg, *A Spark is Struck!*, p. 379.

126   "Any doubt that the Republicans might have voted": Johnson, *The City and County of Honolulu*, p. 221.

126   "should have been a Democrat": Dan Aoki, JABOHP, 25 March 1975, p. 29.

127   Burns lost by only 890 votes: official tabulation—territorial election, Tuesday, 2 November 1954, Archives of Hawaii.

127   "We ran completely out [of money]": Zalburg, *A Spark is Struck!*, p. 377.

127   "Didn't bother me at all": John A. Burns, JABOHP, 5 February 1975, pp. 7–9.

Chapter Eight—Delegate

128   "Fifty-six is another election": Inouye, *Journey to Washington*, p. 249.

129 "We put together . . . seventy, eighty, ninety bills": Tom Gill, JABOHP, 7 November 1976, pp. 19–20.

129–130 "He vetoed a large number of tax and spend bills": Fuchs, *Hawaii Pono*, p. 326.

130 "Callous and wanton disregard of the expressed mandate": HSB, 26 July 1955, p. 7.

130 "I liked him because he was a Democrat": Ben Menor, interview with Dan Boylan, 8 December 1981, from author's notes.

130 Burns publicly credited the ILWU: HSB, 22 November 1954, p. 7.

131 Burns . . . had been "severely criticized": HSB, 24 September 1955, p. 2.

131 "Jack was speaking to an ILWU audience": HSB, 3 October 1955, p. 8.

131 "It is quite natural that Jack is very anxious": HSB, 1 December 1955, p. 8.

132 "a pimple on the path of progress": David Halberstam, *The Fifties* (New York: Villard Books, 1993), p. 250.

132 Burns brought a few investors . . . into his . . . business: John A. Burns, JABOHP, 24 January 1975, tape 4, pp. 13–14.

132 "Politically, it was a perfect set-up": Mike Tokunaga, JABOHP, 12 July 1977, tape 2, p. 16.

133 "Ed, here's your card": John A. Burns, JABOHP, 5 February 1975, tape 10, p. 14.

133 "Your chairman, representing each of you": John A. Burns, *Report of the Chairman of the Territorial Democratic Central Committee*, February 1956, Archives of Hawaii.

134 "In all humility, I am . . . firmly convinced": HSB, 12 May 1956, p. 3.

135 As Masao ("Pundy") Yokouchi recalled: JABOHP, 9 August 1977, tape 1, pp. 15–16.

135 "The only reason you didn't get that New Deal": HSB, 25 September 1956, p. 13.

135 "I wasn't in there to do a lot of politicking": Elizabeth Farrington, JABOHP, 26 May 1976, p. 25.

136 "They were polite and cordial enough": HA, 26 October 1956, p. B1.

136–137 "The Story of Beatrice Burns": John A. Burns, campaign brochure, "The Woman Behind the Man," 1956, Archives of Hawaii.

137   "I support Jack Burns for Delegate": John A. Burns, campaign brochure, "The People Behind Burns," 1956, Archives of Hawaii.
137   "Coffee hours made believers": Mike Tokunaga, JABOHP, 12 July 1977, tape 2, p. 21.
138   "If I had said today what my opponent said": HSB, 26 October 1956, p. 1.
138   "The late Delegate Joseph R. Farrington": HSB, 30 October 1956, p. 1.
138   "Where was Mr. Burns when the blackouts came": HSB, 31 October 1956, p. 41.
138   "I was offered a commission in naval intelligence": HSB, 2 November 1956, p. 6.
139   "I wonder why Burns should be a hero": HSB, 2 November 1956, p. B1.
139   "Hawaii was as close to the realization of its fondest hopes": HSB, 19 October 1956, p. B1.
139   "Did they ask Drew Pearson to publish a retraction": HA, 25 October 1956, p. A3.
139   "If my opponent is the great messiah": HSB, 27 October 1956, p. 1.
140   "How is a person who calls Democrats 'Dixiecrats'": HSB, 30 October 1956, p. 2.
140   "Statehood is opposed by many people right here": HSB, 5 November 1956, p. B1.
140   The final count . . . was 82,166 for Burns: official tabulation—territorial election, Tuesday, 6 November 1956, Archives of Hawaii.
140   "For Hawaii, 1956 was what 1936 had been [on the mainland]": Fuchs, *Hawaii Pono*, p. 327.

Chapter Nine—Statehood

141–142   From "they handed over the Islands" to "78 percent . . . favored statehood": Daws, *Shoal of Time*, pp. 382–384.
142   "There has been too much wall-building": Zalburg, *A Spark is Struck!*, p. 391.
143   "Jack thought he could do anything": Margaret Mary [Burns] Curtis, interview with Dan Boylan, 16 March 1982, from author's notes.
143   Elizabeth Farrington offered him neither office space nor the files: William Miller, *Fishbait: The Memoirs of a Congressional Doorkeeper* (Englewood Cliffs, N.J.: Prentice-Hall, 1977), p. 82.

143–144   "a lot of research" and "a hell of a lot" of public relations: Seichi Hirai, JABOHP, 1 June 1978, p. 24.

144   "Everything Mr. Burns did in Washington": Dan Aoki, JABOHP, 25 March 1975, pp. 18–20.

144   "The chairman ran his committee": Representative Dante Fascell, interview with Dan Boylan, 23 June 1981, from author's notes.

145   "There are many shades and mixtures": Congress, Senate, Senator J. Strom Thurmond of South Carolina speaking against Hawaiian statehood, 86th Cong., 1st sess., *Congressional Record* (1959), pp. 3461–3464.

145–146   From "I am sure that no section of the country" to "our 'Southern Brethren'": John A. Burns, letter to Gregg Sinclair, 10 January 1957, Burns papers, Archives of Hawaii.

146   "I found in the course of getting acquainted": John A. Burns, letter to Nelson Doi, 15 August 1957, Burns papers, Archives of Hawaii.

146   "Burns made friends with as many congressmen": Rep. Jim Wright, interview with Dan Boylan, 21 June 1981, from author's notes.

146   "Jack knew everybody": Senator Eugene McCarthy, interview with Dan Boylan, 21 June 1981, from author's notes.

146   Burns "was constantly talking to people": Representative Dante Fascell, interview with Dan Boylan, 21 June 1981, from author's notes.

146   "He just let you know how he felt": Representative Paul Rogers, interview with Dan Boylan, 26 June 1981, from author's notes.

146–147   "He spent much of his time waiting": Mary Isa, interview with Dan Boylan, 15 August 1978, from author's notes.

147   "He'd come home at eleven o'clock at night": Beatrice Burns, JABOHP, 11 February 1976, p. 38.

147   From "It was nice of him to take me places" to "The Texans liked Jack": Beatrice Burns, interview with Dan Boylan, 30 March 1979, from author's notes.

148   "Since the 1954 Supreme Court decision": Bobby Baker, interview with Dan Boylan, 12 January 1979, from author's notes.

148   "honorary citizens of the State of Texas": John A. Burns, letter to Senator Ralph Yarborough, 15 January 1959, Burns papers, Archives of Hawaii.

149   "Both Burns and Rayburn were externally irascible": Representative Jim Wright, interview with Dan Boylan, 21 June 1981, from author's notes.

149   "Burns was a teetotaler": Bobby Baker, interview with Dan Boylan, 12 January 1979, from author's notes.

149   From "Sam Rayburn learned his politics" to "The sandwich will give you strength": Juanita Roberts, interview with Dan Boylan, 21 June 1981, from author's notes.

150   "Some efforts seem to be afoot": John A. Burns, letter to Oren Long, 14 January 1957, Burns papers, Archives of Hawaii.

150   "If nothing more is secured": John A. Burns, letter to Oren Long, 23 August 1957, Burns papers, Archives of Hawaii.

151   "By 1958, we had the votes for Alaska": Merle Miller, *Lyndon, An Oral Biography* (New York: G. P. Putnam, 1980), p. 219.

151   "When the delegation arrived in Washington": John A. Burns, letter to Shigeo Soga, 14 July 1958, Burns papers, Archives of Hawaii.

152   "If there was one haole in the islands": Fuchs, *Hawaii Pono,* p. 331.

152   "Trust me, I know what I'm doing": Fuchs, *Hawaii Pono,* p. 335.

152–153   Burns was returned to Congress: official tabulation, Tuesday, 6 November 1958, Archives of Hawaii.

153   Momentum had remained with the Democrats: Fuchs, *Hawaii Pono,* pp. 336–337.

153   After the election, Burns left nothing to chance: Fuchs, *Hawaii Pono,* p. 411.

154   On 11 March 1959: Daws, *Shoal of Time,* p. 391.

154   "Enclosed herewith is a contribution": John A. Burns, letter to the Immaculate Conception Shrine, Washington, D.C., 19 March 1959, Burns papers, Archives of Hawaii.

Chapter Ten—False Start

155   "Oh no! Why would he do that?": Beatrice Burns, interview with Dan Boylan, 12 September 1983, from author's notes.

155–156   "As you point out . . . I am entitled": John A. Burns, letter to James Michener, 28 March 1959, Burns papers, Archives of Hawaii.

156   "because that is Jack's favorite": HSB, 30 March 1959, p. B1.

156   "Jack aged when he was delegate": Beatrice Burns, interview with Dan Boylan, 30 March 1979, from author's notes.

156–157   "Jack should have been in the U.S. Senate": Doug Boswell, interview with Dan Boylan, 2 February 1982, from author's notes.

157   "We all feel very strongly here": Zalburg, *A Spark is Struck!,* p. 418.

157   "Herbert, my very real ambition": John A. Burns, letter to Herbert Isonaga, 10 March 1959, Burns papers, Archives of Hawaii.

157 "I do not know where the information came from": John A. Burns, letter to Morris T. Takushi, 10 March 1959, Burns papers, Archives of Hawaii.

158 "A ticket composed entirely of AJAs": John A. Burns, letter to Robert Dodge, 20 March 1959, Burns papers, Archives of Hawaii.

158 "Mr. Burns, run for the U.S. Senate": Dan Aoki, JABOHP, 25 March 1975, pp. 24–25, 28.

158 "Under the present circumstances": Dan Aoki, letter to Paul Tokunaga, 8 April 1959, Burns papers, Archives of Hawaii.

158–159 "Something that concerns me is a rumor": Ed Sheehan, letter to John A. Burns, 18 March 1959, Burns papers, Archives of Hawaii.

159 Hawaii must "thank the ILWU": John A. Burns, letter to Ed Sheehan, 24 March 1959, Burns papers, Archives of Hawaii.

159 "whether it be Governor or Senator": HA, 10 April 1959, p. A3.

159–160 "As we analyze the situation": John A. Burns, address to the ILWU Convention, 9 April 1959, p. 5, Burns papers, Archives of Hawaii.

161 "May I suggest for your consideration": John A. Burns, letter to James Seishiro Burns, 12 May 1959, Burns papers, Archives of Hawaii.

161 "Jack Hall and the ILWU [must remain] silent": Joe Miller, letter to Dan Aoki, 8 June 1959, Burns papers, Archives of Hawaii.

162 "Sparky Matsunaga got mad at us": Mike Tokunaga, JABOHP, 12 July 1977, tape 2, p. 32.

163 "that represents all our people": HA, 24 July 1959, p. A4.

163–164 From "It's very simple" to "I know something about the ILWU": HSB, 27 July 1959, p. 31.

164 "The first governor of our new state": *Hana Uwila*, International Brotherhood of Electrical Workers, 27 July 1959.

165 "I think it was demagoguery the way we presented it": A. A. Smyser, JABOHP, 25 June 1975, pp. 25, 28.

165 The regional director of the ILWU predicted: Zalburg, *A Spark is Struck!*, pp. 420–421.

165 "That son-of-a-bitch, endorsing Quinn": James Michener, interview with Dan Boylan, 19 July 1983, from author's notes.

166 "But if you are really determined to lose an election": SSA, 3 December 1959, second news section, p. 2.

166–167 From "In that case, I won't go" to "The White House had deliberately ignored the man": Dwight C. Dorough, *Mr. Sam* (New York: Random House, 1962), p. 542.

Chapter Eleven—Governor

168   "I think the State of Hawaii is going to have to make good use": HSB, 29 July 1959, p. G1.

169   "The man that really created the East-West Center": Dan Aoki, JABOHP, 3 April 1975, pp. 11–13.

169   "I wanted a 2,000 to 2,500 margin": Ben Menor, interview with Dan Boylan, 8 December 1981, from author's notes.

169   "It was the first definite decision": HSB, 19 September 1962, p. 3.

169–170   "On the office procedure": Mary Isa, letter to Sally Sheehan, 29 September 1959, Burns papers, Archives of Hawaii.

170   "I sometimes lunched with Burns": Richard Kosaki, interview with Dan Boylan, 16 October 1981, from author's notes.

170   "Without Jack Burns, neither Alaska nor Hawaii": Rohrbough, unpublished manuscript, no pagination.

171   "So one day I says, 'Hey, Jack'" to "Hey, Pop, how much would it have cost": Dan Aoki, JABOHP, 29 March 1975, p. 29.

172   Dan Inouye was the leading vote getter: HSB, 23 May 1960, p. 10.

172   The result was a four-way split: HA, 14 July 1960, p. A1.

173   "I have never supported Mr. Blaisdell": HSB, 12 September 1960, p. A1.

173   "[Putting it] bluntly, I need to have recognition": John A. Burns, letter to Bobby Baker, undated, Burns papers, Archives of Hawaii.

174   "I would [accept the position] if the director": Mary Isa, letter to Lillian (last name not indicated), 16 March 1961, Archives of Hawaii.

174–175   From "There was petty bickering" to "I must take responsibility": *Honolulu Magazine*, February 1982, pp. 55–56.

175–176   "Hi, I understand you're a darn good lawyer": Robert Oshiro, JABOHP, 24 February 1977, p. 8.

176   "That news was so electrifying": Robert Oshiro, JABOHP, 24 February 1977, pp. 11, 17.

176   "You should not have lost the '59 election": Robert Oshiro, JABOHP, 24 February 1977, pp. 21–22.

176–177   Oshiro was . . . "a big statistics man": William Richardson, JABOHP, 28 July 1977, pp. 10–13.

177   "The house was unkempt": Robert Oshiro, JABOHP, 24 February 1977, pp. 25–27.

178   "In my book . . . [Burns] was more of an intellectual": Ralph Miwa, JABOHP, 7 March 1977, pp. 18–20.

178 The Party's fact-finding committee had cast twelve . . . votes: HA, 4 February 1962, p. 1.

179 "Wherever [Long] went, most of the people agreed": Mike Tokunaga, JABOHP, 19 July 1977, pp. 1–2.

180–181 "There is an urgency to all of this": John A. Burns, announcement speech, 12 August 1962, Burns papers, Archives of Hawaii.

181 "First, listen to me": Robert Alderman, interview with Dan Boylan, 11 July 1980, from author's notes.

182 "All right fellas, let's go": Dan Aoki, JABOHP, 25 March 1975, tape 13, p. 42.

182 "Quinn had an incredibly fine mind": Roger Coryellas, quoted in Mary C. Kahulumana Richards, *No Ordinary Man: William Francis Quinn, His Role in Hawaii's History* (Honolulu: Hawaii Education Association, 1998), p. 320.

182 "Quinn Given Edge in Lackluster Debate": HSB, 3 November 1962, p. 1.

Chapter Twelve—Getting Started

185–186 From "I was a small kid at the time" to "Politically, he was never a wheeler-dealer": Monsignor Charles Kekumano, interview with Dan Boylan, 26 December 1984, from author's notes.

186 "talent search" at Takabuki's home: Dan Aoki, JABOHP, 31 May 1977, p. 27.

187 "Oh, by the way . . . what's your politics?": Fujio Matsuda, JABOHP, 14 July 1978, pp. 15–16.

187–188 "Governor," Kobayashi noted, "there are so many": Bert Kobayashi, JABOHP, 18 June 1980, pp. 15–17.

188 "The job simply called for common sense": Andrew Ing, interview with Dan Boylan, 22 July 1980, from author's notes.

190 "While I do not particularly like to bring a relative": HSB, 3 December 1962, p. 25.

190 "Racially, the cabinet has an even better balance": HSB, 26 January 1963, p. 5.

191–192 "In August 1962, I accepted the presidency": Samuel Crowningburg Amalu, *Jack Burns, A Portrait in Transition* (Honolulu: The Malama Foundation, 1974), pp. 160–162.

193 "The purpose of having regents' terms": Thomas Hamilton, JABOHP, 25 July 1979, p. 15.

193 "As far as land and fiscal policy [are connected]": Matsuo Takabuki, JABOHP, 22 July 1978, pp. 12–13.

193   "I made it very clear during the 1962 campaign": Robert Oshiro, JABOHP, 17 February 1977, pp. 16–17.

193–195   From "To secure for the people of Hawaii" to "It will be my aim to raise": John A. Burns, inaugural address (1962), Burns papers, Archives of Hawaii.

195–196   "Many of the programs Governor Burns outlined": HSB, 4 December 1962, p. 8.

196–197   "In the past statehood boom" to "the disproportionate concentration of population": Hawaii, *House Journal,* 21 February 1963, pp. 10–12.

198   "He meets the challenge of shrinking tax income": HSB, 22 February 1963, p. 6.

Chapter Thirteen—First Term

199   "In 1959, the new stage government owned 32 percent of all the land": Fuchs, *Hawaii Pono,* pp. 426–427.

200   "One of these was Harry M. Field": George Cooper and Gavan Daws, *Land and Power in Hawaii* (Honolulu: Benchmark Books, 1985), p. 403.

200   "The criticism was thunderous": Ariyoshi, *With Obligation to All,* pp. 54–55.

201   "I was brought up in an atmosphere": SSA, 5 May 1963, p. A3.

201   "The failure of the Maryland Bill": HSB, 4 May 1963, p. 4.

201   The *Honolulu Star-Bulletin* called it a "good session": HSB, 7 May 1963, p. 8.

201   "They warily grant the Governor John A. Burns": *New York Times,* 24 May 1963, p. 52.

202   "nine days out of ten": Beatrice Burns, JABOHP, tape 2, 8 March 1976, pp. 18–19; telephone interview with Dan Boylan, 16 August 1980, from author's notes.

202   "He'd be sitting there . . . with the *Advertiser*": George Chaplin, JABOHP, 5 June 1978, pp. 31–32.

202–203   "He gave you responsibility": Mary Isa, interview with Dan Boylan, 15 August 1978, from author's notes.

203   "He used to work at home": Beatrice Burns, JABOHP, 8 March 1976, pp. 20–21.

203–205   From <total employment had risen by 2,500 jobs> to <Burns expressed particular pleasure>: Hawaii, *House Journal,* 19 February 1964, pp. 21–24.

205	The night before the budget session began: HSB, 19 February 1964, p. 21.
205–206	From <He cut back his expenditure projection> to <being assessed at "highest and best use">: Hawaii, *House Journal,* 19 February 1964, pp. 19–24.
206	the legislature "did juggle the funds": HA, 30 March 1964, p. A2.
207	The charts below show the *Baker v. Carr* implications: SSA, 16 February 1964, p. A4.
208	Burns' plan sought to set the size of the house and senate: Hawaii, *House Journal,* 23 July 1964, p. 8.
208	"The blame is on one man alone": HA, 28 August 1964, p. 1.
208	Gill easily defeated Nadao Yoshinaga: HA, 5 October 1964, p. 1.
208	Fong defeated Gill by 14,000 votes: HA, 5 November 1964, p. 1.
209	"right under Governor Burns' nose": Dan Aoki, JABOHP, 24 March 1975, tape 2, p. 16.
209	A three-judge federal district court panel ruled: HA, 19 February 1965, p. A8.
210	"The court took a fairly firm position on that, didn't it?" HA, 19 February 1965, p. A8.
210	The twenty minute message . . . to the joint session: Hawaii, *House Journal,* 18 February 1965, pp. 8–11.
210	the federal court rejected the legislature's plan: HA, 29 April 1965, p. A6.
210–211	Another eleven months passed before the U.S. Supreme Court: HA, 26 April 1966, p. A1.
211	"Eschewing the spotlight": SSA, 6 June 1965, p. A17.
211	"The legislature was made up": Jack Kellner, interview with Dan Boylan, 15 February 1982, from author's notes.

Chapter Fourteen—A Case of the Hives

212	From "I didn't look forward to" to "By the time she left Washington": Beatrice Burns, JABOHP, tape 2, 8 March 1976, pp. 13–15.
213	From "I had transportation" to "The security men used to say": Beatrice Burns, JABOHP, tape 2, 8 March 1976, p. 20.
213	From <More than 600,000 visitors> to <a $6.3 million surplus was anticipated>: Hawaii, *House Journal,* 16 February 1966, pp. 17–20.
214	"Before the new capitol was built": Doug Boswell, interview with Dan Boylan, 2 February 1982, from author's notes.

214   "At *pau hana* time the reporters would sit out": Tom Coffman, in-
       terview with Dan Boylan, 3 February 1982, from author's notes.
214   "scared the pie out of Jack": Beatrice Burns, telephone interview
       with Dan Boylan, 6 August 1980, from author's notes.
214   "Richardson was regarded as the likely choice": HSB, 18 Decem-
       ber 1965, p. A1.
214   "Well, I'd rather be chief justice": William Richardson, JABOHP,
       2 February 1976, p. 19.
215   Burns "reportedly believes the post would groom Cravalho":
       HSB, 18 December 1965, p. A1.
215   "I felt free to walk up any time": Elmer Cravalho, JABOHP,
       10 August 1977, p. 26.
215   "The Richardson appointment also sets in motion": HA, 26 Feb-
       ruary 1966, p. 26.
215–216 From "There isn't a soul" to "we'll work it out": Elmer Cravalho,
       JABOHP, 10 August 1977, pp. 29–31.
216   "I finally convinced him": HA, 29 March 1966, pp. A1, A2.
216   "I don't like the pomp": Elmer Cravalho, JABOHP, 10 August
       1977, pp. 33–34.
216   "giving serious thought to possibly running": HA, 12 April 1966,
       p. A2.
217   "No way. I love politics, but": Bert Kobayashi, JABOHP, 18 June
       1980, p. 25.
217   "Do you think you'd get hives": John A. Burns, JABOHP, 27 Jan-
       uary 1975, p. 18.
217   "He made it very clear that he'd prefer somebody else": Tom Gill,
       JABOHP, 7 November 1976, p. 48.
217   "I didn't want to run for Congress again": Tom Gill, JABOHP, 7
       November 1976, p. 46.
217–218 What Gill did not say in his 1976 interview: Tom Gill, interview
       with T. Michael Holmes, 3 May 1993, from author's notes.
218   "political observers at the [Republican] convention": HSB,
       23 May 1966, p. A1.
218   "For some city and state workers": Johnson, *The City and County
       of Honolulu,* p. 280.
218   "I guess he said, 'The hell with it'": Herman Lemke, JABOHP,
       19 June 1980, p. 29.
219   "Now that the Republicans have lost their strongest candidate":
       SSA, 22 May 1966, p. A1.

219   The big news from the Democratic Convention: HSB, 25 May 1966, p. A1.

219   "Kamaaina 'Defects' to Demos": HA, 9 June 1966, p. A1.

219   "he's the most intelligent man I have ever known": Kenneth F. Brown, JABOHP, 1 June 1978, pp. 23–24.

219–220 Burns was also attracted to an almost endless list of public organizations: HA, 20 July 1966, p. A2.

220   When Mike Tokunaga . . . first heard the news: Mike Tokunaga, JABOHP, 8 August 1977, p. 9.

220   "So right there, I knew our work was cut out for us": Hiroshi Tanaka, JABOHP, 25 July 1977, p. 37.

220   "Welcome in. The water's fine": HA, 20 July 1966, p. A2.

220   "That was a dumb thing": Tom Gill, JABOHP, 7 November 1976, p. 48.

220–221 The *Honolulu Advertiser* released a poll they had taken in mid-May: 21 July 1966, p. B1.

221   "There's a danger that if we stretch our political tent": HA, 1 August 1966, pp. A1, A2.

221   "Jack [Burns] and I can produce great things": HA, 6 August 1966, p. A1.

221   "I figure when you do a good job": Doug Boswell, interview with Dan Boylan, 2 February 1982, from author's notes.

222   "When the Governor leaves the State": HSB, 20 August 1966, p. A2.

222   "We won in 1962 with a wide base of support": HSB, 20 August 1966, p. A3.

222–223 "I am deeply appreciative of the warm and strong support": SSA, 4 September 1966, p. 1.

223   A lieutenant governor should be "willing to submerge himself": SSA, 4 September 1966, p. A1.

223   "Like Adlai Stevenson": HA, 27 September 1966, p. A2.

224   "I deeply regret . . . that I must be out of the State": HSB, 27 September 1966, p. 1.

224   "a partner, not a competitor": HA, 27 September 1966, p. A1.

224   From "The primary was on Saturday" to "Would you give me those figures again?": Tom Coffman, *Catch a Wave* (Honolulu: University of Hawai'i Press, 1973), pp. 47–48.

224–225 Gill's victory "proved again that political popularity is rarely transferable": SSA, 2 October 1966, p. B2.

225   "In retrospect, things began to go wrong": HSB, 3 October 1966, p. A8.

225   "The people had better stick to the Democratic side": HSB, 3 October 1966, p. A14.

225   "The Governor has made it clear that he cannot work with Mr. Gill": HSB, 3 October 1966, p. 1.

226   "Crossley, whose personal and business counsel was Herbert Brownell": Fuchs, *Hawaii Pono,* p. 324.

226–227   From "They persuaded me to go to New York" to "And that was it": Kenneth F. Brown, JABOHP, 1 June 1978, pp. 29–31.

227   "I don't give a damn whether I get elected": Matsuo Takabuki, JABOHP, 22 July 1978, pp. 26–27.

227   "Jones stuck a mike under his nose": HA, 11 October 1966, p. 1.

227–228   "If they'd planned it for weeks": Tom Gill, JABOHP, 7 November 1976, p. 50.

228   Burns delivered . . . "a fighting speech": HSB, 15 October 1966, p. 1.

228   "I was struck by Lois' intelligence": Beatrice Burns, telephone interview with Dan Boylan, 11 January 1979, from author's notes.

228   "The first piece of legislation we will present": HSB, 9 October 1966, p. 1.

228   When the Democrats pressed Crossley: HSB, 1 November 1966, p. A1.

228–229   "In brief, Hawaii is enjoying more prosperity than ever before": SSA, 30 October 1966, p. B2.

229   Burns and Gill received 108,840 votes: official tabulation—state election, Tuesday, 8 November 1966, Archives of Hawaii.

229   "There are times when I'd rather be alone": HA, 10 November 1966, p. 1.

Chapter Fifteen—Second Term

230   "We put together a pretty good committee": Tom Gill, JABOHP, 7 November 1976, pp. 53–54.

231   From "in particular, those oriented to ocean sciences" to "We have no room for conflicts of interests": HSB, 5 December 1966, p. C2.

232   From <The Democrats still enjoyed a two-thirds majority> to "In the thirty-nine years since I became a legislator": HA, 16 February 1967, p. A4.

233   "The economic outlook is not as clear-cut as it appeared": Hawaii, *House Journal,* 16 February 1967, p. 20.

233 "The two men [Burns and Gill] are enveloped in a capsule of bitterness": HSB, 21 February 1967, p. C1.

234 "I thought he was a very good appointment": Tom Gill, JABOHP, 7 November 1976, pp. 56–57.

234 "Bea insisted on going": Lady Bird Johnson as quoted in letter from Betty Tilson, staff assistant to Mrs. Lyndon B. Johnson, to Dan Boylan, 27 July 1981.

235 "John Connally (Texas) . . . the handsomest man in the room": Lady Bird Johnson, *A White House Diary* (New York: Holt, Rinehart and Winston), pp. 504–505.

236 "the political spoils system now reaches even into the courts": HSB, 8 May 1967, p. A8.

237 "there can be no guarantee of tenure": W. Todd Furniss, letter to Oliver Lee, 29 May 1967.

237 From "there can be no guarantee of tenure" to "encouraging desertion, disposing and destroying of weapons": HA, 6 June 1967, p. A2.

237 "while they were taking some risks of prosecution": HA, 11 June 1967, p. 1.

237 "To tell a group of students to issue a potentially seditious statement": HA, 29 June 1967, p. A2.

237–238 "I have spent a great deal of energy protecting academic freedom": SSA, 24 December 1967, p. 1.

238 Gill characterized Hamilton's resignation as "a grievous blow": HA, 25 December 1967, p. 3.

238 From "Whenever I was about to take a step" to "I might have handled it differently": Thomas Hamilton, JABOHP, 25 July 1979, pp. 34–35.

238–239 The Oliver Lee case finally ended on 11 April 1969: HSB, 12 April 1969, p. A9.

239–240 From "grave problems in Hawaii and in the Pacific region" to "No wave of visitors to Hawaii": Hawaii, *House Journal*, 23 February 1968, pp. 10–12.

240 Hawaii's voters had been quick to say "yes": official tabulation—general election, Tuesday, 8 November 1966, Archives of Hawaii.

241–242 "I do not believe it is proper for me to comment": HA, 30 July 1968, p. A4.

242 Blaisdell's dream of becoming a Bishop Estate trustee was shattered: HA, 31 August 1968, p. A4.

242 "I had no reason to believe I was the favorite son": HA, 5 September 1968, p. 1.

242   "No deals, absolutely no deals": William Richardson, interview
        with T. Michael Holmes, 11 June 1993, from author's notes.

243   Blaisdell took a terrible drubbing: official tabulation—general
        election, 5 November 1968, Archives of Hawaii.

243   "Retired from politics, Neal Blaisdell became": Johnson, *The City
        and County of Honolulu,* p. 286.

243   "when it became apparent that I had lost": Matsuo Takabuki, *An
        Unlikely Revolutionary* (Honolulu: University of Hawaii Press,
        1998), p. 78.

243–244 "He has been *the* outstanding administrator in our government":
        HSB, 18 January 1969, p. B5.

244   Burns . . . feared for the East-West Center: HSB, 4 January 1969,
        p. B1.

244–245 From "The theme is prudent spending" to "Let us clearly under-
        stand that diversity and division are not the same": Hawaii, *House
        Journal,* 20 February 1969, pp. 18–20.

245–246 "Burns always maintained a dreamy vision of Hawaii": Gerry
        Keir, interview with Dan Boylan, 3 February 1982, from author's
        notes.

246   "I've always said, 'If you'd skin him, he's not a haole'": Beatrice
        Burns, telephone interview with Dan Boylan, 3 January 1982,
        from author's notes.

246   The governor . . . agreed to Kobayashi's move with "mixed feel-
        ings": HA, 12 April 1969, p. A4.

246   "Fortunately, I was able to persuade the governor": Takabuki, *An
        Unlikely Revolutionary,* p. 94.

246   "A spiritual . . . pick-up": HSB, 4 November 1967, p. 1.

246–247 From "Burns . . . halted further land-fills" to "in time for Burns to
        plant a ceremonial tree": Coffman, *Catch a Wave,* pp. 66–68.

247–248 "That bill," Yano charged, "does not meet the problem": SSA,
        14 September 1969, p. A6.

248   Those who favored the Yano plan numbered 1,355: HSB, 7 No-
        vember 1969, p. A1.

248   responding to Roman Catholic bishop John Scanlon's character-
        ization of abortion: HSB, 7 November 1969, p. A20.

248   "Do you agree with the State Senate proposal": HSB, 13 Febru-
        ary 1970, p. 1.

248   Inouye gave an early rendition of the classic pro-choice position:
        HSB, 13 February 1970, p. A4.

248   Loo wanted no "abortion-tours" to Hawaii: HA, 26 February
        1970, p. 1.

249	"The abortion bill was sitting on his desk": Gerry Keir, interview with Dan Boylan, 3 February 1982, from author's notes.
249	"He argued that if he vetoed": John Hulten, interview with Dan Boylan, 20 November 1981, from author's notes.
249–250	"I have declined to sign this bill after much study and soul-searching": HSB, 12 March 1970, p. D8.
250	From "the best example of how he had mellowed" to "He agonized over that": James S. Burns, JABOHP, 5 April 1976, pp. 5–6.

Chapter Sixteen—Catching a Wave

267–268	From "I am constrained to describe" to "If a man is hungry": Hawaii, *House Journal*, 22 January 1970, p. 33.
268	"No conference ever solved a traffic problem": HSB, 9 February 1970, p. 2.
269	"You can pump all the money you want": HSB, 27 March 1970, p. A3.
269	"the mechanism for allowing the State to go into massive housing": HSB, 16 April 1970, p. A10.
270	"I'm told that there are those in Hawaii": SSA, 10 May 1970, p. A4.
270	According to the Federal Housing Administration: HSB, 2 June 1970, p. 1.
270–271	From "excluded from all major decisions" to "It's a free country": HA, 10 July 1970, pp. 1, A12.
271	"He didn't. Bob Oshiro did": Beatrice Burns, JABOHP, 8 March 1976, p. 29.
271–272	"I was sorry to see him agree to run again": Edward Burns, JABOHP, 30 April 1975, p. 33.
272	"Had not Tom Gill been the guy running": James S. Burns, JABOHP, 5 April 1976, p. 8.
272–273	From "What I tried to do" to "Bob, I'm no 52-year-old": Robert Oshiro, JABOHP, 24 February 1977, pp. 26–28.
273	From "I didn't have a candidate" to "my answer would be 'yes' to that question": Robert Oshiro, JABOHP, 3 March 1977, pp. 4–5.
273–274	From <The media campaign has been well documented> to <In the decade following 1960>: Coffman, *Catch a Wave*, pp. 9–11.
274–275	Ariyoshi was . . . surprised: Ariyoshi, *With Obligation to All*, p. 69.
275–276	From "I am what I am because of you" to "If any man in Hawaii is to be given credit": Coffman, *Catch a Wave*, pp. 94–95.

276   In a poll taken on 12 and 13 August: HSB, 17 August 1970, p. 1.

276–277   From <Buck Donovan revealed that Shiro Nishimura> to "This
               kind of reporting keeps the government on its toes": HSB, 22 Au-
               gust 1970, p. 1.

277   Burns announced that Bill Cook would be his special assistant:
               HSB, 26 August 1970, p. D9.

277–278   "There are those who would have us believe": HSB, 21 August
               1970, p. C5.

278   fewer than 50 percent of the voters: Coffman, *Catch a Wave*,
               p. 148.

278   From "When I see my dear friend and political father being at-
               tacked" to "So we have to say it for him": HA, 1 October 1970,
               p. A7.

279   Another element of Burns' momentum: HA, 5 October 1970,
               p. A1.

279   On Oahu, the seat of Gill's strength, only 68 percent . . . turned
               out: SSA, 4 October 1970, p. 1.

280   From "Open Letter to the People" to "both of us were lying like
               hell": Tom Gill, JABOHP, 7 November 1970, p. 63.

281   "If the governor had taken a stand on organized crime": SSA,
               25 October 1970, p. A1.

281   "There goes the election": Coffman, *Catch a Wave*, p. 199.

281   In the absence of a Tom Gill-led "Democrats for King" drive: of-
               ficial tabulation—general election, Tuesday, 3 November 1970,
               Archives of Hawaii.

281–282   delivered his third inaugural address: HA, 8 December 1970,
               p. A1.

Chapter Seventeen—End of the Rainbow

283–284   From "Even before the general election" to "He used to call me
               and ask me if I was free for lunch": George Ariyoshi, JABOHP,
               26 July 1979, pp. 36–38.

284   "Right after the 1970 election": Ariyoshi, *With Obligation to All*,
               p .78.

284   "He liked him," she recalled. "We all did": Beatrice Burns,
               JABOHP, 8 March 1976, pp. 30-31.

284   "George, you don't know how good it is": George Ariyoshi,
               JABOHP, 26 July 1979, p. 38.

285   "Why don't you take a look at that": Ariyoshi, *With Obligation to
               All*, p. 79.

285   "You're the boss": George Ariyoshi, interview with T. Michael Holmes, 15 July 1993, from author's notes.

285   "One thing stood out clearly in my mind": SSA, 30 June 1974, p. A1.

285   Acting Governor George Ariyoshi signed a $4.5 million appropriations bill: HA, 6 June 1972, p. 1.

286   "he left the decision entirely up to me": HA, 7 June 1972, p. A13.

286   On 22 July 1971, Edward Y. Hirata ... announced: HSB, 22 July 1971, p. 1.

286–287 Doug Boswell reported in October 1973: 18 October 1973, pp. A1, A4.

287   "If Mr. Fasi paid as much attention to municipal affairs": HSB, 19 August 1971, p. 1.

287–288 On 17 January, the West Coast dock workers struck: HA, 18 January 1972, p. 1.

288   Labor writer Charles Turner outlined the entire litany: HA, 2 February 1972, p. 1.

288   "When the appointment was announced last week": HA, 22 June 1972, p. A4.

288–289 "In the four years that I have served on the bench": HA, 30 June 1972, p. 1.

289   "When it comes to matters of the judiciary, I stay out": HSB, 20 July 1972, p. D20.

289   From "One morning in 1972" to "I was making a big financial sacrifice": Takabuki, An Unlikely Revolutionary, pp. 95–96.

290   "a dark and disappointing day for many of our native Hawaiian people": HA, 22 June 1972, p. A4.

290   "The bells of Kawaiahao Church rang": Takabuki, An Unlikely Revolutionary, p. 98.

290   "The Takabuki protest symbolizes the Hawaiians' first battle cry": Takabuki, An Unlikely Revolutionary, p. 199.

291   Tom Gill prophesied that the appointment: HA, 23 June 1971, p. A12.

291   The story, written by Fasi retainer Brian Casey: Carol S. Dodd, The Richardson Years (Honolulu: University of Hawaii Foundation, 1985), pp. 31, 44f.

291   "I would not resign as long as you people want me": Matsuo Takabuki, JABOHP, 22 July 1978, p. 35.

292   Takabuki quoted Abraham Lincoln: HSB, 30 July 1972, p. A19.

292   "The estimated value of the Bishop Estate: Kekoa Paulsen, interview with T. Michael Holmes, 11 August 1993, from author's notes.

292   "the difference between political animosity and personal animosity": James S. Burns, JABOHP 5 April 1976, p. 8.

292   "I'm doing my job as if I were going to run": HA, 30 July 1971, p. A15.

292–293   "At age 51, Frank Fasi has never been in better shape for a campaign": HSB, 4 January 1972, p. 1.

293   rumors that "Burns people" had approached Tom Gill: HSB, 26 April 1972, p. 1.

293   "the election would cost them two million bucks": Tom Gill, JABOHP, 7 November 1976, pp. 64–65.

294   "Apparently she has been spending too much time in Oregon, Paris, and elsewhere": HSB, 24 June 1972, p. A17.

294   Frank Fasi won the Democratic primary with 52 percent: SSA, 8 October 1972, p. 1.

294   "I'm a Democrat. . . . I don't support Republicans": HA, 9 October 1972, p. A8.

294   Don Horio . . . "worked behind closed doors": HA, 3 November 1972, p. A16.

295   Gerry Keir's analysis of the election returns: HA, 11 November 1972, p. A8.

295   "on the slopes of the Kohala Mountains": HA, 23 August 1972, p. A1.

295   Burns . . . told Ariyoshi that he had a pain: George Ariyoshi, JABOHP, 26 July 1979, p. 43.

296   From "Oh, we'll take care of it" to <Reluctantly, Burns submitted>: Beatrice Burns, interview with Dan Boylan, 5 July 1980, from author's notes.

296–297   "With no regrets, with an unclouded conscience": HSB, 11 April 1974, p. 1.

297   "Burns . . . gave way to tears several times": HSB, 12 April 1974, p. A1.

297   From "I took it very personally" to "I was convinced that George was the best candidate": HSB, 2 December 1974, p. A2.

297–298   "It was pleasant enough. I don't have any hard personal feelings": Tom Gill, JABOHP, 7 November 1976, p. 65.

298   "If your father tells me 'no,' I'll get out": James S. Burns, JABOHP, 5 April 1976, p. 14.

298   "It simply means that he [Ariyoshi] can function more efficiently": HSB, 2 July 1974, p. 18.

299   From <Ariyoshi captured the Democratic Party nomination> to <Doi received 92, 613 votes to Akaka's 77,162>: HSB, 7 October 1974, pp. A16, A20.

300   In the lowest voter turnout since statehood: HSB, 6 November 1974, p. H2.

300–301   From "It was when Ariyoshi was officially declared Governor" to "He's a real Kabuki actor": 3 December 1974, p. 1.

301   "He never admitted he was going to die": Beatrice Burns, interview with Dan Boylan, 30 March 1979, from author's notes.

Epilogue—The Burns Years

303   "Jack kept it together in those bad years; only he": James Michener, interview with Dan Boylan, 19 July 1983, from author's notes.

304   "His achievement was not in terms of legislation": Doug Boswell, interview with Dan Boylan, 2 February 1982, from author's notes.

304   "It was an activist court": Bambi Weil, interview with Dan Boylan, 12 February 1982, from author's notes.

304   "as a symbol of changes that occurred": Byron Baker, interview with Dan Boylan, 17 February 1982, author's notes.

304   From "growth for growth's sake" to "administration to be shut to outsiders": Buck Donham, interview with Dan Boylan, 15 March 1982, from author's notes.

304   From "two clear ideas" to "His first term was the one that mattered": Tom Coffman, interview with Dan Boylan, 3 February 1982, from author's notes.

305   "Burns was like a magnet": Shunichi Kimura, interview with Dan Boylan, 17 March 1982, from author's notes.

305–306   "Burns did much to ameliorate the wartime hysteria": Takabuki, An Unlikely Revolutionary, pp. 67–70.

306   "They called John Burns 'Stone Face'": HSB, 7 April 1975, p. A1.

306   "tremendous loyalty from the young Japanese": Norman Meller, interview with Dan Boylan, 23 February 1982, from author's notes.

306–307   "I think the Democrats and the Burns situation": Malcolm McNaughton, JABOHP, 11 May 1983, p. 28.

307   Hitch . . . spoke of the years from 1959 to 1973 as "the boom years": Thomas K. Hitch, *Islands in Transition* (First Hawaiian Bank/University of Hawaii Press, 1991), p. 183.

307   But the truly striking figures: Hitch, *Islands in Transition*, pp. 170–171.

SOURCES CITED

Alderman, Robert. Interview with Dan Boylan, 11 July 1980.
Amalu, Samuel Crowningburg. *Jack Burns, A Portrait in Transition.* Honolulu: The Malama Foundation, 1974.
Aoki, Dan. John A. Burns Oral History Project, 24 March 1975.
     25 March 1975.
     3 April 1975.
     31 May 1977.
————. Letter to Paul Tokunaga. 8 April 1959, Burns papers, Archives of Hawaii.
Ariyoshi, George R. *With Obligation to All.* Honolulu: Ariyoshi Foundation, 1997.
————. John A. Burns Oral History Project, 26 July 1979.
————. Interview with T. Michael Holmes, 15 July 1993.
Baker, Bobby. Interview with Dan Boylan, 12 January 1979.
Boswell, Doug. Interview with Dan Boylan, 2 February 1982.
Brown, Kenneth. John A. Burns Oral History Project, 1 June 1978.
Burns, Beatrice. John A. Burns Oral History Project, 11 February 1976.
     8 March 1976.
————. Telephone interview with Dan Boylan. 30 March 1979.
     15 July 1980.
     12 September 1983.
Burns, Edward. John A. Burns Oral History Project, 30 April 1975.
     12 February 1979.
————. Undated memo. Burns police file, Archives of Hawaii.
Burns, James S. John A. Burns Oral History Project, 5 April 1976.
Burns, John A. John A. Burns Oral History Project, 2 January 1975.
     16 January 1975.
     24 January 1975.
     27 January 1975.
     29 January 1975.
     5 February 1975.
————. Address to ILWU Convention, 9 April 1959, Burns papers, Archives of Hawaii.

———. Announcement speech, 12 August 1962, Burns papers, Archives of Hawaii.

———. Application for liquor license, Burns police file, Archives of Hawaii, August 1945.

———. Campaign brochure, "The People Behind Burns," 1956, Burns file, Archives of Hawaii.

———. Campaign brochure, "The Woman Behind the Man," 1956, Burns file, Archives of Hawaii.

———. Inaugural address, 1962, Burns papers, Archives of Hawaii.

———. Interview with Helen Altonn, Reported in the *Honolulu Star-Bulletin,* 20 August 1974.

———. Letter to Democratic County Committees, 23 June 1952, Burns papers, Archives of Hawaii.

———. Letter to Interior Secretary Oscar Chapman, 8 May 1952, Burns papers, Archives of Hawaii.

———. Letter to Gregg Sinclair, 10 January 1957, Burns papers, Archives of Hawaii.

———. Letter to Oren Long, 14 January 1957, Burns papers, Archives of Hawaii.

———. Letter to Nelson Doi, 15 August 1957, Burns papers, Archives of Hawaii.

———. Letter to Oren Long, 23 August 1957, Burns papers, Archives of Hawaii.

———. Letter to Shigeo Soga, 14 July 1958, Burns papers, Archives of Hawaii.

———. Letter to Senator Ralph Yarborough, 15 January 1959, Burns papers, Archives of Hawaii.

———. Letter to Herbert Isonaga, 10 March 1959, Burns papers, Archives of Hawaii.

———. Letter to Morris T. Takushi, 10 March 1959, Burns papers, Archives of Hawaii.

———. Letter to the Immaculate Conception Shrine, Washington, D.C., 19 March 1959, Archives of Hawaii.

———. Letter to Robert Dodge, 20 March 1959, Burns papers, Archives of Hawaii.

———. Letter to Ed Sheehan, 24 March 1959, Burns papers, Archives of Hawaii.

———. Letter to James Michener, 28 March 1959, Burns papers, Archives of Hawaii.

———. Letter to James Seishiro Burns, 12 May 1959, Burns papers, Archives of Hawaii.

———. Letter to Bobby Baker, Undated, 1960 or 1961, Burns papers, Archives of Hawaii.

———. *Report of the Chairman of the Democratic Central Committee,* February 1956, Burns file, Archives of Hawaii.

Burns, Sheenagh. "Jack Burns: A Daughter's Portrait," *The Hawaiian Journal of History* 24 (1990).

Coffman, Tom. *Catch a Wave*. Honolulu: University of Hawaii Press, 1973.

Cooper, George, and Gavan Daws. *Land and Power in Hawaii*. Honolulu: Benchmark Books, 1985.

Cravalho, Elmer. John A. Burns Oral History Project, 10 August 1977.

Curtis, Margaret Mary [Burns], Interview with Dan Boylan, 16 March 1982.

———. John A. Burns Oral History Project, 27 July 1979.

Daws, Gavan. *Shoal of Time*. Honolulu: University of Hawaii Press, 1968.

Dodd, Carol S. *The Richardson Years*. Honolulu: University of Hawaii Foundation, 1985.

Dorough, Dwight C. *Mr. Sam*. New York: Random House, 1962.

Esposito, O. Vincent. John A. Burns Oral History Project, 12 June 1975.

Farrington, Elizabeth. John A. Burns Oral History Project, 26 May 1976.

Faschell, Representative Dante. John A. Burns Oral History Project, 23 June 1981.

Fuchs, Lawrence. *Hawaii Pono*. Honolulu: Bess Press, 1961.

Furniss, W. Todd. Letter to Oliver Lee, 29 May 1967, Archives of Hawaii.

Gabrielson, William A. Letter to Flo Burns, 18 December 1935, Burns police file, Archives of Hawaii.

Gill, Tom. John A. Burns Oral History Project, 7 November 1976.

———. Telephone interview with T. Michael Holmes, 3 May 1993.

Ginger, Ann Fagan, and David Christiano, eds. *The Cold War Against Labor*. Berkeley: Meiklejohn Civil Liberties Institute, 1987.

Halberstam, David. *The Fifties*. New York: Villard Books, 1993.

Hamilton, Tom. John A. Burns Oral History Project, 25 July 1979.

Hana Uwila, International Brotherhood of Electrical Workers, 27 July 1959.

Hays, Don J. Fitness report on John A. Burns, Burns police file, Archives of Hawaii, 30 November 1937.

Hirai, Seichi. John A. Burns Oral History Project, 1 June 1978.

Hitch, Thomas K. *Islands in Transition*. Honolulu: First Hawaiian Bank/University of Hawaii Press, 1991.

Holmes, T. Michael. "The Reinecke Case: A Study in Administrative Injustice," *Hawaii Bar Journal* 12, no. 3 (Fall 1976).

———. *The Specter of Communism in Hawaii*. Honolulu: University of Hawaii Press, 1994.

Honolulu Advertiser, 1946–1975.

Honolulu Record, 1950.

Honolulu Star-Bulletin, 1941–1975.

Ing, Andrew. Interview with Dan Boylan, 22 July 1980.

Inouye, Senator Daniel, with Lawrence Elliott. *Journey to Washington*. Englewood Cliffs, N.J.: Prentice-Hall, 1967.

———. John A. Burns Oral History Project, 6 August 1975.

Isa, Mary. Interview with Dan Boylan, 15 August 1978.

————. Letter to Sally Sheehan, 29 September 1959, Burns papers, Archives of Hawaii.

————. Letter to Lillian, 16 March 1981, Burns papers, Archives of Hawaii.

Johnson, Donald D. *The City and County of Honolulu.* Honolulu: University of Hawaii Press, 1991.

Journal of the House of Representatives, State of Hawaii, General Session of 1963, 21 February 1963.

Journal of the House of Representatives, State of Hawaii, Budget Session of 1964, 19 February 1964.

Journal of the House of Representatives, State of Hawaii, Special Session of 1964, 23 July 1964.

Journal of the House of Representatives, State of Hawaii, General Session of 1965, 18 February 1965.

Journal of the House of Representatives, State of Hawaii, Budget Session of 1966, 16 February 1966.

Journal of the House of Representatives, State of Hawaii, General Session of 1967, 16 February 1967.

Journal of the House of Representatives, State of Hawaii, Budget Session of 1968, 23 February 1968.

Journal of the House of Representatives, State of Hawaii, Regular Session of 1969, 20 February 1969.

Journal of the House of Representatives, State of Hawaii, Regular Session of 1970, 22 January 1970.

Ka Lamaka. St. Louis High School Yearbook, Spring 1930.

Kanazawa, Kanemi. Interview with Dan Boylan, 15 July 1982.

Kawano, Jack. John A. Burns Oral History Project, 21 August 1975.

Keir, Jerry. Interview with Dan Boylan, 3 February 1982.

Kido, Mitsuyuki. John A. Burns Oral History Project, 17 July 1975. 31 July 1975.

Kimura, Shunichi. Interview with Dan Boylan, 17 March 1982.

Kobayashi, Bert. John A. Burns Oral History Project, 18 June 1980.

Kosaki, Richard. Interview with Dan Boylan, 16 October 1981.

Krauss, Bob. *Johnny Wilson: First Hawaiian Democrat.* Honolulu: University of Hawaii Press, 1994.

Leehman, Elmer. Telephone interview with Dan Boylan, 6 June 1982.

Lemke, Herman. John A. Burns Oral History Project, 19 June 1980.

Matsuda, Fujio. John A. Burns Oral History Project, 14 July 1978.

Mau, Chuck. John A. Burns Oral History Project, 21 September 1975.

McCarthy, Senator Eugene. Telephone interview with Dan Boylan, 21 June 1981.

McNaughton, Malcolm. John A. Burns Oral History Project, 11 May 1983.

Meller, Norm. Interview with Dan Boylan, 2 October 1981.

Menor, Ben. Interview with Dan Boylan, 8 December 1981.

Michener, James. Interview with Dan Boylan, 19 July 1983.

————. "How to Lose an Election," *Honolulu Star-Bulletin,* 3 August 1959, second news section, p. 2.

Miller, Joe. Letter to Dan Aoki, 8 June 1959, Burns papers, Archives of Hawaii.

Miller, Merle. *Lyndon: An Oral Biography.* New York: G. P. Putnam, 1980.

Miller, William. *Fishbait: The Memoirs of the Congressional Doorkeeper.* Englewood Cliffs, N.J.: Prentice-Hall, 1977.

Miwa, Ralph. John A. Burns Oral History Project, 7 March 1977.

Murai, Ernest. John A. Burns Oral History Project, 8 July 1975.

Murphy, Thomas D. *Ambassadors in Arms.* Honolulu: University of Hawaii Press, 1954.

New York Times, 1963.

Official Tabulation—Results of Votes Cast, Territorial Election Held Tuesday, 11 November 1944, Archives of Hawaii.

Official Tabulation—Results of Votes Cast, City and County Primary Election, Held Saturday, 5 October 1946, Archives of Hawaii.

Official Tabulation—Results of Votes Cast, Territorial Election, Held Tuesday, 5 November 1946, Archives of Hawaii.

Official Tabulation—Results of Votes Cast, Territorial Primary Election, Held 2 October 1948, Vote for Delegate to Congress, Archives of Hawaii.

Official Tabulation—Results of Votes Cast, Territorial Election, Held Tuesday, 2 November 1948, Vote for Delegate to Congress, Archives of Hawaii.

Official Tabulation—Results of Votes Cast, Territorial Election, Held Tuesday, 7 November 1950, Archives of Hawaii.

Official Tabulation—Results of Votes Cast, City and County Primary Election, Held Saturday, 4 October 1952, Archives of Hawaii.

Official Tabulation—Results of Votes Cast, City and County General Election, Held Tuesday, 4 November 1952, Archives of Hawaii.

Official Tabulation—Results of Votes Cast, Territorial Election, Held Tuesday, 4 November 1952, Archives of Hawaii.

Official Tabulation—Results of Votes Cast, Territorial Special Election, Held 31 July 1954, Archives of Hawaii.

Official Tabulation—Results of Votes Cast, City and County Primary Election, Held Tuesday, 2 October 1954, Archives of Hawaii.

Official Tabulation—Results of Votes Cast, Territorial Election, Held Tuesday, 2 November 1954, Archives of Hawaii.

Official Tabulation—Results of Votes Cast, Territorial Election, Held Tuesday, 6 November 1956, Archives of Hawaii.

Official Tabulation—Results of Votes Cast, State of Hawaii, General Election of 1966, 8 November 1966, Archives of Hawaii.

Official Tabulation—Results of Votes Cast, State of Hawaii, General Election of 1970, 3 November 1970, Archives of Hawaii.

Ogawa, Dennis. "A War of Race." Lecture presented at the University of Hawaii, 8 July 1992.

Oshiro, Robert. John A. Burns Oral History Project, 24 February 1977.
3 March 1977.

Paulsen, Kekoa. Telephone interview with T. Michael Holmes, 11 August 1993.

Platform of the Territorial Democratic Party, 1952. Archives of Hawaii.

Richardson, William. John A. Burns Oral History Project, 2 February 1976.
28 July 1977.

———. Telephone interview with T. Michael Holmes, 11 June 1993.

——— (Secretary). *Minutes of the Territorial Democratic Central Committee,*
24 May 1952, Archives of Hawaii.

Roberts, Juanita. Telephone interview with Dan Boylan, 21 June 1981.

Rogers, Representative Paul. Interview with Dan Boylan, 26 June 1981.

Rohrbough, Edward. Unpublished manuscript on the life of John A. Burns.
Archives of Hawaii.

Serizawa, Toshio. John A. Burns Oral History Project, 28 July 1979.

Sheehan, Ed. Letter to John A. Burns, 18 March 1959, Burns papers, Archives
of Hawaii.

Smyser, A. A. John A. Burns Oral History Project, 25 June 1975.

Staats, Mary Beth [Burns]. Interview with Dan Boylan, 17 July 1979.

Strauss, Leon. Interview with Dan Boylan, 6 February 1979.

Sunday Star-Bulletin & Advertiser, 1963–1975.

Takabuki, Matsuo. *An Unlikely Revolutionary.* Honolulu: University of Hawai'i
Press, 1998.

———. John A. Burns Oral History Project, 22 July 1978.

Tanaka, Hiroshi. John A. Burns Oral History Project, 25 July 1977.

Thurmond, Senator J. Strom. U.S. Congress, Senate. *Congressional Record,*
Eighty-sixth Cong., 1 Sess., Washington, D.C., 1959.

Tokunaga, Mike. John A. Burns Oral History Project, 12 July 1977.
19 July 1977.
8 August 1977.

Toland Commission Report. Burns police file, Archives of Hawaii, Undated.

U.S. Congress, Senate. Committee on Immigration and Naturalization. *Immigration to Hawaii.* Cong., 1 Sess., Washington, D.C., 1921.

United States v. Fujimoto et al. Criminal No. 10,495. 1952–1953.

Walker, T. G. S. Letter to Harry Shigemitsu, 6 September 1946, Archives of
Hawaii.

Wright, Representative Jim. Interview with Dan Boylan, 21 June 1981.

Yokouchi, Masao. John A Burns Oral History Project, 9 August 1977.

Zalburg, Sanford. *A Spark is Struck!* Honolulu: University Press of Hawai'i,
1979.

INDEX

Page numbers for photographs appear in **boldface**.